The publisher gratefully acknowledges the generous
support of the Humanities Endowment Fund of
the University of California Press Foundation.

The Life of Cheese

CALIFORNIA STUDIES IN FOOD AND CULTURE
Darra Goldstein, Editor

The Life of Cheese

Crafting Food and Value in America

———

Heather Paxson

UNIVERSITY OF CALIFORNIA PRESS

Berkeley   Los Angeles   London

University of California Press, one of the most distinguished university
presses in the United States, enriches lives around the world by
advancing scholarship in the humanities, social sciences, and natural
sciences. Its activities are supported by the UC Press Foundation and
by philanthropic contributions from individuals and institutions.
For more information, visit www.ucpress.edu.

University of California Press
Berkeley and Los Angeles, California

University of California Press, Ltd.
London, England

Library of Congress Cataloging-in-Publication Data

Paxson, Heather, 1968–
    The life of cheese : crafting food and value in America / Heather
Paxson.
        p.   cm. — (California studies in food and culture ; v. 41)
    Includes bibliographical references and index.
    ISBN 978-0-520-27017-6 (cloth : alk. paper) — ISBN 978-0-520-27018-3
(pbk. : alk. paper)
    1. Cheesemaking—United States.   2. Cheese industry—United
States.   3. Cheese—Social aspects—United States.   4. Food habits—
United States.   5. Local foods—United States.   I. Title.
    SF274.U6P39   2013
    637'.3—dc23   2012026487

22 21 20 19 18 17 16 15 14 13
10 9 8 7 6 5 4 3 2 1

CONTENTS

ILLUSTRATIONS

FIGURES

TABLES

I love cheese. Growing up in southern Illinois, I considered myself a food snob because I loathed soda and would refuse to touch a sandwich adulterated by a waxy slice of Kraft American. I ate only *real* cheese, like nicely sharp, not-too-orange Cheddar, or the Baby Swiss my mother bought thinly sliced at the grocer's deli counter. When I was fourteen, I chronicled the process of making cheese at the Crowley Cheese Factory in Vermont in a photo-story project for my 4-H club. In my twenties, when I stopped eating meat, cheese became even more central to my diet. But really thinking about cheese came later.

The turning point may have been a millennial summer day in New York City, 2000 or 2001, when a student of my (now) husband stopped by with a paper-bag-wrapped gift whose pungent odor reached clear across the apartment. It was a generous hunk of cheese, slightly squashed from riding in a backpack. Beneath a tacky, almost shockingly orange rind, a toothsome interior was invitingly straw-colored. It tasted . . . not as good as the French Époisses we had recently discovered at Murray's Cheese on Bleecker Street. The cheese continued to ripen in our refrigerator, and I think I actually threw out the last bit of it. But I was intrigued. The student had purchased the cheese at the Union Square Greenmarket. This smelly, sticky, decidedly handmade cheese originated within two hundred miles of Manhattan. *Who made it?* I wondered. *How? Why?*

Only later, after I had moved to Massachusetts and was plotting the anthropological research behind this book, did I realize that the Greenmarket cheese must have been Hooligan, a washed-rind cheese made at Cato Corner Farm in Colchester, Connecticut, by Mark Gillman. Back in the late 1980s, Mark Gillman and I attended the same liberal-arts college. He did yard work for the woman whose house I cleaned weekly. I was thrilled to be able to purchase Mark's cheese (as I now thought of it) from a shop within walking distance of our Cambridge apartment. When not the worse for wear, the cheese is pretty wonderful.

Moving from consumer of cheese to ethnographer of cheesemaking, I visited Mark and many others who are devoted to making a life and a living by making cheese. I came to recognize their vocational project as also a moral project. This book describes what goes into handcrafting cheese, and it analyzes what artisanal work means to the women and men who have chosen to pursue it. As an anthropologist, I am in the business of discerning and interpreting the cultural meanings that both motivate and are conveyed by quotidian aspects of people's lives. Through manual effort and the rhetorical power of narrative, today's cheesemakers not only craft cheese, they also craft themselves as artisans, entrepreneurs, farmers, and families. In the process, they rework patches of American landscape, transform rural economies, and rewrite the script for American food politics. This book explores the meanings and also the values of artisanal cheese in the United States today.

ACKNOWLEDGMENTS

For introducing me to the life of cheese—in all its forms—I thank first the cheese-makers, mongers, consultants, scientists, and others I visited and interviewed for this book, including those whose stories did not make it onto the final pages. Early conversations with Ihsan Gurdal and Robert Aguilera of Formaggio Kitchen pointed me to David Major and Cindy Major and to Mateo Kehler and Andy Kehler, who played formative roles in my research. I thank them for their hospitality as well as their insights.

Other members of the artisanal cheese world who contributed in substance and form to this book include Barbara and Rex Backus, Marcia Barinaga, Jill Giacomini Basch, Beatrice Berle, Jennifer Bice, Jim Boyce, Tim Bucciarelli, Joe Burns, Liam and Cindy Callahan, Jeanne Carpenter, Dan Carter, D. J. D'Amico, Sasha Davies, Pascal Destendau, Debra Dickerson, Peter Dixon, Catherine Donnelly, Rachel Dutton, Jody Farnham, Gari Fischer, Mark Fischer, Laini Fondiller, Tom Gilbert, Mark Gillman, Mike Gingrich, David Gremmels, Barbara Hanley, Jerry Heimerl, Gail Holmes, Gemma Iannoni, Matt Jennings, Brenda Jensen, Lisa Kaiman, Patty Karlin, Rob Kaufelt, Mary Keehn, Angie Kehler, Paul Kindstedt, Michael Lee, Willi Lehner, Elizabeth MacAlister, Christine Maguire, Qui'tas McKnight, Angela Miller, Norm Monson, Elizabeth Mulholland, Peter Mulholland, Diana Murphy, Myron Olson, Charlie Parant, Marian Pollack, John Putnam, Marge Randles, Vince Razionale, Jeff Roberts, Matt Rubiner, Judy Schad, Al Scheps, Michael Scheps, David Seaton, Eric Smith, Tricia Smith, Diana Solari, Ann Starbard, Bob Stetson, Marjorie Susman, Dawn Terrell, Anne Topham, Maria Trumpler, Juliana Uruburu, Lori van Handel, Ig Vella, Karen

Weinberg, Joe Widmer, Bob Wills, Bruce Workman, and Jon Wright. I am also grateful to the 177 participants in my 2009 survey.

Monty Python reminds us that "blessed are the cheesemakers"; so too do we cheese scholars feel blessed. My thanks to the Cheese Scholars Collective and especially to Cristina Grasseni, Elia Petridou, Colin Sage, and Harry West for *all* our collaborative efforts at Schumacher College in Devon, U.K. And to Ken MacDonald for talking, and shopping for, cheese in Toronto.

For organizing conference panels, for inviting me to speak in classrooms and at colloquia, for critically reviewing drafts of this work, for suggesting helpful citations and contacts, and for ongoing conversation, I thank Rebecca Alssid, Tom Boellstorff, Ted Bestor, Rachel Black, Sarah Bowen, Bodil Just Christensen, Jane Collier, George Collier, Carole Counihan, Marcy Dermansky, Kathryn Dudley, Joe Dumit, Jim Faubion, Robin Fleming, Xaq Frolich, M. Amah Edoh, Darra Goldstein, Sherine Hamdy, Deborah Heath, Chaia Heller, Michael Herzfeld, Line Hillersdal, Linda Hogle, Gry Skrædderdal Jakobsen, Chris Kelty, Eben Kirksey, Hannah Landecker, Vincent Lépinay, Victor Luftig, Bill Maurer, Anne Meneley, Natasha Myers, Annemarie Mol, Cris Moore, Kristina Nies, Chris Otter, Canay Ozden, Gísli Pálsson, Verena Paravel, Bronwen Percival, Tobias Rees, Juliette Rogers, Sophia Roosth, Russ Rymer, Dorion Sagan, Caterina Scaramelli, Hillel Schwartz, David Sutton, Karen-Sue Taussig, Megan Tracy, Mitali Thakor, Maria Trumpler, Deborah Valenze, Wendy Walker, Charles Watkinson, Corky White, Brad Weiss, Barbara Wheaton, Richard Wilk, Joby Williams, Rebecca Woods, and Ken Wissoker. Susanne Freidberg and Amy Trubek were especially generous and helpful.

I am ever grateful to the tireless critical engagement and sustaining camaraderie of my super-smart writing group: Elizabeth Ferry, Smita Lahiri, Ann Marie Leshkowich, Janet McIntosh, Ajantha Subramanian, and Chris Walley.

In MIT Anthropology, I have the best colleagues in the world: Manduhai Buyandelger, Michael Fischer, Stefan Helmreich, Jim Howe, Jean Jackson, Erica James, Graham Jones, Susan Silbey, and Chris Walley. The workshop in which they politely shredded an early, partial draft of this manuscript was pivotal. Thanks, too, to Kieran Downes, Irene Hartford, Rosie Hegg, and Amberly Steward, and, in neighboring programs, Chris Boebel, Deborah Fitzgerald, David Jones, David Kaiser, Anne McCants, Harriet Ritvo, Natasha Schüll, and Roe Smith.

Holly Bellocchio Durso, Louisa Denison, Lily Higgins, Kirrah Jones, Christie Lin, Patricia Martinez, Alyssa Mensch, Caroline Rubin, Aayesha Siddiqui, and Emily Wanderer transcribed interview recordings and helped with other essential tasks. I owe a special thanks to Elizabeth Page Velasquez, a wiz with Excel, who made legible to me the quantitative data generated by our massive survey.

My research was made possible thanks to the generous support of the Wenner-

Gren Foundation for Anthropological Research (Gr. no. 7641), the Marion and Jasper Whiting Foundation, the James A. and Ruth Levitan Prize in the Humanities, and the MIT Class of 1957 Career Development Chair. As a Mary I. Bunting Institute fellow, I wrote the majority of this book during a year in residence at the Radcliffe Institute for Advanced Study (2009–2010), for which I am deeply grateful. At the University of California Press, Kate Marshall's enthusiasm for my project and confidence in my writing have been tremendous, and it has been a real pleasure to work again with Jacqueline Volin, my production editor. Many thanks, too, to Jürgen Fauth for taking the gorgeous photo of Consider Bardwell cheese at the Londonderry, Vermont, farmers' market (while visiting us during my fieldwork) and allowing me to put it on the cover of this book.

My interests in cheese and culture reach back to my childhood; my parents, Tom and Judi Paxson, nurtured my curiosity in both. In recent years, they have stepped in to provide childcare at crucial times to enable the completion of this book, and my dad's careful reading of chapters kept me on track. Mary and Eric Helmreich clipped articles about California cheese, provided a key contact, and reminded us to relax.

At age six and a bit, Rufus Paxson Helmreich has lived with cheese, and my research on cheese, his entire life. Perhaps this is how, entirely on his own, he thought up the title for this book. Thank you, Rufus. I look forward to a life together with less cheese-related distraction, if not less cheese. Stefan Helmreich, my partner in all things, contributed in more ways than I can count to the research and writing of this book. I thank him for his willingness to organize summer months around my fieldwork, his sharp anthropological insight, his patient reading of endless versions of my arguments, his tireless taste for cheese, and, above all, for his unwavering faith in me.

Arguments I originally developed in the following articles are reprinted with permission:

Post-Pasteurian Cultures: The Microbiopolitics of Raw-Milk Cheese in the United States. *Cultural Anthropology* 23 (1): 15–47. Published Wiley-Blackwell, © 2008 American Anthropological Association.

Cheese Cultures: Transforming American Tastes and Traditions. *Gastronomica: The Journal of Food and Culture* 10 (4): 35–47. © 2010 University of California Press.

Locating Value in Artisan Cheese: Reverse-Engineering *Terroir* for New-World Landscapes. *American Anthropologist* 112 (3): 442–457. Published Wiley-Blackwell, © 2010 American Anthropological Association.

The "Art" and "Science" of Handcrafting Cheese in the United States. *Endeavour* 35 (2–3): 116–124. © 2011 Elsevier.

American Artisanal

Andy and Mateo Kehler started milking cows and making cheese at Jasper Hill Farm, in northern Vermont, in 2003. Just one year into production, their Bayley Hazen Blue and Constant Bliss were featured in restaurants and gourmet shops from Boston to Chicago. Jasper Hill exemplifies the New American Cheese, the artisanal fabrication of cheeses by hand, in small batches, in the fashion of a European culinary style.[1] These cheeses are intended to be savored on their own, or perhaps with a glass of wine. The Kehler brothers represent a new kind of American food producer: college educated and urban raised, they are becoming farmers, investing in their land and local community, and dedicating themselves to mastering the entire process of cheese production, from pasture to plate.

I first visited the Kehlers in March 2004. To reach Jasper Hill Farm, I drove through wooded hills dotted with crumbling buildings and rusted farm equipment. Lacking a major waterway, Vermont's Northeast Kingdom, a trio of optimistically named counties south of the Canadian border, missed out on the state's nineteenth-century logging boom and still retains the feel of a frontier territory. Andy and Mateo enjoyed childhood summers up here on Lake Caspian, following a family tradition reaching back to the 1920s. They remember their grandmother, the daughter of a traveling salesman who had bought a lakeside fishing hut here, telling tales from her youth of local residents descending from hilltop farmsteads dressed in home-styled furs.[2] Today, at least during the spring mud season, many farms up here look more desperate than quaint.

Arriving at the farm, I was greeted by Andy, the brother in charge of the Ayrshire cows we later visited in the barn. I tugged hygienic hospital booties over my shoes before entering the sunlit cheese room the Kehlers built beside the milking parlor. Here, Mateo, his wife, Angie, and Andy's fiancée, Victoria—all then in their early to mid-thirties—were at work making an English-style cheese they called Aspenhurst. While Mateo fed heavy, rectangular slabs of pressed cheese curd through a noisy shredding machine, Andy leaned over the vat to join Victoria in agitating the shredded curd with his bare hands to prevent clumping. They stirred in a generous amount of salt, too. In Wisconsin, people snack on fresh cheese curds much like these, but in Vermont curd is merely a step along the way to making cheese. Using handheld scoops, the Kehlers hooped (that is, packed) the curd into cylindrical molds that they slotted into another machine, called a horizontal gang press, to squeeze out the remaining whey. It was steamy-hot, physically demanding work using shiny new models of the sort of equipment that would have been employed a hundred years ago by tradesmen working in cheese factories throughout New England's dairying regions, before industrial automation took over in the middle of the twentieth century.

As curd was being shredded, salted, and packed into wheels, Mateo shared their vision: "We wanted to make some money" and live in Vermont, "the most beautiful place in the world." Andy, a carpenter who worked as a building contractor after graduating from the University of Vermont, had been looking for an alternative occupation because as a contractor, "you make money off of other people's labor." Mateo, who studied international development at a Quaker college in the early 1990s and worked with a microfinance development organization in India after graduation, was politically committed to sustainable agriculture. Vermont, Mateo told me, is just as much in need of agricultural development as any struggling farm community the world over; his adopted state had lost fifty dairy farms the previous year.[3] The Kehlers set out to create a precedent for agricultural entrepreneurialism that might reverse the trend of farm closures. From the beginning, their plan was to help develop the local economy in a way that would compromise neither what they described as the "culture of independence" of Vermont's people nor the "working landscape" of its environment. In 1998, using savings and some family money, the brothers bought 223 acres with a dilapidated barn. One of their early business models explored the market potential for organic tofu; another considered a microbrewery. But then they "looked around and said, 'Why not cows?'" Cows, they explained, are not only part of the existing landscape; they are central to Vermont's identity.

Labor-intensive, handmade cheese became the key to their plan. Dairy may be "the basis of the Vermont economy," Mateo explained, but fluid milk, sold by bulk tank to processing plants, has become a "failed industry" for the state. "We can't compete with the economies of scale in California," he said, citing a dairy in Barstow with nineteen thousand cows. In 2002, half of Vermont's dairy farms housed seventy cows or fewer. "California is going to bury Vermont in a tidal wave of cheap milk," Mateo predicted. As the Kehlers see it, Vermont's dairy

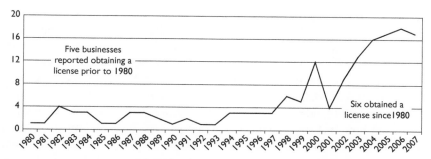

FIG. 1. Years in which artisan creameries became licensed for commercial business, 1980–2007, based on survey data collected in February 2009 (n = 164).

future lies in artisan-made cheese. A family here can make a decent living with twenty-five or thirty cows, they told me—if they add commercial value to the milk by processing it into high-end cheese for a high-end market.

Today in the United States, upwards of 450 enterprises handcraft cheese from milk purchased from nearby farms or produced by the cheesemakers' own animals.[4] The Kehlers are riding the crest of a wave of new artisan cheesemaking enterprises whose force has more than doubled since 2000, as indicated in fig. 1.[5] Over the past thirty years, former professionals and recent college graduates have followed ex-hippies in renovating run-down farms and reinventing "farmstead cheese," an informal designation for cheese made artisanally on the dairy farm that supplies the milk. The vanguard was young women moving back to the land in the 1970s and commercializing their vocation in the 1980s. Today's cheesemakers come from wide-ranging backgrounds, including business management, nursing, homemaking, fine arts, science education, and gourmet retail. Heritage dairy farmers, who inherited their farms or married into farm families, represent a growing number of farmstead cheesemakers.

Here is a deceptively basic recipe for making cheese: Heat milk; sour it by adding bacterial cultures to convert milk sugar (lactose) to lactic acid; add an enzyme (such as rennet) to help coagulate the fermenting milk. Once the milk has set into a gel-like substance, use long blades to cut the curd into pieces and release the watery whey, drain, salt, and pack the curds into molds. Endless variations—including the choice to start with goat's, sheep's, or cow's milk; the selection of added bacterial cultures; the timing and temperature of the steps of the cheesemaking process; whether a cheese is eaten fresh or aged for months or even years—result in hundreds if not thousands of varieties of cheese. In his 2007 *Atlas of American Artisan Cheese,* Jeff Roberts catalogued newly invented artisanal cheeses rubbed with cocoa and lavender, washed in buttermilk and hard ciders, or covered with bloomy coats of edible mold. The novelty of such new American cheeses is secured in no small part by whimsical names (Purple Haze, Barely Buzzed, Fuzzy Wheel, Hyku) that convey the personal imprint of an individual producer and mark a contrast with Europe's place-based cheese names (Comté, Taleggio), which carry the historical weight of collective regional traditions.[6]

"The art of cheesemaking," writes dairy scientist Paul Kindstedt, "is really about working with, shaping, and to some extent controlling the forces of nature," and so in examining the artisanal culturing of cheese we encounter broader questions about how "nature"—environmental, microbial, animal, human—should best be inhabited, incorporated, and regulated.[7] As people work pastureland, tend livestock, handcraft cheeses, and ready them for market, they manage forces that are symbolic and institutional as well as organic. *The Life of Cheese*, then, refers both to the working lives of people dedicated to cheesemaking, and to the liveliness of the substance with which they work. Idiosyncratic and future-oriented, celebrating entrepreneurial innovation rather than consensual customs of the past, the culture of artisan cheesemaking in the United States is decidedly American.

WHAT MAKES GOOD FOOD GOOD?

Reporting on ethnographic research carried out in New England, Wisconsin, and California dairy regions, this book travels onto farms and into creameries to investigate efforts to produce American cheese as good food. Cheese may be considered to be good on the basis of taste and healthfulness and also on the basis of whether it is produced well—in other words, thoughtfully, even ethically. While handmade cheese undoubtedly generates gustatory pleasure and social status for its consumers, this book focuses on the values that making cheese generates for its rural and peri-urban producers.[8]

The value of food to humans endlessly transcends quantitative measures, whether of kilocalories or grams of fat, or in dollars and cents. Beyond providing a source of nutrition and an economic livelihood, food is everywhere a medium of cultural and social exchange.[9] Its preparation invites creativity and requires an investment of material resources, while eating and feeding offer opportunity for pleasure as well as denial. Through food, people solidify a sense of self and connectedness to (or distance from) others.[10] Food offers a strong anchor for identity because eating well—adequately, appropriately—holds not only the promise of being well (healthy) but also of being good (moral). Think of the role of food as the nutritive medium of motherhood, or as the virtue of generous hospitality. Consider too, though, how food may constitute a bone of contention, a site for playing out social conflict, discord, or resentment.[11] Food does not merely symbolize status and prestige; it is a transformative substance through which social relations are manipulated and power is enacted.[12]

Food's goodness may thus be evaluated in terms of bodily and social well-being, purity, status, emotional impact, ease of preparation, cost, and, not least, deliciousness. The layering of multiple values that constitute food's goodness can make fraught the politics of eating: how we enact the adage "We are what we eat," or pose the accusatory challenge "You are what you eat." Ethical trade-offs and inconsistency in food choices are hardly surprising, since what makes food culturally and culinarily desirable is not always the same as what is understood to make food nutritionally or socially beneficial.[13]

Similar qualifications manifest in producing food. Artisan producers want to make healthful and delicious food, but more than that, in making good food they want to make a good life for themselves, pursuing engaging and gratifying work. Insofar as these rural entrepreneurs are guided not solely by profit but also by sentiment, artisan cheesemakers in the United States are similar to the winegrowers of Bordeaux, chocolatiers in Paris, and fish traders in Tokyo studied by my anthropological colleagues.[14] While the Kehler brothers may pitch their enterprise in political terms of remaking a segment of the food system, others are engaged in far more modest, even idiosyncratic endeavors.[15] Most neither proselytize nor pretend to offer solutions to entrenched structural problems with our current food system, such as inner-city landscapes, called food deserts, that are denuded of grocery stores yet cluttered with cheap fast-food outlets.[16] Rather, they are mindful of the everyday practice of their own lives. Anthropologist Judith Farquhar suggests, "Agency in everyday life is a form of craftwork involving intimate collaborations among embodied humans and material objects like food. Like recipes and the cooking skills on which they rely, like tasting food and savoring the company of others, the crafting of a good life is an improvisational project in which a great deal goes without saying."[17] *The Life of Cheese* offers close attention to how the crafting of cheese and the crafting of a life mutually inform each other.

By what accounting might it seem sensible to employ nineteenth-century-era machinery and craft techniques to make cheese for commercial sale when a fully industrial food system has accustomed us to more efficient, less expensive, and more consistent ways of producing food? Those who handcraft cheese in the United States today do so because the value they gain by doing it exceeds its limited potential to generate income. Although the daily discipline of artisanship varies as cheese is made in fifty-gallon kettles or fifteen-hundred-gallon vats, from raw or pasteurized milk, by third-generation cheesemakers or former housewives or business executives, artisan cheesemakers are united by a belief that the qualities that make their cheeses taste good are fundamentally connected to personal values that make the cheeses good for them to make.

This book brings the interpretive analysis so richly applied to food consumption to the study of its commercial production to explain why cheesemakers believe in the goodness of their endeavor and of their cheese. How do culinary and moral values influence producers' practical encounters with pastureland, dairy animals, and the biochemical substance of milk that they transubstantiate into cheese? How are those values conveyed to a consuming public and translated (or possibly undermined) through market exchange? What can we learn from artisan food-making about the politics of nature and the ethics of the market-place in the United States at the beginning of the twenty-first century?

THE VALUE OF ARTISAN CHEESEMAKING TODAY

Artisan cheesemaking is part of a broader cultural transition in the United States as key cultural values have been challenged by, or are being adapted in response to, deleterious legacies of twentieth-century industrial agriculture. Our supply of cheap food comes at the cost of farm closures, periodic outbreaks of food-borne illness, and the inhumane treatment of farmworkers and livestock; in this light, the technoscientific promise of unlimited progress through rationalized, industrial efficiency rings hollow.[18] From the best-selling book *Fast Food Nation* to the Academy Award–nominated film *Food, Inc.,* popular exposés fuel public critique of agribusiness as usual.[19] At the same time, disillusionment with cor-porate America following urban deindustrialization and scandals of executive malfeasance has precipitated a groundswell of interest in making do for one-self.[20] Half a century ago the American Dream promised a union-negotiated family wage to workers who drove cars they helped build and owned houses they could afford; today, the collective mythology of rugged individualism and self-realization carries on in a very different register as do-it-yourself craft and gardening collectives are moving into postindustrial urban landscapes, while suburban chicken coops have become "The Most Exciting Backyard Accessory since Lawn Darts."[21] Artisan cheesemaking represents not a new cultural trend so much as (for those who take it up) a reordering of values that are pervasive and enduring in American culture—autonomy and self-determination, belief in the virtue (and reward) of hard work, a communitarian ethos of neighborliness, concern for the natural environment, and faith in future progress.[22]

While some cheesemakers got into artisanship as a sustainable retirement project, others work to earn a living for themselves and their families. Like the Kehlers, many are new farm families, new to farming and also new families: young couples moving to the countryside to raise children; lesbian women and gay men making a life and a living together; multigenerational constellations of reconvened family members united by commitment to collective enterprise. But the story of America's farmstead cheesemaking resurgence is also a tale of multigenerational dairy farmers hoping to escape the dilemma of industrial agriculture: either get big (and squeeze out your neighbor) or get out.[23] Both groups wrestle with multiple, sometimes competing values as they pursue work they find personally satisfying.

Through the stories I tell and interpret in this book, I aim to demonstrate the complexity of cheesemakers' decisions and actions. My intent is not to make judgments about what cheesemakers do and decide. When people are motivated to become artisan food-makers out of concerns that they share with consumers of local and Slow foods—support for rural economies and communities, commitment to feeding their families healthy yet tasty food—I ask: how might such sentiments inform and be modified by the practical concerns of animal husbandry, product development, and business growth? Working to realize multiple values simultaneously can create moral ambivalence as well as economic uncertainty. Many cheesemakers struggle to discover how they might grow big enough as a business to cover their bills, pay themselves a modest salary, and put away some savings, but without growing so big that they find themselves sitting in an office doing managerial work, rather than outside with their animals or submerging their arms in sweet-smelling curd, realizing the personal values they initially pursued in becoming commercial cheesemakers. Producers' uncertainty is exacerbated when a product's strongest selling point may be the subjective value it embodies for its maker: the four generations a family has lived and worked on a farm, say, or the personal names given to dairy goats. In marketing the personal values they derive from making cheese, artisan cheesemakers risk exaggerating the influence of those values in generating a cheese's material qualities, its apparent intrinsic goodness.

The figure of the artisan within an industrial society is an uneasy one, embodying cultural anxieties about middle-class status and security.[24] In Europe, artisans are prone to being considered throwbacks to a premodern era, holding static the tradition against which the rest of society measures its modernization.[25] French chocolatiers, in Susan Terrio's analysis, for example, "represent what the French like to tell themselves about themselves in terms of a traditional work ethic, family values, community cohesion, and the noncompetitive practices of small business," but at the same time they remain "manual workers whose businesses require considerable self-exploitation."[26] Their self-employment affords economic upward mobility but without the refinement that higher education affords. Deemed insufficiently cultured, artisan entrepreneurs in France are suspected of being "vulnerable to economic greed," liable to overcharge customers and exploit workers. In the United States, artisan cheesemakers may also represent what many Americans like to tell themselves about their own work ethic, family values, and community cohesion, but here romanticizing farming and artisan enterprise as honest work can generate unrealistic expectations for moral purity. Popular celebrations of local and artisanal foods wax poetic about the agrarian Good Life—think of novelist Barbara Kingsolver's 2007 best seller *Animal, Vegetable, Miracle,* recounting a year procuring food from neighboring farms and her family's own backyard—but rural entrepreneurs must be practical. In the words of one veteran cheesemaker, "People who really cared about what they ate in the sixties grew up to have businesses that have to survive." Pragmatism and compromise are part of their moral reasoning.

In their dual roles as craftspeople and small-business owners, American cheesemakers risk being represented—or may judge one another—as hypocritical "sell-outs." In a striking inversion of the French stereotype of artisans lacking in cultural refinement, American artisans are instead suspected of granola-coated elitism, playacting at manual labor as a means of denying their privileged class status. There are problems with this generalizing presumption. First, it disregards as artisans the dairy farmers who have taken up cheesemaking to add commercial value to their milk, as well as the third-generation owner-operators of artisan factories who have resisted mechanical automation. It also disregards the influence of consumer expectations on marketing rhetoric; marketing the pastoral romance that appeals to consumers obscures what producers know to be a far less romantic reality of unpaid bills, rising property taxes, and animal slaughter. Finally, the judgment that commercial artisans may be moral sell-outs reproduces a dichotomy between quantitative market value and qualitative social values, such that the pursuit of one is assumed to diminish the other. This book refutes that view.[27] Indeed, I propose that the struggle to realize potentially competing values itself constitutes a source of value for producers: it is the moral struggle, and not necessarily its resolution, that makes artisanship worth undertaking.

Although the revival of artisan cheesemaking emerged from the back-to-the-land movement of the 1970s, as it has grown it has largely shed its countercultural ethos. Artisan cheesemaking remains a marginal economic enterprise but has become a mainstream cultural project. It reflects a postindustrial reconfiguration and reimagination of the American landscape, one produced by new social traffic between the country and the city as well as by a growing sensibility that "nature" as we know it is clearly a product of human activity. Whether carried out by rural newcomers fleeing desk jobs or by heritage dairy farmers, artisan cheesemaking gives new life to run-down farms, provides new jobs to rural residents, and expands culinary tastes. It is part of the emergence of an agrarian form of life that is more future-oriented than nostalgic for a mythical pastoral; an ethos that seeks—in contrast to industrial agriculture's technoscientific domination of nature—to work in collaboration with the agencies of pasture ecologies, ruminant life cycles, and milk fermentation. In many ways, contemporary artisanship is guided by what I call a *post-pastoral* ethos.[28]

FROM INDUSTRIAL TO ARTISANAL PRODUCTION

First, to grasp the emergence of what Carlo Petrini, a founder of the Slow Food movement, impressionistically calls America's artisan cheesemaking "renaissance," it is important to consider what American cheese has been.[29] What is today celebrated as farmstead cheese, namely, cheese made by hand on a dairy farm, was a household staple in preindustrial agrarian America (this history will be elaborated in chapter 4). For generations, farmwomen made cheese for domestic use and commercial trade. By the late nineteenth century, cheesemaking had moved into factories where specialized, skilled tradesmen processed milk pooled from area farms. Food scientists soon scaled up the process, breaking down the chemistry of turning milk into cheese and building it back up as the industrial processing of a safe, predictable, commodity food. Factories were consolidated and, in most plants, automated assembly displaced artisan workers—although, as chapter 4 details, a few artisan factories still turn out cheese in much the same way as they did a century ago. Meanwhile, in 1997 commodity cheddar (made using a different process than true Cheddar) began to be priced alongside pork bellies on the trading floor of the Chicago Mercantile Exchange. Kraft Foods, Sara Lee, and McDonald's are among the corporate players trading barrel cheese by the carload.[30]

Dairy farms have undergone similar transformations. Over the past century, dairy farming, like the production of wheat and other staple crops, has come to be organized by an industrial logic guided by faith in capitalist and techno-scientific rationality to realize the singular goal of maximizing production and profit.[31] Throughout the twentieth century, small dairy operations were forced out of business by higher equipment prices, declining milk consumption, and health regulations that increased the costs of production (e.g., mandates in the 1950s for concrete-floored milking parlors and the replacement of metal milk cans with bulk tanks).[32] Between 1970 and 2006, the number of cow dairy farms in the United States fell by 88 percent.[33] The U.S. Department of Agriculture has regarded subsequent rural depopulation as a measure of the success of agriculture's industrial logic, offering "evidence of technological mastery."[34] Fewer and larger farms continue to produce more milk at lower prices (see fig. 2).[35] Industrial agriculture has undoubtedly provided the United States with cheap food. As a whole, Americans spend less than 10 percent of their disposable income on food (within low-income households that figure rises to 21 percent).[36] But cheap food, as Mateo Kehler reminded me, is produced by economies of scale that have not only displaced small farmers but also rent the social fabric of rural communities while depleting the fertility of agricultural lands.

In 1970, Margaret Mead argued that commercial agriculture had lost sight of food's significance as a source of bodily and social nourishment.[37] Instead,

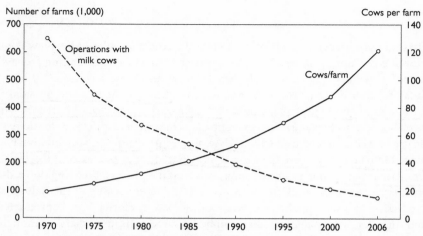

FIG. 2. Dairy farm size rises as farm numbers decline. Data and graph from the U.S. Department of Agriculture (MacDonald et al. 2007).

food production had become redefined in terms of staple crops (on which the prosperity of an entire region or even country might depend) and as potential profit for agribusiness. Such economistic thinking, according to Mead, led to the tragic paradox of our global commodity food system: dire food shortages exist alongside food surpluses. Thousands of tons of food lie rotting because bringing it to market would upset prices. The iconic symbol of commodity food policy's illogic may well be the Reagan-era "government cheese" giveaway. Only after the national press reported that tons of price-supported surplus dairy products were rotting in refrigerated warehouses where they were stored at great public expense—and, more gallingly, at a time when the reach of the federal food stamp assistance program was being slashed—did the Reagan administration in 1981 release thirty million pounds of government surplus cheese to feed "the needy." The poor and the elderly stood in long, televised lines to receive blocks of the generic, processed surplus dairy product turned out by assembly-line manufacture, a product known as "American cheese." Recipients were instructed to scrape off any nontoxic mold that might have formed on the surface during storage.[38] Not only did the giveaway symbolically taint processed cheese as the food of poor people, it did nothing to reduce the volume of surplus that was eroding dairy farmers' profits. At the behest of the National Cheese Institute, cheese buyout and redistribution was replaced with another federal initiative to restore market balance: the Dairy Termination Program. Otherwise known as the Whole Herd Buyout, this federal program paid farmers to submit herds of dairy cows for slaughter.[39] Dairy farmers were told by their government to get big or get out.

Hoping to forge a viable middle way, the state governments of Vermont and Wisconsin have thrown their support behind what are called "value-added" farm products. Instead of expanding herd size to produce more milk to sell at commodity prices to regional processing plants, midsize farmers are now encouraged to downsize and add commercial value to high-quality milk by processing it themselves into butter, ice cream, or cheese for direct sale.[40] Since 2004, state institutions such as the Vermont Institute for Artisan Cheese (VIAC), affiliated with the University of Vermont, and Wisconsin's Dairy Business Innovation Center (DBIC) have provided technical support for value-added dairying. These states promote dairying, but their historically smaller farms struggle to compete in national fluid milk markets dominated by and calibrated to California's vast valleys, mild winters, and pro-agribusiness political climate.[41] Value-added agriculture attempts to expand niche markets in which small-scale farmers might capture a greater portion of the consumer dollar. Government support is aimed at rural economic development through job creation and preserving agricultural or open land-use.[42]

Institutional initiatives for transforming dairy farming are inspired by the apparent success of homesteaders and other rural in-migrants who have been buying abandoned farms and making cheese from Maine to California since the 1980s. Well-capitalized operations (early ones include Coach Farm and Old Chatham Sheepherding Company in downstate New York) made a name for American artisanal cheeses, paving the way for newcomers with more modest start-up funds and less expansive market networks. At the same time, artisan cheese factories that resisted automation in the twentieth century began to repackage their specialty cheese for a twenty-first-century artisanal food market.

Whether "lifestyle migrants" escaping office jobs or longtime dairy farmers shifting strategies, today's artisan cheesemakers want to make and sell food that is better than industrially produced food: with fewer social and environmental costs, and with more complex taste, greater nutrition, and higher commercial value.[43] To do so, they work artisanally. Instead of processing vast quantities of standardized milk using automated assembly, they make cheese in small batches using minimally modified milk, employing machinery and other tools to extend rather than replace their practical knowledge. They purchase milk from or operate themselves what sociologist Douglas Harper calls "craft farms," comprehensive small-scale operations in which members of a farm household perform, or at least participate in, all the tasks of the production system. In craft dairying as in artisanal cheesemaking, "the worker controls and directs the machines rather than vice versa," Harper writes.[44] Buying dilapidated farms on which to substitute artisanal for industrial modes of production, the Kehlers and others like them hope to revitalize agricultural land and rural communities scarred by industrial farming. It is telling of the class politics and economics involved that many of the new artisan enterprises were enabled by government foreclosure on older farms that were let down by the promise of industrialization.

Artisan-made or artisanal cheese is not cheap food. As one goat cheese producer who grew up on a conventional dairy farm said to me, "You don't go to farmers' markets now looking for a bargain. That's one thing that's changed from even twenty to twenty-five years ago." Farm produce prices have not risen because small farmers today demand more money for their produce than in the past. Rather, farmers' market prices seem expensive because industrial-scale farming practices, government subsidies, deregulated transportation, and global trade have artificially deflated the price of supermarket food.[45] The issue is not simply a matter of industrial machinery, but of political decisions. Prices that compensate low-intensity dairying and artisan labor—prices that boosters hope may revitalize pockets of rural America—are out of reach for many, even most, consumers not because such producers overestimate the value of their labor, but because the United States government subsidizes large-scale industrial dairy enterprises (but not, as in Europe, artisan food production). More of the costs of producing cheese are borne by artisan producers in the United States, as compared to both industrial and European artisan production. So while artisan cheesemaking has been upheld as a bellwether for American agricultural enterprise, one that might presage new alternatives to industrial foods, legislative work is required to move away from one-size-fits-all agricultural policies before any durable systemic change can take place.[46]

Anthropologists seek to understand how social change manifests not only materially—for instance, in institutional policies and standards of living—but also in less tangible ways, in how people think and feel about what they do. As a commodity sold in a market, artisanal cheese is surely a manifestation of capitalist economic enterprise, but its production is not strictly governed by the industrial logic of economic efficiencies. As an entrepreneurial enterprise and as a mode of production, artisan cheesemaking is guided by an understanding that economic values and personal sentiments explicitly, though not neatly, inform one another.[47] Deliberations over what kind of cheese to make, how to market it, and how large to grow a business entail negotiating economic and moral values. Such negotiations also appear in debates over the meaning and worth of designations—*local, organic, artisanal, farmstead,* terroir—that both establish commonalities and differentiate among cheeses as commercial goods and as good foods. Although craft farmers and artisan cheesemakers are keen to integrate moral and economic values, they nevertheless work within a market economy whose mythology claims that capitalism primarily rewards unsentimental, rational self-interest. Caught between competing value hierarchies, their optimism is often coupled with anxiety.

Artisanal cheese, I argue, attains meaning and significance not only in opposition to industrial cheese in terms of how it is *made,* but also in opposition to commodity cheese in terms of how it is *valued.* If the aim of twentieth-century industrial food production was to make "every farm a factory," as historian Deborah Fitzgerald has detailed, then a central aim of twenty-first-century artisan food production is to make every farm a working landscape—one that generates, and will continue to generate in the future, multiple values: decent livelihoods, healthy ecologies, beautiful vistas, and, most immediately, good food.[48]

REALIZING VALUE IN AN UNFINISHED COMMODITY

Through detailing how people work to make a good life and a decent living by crafting cheese, *The Life of Cheese* demonstrates how economic, moral, and social actions are fundamentally, inseparably implicated in one another.[49] Cheesemakers are by no means alone in struggling to reconcile multiple values—in searching for worth, as sociologist David Stark puts it—because this is how we all operate in a market society.[50] In addition to earning wages or salaries with which we purchase goods and services, we may also receive inheritance or cash gifts from relatives, swap baby-sitting services with friends through play dates, grow vegetables in a garden that a neighbor waters while we are away, and so forth. The value of such actions is equally material and symbolic. What anthropologist Stephen Gudeman names "economy's tension," the dialectic between market competition and the "mutualism" of nonmarket transactions on which we all rely, underwrites an ongoing quest for meaning in labor.[51] Artisan cheesemakers illuminate this broader reality because their struggle to realize multiple values in and through their business enterprise is both self-conscious and valorized by others, whereas elsewhere the interplay of economic and moral values is often obscured through language that separates spaces of "work" from "home" and distinguishes actions carried out for money from those we do for love.

By continually confronting the tension between principle and pragmatism, artisan cheesemakers craft a sense of themselves as ethical subjects of production. I am by no means suggesting that the practice of making cheese is inherently moral. Instead, my point is that commercial artisan cheesemaking lends itself to ethical self-fashioning, to the evaluation of oneself as a good person, because the value of American artisanal cheese is not fully determined.[52] Artisanal cheese is what I call an *unfinished commodity.* It has not (yet?) been reduced to an apparent equivalence between intrinsic value and market value. The unfinished character of artisanal cheese as a commodity calls attention to the instability, and hence open promise, of its heterogeneous forms of value.[53]

A finished commodity would be one in which the appearance of value has been effectively reduced to an economic equivalency between use value (what someone gets out of a purchase) and exchange value (what is paid for that purchase). A box of cereal can illustrate. Entire supermarket aisles are packed with innumerable varieties priced roughly the same. As consumers, we have little idea of what went into each box by way of labor, research and development, product design, sourcing of ingredients, environmental costs, marketing, and packaging. All commodities have biographies or "social lives" of production.[54] In finished commodities, these backstories are obscure to consumers. In the place of labor and indirect costs, new stories are written for commodity goods through corporate branding and marketing.[55] Precisely by keeping the experiences, sentiments, and interests of those who designed and produced the item out of the experience of commodity exchange can the desirability and functional capacity of an object (its use value) be figured as having worth equal to what people are willing to pay for it (its exchange value). Value is thus figured as intrinsic to the object; this is what Karl Marx called labor alienation and commodity fetishism.[56]

In contrast, cheesemakers bring select elements of the social and material backstory of an artisanal cheese's fabrication to the foreground. Marks of the artisan's labor are retained to enhance a cheese's consumer appeal. In a shop or at a farmers' market stall, a photo of the farm where a cheese came into being may be displayed alongside samples for tasting. Cheese names that sound like nicknames (Fat Bottom Girl, Square Cheese), in contrast to more familiar names that place a cheese within a classificatory system of belonging (Cheddar, washed-rind), are intended to carry the identities of their producers in them.[57] In calling attention to their own labor, as well as to the productive contributions of farm animals, bacteria, and fungi, cheesemakers seek to provide a demystified life for artisanal cheese, one distinct from conventional commodity cheese.

Less intentional pointers—a cheese's mottled surface appearance, lopsided shape, or barnyardy odor—also suggest the handicraft of an individual rather than assembly-line production. While such variations may be promoted as a valued manifestation of artisan labor, if a cheesemaker produces results that are consistently more erratic than merely variable, this may undermine a product's market value. In the eyes of consumers accustomed to supermarket shopping for finished, standardized commodities, imperfectly formed cheeses—discolored, uneven, unclassifiable as a familiar type—may appear incomplete as commodity goods.[58] How can consumers evaluate whether an unfinished commodity is worth its labeled price per pound? From many of their names—Pleasant Ridge Reserve, Carmody—we can only guess what a cheese might look, smell, and taste like. Nevertheless, unfinished commodities are sold and purchased every day by restaurants and at farmers' markets and specialty shops. Producers, traders, and consumers need not come to a consensus on how to value artisanal cheese. Certainly consumers do not have the final word on what making cheese signifies and generates for those who make it.

The unfinished commodity character of American artisanal cheese is a material instantiation of a market economy's constitutive tension.[59] From one batch to the next, does variation in quality characteristics (color, texture, taste, odor) reflect the hands-on aspect of skilled artisanship, or the influence of natural environmental conditions, or sloppy workmanship? As a commodity, does artisanal cheese represent an elite consumer treat or, more nobly, in the words of *maître fromager* (cheese master) Max McCalman, "a vehicle for rescuing [dairy] operations destined to fail"?[60] Such questions, explored in the chapters to come, remain open. In the meantime, artisanal cheese generates moral value for producers largely because it is an unfinished commodity.

The unfinished commodity character of artisanal cheese suggests further that people may be motivated to make and sell it not only for what it offers them now, but also for what it might offer in the future.[61] As food producers reconfigure their personal values, they are also brokering changes in the land and landscape. One Vermont dairying family I met transitioned to organic production as an economic strategy but then came to believe in an organic ethic of care for their cows, whose veterinary bills declined after being fed pasture grasses. Practices of producing, exchanging, and eating food construct broader social and material realities, often in unforeseen ways.[62] Rural in-migrants may pride themselves on keeping land in agricultural use and buying hay or milk from their neighbors at fair prices, but when they invest urban-earned money in rural communities they may also contribute to rising rural property taxes and the displacement of long-term residents. Far from representing a romantic return to nature, artisanal cheese offers a means to bring into being a "working landscape," one worked by humans and other animals to produce multiple values that may shift over time.[63]

THE POST-PASTORAL

Artisanal cheese contributes a new chapter to the American Pastoral. In the classic pastoral imaginary, nature and culture are defined in opposition, while production and consumption are considered to take place in separate, rural and urban locales. Premised on caricatured contrasts between the country and the city, escaping from the hustle-bustle of urban society to a countryside idyll has been an enduring theme in American narrative, embodied in the writings of American authors such as James Fenimore Cooper, Henry David Thoreau, and Robert Frost. "From the beginning of its long history," writes literary theorist Terry Gifford, "the pastoral was written for an urban audience and therefore exploited a tension between the town by the sea and the mountain country of the shepherd, between the life of the court and the life of the shepherd, between people and nature, between retreat and return."[64] Pastoral imagery conveys a view of land seen from a remove, as a landscape.

Artisanal cheese, particularly when made on dairy farms, often trades on the mythic quality of the pastoral.[65] Miles and Lillian Cahn—to take one prominent example—sold a luxury goods business, Coach Leather, and in 1983 bought an abandoned farm in New York's Hudson River Valley, soon launching Coach Farm goat dairy and creamery. At a New York City Slow Food event in 2001, I heard Miles Cahn tell their story, retold in the photo-filled *Perils and Pleasures of Domesticating Goat Cheese*: "We had this idea about moving to a farm," he recounted to a rapt audience. "We were Manhattanites. I definitely had a particular image of a farm in my head. I'd seen this cartoon, with a red barn and a silo and Farmer Brown on his tractor, talking to a cow. And that's how I thought of it, as me and the animals talking to each other."[66] Cahn writes in his book, "It all began with the idea that it would be nice to have a place in the country—a farm actually—where we could enjoy a change of pace on the weekends."[67] Cahn's imagery is self-consciously pastoral and might seem parodic if it did not conform so well to type.

While pastoral imagery has tended to be overly romanticized or sentimentalized in popular discourse, Leo Marx has shown that in American literature the pastoral ideal is continually interrupted: into the contemplative wilderness chugs the locomotive, that noisy engine of industrial progress.[68] Naming this device the "machine in the garden," Marx calls attention to a paradox at the heart of American industrialism, that nature is simultaneously reduced to raw material for human cultural and technological transformation and, in its purportedly pristine form, upheld as an object of reverence and means of contemplative self-realization. While *land* is seen by agricultural and mining industries as a resource for value extraction, *landscapes* are framed as objects of contemplation and sites of relaxation. What Marx calls "complex pastoralism" wrestles with what this paradox might mean for what counts as progress in American culture.

In *The Country and the City*, Raymond Williams argues that the paradox of complex pastoralism is ideological. For Williams, it is not merely poetic that "The means of agricultural production—the fields, the woods, the growing crops, the animals—are attractive to the observer."[69] In aestheticizing agricultural fields and pastures, the pastoral divide between country and city masks rural exploitation when that exploitation is enacted in courts of law, money markets, and opportunities for conspicuous consumption—all of which are found in the city.[70] Bucolic pastoral imagery has had durable effects in the world, as starkly evident in the history of farm labor. In Depression-era California, landowners traded on the promise of a rural idyll to lure farmworkers from the heartland; upon arrival these labor migrants, derogatorily named Okies, were exploited and dispossessed.[71] By telling their tale, John Steinbeck's *The Grapes of Wrath* gives us a powerful anti-Pastoral. Pastoral mythology continues to mask the structural inequalities, from health-care disparities to seats of regulatory authority and advisory power, reinforced when capital flows from rural to urban areas.

If at first glance Mateo and Andy Kehler seem to repeat a Thoreauvian ...ment in agrarian living, their self-narrative—and those of other chees... in this book—tells not of an ambivalent "complex pastoralism," nor of a ...u...al anti-pastoralism, so much as an optimistic *post-pastoralism.* Their ideological anchor is a revised pastoral that critiques industrial capitalism's wholesale exploitation of nature and culture yet retains, while modifying, an opposition between city and country—and it hopes to offer a better way forward. Far from being denied or debated, the "machine in the garden" at Jasper Hill Farm is proudly front and center—in the form of the cheese vats, pneumatic presses, walk-in coolers, vacuum-packaging machines, and steady stream of UPS trucks necessary to produce cheese and deliver it to a distributed marketplace. Their dreams share many features with what Terry Gifford has identified as a twentieth-century, environmentalist post-pastoral literature, from the naturalist essays of John Muir to the poetry of Ted Hughes.[72]

Taking Leo Marx's machine in the garden as a point of reference, the "machine" of artisanal cheese production is integrated into a post-pastoral landscape, meant not to displace nature but to work in collaboration with organic agencies in a productive fashion. The machine may indeed be mechanical, but it remains human-scale. The labor of artisanal cheesemaking is slow, thoughtful, even sensual. Its temporal pace is freed from the factory clock. Artisans prefer to pasteurize milk used for cheesemaking by heating it gently and gradually—a process that takes more time but is less detrimental to the enzymes in milk than the almost instantaneous high-temperature, short-time pasteurization method used in industrial fabrication. Rather than follow a preprogrammed procedure, artisan cheesemakers reach into the vat, thrusting fingers into coagulating curd to ascertain when it is ready to be cut and drained from the whey. Artisanal manufacture represents an extension of the craftsperson's body into the productive process rather than its replacement by computer-programmed machinery.

The "garden" of the artisan post-pastoral is neither wilderness nor country estate, but instead a working landscape. Urban and suburban migrants relocate to the countryside not merely to observe and contemplate the natural beauty of its landscapes, but to work and to steward the land. Agricultural newcomers such as the Cahns and the Kehlers have purposefully set out to keep land in agricultural use, protecting it from being otherwise developed by encroaching exurbs (as in New York's Westchester County) or small-town real estate developers (as in the Massachusetts Berkshires or California wine country)—or, in Vermont, preventing tree regrowth from covering fields as they are kept open by the nibbling of grazing livestock. Placing sentimental as well as material value on the working landscape, cheesemakers articulate a synthesis of land (resource extraction through labor) and landscape (bucolic vista). While valuing, even sometimes romanticizing the potentiality of nature, they are under no illusion that that nature is simply there, awaiting labor to be mixed with it. Instead, they understand that nature's generative potential must be realized through proper care—that is, through post-pastoral artisanship.

Here is how Steve Getz, who after 9/11 quit his job as a business consultant and moved with his family from suburban Pennsylvania to rural Vermont, intending to make cheese, describes his farm:

> It has mountain views in every direction, which is really nice. It's a very pleasant place to farm, but this is a farm in transition. . . . We bought this farm [from] a young man [who had] the cows locked up 365 days a year, heavily drugged, [and] the fields plowed edge to edge for corn silage. I took two contractor bags of syringes out of the manure pile. And so it's been a series of cleaning this up from what was done to this farm over time. So I see a farm going back to the future, going *back* to some of the traditional techniques of grazing and making dry hay. . . . [But] we're using some newer techniques, too. . . . We put up this solar barn, which we bed with deep straw, and that's where our cows live in the wintertime. It's their choice, though—be outside or come inside on that deep straw.[73]

Such narratives construe cheesemaking and the craft dairy farming on which it is based as a form of counterindustrial agricultural remediation.

A post-pastoral ethos recognizes that culture and nature are not in fundamental opposition to each other; instead, nature, no less than culture, contains and unleashes creative as well as destructive forces—and therefore requires responsible human guidance. Cheese itself exemplifies *cultured nature,* the product of human skill working in concert with the natural agencies of bacteria, yeasts, and molds to transform a fluid made by ruminant animals.[74] In "recognition of a creative-destructive universe equally in balance in a continuous momentum of birth and death, death and rebirth, growth and decay" that Gifford identifies as fundamental to post-pastoral literature, the post-pastoral artisan teams up with beneficial microorganisms in a collaborative effort to defeat those germs that might derail fermentation or introduce pathogens into a food destined for human ingestion.[75] While human-crafted, cheese has a life of its own. So-called natural cheese, *real* cheese, is said to "age" and "mature." Wisconsin cheesemaker Anne Topham once said to me, "I've always thought that the cheese just has a life of its own and, once we really got going, my job was to follow it around and make it."

Artisan post-pastoralism is "after nature" in the sense described by Marilyn Strathern—at once post-nature, recognizing that there is no pristine natural world outside human cultural activity, and also ever in pursuit of some kind of remade nature as a ground for appropriate human action.[76] The post-pastoral remains haunted by, even indebted to, the pastoral: in sharing its aesthetic values, in looking to the natural world as a source for self-realization—though now more through work than through restful contemplation. Many of today's rural in-migrants who engage in the day-to-day labor of dairy farming and artisanal production hail, too, from a demographic that in the past enjoyed the country as recreational vacationers rather than residents. It is not incidental that the Kehlers now farm where their grandmother once summered. In *All Creatures,* a cultural history of natural history collecting in the United States, historian Robert Kohler draws a connection between the late-nineteenth-century rise of middle-class outdoor vacationing and a scientific interest in nature: "Natural history was an outdoor activity that particularly embodied the idea of active, improving recreation. It was a kind of work (and play) that was easily assimilated, morally and logistically, to the practices of middle-class vacationing."[77] Artisanal cheese-making, when practiced by rural in-migrants, might be viewed as a kind of work (and play) that assimilates the improving recreation favored by the middle class into the marketplace. If the pastoral-inspired, middle-class penchant for buying abandoned farms as vacation homes paved the way for early twentieth-century natural science collecting, three generations later some of the same properties provide opportunities for commercial cheesemaking.[78] The artisan post-pastoral builds upon those capitalist economic structures that, according to Williams, the pastoral ideal has long legitimated.

By the same token, artisanal cheesemaking not only poses a critical response to industrial agriculture, it has been enabled by it. The infrastructure of highways and long-haul refrigerated trucking necessary to get rural-made cheese to afflu-ent urban markets is the same infrastructure that paved the way for the Wal-Mart economy that now accounts for a significant portion of the grocery market in this country.[79] And it is no coincidence that the beginning of the American artisanal cheese revival in the 1980s coincides with a decline in small family dairying when a new wave of rural in-migrants bought deteriorating farms and restored old barns and farmhouses—the very farms, in many instances, that were casualties of industrial agriculture. Almost without realizing it, Miles Cahn of Coach Farm hits on the historic conditions in which his dream could be realized: "In my fantasy, the farm we were looking for was going to be a real working farm. . . . We soon learned, however, that if it was a real working farm, it wasn't for sale. And if it was for sale, it was surely not working."[80] In her anthropological study of the fallout from 1980s midwestern American farm closures, Kathryn Dudley argues that cultural romance with an idealized rural way of life obscured from public view the social trauma of the U.S. farm crisis: "The disappearance of a family farm system of agriculture has not yet registered in the consciousness of the nation. The paradox of the pastoral ideal has allowed us to entertain the illusion that any family with the right combination of skill, ambition, and luck can make a decent living on the land."[81] Artisan cheesemaking is unfolding as a sequel to the 1980s farm crisis insofar as the "nature" that today's cheesemakers have inherited or, more likely, purchased, is not bucolic pastoral landscape but instead industrially configured agricultural land. This book offers a partial sequel to Dudley's story, too, in telling of suburbanites and city dwellers, hoping to alight upon the right combination of skill, ambition, and luck, who are setting out to forge a new post-pastoral ideal.

In the post-pastoral vision of a working landscape, cultured nature—cows grazing on a hillside pasture, or the microbial activity that creates a "natural" rind on a wheel of cheese—is both productive of commercial goods and also a vehicle for social and aesthetic value. While in many ways the practice of artisan cheesemaking challenges a familiar divide between country and city—"here nature, there worldliness," to borrow a phrase from Raymond Williams—that is enshrined in popular, romantic representations of the pastoral, such familiar oppositions do often pervade cheesemakers' own marketing.[82] Mary Keehn, founder of Cypress Grove Chevre in Arcata, California, told me in an interview, "I wrote in an article that you have to have a lot of different footwear, from your boots in the barn to your clogs in the creamery to your high heels to go to town [to market cheese]. People see it at the high-heel level and they want to romanticize all the rest." Nevertheless, Keehn's company's Web site declares: "In our cheesemaking process, we let as much local environmental influence into our creamery as regulations allow. What does that environmental influence look and feel like? Well, stunning vistas and moist air. We're located in rural Humboldt County, in the northern most reaches of California. It's rugged and remote here, a place where the legend of Bigfoot is celebrated with a yearly festival. . . . Our creamery sits where the redwoods meet the Pacific Ocean, the perfect vantage point to watch the fog roll in."[83]

Although artisans make pragmatic business decisions and their fabrication methods are often technologically sophisticated, their cheese's commercial value still trades on classic pastoral romance. Within the artisan post-pastoral lie not only the seeds of a powerful cultural critique of industrial capitalism, but also the potential for a new myth of labor and value. A working landscape is not fastidiously cultivated to demonstrate wealth but suggests instead a democratic ideal in a "hard-working American" kind of way.[84] Still, as with the classic Pastoral before it, idealization of the working landscape can paper over real economic differences among working farmers and artisans.

QUESTIONS OF CLASS

How might we think about social class in rural settings in an era not of gentleman farmers, but of former professionals whose second career has them rising at dawn to milk animals and whose weekends are spent behind a folding table making change at a farmers' market? Among artisan cheesemakers are some economically privileged landowners who bring refined cultural tastes to their productive activity. A few are wealthy indeed; not coincidentally, these tend to be the ones profiled in the *New York Times* and *Wall Street Journal* as models of what can be achieved by returning to the land. At the same time, a few producers of highly sought-after cheeses live near the poverty line. Although income measures can be deceptive, among cheesemakers participating in a nationwide survey I conducted in 2009, 14 percent (n = 143) reported annual household incomes under twenty-five thousand dollars. Those who lived on the least amount of money were also those whose income depended on sales of cheese and other farm products, without the off-farm income of a spouse or the investment income generated by savings from a prior occupation.

It is not strictly the case that these households are unable to make more money. Rather, money is not the measure of the life these farmers and artisans seek. Still, choosing not to pursue wealth for its own sake does not make poverty a lifestyle choice. The structural conditions within which people confront everyday economic decisions are an important part of the "moral ecology of the market."[85] In the United States, as artisanal production demonstrates, these conditions favor the interests of large corporations at the expense of small entrepreneurs, as well as the potential of initially well-capitalized operations at the expense of more modest upstarts.

We need a more complex understanding of social class than the familiar model of whether someone owns the means of production to understand contemporary rural social dynamics.[86] We need to unravel the symbols and processes through which economic and cultural capital—that is, money and taste—map onto and reinforce each other. "Cultural capital" is a term elaborated by Pierre Bourdieu to call attention to how taste, while it may feel subjective and personal, is in fact shaped by the class position of the taster.[87] When hiring practices transmit cultural capital into earning power, belief that taste is an intrinsic matter of character may seem to legitimate class hierarchies. As with artists and educators, the social position of unconventional farmers and artisan food producers often complicates this equation. Hippie cheesemakers may be decidedly cash-poor yet exhibit tastes that run to the cosmopolitan, naming their goats after Greek goddesses or female reporters for National Public Radio. And when dairy farmers develop artisanal skills hoping to generate additional income, they may acquire new tastes.[88] Cultural capital can be accrued through the production no less than the consumption of status goods, though this is not always obvious to consumers.[89] Commenting on my research, a graduate student once asked me, "You mean frou-frou cheese?" His disapproving tone suggested that cheese that appeals to elite tastes must surely be made by elite people. Demonstrating naïveté about the means and mode of artisanal production, such a portrayal is reminiscent of the 1990s demographic that David Brooks skewered as "bourgeois bohemians, or Bobos."[90] Based on analyses of patterns and rationales of consumption, such accounts offer little to help us understand the artisanal production of goods, even when artisan markets may rely on "Bobo" consumers.[91] The "frou-frou" characterization is rooted in a class-based critique of "sentimental pastoralism" that obscures a more complicated dialectic of economic and moral activity enacted by artisans across the country.

By implying that handcrafted goods must be the province of those who do not work to make money, the charge of elitism also reflects the marginal, ambiguous status of artisanship in a hyperindustrial society.[92] The artisan, like the independent farmer, is neither a quintessential capitalist, living off the labor of others, nor an alienated wage-worker. Artisanship confounds familiar class categories. Smaller enterprises may see wealthy landowners assuming the physical labor of dairying and cheesemaking; larger enterprises may see employees innovating new production methods and creating new cheeses. Those who have taken up cheesemaking as a second career might be characterized as belonging to a "creative class," a growing segment of the American workforce—scientists and engineers, artists and designers, new media producers, university professors— paid to "create new ideas, new technology and/or new creative content," according to Richard Florida.[93] But not every maker of artisanal cheese working today fits this characterization.

Those who start cheesemaking businesses are, though, predominantly white.[94] There are many reasons for this, including European and Middle Eastern traditions of cheesemaking and cheese eating, a history of racial discrimination in agricultural loans and federal assistance from the U.S. Department of Agriculture, and a history of segregated vacationing in rural landscapes. All across the country, however, agriculture and food-processing industries, including a few of the larger artisan enterprises in this book, rely increasingly on immigrant labor.[95] As far north as Vermont and Maine, dairy farms (larger than the ones I visited in my research) are sustained by the low-wage labor of Mexican and Latin American farmworkers.[96] Among these farmworker populations are women and men who, working on the side in unlicensed facilities, turn milk into *queso fresco* and other "Hispanic-style" cheeses for domestic consumption and informal trade. Their stories, like those of Amish cheesemakers now flourishing in Wisconsin, are in many ways parallel to the story I tell here.[97]

Recent signs suggest that the artisan cheese community of which I write is beginning to diversify. In Wisconsin, Cesar Luis, an auto mechanic who emigrated from Mexico to find work in his teens and who missed eating the Oaxacan rope cheese that his grandmother taught him to make, spent his weekly day off taking cheesemaking classes to earn his license (Wisconsin is the only state that licenses commercial cheesemakers).[98] After renting vat time for one year, he and his wife, Heydi, bought and installed a cheese vat at a dairy farm in eastern Wisconsin; two days a week they make cheese curd for the farm to sell, and on other days they make Mexican-style cheeses to sell under their own label, Cesar Cheese.[99] In the 2010 competition of the American Cheese Society, Cesar and Heydi won First Place for their Queso Oaxaca in the Mozzarella Type category.

METHOD

Because I am most interested in artisanal production, the bulk of my research has been carried out by visiting dairy farms and creameries and by interviewing cheesemakers.[100] While most of the people I interviewed are owner-operators of small businesses, a few co-own or manage farms or larger creameries that employ artisans.[101] I formally interviewed forty-five artisan cheesemakers and/or owners representing forty-two businesses centered within three major dairying and cheese-producing regions: New England, Wisconsin, and Northern California.[102] This figure represents approximately 10 percent of all artisan cheese enterprises across the country. I have spoken informally with dozens of additional cheesemakers at farmers' markets, tasting events, and other public venues.

Although I always arranged appointments in advance, I never knew what to expect when I arrived for an interview. Often I was invited into a cheesemaker's home, where we would have a leisurely talk over a cup of coffee or a light lunch before touring the farm and/or cheesemaking facility. Other times I accompanied farmer-cheesemakers as they carried out their daily routine, scribbling notes as we talked, aware that the audio recording would be difficult to decipher over the rush of wind as we walked around a farm or the din of clanging metal and running water as cheese molds were washed. Always, it was instructive to see the facilities: Was the equipment cutting-edge or repurposed? Was the workspace designed with a picture window overlooking a cow pasture or tucked into the corner of a garage?

In the spring of 2004, I spent twelve days as a resident anthropologist at a sheep dairy farm in Westminster West, Vermont, sleeping in David Major's barn and helping to make and cure wheels of Vermont Shepherd cheese. Anthropologists call this mode of learning by doing—and more, by experiencing the quotidian instances and interactions of everyday life among those whose vocations and concerns we study—*participant-observation.* Sharing a barn bunkhouse with David's intern, no less than working alongside David in managing rotational grazing, delivering lambs, milking ewes, and culturing, molding, curing, and packaging cheese, provided invaluable access to the daily experiences of sheep dairy farming and cheesemaking. It also gave me a firsthand feeling for how milk becomes cheese—for the smooth touch of coagulated curd, for the warm humidity of the immersive environment of the cheese room, for the endless washing and sanitizing. In working on Major Farm and enrolling in several hands-on cheesemaking workshops in Vermont, I was becoming not so much a cheesemaker as an anthropologist of cheesemaking. My rudimentary experience in working with sheep and curd became invaluable to me when later conversing with cheesemakers as they struggled to convey the tacit knowledge of their craft.

Cheese is a material artifact, shaped by human craft. Like any artistic work, however, cheese is fabricated, packaged, and presented, and bestowed aesthetic value through the aggregate, if not always collaborative, efforts of numerous people. In addition to cheesemakers, these include office managers, equipment sales representatives, summer interns, specialty foods distributors, retailers, technical and business consultants, chefs, food writers, judges at cheese competitions, and consumers. I refer to this distributed community as the artisan cheese world.[103] The American Cheese Society (ACS), a nonprofit organization founded in 1983 by a Cornell University dairy scientist to help develop and support artisanal cheese production, represents a significant slice of this world. With blue ribbons won at its annual competition translating into media attention and increased sales, the ACS has been instrumental in revising popular understandings of "American cheese."[104] Its annual meetings provided a crucial venue for participant-observation, offering me unparalleled opportunity to learn about the concerns of and debates among people in the artisan cheese world, for instance: building facilities to government code, working with raw versus pasteurized milk, branding and trademarking, finding a market, and defining *farmstead* and *artisanal,* terms that help organize this emergent enterprise. I have attended four ACS meetings over a seven-year period (2005, 2007, 2008, 2011), allowing me to track cheesemakers' conversations—among themselves but also in dialogue with retailers and distributors as well as food-industry and dairy-science consultants—from coast to coast and from year to year.

This book tells stories about people who populate the world of American artisan cheese. My mode of analysis is to interpret these stories by offering multiple perspectives—including but not exclusively my own—on what it takes and what it means to make cheese artisanally. Because people's individual stories and perspectives are so central to this text, I have decided not to use pseudonyms. Although my analysis is informed by the composite of my research, I have had to be selective here in telling only the most vivid stories, or those that best represent conclusions I have drawn from years of research. I regret that I am unable to tell more stories of more people. Those persons named in this book have given approval for my use of attributed quotations from my interviews.

I should mention two additional research methods. First, there is eating. It was as a consumer that I first encountered and thought about American artisanal cheese, and I have continued to eat quite a lot of it. In shopping for and tasting cheese I have been able to discern producers gaining skill in their craft, apparent to me through greater consistency from one batch to the next as well as in the qualities of any particular wheel or wedge. I have watched retail prices rise. I have seen cheese varieties, and entire businesses, appear and disappear from the market.

Finally, in January and February 2009 I conducted an extensive, nationwide survey of artisan cheesemakers—the first social science survey of its kind—to provide a contextualizing data set on cheesemakers' ethnicity, age, gender, and household composition; educational background and occupational experience; land ownership and financing strategies; household income; and scale and profitability of business operations. I distributed the survey to 398 businesses, yielding 177 responses (a 45 percent response rate).[105] The survey gathered additional data on how, when, and for what initial reasons people learned to make cheese; through what venues businesses market their cheese; whether farmstead operations also buy milk for cheesemaking; as well as other business-related matters. A report on survey results was sent to all survey participants as well as to the ACS and a few regional cheese organizations.

Although I did not set out to conduct a systematic regional comparison in my research, a few patterns emerged. In New England and California, where open pastureland is under threat of development, selling use rights to land trusts is a popular way to capitalize the expansion of cheesemaking facilities. In Wisconsin, where land is less at a premium, no one spoke of the need to preserve a "working landscape" (as they did in Vermont), nor did farmers sell development rights to land trusts; the story I heard there was that artisanal cheese provided a means of carrying into the future Wisconsin's "rural way of life." People, as farmers and artisans, were drawn in sharper relief in Wisconsin, while, rhetorically speaking, land and landscape were more fully in focus on the coasts. At the same time, the majority of New England's cheesemaking artisans are college graduates, often from elite schools, who have returned to family land with new class dispositions and business sensibilities or who have adopted a state like Vermont or Maine as a land of environmentally sound business opportunity. In Wisconsin, the only state that requires cheesemakers to be licensed through internship and examination, cheesemaking has been and continues to be a viable, visible profession. Here, where rural newcomers live and work alongside third-generation farmers and artisans, cheesemakers are said to exemplify a "midwestern work ethic" that was cited to me as frequently in Wisconsin as the "working landscape" was in Vermont.

A NOTE ON CONSUMER INTEREST

Although this book focuses on the producers and production of cheese, a consumer market is essential to their projects. Ihsan Gurdal, whose Formaggio Kitchen in the Cambridge, Massachusetts, neighborhood where I live was the first cheese shop in the United States to install a French-style cheese "cave" for ripening cheeses, told me that from his perspective as a retailer, consumer interest in domestic cheese has piggybacked on broader consumption of European cheeses. This interest took off in the 1990s as a strong U.S. dollar and domestic economy encouraged Americans to travel to European cities and country inns where, Gurdal said, they "were exposed to cheese" and to the way Europeans eat cheese, as a discrete course in a meal. Meanwhile, he noted, people were beginning to realize that the eighties' "cholesterol scare was overdone." American diners requested that restaurants offer after-dinner cheese plates, and chefs were only too happy to oblige. Middle-class consumers have since flocked to educational and recreational cheese-tasting workshops held at restaurants, bars, and retail shops, just as they had begun exploring wine in the 1970s. Cheese is the new wine: a mark of educated good taste. Meanwhile, the low-carb diet craze of the early 2000s did even more for hedonistic cheese consumption than the news about good cholesterol. In 2004, a retailer at Formaggio Kitchen told me of new customers, people who had previously never thought of cheese as a food in its own right, walking in the door and announcing, "I'm on Atkins! Give me some cheese! Fat is no problem!"

If high-end cheese consumption is on the rise, how much of this market is dominated by European imports and how much is filled by domestic production? This turns out to be a difficult question to answer. There are no direct data available on production and sales volumes for U.S. artisanal cheese. State and federal statistics do not differentiate between artisanal and specialty cheese; "specialty" includes industrially fabricated cheeses of foreign origin (e.g., Feta, Asiago, Hispanic-style) as well as specially designed cheeses in limited supply (e.g., industrially made, waxed Cheddar cut to resemble the geographic outline of the state of Wisconsin). Furthermore, the U.S. National Agricultural Statistics Service declines to release production data on cheese made from goat's milk and sheep's milk; producers are so few, particularly at the high-volume end, that release of data might compromise proprietary information for the largest facilities.[106] What can safely be said is that the market for domestically produced artisanal cheese continues to grow.

While the strong U.S. dollar of the 1990s spurred American consumption of European cheeses, the strong euro of the 2000s helped to widen the market for domestic cheeses. In Sonoma, California, I asked eighty-year-old Ignazio Vella, venerable second-generation maker of Vella Dry Jack, what he made of what was being called a domestic artisan renaissance. Leaning forward in his office chair, his customary, crisply folded paper hat cocked to one side, Ig Vella's eyes widened as he replied: "What has driven this has been the euro. The euro began to climb, and all of a sudden"—he lowered his voice to a mock-conspiratorial whisper—"*cheese made in America wasn't bad at all!* . . . When the euro went up and is staying up, our cheese is good. *That's* your renaissance." Indeed, the last time the U.S. dollar exchanged at a higher rate than the euro occurred in the fall of 2002, just as Jasper Hill and so many other domestic cheese producers were preparing to enter the market. The weak dollar of the past decade brought the price of European cheeses, generously subsidized by state governments, up to the range of American prices. When European cheeses are not the comparative bargain they once were, a retailer confirmed, even the most Europhilic consumers are more willing to take a chance on American cheeses. But while heightened interest in sophisticated European cheeses may have helped open a market for domestic varieties, it also raised the bar. Another retailer suggested to me that increased sophistication might have made consumers "more suspicious" of American cheeses, not more curious about them. The American artisanal cheese industry has taken off amid increasing pressure to be good in another way—to produce high-quality cheese consistently.

Reinforced by the growth of farmers' markets and food-themed television programming, consumers are expressing an interest in learning about where their food comes from and how it is produced. The U.S. adoption of Slow Food, an organization begun in Italy to protect customary food-making knowledge and to cultivate in a new generation a taste for "traditional" foods enjoyed in convivial settings, is symptomatic of such interest. While Slow Food in Europe has been a producer-driven initiative, Slow Food USA has been consumer and retailer-driven. Locally sourced foods are à la mode. Cheese, another retailer said to me, is becoming "the darling of chefs," citing a restaurant fad of featuring "one perfect cheese" if not a wide cheese selection; with broader emphasis on regional produce, more featured cheeses are produced domestically. Since *New York Times* writer Marian Burros named Mateo Kehler (shortly after my initial visit to Jasper Hill) the "rock star of the cheese world," the Kehlers and a handful of other cheesemakers (and their cheeses) have appeared on *Good Morning America* and *The Martha Stewart Show* and in the pages not only of gourmet food magazines but also of *Fortune* and *Details*.[107] It would not be surprising if such attention influenced producers' own hierarchy of values.

MENU

The chapters of this book unfold the stories of particular cheesemakers while developing a set of arguments. Chapters 2 and 3 concentrate on the people behind the artisan resurgence that began on the coasts in the 1980s and spread inward across the country, while chapter 4 settles in Wisconsin and provides a historical overview of American cheesemaking since colonial times, bringing into view artisan factories, some still in operation, that long predate today's post-pastoralists. Chapters 5 and 6 draw from science and technology studies to analyze the craft practice and regulatory conditions of commercial cheesemaking. Chapters 7 and 8 situate artisanal cheese production and consumption within contemporary agricultural and food politics.

Chapter 2, "Ecologies of Production," draws from my stay on David Major's farm to detail what goes into producing cheese and to analyze how producers draw meaning from that labor. Vermont Shepherd cheese's farm-based ecology of production includes the pasture grasses, sheep, and microorganisms that contribute to the development of the cheese and its sensory qualities. In telling and selling a story of how cheese is made on a farm, cheesemakers depict livestock and microorganisms as sorts of co-laborers, a move that reflects an appreciation for their animals and the organic agencies of fermentation and cheese ripening. Because commercial stakes are involved, however, which particular properties of farm-based production should be considered value-enhancing is a matter of debate carried out over the meaning of "farmstead" cheese.

If chapter 2 examines "the life of cheese" in an ecological sense, chapter 3, "Economies of Sentiment," zeroes in on the life of cheese as a vocation for those who pursue cheesemaking commercially. It begins by surveying the motivations and goals that have led a variety of people to start artisan cheesemaking businesses. It then shows how, in price setting, marketing, and calibrating business growth, rural entrepreneurs struggle to reconcile their principles and pragmatic needs in ensuring that their enterprises are both personally fulfilling and financially viable.

Chapter 4, "Traditions of Invention," retraces the history of cheesemaking in the United States to argue that continuities in artisanal fabrication methods between factory and farmstead creameries are obscured by changes in the organization and significance of artisanal production. Juxtaposing the artisanal practices and sensibilities of third-generation factory cheesemakers in Wisconsin and first-generation farmstead producers in Vermont, I show how cheesemakers in this country continually reinvent an American tradition of entrepreneurial innovation.

Chapter 5, "The Art and Science of Craft," investigates what makes artisanal cheese artisanal. In contrast to industrial cheesemaking, which begins with standardized ingredients and hypersterile conditions to produce an utterly consistent product, artisan cheesemakers adjust their method to work with rather than against seasonal and climatic variations in milk that affect fermentation and coagulation as well as the color and flavor of cheese. What distinguishes a cheese as artisanal is the *synesthetic reason* of the artisan, engaging her senses to evaluate the empirical conditions and behavior of curd as it forms in the vat and matures in a wheel of cheese. I unpack the significance of the fact that cheesemakers speak of this skill not as a craft but rather as a balance between art and science.

Chapter 6, "Microbiopolitics," considers the regulatory dimension of food production. While the U.S. Food and Drug Administration views raw-milk cheese as a biohazard, potentially riddled with pathogenic microbes, many artisans and consumers see it as a traditional food processed for safety by the action of beneficial microbes that can outcompete "bad bugs" that may be lurking in milk or can settle on the surface of an aging cheese. Revisiting ecologies of production at a microscopic scale, I develop the concept of *microbiopolitics* to analyze how farmers, cheesemakers, food microbiologists, safety regulators, retailers, and consumers work variously to reconcile Pasteurian (hygienic) and post-Pasteurian (probiotic) attitudes about the microbial agents at the heart of cheese.

Chapter 7, "Place, Taste, and the Promise of *Terroir*," revisits the theme of value creation by investigating American experiments in translating for American cheese the French notion of *terroir*, which links the taste of comestibles to the geographical and geological features of agricultural lands. While some cheese-makers describe distinctive relations among land, climate, cheese type, and flavor, others work in a more avowedly constructivist and, indeed, American, register, invoking *terroir* to speak to the instrumental values of artisanal production. To many, artisanal cheese has the potential to revitalize agricultural landscapes, reinvigorate rural economies, and even create new places. Through the vocabulary of *terroir*, producers seek to concretize their visions of the value of handcrafted—and handcrafting—cheese.

In a brief conclusion, chapter 8, "Bellwether," meditates on what artisanal cheese might suggest about the future of agricultural practice and food politics in the United States.

Ecologies of Production

With its golden brown rind and rustic shape, every wheel of Vermont
Shepherd is distinctive. The texture is smooth and creamy. The flavor is
sweet, rich and earthy, with hints of clover, wild mint and thyme. . . . Like
many fine foods . . . strawberries, Beaujolais and morel mushrooms, our
sheep's milk cheese is seasonal. The cheese is made when our pastures are
abundant with wild herbs and grasses.

—VERMONT SHEPHERD CHEESE MARKETING BROCHURE

In southeastern Vermont, a picturesque region of rolling hills, neighborly general stores, and cozy bed-and-breakfasts, David and Cindy Major began making Vermont Shepherd cheese in the early 1990s. David grew up in a house across the road, where his parents still live. The family raised sheep for meat and wool to supplement the income that David's mother earned teaching kindergarten and his father made by working as a real estate agent, but mostly they did it for fun. After graduating in 1983 from Harvard College, where he studied international development and engineering (and was disappointed not to learn practical skills, such as well digging), David returned to his parents' farm with the idea of making a living by working the land. He was trying, and failing, to make it in the wool and lamb business when he met Cindy, a student at nearby Marlboro College. It was Cindy's father, owner of a dairy processing plant in Queens, New York, who suggested to the couple that they might milk the sheep—something that had not occurred to the Majors, who regarded their flock as meat, wool, and pets. By 1993, Cindy and David were transforming raw sheep's milk into wheels of Vermont Shepherd, a farm-based product that, by the time I visited in 2004, sustained their family of four plus a handful of employees. Since then, David and Cindy have divorced. Today David farms and makes cheese with Yesenia Ielpi Major and their blended family.

Cheese begins on dairy farms. David Major considers himself a sheep farmer who also makes cheese. During spring lambing season he sleeps in the unheated barn, ready to assist ewes with difficult births. He does the shearing and takes shifts in the milking parlor. With their neighbors' help, the Majors cut and bale hay from fields nourished with composted manure and whey, the protein-rich liquid by-product of cheesemaking. David serves as a farmer representative on numerous local and state agricultural committees. His trajectory from college student to sheep dairy farmer and commercial cheesemaker represents a quest for a post-pastoral form of life.

When I first visited Major Farm on a chilly afternoon in March 2004, David took me on a walking tour of the cheesemaking facilities, comprising a free-standing cheese house where milk is transformed into fresh wheels of cheese and a separate aging "cave" where cheeses ripen. Crossing snow-covered fields with a pair of border collies at our heels, we stopped to feed the sixty-five ewes sheltering in David's parents' barn. It soon became apparent that the way of life David was beginning to describe to me was not ultimately about the cheese. To him, making cheese for commercial sale represents a means to spend much of his time outside, "directly engaged with the land." Of the entire process of farmstead cheesemaking, which this chapter details, David most loves grass pasturing: shepherding animals over hills kept lush with clover, wildflowers, and grasses by intensive rotational grazing. David is also fond of the sheep, descendants of animals he tended as a child. As I gave him a hand pulling apart bales of hay to stuff into feed troughs, he pointed out ancestral traits among the sheep, such as a distinctive facial freckling from one of his best-producing ewes, which he bred specially with an East Friesian stud. David's sentimental orientation toward the origins of the milk rather than the eventual dairy product may help to explain why, for more than a decade, Vermont Shepherd—a cheese whose very name conveys pastoral origins—was the only cheese he made from his sheep's milk.[1]

That afternoon walking the pastures with David Major first brought into focus for me how grass, animals, wool, meat, milk, and cheese are all part of the same agricultural process. In order to produce the milk that will become cheese, ewes must first get pregnant and give birth. Behind cheese lie animal genealogies and the logistics of breeding, the management of sex ratios through the slaughter of young males for meat, and the daily routines of pasturing and milking. Artisanal cheese may be made largely by hand, but humans do not make it alone: ruminant animals, herding and guard dogs, and bacteria, yeasts, and molds also contribute.

Understanding how cheese is made entails grasping its full production, by which I mean assemblages of value-making activities held together by histori-cal, economic, social, and regulatory forces. This chapter traces the develop-ment of both a wheel of cheese and a rural business enterprise to argue that Vermont Shepherd comes into being through a particular *ecology of production,* an assemblage of organic, social, and symbolic forces put into productive play in the service of a post-pastoral form of life, one that seeks to work with the agencies of the natural world in a way that revitalizes rather than depletes those forces.[2] The word *ecology,* derived by Ernst Haeckel in 1869 from the Ancient Greek *oikos,* meaning "home" or "house," may be viewed as "the study of the 'home life' of living organisms." Elaborated as an academic field, ecology refers to the "study of the interactions between organisms and their environment."[3] By situating artisan cheesemaking within ecologies of production I mean to call attention to the multiple agencies that contribute to agricultural enterprise, while also emphasizing that the dynamic capacities of a farm are harnessed through a capitalist mode of production to generate food for commercial trading as well as for eating. Far from being rural isolates, commercial farms are connected to industrial manufacturing and urban markets and are embedded in county, state, and federal polities.[4] Ecologies of production, then, encompass nested spheres of productive activity: first, the multispecies activity on a farm; and second, how that farm activity is made possible, organized, and constrained by broader social, economic, and legal forces.[5]

I returned to Major Farm in May 2004 as a resident anthropologist, helping to milk sheep and move flocks between pastures, bottle-feed newborn lambs, keep the records entailed in livestock husbandry, and make and cure cheese. I gained an appreciation for the work that goes into producing a wheel of Vermont Shepherd both as good food and as good for the Majors to make, in that the cheese provided an engaging life and a comfortable living for them. That work is both manual and rhetorical. Consider, for example, how the description of Vermont Shepherd quoted from a farm brochure in this chapter's epigraph invites consumers to imagine the flavors distinctive to this cheese as emerging from equally distinctive clover-filled pastures, locating the cheese, and its maker— the Vermont shepherd—in a pastoral landscape emblematic of Vermont. Such imagery appeals to consumer fantasies of pastoral romance, but it also reflects producers' genuine belief that what makes their cheese taste delicious, and distinguishes it from industrially made cheese, is that it emerges from ecologies of production, or what Vermonters often describe as a "working landscape." On this view, agrarian nature should be approached not as an objectified resource for value extraction but rather as a collaborator in the production of material and symbolic value.

In a working landscape, grazing livestock are seen to "work" with human agents to produce value. In telling—and selling—the farm-based story of how cheese is made, producers direct attention to how various forms of labor and life—from grazing animals to metabolizing microorganisms to skilled humans— come together on a farm to generate the particular qualities of a cheese. This idea is encapsulated in the "farmstead" designation to distinguish an artisanal cheese produced on the same farm where the animals that provide the milk for it are raised. The farmstead label both valorizes and capitalizes on a particular ecology of production; through it, cheesemakers establish their products as intrinsically good (natural, authentic) and as virtuously produced. The biological activity of sheep and microorganisms, no less than the industry of humans, can be narrated as producing commodity value because the story taps into wider cultural values regarding the virtue of hard work. Hard work is the cornerstone of the American Dream and the ideological basis of the meritocracy that many Americans believe forms the bedrock of social strata; hard work (on this view) makes things as they should be. John Locke provided an early and influential articulation in the seventeenth century, writing that "'tis *labour* indeed that *puts the difference* of value on every thing."[6]

At the same time, by extending Locke's theory that labor creates value into the animal and even microbial world, the making and marketing of farmstead cheese would seem to *naturalize* a labor theory of value—making it appear to be fundamental, inevitable, and morally good.[7] Nevertheless, as we will see, cheese-makers disagree over which specific elements of "farmstead" production should legitimately be recognized as adding value to an artisanal cheese. Value making is neither natural nor self-evident after all.

This chapter tracks material and rhetorical elements of Vermont Shepherd's fabrication, from pasture to milking parlor to cheese house to cave and beyond.[8] As an anthropologist, I believe it is important not only to delineate such networks of productive relations but also to inquire *why* human actors believe in the moral rightness of a particular assemblage, in the ethos of a particular form of life, and are therefore committed to tinkering with it to get it to work.[9] Why are people like David Major so committed to farmstead cheesemaking as a way of making a life and a living, and how might this commitment enable, or perhaps constrain, the ecologies of production he orchestrates? To find out, we must visit the farm.

SHEEP DAIRYING AND THE SYSTEMATIC PRODUCTION OF GOOD MILK

It was a Saturday afternoon when I pulled up in my rental car to the barn's bunkhouse adjacent to the milking parlor on Patch Farm, down the road from the Majors' farmhouse (fig. 3). When Patch Farm had been put up for sale in the mid 1990s, the Vermont Land Trust had asked the Majors to buy the neighboring property as a means of expanding their operation while preserving the work-ing landscape from nonagricultural development, the most likely threat coming from new-construction second homes for city dwellers. Working with the land trust and state housing conservation board, and thanks to financial help from Cindy's parents, the Majors were able to buy the farm. Patch Farm's barn had been built in the nineteenth century as a sheep barn; during David's childhood it was converted to shelter cows. David is thrilled to keep it in agricultural use, again housing sheep.

FIG. 3. The Patch Farm barn. The stairs at left lead to the bunkhouse. The pickup truck is backed up to the entrance to the milking parlor, preparing to transport milk cans to the cheese house on Major Farm. Photo by author.

In the milking parlor I found Lucy, the Majors' summer intern and a recent Smith College graduate, with whom I was to share the adjacent spare but comfortably furnished two-bedroom bunkhouse. I followed Lucy to the pasture behind the barn to collect the sheep for milking. The herding border collies, Chet and Casey, were with us, ready to do their job. Standing at the foot of the sloped pasture, the dogs safely off to one side, Lucy called out, "Here, sheep!" Immediately, more than a hundred shorn creatures obediently tramped down the hill following a worn path to the barn, though Lucy had to coax them a bit when they came abreast of the dogs. The sheep milled about, nibbling hay as they awaited their turn in the milking parlor.

A sheep dairy farmer and cheesemaker in Wisconsin once told me that when she sells cheese at farmers' markets, conventional dairy farmers (who milk cows) sometimes approach her and insist, "You can't milk sheep!" Historically, sheep were milked (and bred for milk production) long before cows were, though sheep dairying has remained concentrated around the Mediterranean Sea, stretching into southern Europe. Roquefort, Pecorino, and Feta are all traditionally made from sheep's milk. The Majors started the first commercial sheep dairy in New England, with Old Chatham Sheepherding Company in New York following the next year, 1994.

The sheep-milking stanchion at Patch Farm utilizes a cascading headgate that a high-school friend of David's, a welder, built for him on a European design (David, leveraging his engineering major, applied for a U.S. patent on the design in 1987). It is a human-scale "machine in the garden." A tug on a rope opens a door at the side of the milking platform, raised about three feet off the ground; ewes file in and stumble along the platform (fig. 4). As the first ewe sticks her neck through an open gate to reach a feed bucket, the yoke closes and triggers the opening of the gate to her left. Every now and then a recalcitrant or confused animal must be prodded to queue up properly, but in general the sheep are orderly and compliant. Once sixteen ewes are secured, a human milker (we work in pairs) walks down the line with a plastic bottle, squirting sixteen pairs of teats with an antibacterial iodine solution (the udders of sheep, like goats, have two teats; cows' udders have four). The udders are close to our faces and it is easy to see any dirt or crusty manure, which we wipe away with brown paper toweling. The digestive system of ruminants turns grass into milk, but this simple hygienic step to remove any possible E. coli or other problem-causing microorganisms that thrive in manure is crucial for turning milk into viable cheese.

As soon as we place vacuum-pressurized milking cups on the sheep's teats, milk shoots down through plastic tubing and collects in an old-fashioned milk can. Milking easily and efficiently requires a tactile sensibility that takes practice to develop. Some sheep stamp their hind hooves, fighting the milking machine (the back of my hand became covered with hoof scratches), while others part their hind legs to make way for the milking cups. Lucy, who can identify trouble-makers at a glance, would warn, "Here comes the crazy one!" Above the constant whir of the pressurized milking system a small boom box blasts music or news from National Public Radio. The sheep seem soothed by reggae and Irish folk music. While extracting milk we are also looking after the sheep (by treating hoof problems, for example) so they can continue as milk producers. After disengaging the milking machinery, we again walk down the line squirting teats with iodine. This application is to prevent mastitis, an inflammation of the mammary gland caused by physical injury, stress, or bacterial infection. When I was on the farm, we milked seven groups of sixteen ewes. Occurring twice a day, each milking takes two people about two hours to complete, although the first time I assisted Lucy we were at it for close to three hours.

Dairy farmers regard their animals as farm laborers. The sheep, cows, and goats who live and work on the craft farms run by cheesemakers I visited are not, however, pushed to maximize milk volume according to industrial efficiencies. Unlike the ruminant animals on industrial dairies, which are fed high-protein grain rations, injected with subtherapeutic levels of antibiotics to promote growth and enable a grass-free diet, or milked three times a day, dairy animals on cheesemaking farms are generally fed a mixed diet that includes quantities of hay as well as seasonal grass pasture or, for goats, woodland browse. On Patch Farm, the daily routine during milking season includes "making pasture," moving portable fencing to create delineated grazing zones. Intensive rotational graz-

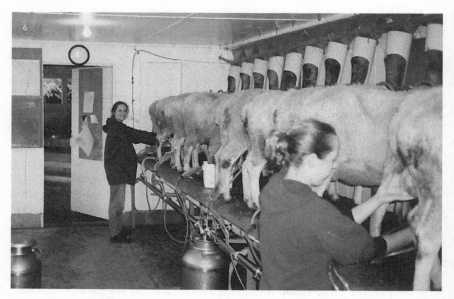

FIG. 4. The author (left) with Lucy milking sheep on Patch Farm. Photo by David Major.

ing offers the sheep a variety of grasses and wildflowers to consume; I identified dandelions, clover, buttercups. The ewes are moved to a fresh patch of pasture after every milking. To reduce pasture stress, every three to five days David and the dogs herd the flock to an entirely different area of the property. The yearlings, one-year-old sheep that David will not breed or milk until the following season, contribute labor as the "clean-up crew," consuming the plants rejected by the lactating ewes to ensure that these less desirable species will not come to dominate the pastures. Through such human, canine, and ovine activities a working landscape is cultivated as value-producing.

The working landscape of sheep dairying is tied to three different markets: cheese, meat, and wool.[10] David had shorn the animals of their winter wool earlier in the spring. A local spinnery buys the Majors' finest, cleanest wool for a dollar a pound to sell as yarn to hobbyist knitters, but David must first send the wool to Texas for washing, as no wool washing factories remain in New England.[11] In explaining to me the history of the wool market, David revealed much about the history of sheep farming in Vermont. In 1811, William Jarvis, the American consul in Lisbon and a Vermont native, took advantage of Napoleon's conquest of Spain to convince the Spanish nobility to sell him Merino sheep, a Spanish breed famed for luxuriantly woolly fleece, arguing that exportation to America would spare the animals from being eaten by hungry French soldiers.[12] Jarvis sent a prized flock of four hundred to his farm in Wethersfield, Vermont, and subsequently sold breeding stock throughout the state.[13] In the 1820s and 1830s, Merino wool sold for eighty cents to a dollar per pound. Since sheep could graze the state's rocky hilltops, which were proving unsuitable to wheat cultivation, wool was good business, and by 1840, sheep outnumbered people in Vermont six to one.[14] In the 1840s, however, expanding railroads flooded the New England market with cheap wool from the western frontier. Prices plummeted.[15] Vermont sheep farmers slaughtered entire flocks to escape a failing market.[16] Wool prices shot back up during the Civil War with the demand to supply soldiers with woolen uniforms, but the domestic textile industry did not endure into Reconstruction.[17] Today the only commodity market for David's wool is in China. One afternoon Lucy and I were tasked with filling huge burlap bags with the lower-grade wool that would be sold to a dealer and sent to China for washing. Barefoot, I rolled up my jeans, stepped into an empty bag far taller than I, and gradually rose high off the ground as I stamped on the wool that Lucy fed down to me.

Another morning, David and I drove to his parents' farm to check on the lambs. To stagger lambing times, the sixty ewes living there are bred a little later in the season than the larger flock at Patch Farm. When we arrived we found that six lambs had been born to three ewes in the previous two hours. Lambs typically come in pairs, though singletons and triplets are not uncommon. I recorded the births on a clipboard, charting their sex and David's estimation of their weight. A fourth ewe was in active labor, struggling to give birth. As David pulled on a pair of elbow-length plastic gloves, I crouched down and put my arms around the ewe to keep her still, until she knocked me over. I was holding the mother on my lap when David pulled out her twin lambs, one after the other. Newborns emerge covered with blood and embryonic fluids that act as a painkiller. The mother licked her lambs clean. After just an hour the lambs were standing and hobbling around, ready to nurse. If they failed to nurse the colostrum within twenty-four hours, they would die, David told me. "Was that your first birth?" he asked as we stood before the two new lambs. I nodded. "Congratulations," he said, smiling.

Not all mothers survive birthing. When I first visited the farm I learned that a ewe had recently died giving birth to triplets. We now checked on the orphans, penned in with two ewes that had each recently birthed a singleton. The ewes' heads were immobilized between wooden slats to keep them from interfering with the lambs' nursing. After a few days of nursing and living alongside a ewe's birth lamb, an orphan will smell to the ewe like her own and the mother will "adopt" it.[18]

Before the lambs are turned out to pasture, their tails will be docked. Using a device called an Elastrator, a strong rubber band is slipped over the tail. The constriction limits the flow of blood and, in about three weeks, the tail falls off. Anticipating objections to this standard practice, meant to prevent the develop-

ment of a long woolly tail prone to becoming caked with manure, sheep farmer
Chuck Wooster, in *Living with Sheep*, paraphrases an old shearer's words of
wisdom, "'There's nothing natural about a sheep walking around with a dozen
pounds of wool on it, and nothing natural about a sheep with a wooly tail.
Natural's got nothing to do with it. Unless you want to watch your lambs walking
around with tails covered by maggots and flies, cut the tails off.'"[19] Livestock have
evolved to their present biophysical conformation through generations of selective breeding by humans guided by their own interests—in milk volume or butterfat and protein content, wool quality, size of newborns, or animal sociability.[20]

American dairy farmers who produce milk to transform into cheese (rather
than sell by bulk tank to a processor) tend to continue milking their animals far
longer than the industrial standard; I have met farmers who milk fifteen-year-old
goats. David Major first breeds sheep as two-year-olds, and they remain on the
farm as long as they continue lambing and producing milk. A "good" sheep will
do this for the duration of her life, up to twelve or thirteen years, though only
about a quarter of David's ewes make it that long.[21] In the end, David's sheep
are auctioned at a livestock market in Massachusetts and eventually end up "in
Indian restaurants in Boston."

Cheese is inescapably tied up with the politics and ethics of meat.[22] Sheep
farmer and cheesemaker Karen Weinberg, who owns and operates 3-Corner
Field Farm in Shushan, New York, across the Vermont border, spoke forcefully
to this issue as we drove around her pastures on a four-wheeler, refilling water
troughs on a hot summer day in 2007. Like David Major, Karen raised sheep for
meat and wool before adding dairy products. At the Union Square Greenmarket
in Manhattan, she sells cheese and yogurt alongside legs of lamb, lamb sausages,
sheepskins, and wool yarn. Karen, a fit woman in her mid fifties with a no-
nonsense short haircut and a degree in psychology, complained to me about the
naïveté of some of the market customers.

> Constantly, I get the, "Oh, I can't even look at the meat! Don't even show it to me,
> I'm totally disgusted—But what do you have for cheese?" But you know, that cheese
> wouldn't exist if these lambs didn't exist; "Do you understand the connection?"
> "Oh, but you don't need to kill the sheep in order to drink their milk." But the
> lambs have to go somewhere! "Don't you understand that lambs die in the service
> of producing milk?" McDonald's exists because we have a dairy industry in the
> U.S., not because people wanted hamburgers that badly. Because people drink so
> much milk—so much cow's milk—those cows had to have a place to go. They're all
> part of that system. Just like these lambs are part of our system. They're going to
> end up being slaughtered, so you're just arguing that I shouldn't be responsible for
> their slaughter, someone else should be responsible. My thought is that I brought
> them into the world, at least I can ensure that they live a good life, and that their
> death is as painless and stress-free as possible.

For Karen, marketing lamb meat alongside cheese made from milk that exists only because those lambs were born is not only economically efficient but also morally honest. Lamb chops are not merely a by-product of cheese, the economical solution to culling male lambs from a herd; Karen views lamb, cheese, yogurt, fleece, sheepskins, and lambskins as complementary parts of a nonwasteful—ethical as well as efficient—economy of production.

Far from being callous toward the lives of lambs produced in the course of making milk, Karen works to give them a good life and then a good death.[23] She raises all her lambs on pasture whether they are destined for the farmers' market or nurtured to replace milkers culled from her flock. At about three months old, she separates "the boys and the girls" because otherwise the "boys" will bother the "girls" and "make their lives miserable." She pays a small, independent slaughterhouse to do her butchering. Husbandry's inescapable tension between beneficence and coercion, love and instrumentalism, are in play and at work, Donna Haraway says, "when species meet."[24] Such connections, though, are readily pushed out of sight and mind. What frustrates Karen about many of us who approach food politics only from the vantage of consumption is,

> A lot of people don't understand what the issues are, but they all have opinions. And a lot of those opinions are based on ignorance. I can't tell you how many people don't understand that in order for the animal to produce milk it has to be pregnant! I'll even say to some of them, "Well, how did you think they started to produce milk?" And they'll say, "Well, when they get to a certain age." And I'll say, "Did *you?* Did milk start pouring out of your mammary glands when you got to a certain age?"

Those who have been raised away from the business of growing and raising food while being exposed to the nutrition pyramid might think of meat and dairy as separate "food groups," but to Karen they are clearly part of the same ecology of production. "I would like people to know," Karen said to me, that "the old cow who stops producing is not going to be given a big burial out in the backyard. She's going to be for meat. That's the system." All is not prettified pastoral.

Some elements of this system are determined by the agricultural origins of milk, dependent on weather conditions and other uncontrollable variables, while other elements, explored in the next chapter, are social, determined by the capital needs of commercial agriculture (farm equipment is expensive), market relations, and regulatory limitations (by law, farmers cannot slaughter their own animals if the meat is to be marketed and instead must pay a licensed slaughterhouse). Good milk—flavored by pasture grasses, rich in butterfat, free of pathogens—is materially produced through rotational grazing, hygienic milking, and caring animal husbandry. But milk is also rhetorically produced as good when biological processes of animal gestation, birthing, eating, rumination, digestion, and lactation are narrated *as labor*, since labor (in this theory) is what produces value. At the same time, when farmers credit farm animals as collaborative (if subordinate) laborers, they invite scrutiny of their husbandry practices. Through such chains of association, the qualities that make milk good are associated with qualities that make its production ethical.

Mateo Kehler writes of the farmstead cheesemaking operation that he runs in Vermont with his brother, Andy:

> Jasper Hill is our response to globalization. It is in this spirit that we take cheese, a distillate of grass, the product of sunshine, and put it away, deep underground where it increases in value over time and becomes more delicious.... In an age of synthetic collateralized debt obligations and a virtual economy divorced from natural laws and limits, at a time when the extractive efficiency of capitalism and its compounding capacity to concentrate wealth threatens to collapse the planet's natural systems, it is totally appropriate to remember that all capital originates with sunshine and soil.[25]

In suggesting that farmstead ecologies of production are *by nature* productive of surplus value (that is, profit), Mateo implies that farmstead cheese represents an originary, even pure—and morally proper—form of capitalism.[26] But while sheep, goats, and cows (and herding and guard dogs) certainly contribute to the making of cheese, they do not do so under conditions of their own choosing. The ethic of care in animal husbandry is paternalistic.[27] So when Mateo Kehler and New Jersey farmer-cheesemaker Jonathan White describe what they do in a pastoral turn of phrase as "turning sunlight into cheese," it should be kept in mind that this entire assemblage of photosynthesis, rumination, lactation, and fermentation is imagined, orchestrated, funded, regulated, and appreciated by humans operating within broader political economies.

SHEEP, GOATS, COWS

One morning as I was assisting David in making cheese he suggested that in order to understand cheesemakers I should "look at the animals." David proposed what could be viewed as an animal anthropology of American farmstead cheese, an approach that would consider how cheesemakers perceive and engage with ruminant natures and socialities as a way of getting at the meanings they draw from their vocation. Goat people, David thought, get into cheese because they love the animals. Sheep people like him are oriented toward the pasture-lands that sustain the grazing animals. And cow people, he mused, seem fond of big machinery. While animals have long served as both "mirrors and windows" for human concerns—they show us reflections of our preoccupations and offer perspectives onto nature more broadly—David pointed me toward a more material entwining of animal and human socialities.[28] Humans live and work with animals to accomplish many of our projects, including making food.[29] In the process, animals' characteristic "natures" are both capitalized upon and modulated by their human keepers while people's embodied dispositions are also reshaped; rising before dawn for morning milking is only the most obvious example.[30] Regarding livestock keeping in colonial America, Virginia Anderson writes, "animals not only produced changes in the land but also in the hearts and minds and behavior of the peoples who dealt with them."[31] Farm animals contribute to ecologies of production, their bodies' capacities pressed into the system of commercial agriculture, but animals also contribute to enskilling humans as farmers and cheesemakers.

A love of goats, as David suggested, did indeed lead many women (in particular) to take up cheesemaking. On a field trip associated with the 2005 American Cheese Society (ACS) conference in Louisville, Kentucky, I visited the upscale-rustic southern Indiana farm of Judy Schad, maker of Capriole cheeses. Inspired by pastoral sentiment, in 1976 she started looking at farm properties because she had an idea that she wanted a cow. With her lawyer husband and three young children she moved from the suburbs to a run-down farm, but she never got her cow.[32] Her new neighbors advised, "With cows you have to go out to the barn when it's twenty below and it's awful. You want goats." She bought goats. Her kids (the human ones) got into 4-H and started showing goats at fairs. More kids (goat ones) meant "we had all this goat milk and no one would drink it." (Judy tried sneaking it past her youngsters by filling used cow's milk cartons with goat's milk, but to no avail.) In the early 1980s when they were up to fifteen goats, Judy Schad tasted her first bite of chèvre, fresh goat cheese, made by Laura Chenel in California, and thought, *That's what goat's milk is for!* Her neighbor's advice notwithstanding, Judy cautioned that goats require the same amount of work as cows, yet they yield only one-seventh the amount of milk per animal.[33] "There's no advantage to having goats," Judy said, "except that you like them."

That individual goats have distinct personalities is often cited as the reason people like them.[34] As Tricia Smith walked me around her suburban goat farm in Carlisle, Massachusetts (since moved to Hardwick), a young buck named Adair jumped up and clamored for attention by placing his forehooves on my chest—*so like my two-year-old son,* I thought. Tricia repeatedly interrupted our conversation to speak gently to her goats, "Yes, you've had a hard life, but not as hard as Adair"; "Alys, don't do that, okay?" When I commented that she sounded as though she were disciplining the goats, as if she could actually influence their behavior through her words, Tricia, who once studied Japanese snow monkeys toward a doctoral degree (not completed) in biological anthropology, replied, "They're social mammals." Not only do the goats tune in to and respond to her communicative signals, she said, "They give one another subtle signals, too."

One cheesemaker I interviewed, who has bred and milked both cows and goats on her farm, gave goats a favorable review, telling me that in addition to being approachably human-size, goats are smarter and "more personable" than bovines. "They kind of test you, which I think is fun. They want to see if you're paying attention to them." She pointed out the window at a strawberry patch, half of which was brown; the goats had ducked beneath the fencing to get at the berries. This makes her husband crazy. "He wants to control the goats, but you can't," she said, laughing. "You have to control the fencing, because they can't help it." In his history of the countercultural natural foods movement of the 1960s and 1970s, Warren Belasco notes, "In grazing preferences, the goat was in fact the animal equivalent of the hip survivalist—a rather undisciplined, easily bored deviant who preferred scavenging wild berries to clipping carefully tended lawns."[35] Compared with cows, goats are seen to be more like us. Recognized as individualists, they are readily anthropomorphized as the class clown or the queen.[36]

Sheep are more apt to be pigeonholed *en masse*. In *Living with Sheep*, Wooster warns prospective shepherds that sooner or later, "every friend and acquaintance" will ask "something to the effect of, 'Aren't sheep the stupidest animals in the barnyard?' 'Aren't they dumber than posts, dumber than the fence that holds them in?'"[37] Eugenicist Francis Galton witheringly likened the mediocrity of garden-variety humans to the "mindless gregariousness of herd animals."[38] The problem, Wooster writes, is that humans view sheep anthropocentrically. Sheep are herbivores, a prey species whose best defense is safety in numbers. The apparent lack of independent initiative that the ovine-ignorant interpret as stupidity should instead be regarded, says Wooster, as a species-being response to perceived threat. His own opinion of the woolly ruminant was transformed by an experience of sitting in a sheep pen when, disturbed by an unexpected presence, the creatures moved collectively into huddle formation. "With my eyes near ground level—and very near the level of a wolf's or coyote's eyes—the effect was startling. A dozen individual animals suddenly morphed into a great, twenty-four legged, wooly blob with ... no obvious place to gain a ... canine tooth-hold."[39] Sheep, Wooster maintains, have been unfairly maligned by bipedal predators who expect to know cunning when they see it.[40]

Still, guard dogs or llamas are necessary companion species on sheep farms. The previous year the Majors lost eighteen sheep to coyotes when Tosca, a white Maremma—a dog bred for centuries by Italian shepherds to guard livestock— was out of commission with a bad back, and the coyotes "knew" it. Sheep dairies, then, also provide engaging lives to working dogs bred, as with border collies, to round up sheep or, as with Maremmas, to guard small livestock from predators. At least one farmstead cheesemaker, Dr. Pat Elliott of Everona Dairy in Virginia, got her start after falling for a border collie. Wanting to give the dog meaningful work to do, Pat bought some sheep for her to herd. Keen to have the sheep pay their own way, Dr. Elliott took up commercial cheesemaking alongside her medical practice.

Unlike goatherds, who tend to recognize the idiosyncratic personalities of their animals by bestowing individual names on them, shepherds, including David Major, view their flocks as aggregates of grazers embedded in a pasture ecology. It is not for nothing that the word *sheep* is both singular and plural. Since ewes yield less milk per animal per day than do cows or even does (female goats), sheep dairy farmers by economic necessity handle great numbers of animals, whereas I have encountered successful farmstead cheese operations with just seven cows or a dozen goats.

When David suggested that sheep people are oriented toward the land and landscape that grazing sheep rely on and preserve, he opened another line of analysis: as a contemporary sheep farmer, David is more invested in what sheep do—graze on pasture—than in what they represent as a species or as individual animals. His experience of animal-human relations as relations of production leads him to treat animals as subjects and not just as objects.[41] Unlike goats, who prefer to eat leaves and shoots while standing upright ("They always eat up, not down, because they avoid a lot of intestinal worms that way," a goat keeper told me), or cows, who some would argue can get by just fine on hay and grain, sheep—in order to stay healthy and maintain milk production—must be shepherded from one fresh pasture to another. Their nibbling maintains a "working landscape" kept open from reforestation (and clear of development). Bearing out David Major's prediction, I found that cheesemakers who arrived via goats tended to be primarily attached to their animals, and people who got into cheese via sheep began with an attachment to the land.

Wanting to trade city living for wide-open space, in 1986 Cindy and Ed Callahan moved from San Francisco to thirty-five acres in Sonoma County, California. As their son, Liam, told me the story, "by the end of the summer the grass was over six feet tall." Their land was pasture, not a huge "yard." Wanting to avoid paying for a mowing machine to come each year but needing to guard against brush fires, Cindy bought sheep to serve as cheap lawnmowers. Once they had sheep, the Callahans quickly had lambs. Soon there was more lamb than friends to eat it, so Liam, from his Berkeley dorm room computer, created a form letter introducing their lamb to area restaurants. An early customer was Alice Waters's restaurant, Chez Panisse. The Callahans bought more sheep and raised more lambs, until a friend mentioned how in the Middle East sheep's milk is particularly valued for yogurt and cheese. Cindy learned from U.S. Department of Agriculture statistics that sixty million pounds of sheep's-milk cheese had been imported to the United States the previous year, while only a couple of domestic producers, including Vermont Shepherd, were making it. Between 1990 and 1992,

Cindy converted Bellwether Farms to a sheep dairy and creamery, and Liam, recently graduated from college, signed on as cheesemaker. Wanting land, the family ended up, via sheep, with cheese.

Like the Callahans, David Major started a sheep dairy with a flock bred for meat and wool, not milk. David grew up with Corriedales (a wool breed) and Dorsets (a "second-tier" wool and meat breed, according to Wooster) whose milk was utilized only by the lambs. I asked David if he thought differently about the sheep after he started milking them. He laughed and said, "They think differently about me!" They became "bolder and more talkative. If they want something and see someone who can get it for them, they let their demands be known. They're pushier and more demanding"—a clear contrast to the sheep's "flightier and quieter" comportment before they were milked. When David started milking, he began selectively breeding ewes based on milk volume rather than wool quality or the size of their lambs. Selecting for milk production, he explained, "doesn't mean big udders." Rather, he equated good milk production with ewes' ability "to relax around people and let their milk down." (Large commercial dairies, particularly those located in cooler climates, may inject dairy animals with oxytocin to help them relax.) The traits associated with good milk production go along with an increased ovine sociability with people.[42] Symbolized by the cascading headgate of the milking parlor, the practices of dairying represent a machine in the post-pastoral garden that has produced a dramatic change in the sheep's personalities, in how they think about David. David's story suggests further that, in addition to figuring animals as material agents in anthropological accounts, anthropologists might also make room in our theories for the ways animals can *be* anthropologists, interested students of human behavior.

To view human-animal relations as a mutual encounter joins the modern meaning of culture—as that which distinguishes humans from animals yet also distinguishes among human groups—with its more archaic meaning as the practice of cultivating something, particularly another species.[43] Dairy farmers guided by principles other than, or at least in addition to, maximizing production volume often pride themselves on husbandry practices that let sheep be sheep and cows be cows—by grazing grass rather than being fed grain rations, for instance. Such agencies are important components of post-pastoral ecologies of production. The animal husbandry practiced on farmstead cheesemaking operations I have visited bears scant resemblance to industrialized agriculture in which, as Nigel Clark writes, "technologies of control and modification are applied to ever-more-intimate aspects of biological being."[44] This is not to suggest that craft farms are more "natural" than industrial farms. As with ducks described by Deborah Heath and Anne Meneley as calmly waiting their turn to be funnel-fed in an artisanal process designed and carried out by humans to fatten their livers for foie gras, it is impossible to disentangle the natural from the cultural in a dairy animal bred to lactate long after her offspring are removed and who might, as an individual, participate in her milking by standing still in a milking stanchion, even parting her legs to accommodate the milking cups of a vacuum system.[45]

Vermont dairy farmer Lisa Kaiman, whose Jersey milk is turned into cheese at Consider Bardwell Farm, has trained her cows not to defecate in the milking parlor. If she sees a tail begin to rise she yells, "Put down that tail!" and the cow usually complies. Her immaculate milking parlor, open to the fresh air, does not need to be hosed down after each milking; she simply sweeps it clean. A dry milking parlor is microbiologically hygienic compared to a wet one. Lisa is confident selling raw milk from her farm because she feels that she and her cows have an understanding of what it takes for them together to produce it safely. Again, Lisa's milk is no more "natural" than milk that should be pasteurized before humans could safely drink it; it is differently cultured.

Humans and animals cultivate one another in particular landscapes, but as Karen Weinberg pointed out, they do so within particular ecologies and economies of production. In a post-pastoral ecology, dairy animals are cultivated as farm laborers tasked with processing grass and twigs into milk, the central component in "turning sunlight into cheese." Cows, the largest of the milk makers, are less frequently sentimentalized. Mateo Kehler speaks of Jasper Hill's cows in more machinic than pastoral terms, describing cows going out to the fields to eat and make milk, returning to the barn for milking, and going back out to eat more grass. Describing cows as "our workers who harvest a piece of grass and bring it to the parlor, where we relieve them of it," Mateo condenses the coordinated, "hard-working" agencies of cows and humans into a sort of value-producing machine in the post-pastoral garden of flavor-filled grasses.[46]

Still, ruminant nature-cultures may also contribute more directly, on their own terms, to the character of particular cheeses. What dairy animals eat— wildflowers and legumes, fresh green grass, dried hay, or fermented corn silage— affects the nutrition and taste of milk. But it seems, too, that the habituated practice of *how* ruminants eat also contributes. Goats, I am told, are "nervous animals," ever afraid they will not get enough to eat, and so they end up eating everything in sight; if milk flavor is a concern, then goats' eating must be regulated. Michael Lee, who makes Twig Farm cheese in Vermont, takes his goats on a leisurely woodland walk twice daily to ensure that they sample the tastiest shrubs around. Sheep, in contrast, nibble delicately at the tops of grasses, and so (provided they are moved to a fresh pasture after every milking) their cheese tends to be fairly mild and uniformly flavored. Cows bite big hunks of grass, getting the roots and even some soil, and they chew and chew, processing strong flavors. Cow's-milk cheese expresses pronounced flavors of pasturage. Claims to conveying the taste of the place of production (what the French term *terroir*) would, on the basis of how ruminants eat when given access to outdoor dining opportunities, seem strongest with cow's-milk cheese.[47] This suggests, too, that the "hard-working" productive agencies of cows, goats, and sheep—not to mention the bacteria, yeasts, and molds still to come—may in fact thwart human attempts to control "the system" of production.

Anne Topham started raising goats and making cheese in southern Wisconsin in the early 1980s. During my 2008 visit to her modest farmstead, she described her goats as contributing to the development of her cheese in a more empathic way. A few years ago, when Anne's ailing parents required her attention, she boarded her goats with a goat-keeping friend and neighbor. To make cheese, Anne used milk pooled from their combined herds. The cheese she made that summer was just not the same—not because "her" milk was diluted from being mixed with her neighbor's, but because Anne's goats were away from home. When the animals returned, the cheese improved. Anne told me:

> I always have thought it was because of having that close-tied relationship to the animals. I remember one Sunday afternoon, it was just really, really quiet, it was a beautiful day, and I was hand-ladling the cheese and I was feeling all of the goats in the room. It's like they're there every time I do the cheese. And I need that. I need that relationship. I make lots better cheese when I have that. I don't think you could measure the difference in the milk [as with seasonality or change in fodder]. It's another kind of difference. It's about their life here.

Economies of production are far from dispassionate.

MAKING CHEESE

Vermont Shepherd is made when sheep provide milk, from mid-April through November, at which time the animals are "dried off" in preparation for spring birthing. A seasonal cheese, it is available on the market beginning in August and lasting until that season's inventory sells out. I made cheese with David on four different days, following a process that is schematized in fig. 5. So as not to track in stray bacteria that might foil fermentation, I was outfitted with hygienic gear that never left the cheese room: knee-high rubber boots, a long white plastic apron, a baseball cap, and surgical gloves. Our first task was to haul in the milk cans, each weighing ninety pounds when full. Setting aside the cans from the morning milking, we poured chilled milk from the previous evening (or, on Mondays, from the weekend) into a rectangular vat. David tested the milk for antibiotics. Antibiotics residue from veterinary treatment of animals could kill off the bacteria necessary for fermentation; since it might also cause allergic reactions in consumers, its presence would make the sale of the cheese illegal. David recorded the results on a clipboard by the door "for the inspectors," but this was a matter of form. David used antibiotics only for deworming the sheep or

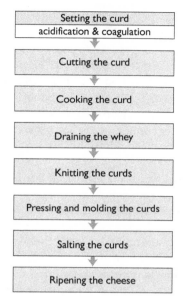

| Setting the curd |
| acidification & coagulation |

↓

| Cutting the curd |

↓

| Cooking the curd |

↓

| Draining the whey |

↓

| Knitting the curds |

↓

| Pressing and molding the curds |

↓

| Salting the curds |

↓

| Ripening the cheese |

FIG. 5. The eight basic steps of cheesemaking, adapted from Paul Kindstedt, *American Farmstead Cheese.*

treating mastitis or other illnesses, and any animals undergoing such treatment were milked by hand into a bucket to remove their milk from the cheese supply.[48]

While whole, raw milk heated gently in the vat, I whisked a powdery starter culture of freeze-dried *Lactobacillus* bacteria into a pail of the morning milk, still warm from animal bodies (73°F–83°F). Feeding on lactose, the bacteria produce lactic acid as a waste product; this starts the fermentation process, called acidification, by which milk becomes cheese. These bacteria are called starter cultures. Selected from benign natural residents in milk, starter cultures can outcompete harmful pathogens and are crucial agents in producing a food safe for human consumption. They also contribute to the resulting flavor, consistency, and identity of a cheese. David seeded the milk—which was not pasteurized— with direct-set mesophilic bacteria cultured in a French lab. Every couple of weeks he alternates strain mixtures to maintain microbial variety in the cheese room and to prevent the accumulation of bacteriophage, a virus that eats bacteria and disrupts fermentation.

Once the milk reached a uniform temperature between 70°F and 80°F, David stirred in rennet, added in a dilute solution with a couple of quarts of cold tap water. Rennet is an enzymatic agent used to speed up the second key chemical process in cheesemaking after acidification: curdling, the coagulation of milk into curd. Since England's "mad cow" disease (bovine spongiform encephalopathy) epidemic, David has used a mold-derived rennet rather than the standard sub-

stance extracted from the lining of the fourth stomach, the abomasum, of suckling ruminants, which he had previously imported from England. Commercial
calf rennet is a by-product of the veal industry. Because animal rennet is also the
most expensive coagulant available, many American cheesemakers use an alternative. In Britain, vegetarian consumers often seek out cheese from mold-derived
rennet, also called "vegetable" rennet; David said "vegetarian" rennet is not much
of a concern in the United States, at least among consumers of high-end table
cheese such as Vermont Shepherd. His other option would be a genetically modified coagulant, but David expressed wariness about introducing GM applications
into his ecology of food production.

About twelve minutes after the rennet was added, the milk hit the flocculation point—from one second to the next it suddenly thickened. During the half
hour the curd took to set fully into a gel-like substance, David and I kept busy
scrubbing and sterilizing milk cans. Using a handheld "cheese knife" (also called
a cheese harp), a series of wires strung on a rectangular metal frame attached to
a long handle, David cut the soft curd to release the whey. Actually, he used two
different knives: one cut vertically to create long strips of curd, and the other cut
those strips horizontally into centimeter cubes. We both reached in for a taste—
the warm curd was sweet and rich, tasting like custard (sheep's milk contains significantly more fat than either cow's or goat's milk).[49] While I simply savored the
sample, David was making a sensory evaluation; any off flavors would be an indication of something gone wrong. Stirring constantly with a large paddle, David
cooked the curd at 101°F, just about the body temperature of a sheep, for thirty
minutes, helping to separate the curds and whey. I finished washing the cans.

Reaching deep into the vat, beyond our elbows in whey, we pressed down on
the now-rubbery "cooked curd" with our palms to consolidate it into a solid mass
at the bottom of the vat. David laid over the curd a couple of lengths of fine-mesh
plastic fencing, and we began to bail out the whey. Whey, like the wastewater
from washing milk cans and cheese molds, is considered by law an industrial
waste and cannot go down a household septic system. Viewing whey as a cultural
resource rather than a waste product, David spreads his whey, rich in protein and
teeming with microbial life, on the sheep's pastures as fertilizer. Other farmstead
producers feed whey to pigs or heifers.[50] We topped the mass of exposed curd
with David's cheese weights, fashioned from lengths of PVC tube filled with
food-grade salt (if a weight were to come open, a bit of spilled salt would not hurt
anything).

After removing the weights and fencing, and using a long knife resembling a
domesticated machete, David cut the solid mass of curd in a way that reminded
me of slicing a pan of brownies. We carried thirty-two blocks of curd, representing the number of wheels of cheese this batch would yield, to a long, sloping
drainage table for pressing and molding.

Each cheese is formed very much by hand. Going down the line, we briefly kneaded each block of curd, smooshing in the corners with the heel of one hand, rotating the cheese much as if we were working with impossibly stiff pastry dough. Each cheese was flipped and pounded four times to "knit" the curd together so it would produce a smooth consistency as the cheese aged. Each lump of curd was placed in a plastic bowl with holes punched in the bottom. These simple bowls, which give Vermont Shepherd its distinctive shape, were purchased years ago from a discount store. The fourth time the cheeses were turned and kneaded, we topped them with a thin plastic form cut in the shape of a sheep (Vermont Shepherd's logo) and the number 15, marking the batch number, and then wrapped them in cheesecloth. The cheeses sat, draining, while we scrubbed out the vat and washed the tools we had used.

After breaking for a late lunch, we reconvened to turn out and flip the cheeses in their plastic molds one last time, carefully pulling the cheesecloth smooth. I wheel-barrowed the fresh cheeses a few hundred yards to the cheese cave, where they drained overnight in their bowls. I returned to the cheese house to help with the final washing up and rinsing down. It was 4:30 in the afternoon. My arm muscles screamed from lifting milk cans in and out of soapy water, and my fingers were stiff and clumsy from kneading curd. After one of these ten-hour sessions, I declined David and Lucy's invitation to join them for a West African–Brazilian dance class.

Noting, in retrospect, that my fieldnotes from those days are filled with carefully detailed descriptions of the tasks in which I was enlisted, annotated with reflections on my experience of carrying out those tasks but containing only cursory reports of nonwork social encounters, I realize that I, too, am prone to fetishizing labor—to thinking of labor not only as inherently value-creating, but as a value in and of itself. Making cheese by hand *is* hard work. More than one cheesemaker I interviewed commented that they might never have gone into the business had they realized earlier just how physically demanding it is. I am sympathetic to cheesemakers who call attention to this labor in their marketing.[51] My point is that when "hard work" is itself understood to produce valued qualities in a cheese (taste, healthfulness, uniqueness), qualities for which consumers might reasonably pay more money than for industrially manufactured cheese, this reflects the contingent fact that cultural value is invested in the virtue of labor—a value, indeed, that earlier generations subjected to cultural critique by embracing industrialization's labor-saving mechanisms.

CHEESE IS A LIVING SUBSTANCE

At the Majors' farm, Tuesdays, Thursdays, and Saturdays were "cave days." On those days, after milking and breakfast, I joined Lucy at the cheese cave, fashioned from repurposed concrete culverts sunk into a hillside, to brine the cheeses that had been made the previous day. No salt had been added to the curd during its "make," but salt, intolerable to many undesirable microorganisms, was crucial to the future of these cheeses. We weighed each cheese to determine how long, between twenty-four and thirty-six hours, a wheel would float in the brine bath with rock salt covering its exposed surface. Lucy tested for pH, a measure of the cheese's acidity. It registered at 4.90, safely within the normal range for Vermont Shepherd at this point in its development. We recorded this number, along with all the cheese weights, on the record sheet for that day's brine batch.

Vermont Shepherd is a "natural-rind" cheese, its outer surface hardened by exposure to air. Natural rinds are an artisanal alternative to waxing or encasing young cheese in plastic to protect it from unwanted mold growth.[52] A natural rind is not simply dried out; it is the result of carefully nurtured biochemical reactions—basically, controlled rotting. Bacteria, yeasts, and molds represent a crucial force in the ecologies of artisanal cheese production. Present in raw milk, microorganisms are also introduced in the form of commercial strains of starter and adjunct cultures and as ambient microorganisms that settle on the exposed surface of a cheese as it ripens. "It's the bacteria who do all the work of making the cheese," Maria Trumpler, who developed Vermont Ayr cheese, once assured me; "they make the flavor, they make the texture. All we have to do is not get in their way." Harry West and Nuno Domingos write similarly of Portuguese cheesemakers who depict their cheeses as "working" in the aging rooms to accomplish fermentation.[53] Enlisted as microscopic laborers, bacteria and fungi are credited with helping to produce the gustatory value of an artisanal cheese. Moreover, by drawing an association between their own labor and the "work" of microorganisms and livestock, cheesemakers moralize their own endeavors as part of a "natural" process.

Labor, however, is not an inevitable metaphor here. *Care* is an alternative way to talk about active engagement with nonhuman agencies.[54] Speaking in an ecological idiom, cheesemakers often describe wheels of natural-rind cheese as an *ecosystem* or microcosmic farm, with microbial flora and fauna to be carefully tended, cultivated, and cultured. One cheesemaker explained the process of curing cheeses by drawing an agricultural analogy: "We want to cultivate the right soil, if you will, for the right things to grow." To cultivate desired microorganisms and weed out undesirable ones, cheesemakers work to manage the environment of a cheese ecosystem. The Majors' cave is kept at 55°F and 95 percent humidity; elevated humidity is maintained by throwing a bucket of water on the floor when necessary. The French have a word for this practice of controlled rotting: *affinage,* or "finishing." It represents what Claude Lévi-Strauss might call the cultural elaboration of the raw by natural means.[55]

Lucy and I turned our attention to flipping the cheeses that had been brined

FIG. 6. Wheels of Vermont Shepherd cheese aging on drain boards in the cave at Major Farm. Photo by author.

in the previous couple of weeks and were now shelved on ash wood boards in the brining area of the cave (fig. 6). Lucy referred to these cheeses as "toddlers," placing them on a developmental trajectory. After a week or so of drying out, the cheeses begin to grow a gentle white mold that looks something like a sprinkling of baby powder. At this point the young cheeses "hit puberty," as David put it to me, and "graduate" to the shelves around the corner. In a biological idiom, a wheel of natural-rind cheese is also spoken of as an *organism* that "matures" and "ages." Microbial life not only contributes a kind of labor to the production of cheese as a fermented food, it also confers vitality upon them. Wheels of Vermont Shepherd have biographies. When I later purchased a wedge of cheese directly from Major Farm, my FedEx package included a card detailing the weather and special farm conditions (such as the presence of a visiting anthropologist) on the day my cheese was "born" in the vat.

After witnessing variability in the development of different batches and even different wheels of cheese, it becomes quite easy, David said, to anthropomorphize cheese as having a life of its own. I certainly found it common practice. One cheesemaker I met elaborated the stages of her cheese's aging in terms of moving from "preschool" to "kindergarten" and eventually "graduating" from college. There is cross-cultural evidence for imputing life to a cheese. In the Basque country, within a rich tradition of transhumant shepherding and cheesemaking, procreative metaphors join developmental ones. In "Aristotle among the Basques: The 'Cheese Analogy' of Conception," Sandra Ott details how Basque shepherds subscribe to Aristotelian theories of procreation that have men's semen acting on the matrix of female blood *in utero* to form a fetus, much as the force of rennet acts on the material of milk to form cheese.[56] Not only do the Basques believe in the generative force of male creation in human procreation, the cheesemakers— exclusively men—speak analogously of birthing their cheeses: "On one occasion when I watched a shepherd [pull a steaming cheese from the whey-filled kettle] . . . he held the newly made cheese at arm's length and proudly exclaimed, 'my little baby!' (*ene nini txipi!*)."[57] The Basques, Ott continues, have analogously treated cheese and babies alike in ritual ways: both are held over an open fire to "strengthen its bone"; both have been confined to a prescribed "space" for the initial three months of life.[58] Moreover, men's generative creativity in procreation as in cheesemaking is believed to convey not only form but also identity. Basque cheeses, no less than children, have paternity and come from patrilineages.

Early in their cheesemaking career, David and Cindy Major traveled to southern France to learn cheesemaking techniques from Basque shepherds. When I first visited Major Farm and was explaining to David my early thoughts about an anthropological research project, he asked, "Oh, you mean like Sandra Ott?" and pulled down from a bookcase in the kitchen, shelved next to the *Moosewood Cookbook*, a copy of Ott's ethnographic monograph, *The Circle of Mountains*.[59] David acknowledged that they got the idea to impress their cheeses with a logo representing their farm from the Basques, who give their cheeses the "mark" of their "houses."[60] In the United States, though, the mark of the house of production does not convey patrimonial belonging so much as a sense of commodity fidelity, in the way that a logo or legal trademark "operates as a signature of authenticity."[61] Through such marks, including the often fanciful names they choose for their cheeses, cheesemakers endeavor to convey the unique specificity of their product through a semiotic transfer of their own "hand" in crafting it, registering, as Rosemary Coombe writes, "a real contact, a making, a moment of imprinting by one for whom it acts as a kind of fingerprint: branding."[62]

But as I suggested in chapter 1, the mark of the artisan left on a cheese is more material than merely that of trademark and brand. Wheels of Vermont Shepherd fluctuate in size from seven to nine pounds and in shape from disklike to domed. The seam lines produced from being pressed in plastic bowls jerry-rigged to serve as molds fall at the center line of some cheeses, while on others the line is noticeably off-center. On some wheels I handled in the cave, the cheesecloth had been pulled smooth and taut; removing it revealed an aesthetically pleasing fine-mesh pattern imprinted on the surface. Other wheels show evidence of the cloth being unevenly bunched. The mottling of fungi on the surface of a natural-rind cheese is just one element of the natural-cultural variation that contributes to the feeling that each wheel of cheese is an individual—something that can enhance the artisanal value of a cheese by distinguishing it from a standardized, industrial product and making it an unfinished commodity.

Natural-rind cheeses are more expensive to buy than shrink-wrapped cheeses not only because they might look more authentically artisanal, but also, again, because it requires considerable labor to cultivate a natural-rind cheese. To cure Vermont Shepherd, twice a week Nicholas, the Majors' young farm manager at the time, "washed" the wheels, a process also referred to as "turning" the cheeses. This was not an immersive bath. Instead, holding an eight- or nine-pound cheese on his left forearm and just barely dipping the gloved fingers of his right hand in the brine solution, Nicholas carried to the cheese salt, bacteria, and moisture as he gently pressed down a newly accumulated microbial bloom to build up a semipermeable crust that allowed gases and moisture to escape. The brine wash keeps mold growth under control. "It's like mowing your lawn," an experienced *affineur* told me. Just as an unmown lawn will become overgrown with weeds, if a wheel of Vermont Shepherd is allowed to sit without being washed with brine, a secondary growth of unappealing greenish mold will appear. Rinds that can be up to 20 percent salt protect the interior from pathogens while nurturing "good" microbes, such as the sharply aromatic *Brevibacterium linens,* that contribute to an aged cheese's complex flavor. At some point in their development the cheeses are no longer washed but are instead brushed with a stiff scrub brush (it was early enough in the season still that we were washing all the cheeses on the shelves). Over the duration of its aging, a wheel of Vermont Shepherd will be handled more than eighty times.

After first working alongside Nicholas in turning the cheeses, my throat and lungs felt irritated and I developed a shallow cough. The next time I worked in the cave, I wore a protective mask. David does little of the curing because he is sensitive to mold. And while Cindy Major once did most of the cheesemaking, the physical strain got to be too much owing to long-term effects from a bicycle accident. David and Cindy's division of labor was in part bodily based, though not in a gendered way.

Responding to cheese's perceived aliveness, some producers suggest that their own ill-tempered moods might deleteriously effect cheese's development through a sort of associative contagion. One Wisconsin cheesemaker told me that she avoids working in the cave when she is in a foul mood, implying that the spirits of a cheesemaker may influence the fate of a cheese.[63] Such cheesemakers guard against harming a ripening cheese through protective practices that anthropologists call magical thinking and cheesemakers are apt to laugh off as "superstition." Both magic and science, argued twentieth-century anthropologist Bronislaw Malinowski, are based in a belief that humans can dominate nature to their own ends, but whereas science proceeds through direct intervention in the natural world, magic proceeds through spells and ceremonies designed to prompt the supernatural to intervene in the natural world. Interpreting why South Pacific islanders incant spells over their well-tended gardens or expertly constructed canoes, Malinowski remarked that even the keenest scientific rationality cannot make the sun shine or hold storms at bay; "To control these influences and these only," the Trobriand Islander "employs magic."[64] Magic, on this view, reflects humility before the forces of nature. Confronted by the aliveness of cheese, cheesemakers share that humility.[65] At the same time, imparting a "life of its own" to a batch or an individual cheese may also let the cheesemaker off the hook for less-than-scrupulous care. Indeed, magical thinking about organic agents reinforces a fetishism of their productive contribution to crafting cheese.

By the time a Vermont Shepherd has "matured," the rind has grown hard and brown and the interior paste has become smooth and toothsome. In the United States, any cheese made from raw (unpasteurized) milk must be aged at least sixty days before being sold (see chapter 6). The mandatory aging period is meant to "provide a measure of pathogen reduction," the idea being that the drying and acidification associated with aging proves increasingly inhospitable to pathogens.[66] David offered me an additional rationale: if something is going wrong in the cheese, by sixty days it will become apparent through explosions of gas bubbles, malodor, or other organoleptic or sensory signs.

Between the time of my first visit in March and my return at the end of May, Major Farm had ordered a voluntary recall of a line of cow's-milk cheeses that their (then) *affineur* had made elsewhere and aged in the Majors' cave, alongside Vermont Shepherd. The Majors ordered the recall after several restaurants contacted them; among diners who had complained of stomach distress (symptoms indicated a *Staphylococcus* infection), the common denominator was Major Farm cow's-milk cheese. Food and Drug Administration testing of the cave's remaining cheese uncovered no pathogens, but not wanting to take chances with the health of consumers or with the future of their business, the Majors recalled two months' cheeses still on the market and went further still: they discontinued the line of cow's-milk cheeses and laid off the *affineur*. Those cheeses no longer exist. The Vermont Shepherd recall reminds us that the "life" of an artisanal cheese not only reflects commodity fetishism; it is subject to the expert knowledge and systemized control of state institutions.[67]

TELLING AND SELLING THE STORY

The coming-into-being of Vermont Shepherd is as much a story of successful marketing as it is a tale of sheep dairy farming and craft food production. It is also a story that has been told repeatedly, if selectively, by the Majors and others;

through such narratives, Vermont Shepherd emerged not only as a cheese but also as a brand.[68] As Fritz Maytag (of Iowa's Maytag Blue and also a member of the family behind Maytag appliances) is reported to have quipped, "A brand is a good story that is true."[69] While the story conveyed in a successful brand may not be made up, it is selectively told. The "story" of Vermont Shepherd (circa 2004) is a partial account of the Majors' social production as farmer-artisans: how they developed the capacity to make sheep's-milk cheese commercially and also gained public recognition as farmstead cheesemakers. Emphasizing how the Majors acquired craft skill, built and equipped workable facilities, and developed market relations, the story omits other elements of their social production. Omitted from the story is the private, behind-the-scenes experience of being married to and raising children with one's business partner; sources of capital investment; and some of the more tragic—and serendipitous—episodes behind their eventual success. Omitted, for example, is a near-fatal bicycle accident that Cindy suffered shortly after their marriage; the insurance settlement from the accident apparently provided initial capital with which they built their cheese house. The story is also ongoing. In a marketing brochure that Major Farm mailed to me in 2009, Cindy Major is absent from the story of Vermont Shepherd.[70]

In 2007, after David and Cindy had divorced and Cindy had left the business, I heard Cindy (who now goes by Cynthia) deliver a version of the Vermont Shepherd story as part of a presentation on marketing slated during a two-day workshop, run by cheesemaker Peter Dixon, on how to start up a farmstead cheesemaking business.[71] Marketing is discursive labor that helps to create symbolic capital and to establish the use value—in this case, edibility—of a commercial product. Cindy in essence advised that the economic value of an artisanal cheese—the price it can fetch on the market—depends on the successful communication of how one's social and moral values contribute to the crafting of a cheese and to the development of a business. At the workshop, whose participants included two dairy-farmer couples considering cheese as a value-added product, Cindy demonstrated her central marketing lesson: tell your story. Handmade cheese, she instructed, will not sell on taste alone at the price you need to survive; you have to sell the story of what goes into the cheese.[72] It might be a tale about farming tradition and farmland inherited from prior generations, or the ups and downs of learning to live with livestock, or even a personal romance. Under the heading "Our Story," a Major Farm brochure I acquired in 2004 begins, "It all started when David and Cindy met in 1983." Consumers are attracted to a romantic notion of artisanship and small-scale family farming. Everyone in the room knew full well that a reality of exhausting work, economic insecurity, and uncertainty about the future is obscured by the idealized postcard image of agrarian living. But that is part of marketing, Cindy acknowledged: selling the consumer what they think they want, regardless of whether it is really, or only, what they are getting.[73]

Once, as I was leaving Mark and Gari Fischer's renovated Vermont farmhouse, I gestured out the French doors off their open-plan kitchen, exclaiming with some envy, "You have *sheep* in your backyard!" With a sigh, Mark replied that the vista, the bucolic view, is an asset they have to market along with their cheese (fig. 7). From our conversation it was clear that he would just as soon sell the sheep and buy milk from another farm to be able to concentrate on what he really enjoys and excels at, which is making cheese. But he understands that the sheep represent symbolic capital that enhances the exchange value of his cheese when attached to a farmstead designation. This opportunity, which may be experienced as a burden, is not restricted to Vermont or even the United States. The head of an Italian dairy firm in the Taleggio Valley told anthropologist Cristina Grasseni, "'I don't sell my cheese because it's good. I sell it saying, "Look at where we live, look at our landscape." Our firm is therefore part of a context that sells well.'"[74] One goal of this book is to get beyond the strategic imagery that suffuses agricultural marketing and which, I believe, does many producers an injustice by failing to convey the struggles and compromises they face while pursuing the "good life" of agrarianism. Behind much of the beautiful scenery of the working landscape featured in farmstead cheese brochures and Web sites are heavy debts, uninsured family members, and scant savings for retirement. But if taste is insufficient to sell cheese, advertising one's property tax rate will probably not help.

At the 2007 workshop, Cindy related Vermont Shepherd's inspirational story as a humorous tale of idealism, naïveté, and the eventual overcoming of persistent failure. Reflecting back on the roller-coaster ride of learning to make and market a natural-rind sheep's-milk cheese, Cindy commented sincerely, "We used failure as a marketing tool." Even before the trend of marketing locally sourced farm-based food products took hold, people were partial to the Majors' underdog story. Cindy learned to market that.

In 1988 the Majors started milking their ewes and became a licensed dairy. For a time, they froze milk, driving it every two weeks to a yogurt manufacturer upstate, but that opportunity did not last. Cindy was about to go back to school when they received a telephone call from a nearby boarding school, offering them the use of the school's licensed cheesemaking facility. This is a rural community of small-town neighbors; the travails of their nascent dairy were common knowledge. At the same time, the Guilford Cheese factory, Peter Dixon's family's creamery, was going out of business. Peter and David had been childhood friends, and so in 1990 Peter joined forces with David and Cindy to experiment with making cheese at the local school. Although Peter had prior experience making Brie and Camembert, Cindy's father, owner of a dairy processing plant, warned, "Don't do a fresh product! You live out in the middle of nowhere and you'll drive yourself nuts" trying to distribute a product with a brief shelf life. They converted a sawdust pit into a ripening room and began searching for a

FIG. 7. Sign marking Mark and Gari Fischer's Woodcock Farm in Weston, Vermont. Photo by author.

hard, aged cheese that would fit their ecology of production by traveling well and surviving storage for a number of months.

With David occupied with sheep farming and grass pasturing, it was Cindy who initially devoted herself to developing a viable product and pioneering the marketing of domestic sheep's-milk cheese. For three years they made cheese at the school. "It was really terrible," Cindy said, referring to the cheese and wrinkling her nose. Working with frozen sheep's milk, they tried Feta, Gouda, and a blue-veined cheese and set up a stand at the Brattleboro farmers' market. The blue cheese "never turned blue" but it was their best seller at the market, so they changed its name to Shepherd's Sharp. "It wasn't even sharp," Cindy said, laughing, "but people liked it"—at least more than the mushy Feta or the Gouda, which invariably grew unpleasant green mold beneath its wax coating.

After three unsuccessful years working to develop an air-dried natural rind on Shepherd's Sharp and throwing "a lot of cheese on the manure pile," Cindy had an epiphany: "We need to go to Europe." There was no one to turn to in this country for help in making raw-milk, naturally aged sheep's-milk cheese on a small commercial scale. The Majors were the first. Cindy wrote to British cheese writer Patrick Rance for advice, describing their problem with rind development and enclosing photos of their farm and sheep. Rance's handwritten reply—which Cindy showed me as we shared a pot of tea on a stormy evening during my stay at the farm—suggested the French Pyrenees as a close analogy to the rolling hills and long winters of Vermont. Perhaps there the Majors might learn how to make an aged sheep's-milk cheese. Roquefort makers would be of no help, Rance wrote testily, since they had ceased curing natural rinds, opting instead to wrap their cheese in metal foil.

In 1993 the Majors packed up their young children, then ages one and four, along with photos of their farm and samples of their cheese and flew to France, the inescapable reference point within a Eurocentric hierarchy of culinary values for authentically artisanal cheese.[75] As Cindy related to participants in Peter's workshop, the Basque shepherds hated their cheese so much, and were so shocked to hear they were working with frozen milk, that they *had* to teach them how to do things properly.

Back in 2004, Cindy shared with me a photo album from the trip "that changed our lives." They visited and made cheese with Basque shepherd families who practiced seasonal transhumance, with shepherds accompanying sheep to high-elevation alpine valleys during the summer months and spending snowy winters in mountain villages. One farm family they visited hand-milked two hundred sheep standing out in the pastures; to make cheese, each member of the family worked in a kettle hanging over a gas burner to create a single wheel.[76]

After two weeks in France, the Majors returned home and adjusted their plan of action. First, they decided to build a creamery on their farm so they could do more to engineer the product. Second, they stopped freezing milk. They also converted their cheese vat so that it would be able to reach the temperatures required for their new recipe: they would make the same type of cheese as all the cheesemakers they visited, called Brebis d'Ossau in the Béarn region and Etorki in the Basque country. In the photos, I could recognize from working with David techniques they had adapted from the Basques to fit available equipment as well as U.S. regulatory standards. There were photos of shepherds hand-kneading curd in plastic bowls almost exactly as we had done (David later confirmed that this was where they got the idea to use plastic bowls as molds). The members of the family with the kettles were pictured with their hands hidden beneath the whey; they were consolidating the "prepressing," accomplishing what David and I had done with plastic fencing and salt-filled PVC tubes.[77]

By April 1993, the Majors were ready to begin making their new cheese. In June, they cracked open a wheel for an initial test. Nervously, Cindy selected the ugliest, most pitted and grayish-colored wheel she could find. They were happily astonished by its smooth, ivory-colored paste and sweet, mushroomy taste. That summer they won their first national award, a First Place in the Farmhouse category, at the ACS's annual competition. In 2000, Vermont Shepherd took the ACS's Best of Show prize.

If the 1993 trip to Europe was the turning point for Vermont Shepherd cheese, the ACS award that year was the turning point for the business. Until then, the Majors had marketed their cheese at farmers' markets and in local food stores. As soon as the award was presented, their telephone started ringing with distributors and retailers across the country wanting to stock their cheese. In time they were able to phase out the farmers' markets, which came as a relief to Cindy, as she hated driving and preferred to spend weekends at home with her children. The main source of income from Vermont Shepherd has been direct-sale wholesale, meaning that the Majors sell cheese at a wholesale price (nearly half what they get when they retail through their Web site or honor-system farm store) directly to retailers, both specialty shops and restaurants, without going through a distributor. Telephones, fax machines, cold packs, UPS trucks, and high-speed Internet are very much part of the ecology of Vermont Shepherd's production. Since the Majors started out, the infrastructure supporting artisanal cheese has expanded to include celebrity chefs who feature domestic cheese on their menus, Food Network programming, and journalists who write feature stories for the food pages of national and local newspapers and food magazines—not to mention three glossy magazines devoted to cheese launched between 2008 and 2010.[78]

Success in direct wholesale requires developing trusting relationships with retailers. Addressing dairy farmers considering making cheese, Cindy advised, "If you're invited to do an in-store tasting, go"—and go yourself; do not send an envoy. More significant than meeting ten customers and getting them excited about your cheese is meeting a retailer who can then share with twenty customers over the following months his or her own story of meeting the cheesemaker. Through personal relationships, producers can instruct retailers to expect product variation owing to seasonal production (and to distinguish this from variation caused by poor manufacturing technique). When retailers count a cheesemaker as a friend, Cindy concluded, they may be more apt to pay their bills on time and to serve as an enthusiastic representative of your cheese to potential customers. And in the worst-case scenario, if a cheese must be recalled following the discovery of a pathogen during routine testing or after an outbreak of foodborne illness, having a personal relationship with one's retailers can be essential for business survival.

Telling the story does not just sell cheese; it conveys a sense of what values the producer brings to a cheese's production. A bit of the cheesemaker would seem to linger in the cheese, one reason I have called American artisanal cheese an unfinished commodity. But might telling and selling the story also serve to package cheese as a kind of gift? Part of a gift's value derives from its ongoing attachment to the giver (which can make cash a less memorable gift than a hand-knitted sweater), and part of what distinguishes artisanal goods from generic (finished) commodities is that they bear the mark of their producers.[79] Gifts, even after they have been given away, still feel as though they belong in some sense to the giver.[80] What do producers get out of such a transaction? To be sure, by appealing to consumers' desire to get something extra beyond nutrition and taste, "giftifying" a food commodity may enhance the exchange value of their cheeses; as Angela Miller acknowledges of customers who buy cheese made at her Consider Bardwell Farm, "Their candied visions are included in the price of the cheese."[81] But I believe more is going on. Through sharing elements of their story with an appreciative audience, cheesemakers may reinforce their own sense that their significant life changes and ongoing labor are worthwhile.

THE POLITICS OF "FARMSTEAD" VALUE

As this chapter has demonstrated, belief in the natural generativity of well-stewarded pastureland and well-cared-for dairy animals lends itself to cheese-makers' claims to produce good food well. In the two decades since Vermont Shepherd was established, *farmstead* has become a marketable appellation to define an ecology of production in which these elements are brought together on the same site. In 2005, I attended a panel session at the ACS annual meeting devoted to the pros and cons of promoting a farmstead appellation to distinguish artisanal cheeses made on dairy farms.[82] A second-career Vermont farmer-cheesemaker suggested that the farmstead category is meaningful in calling attention to "the farm, not just the cheese" and conveys the "extraordinary care of the animals" that happens on small operations such as his. But does making cheese on a dairy farm ensure that extraordinary care is taken? Are farmers who sell milk to cheesemakers rather than process it themselves precluded from taking such care? The farmstead label (which is not a legal category) is far from stable within this community. When the social, moral, and gustatory values of making cheese on a farm are brought into an exchange relation with economic value, this raises the question of which specific ecologies of production can count as "farmstead." Which values are worth valuing? To conclude this chapter, I discuss debate over the farmstead designation to illustrate how ecologies of cheese production are evaluated to imply, if not set, standards for practice.[83]

Although it became clear during the ACS panel discussion that on-farm cheesemaking is a heterogeneous practice, a consensus grew in the room that, by its own definition, the ACS expected all milk used in farmstead cheesemaking to come from that farm's animals, but did not require that all the milk from that farm's animals be used to make cheese.[84] Based on that definition, a tiny farm with a dozen cows or a score of goats would jeopardize its cheese's farmstead status if it were to supplement its own milk with that of neighboring farms, while a ten-thousand-head ranch could legitimately market cheese as farmstead while also selling millions of gallons of milk to commodity processing plants (and possibly producing potentially hazardous manure lagoons). This logical outcome does not sit well with some cheesemakers and retailers committed to supporting small farms—as one member noted, under this definition and contrary (she asserted) to public perception, there is no necessary connection between *farmstead* and *small-scale*. Then again, small and large are relative categories; a large dairy in Vermont resembles a rather small one in California. Moreover, as Jennifer Bice (whose own rather large California goat dairy is Humane Certified) noted, small dairies do not necessarily take particularly good care of their animals, let alone better care than larger operations.

Skirting the limits of the farmstead designation, some farms have begun to buy the milk of different species than they raise to create a parallel line of not-necessarily-farmstead cheeses. Consider Bardwell Farm in Vermont is one example: it is a goat dairy that produces farmstead goat's-milk cheeses as well as a line of cheese made from purchased Jersey cow's milk. This farmstead operation (based on its goat's-milk cheeses) may be better known for cow's-milk cheeses, which are not (by ACS definition) farmstead. The irony here calls attention to the fabricated and political nature of the farmstead designation.

As buying milk becomes increasingly common on cheesemaking farms as a means of expansion without increasing the labor of dairying (which also has an ecological limit in terms of land available for grazing and foraging), I find that producers and retailers are becoming more comfortable with looser interpretations of "farmstead cheese." New England retailers assure me that while consumers are often pleased to learn that cheese is made in proximity to lactating livestock, on a farm rather than in a factory, they are not sticklers about any particular parsing of the farmstead designation.

For all the counterexamples and cautionary tales aired in the room at the 2005 ACS session, Jaime Montgomery, representing England's farmhouse family that produces Montgomery Cheddar, urged the American crowd to be grateful for their "ability to draw this line in the sand" and define for themselves the meaning of "farmstead" cheese. In the United Kingdom, he explained, the Milk Marketing Board patented the word *farmstead* in such a way as to describe block cheese (rather than traditionally shaped wheels) made from milk sourced from multiple farms; the legal definition allowed for other industrial-scale practices against which the ACS is defining farmstead fabrication. "You need to take ownership of 'farmstead'" through consistent use—not legal channels—he urged.[85]

Even if used consistently, however, *farmstead* has geographically limited marketing appeal in the United States. A second-generation dairy farm in New York State added a cheese processing facility in 2008. They had thought to name their business the Argyle Cheese Factory, in honor of the region's rich cheesemaking history and, in particular, of the defunct Argyle Cheese Factory a mile down the road to which their family's farm sold milk in the early 1900s. But as I heard the story from the farmwife, who quit her job as a CPA to become the family's cheesemaker, they decided that today the word *factory* has "the wrong connotations," suggesting a larger, more industrial operation. They settled on Argyle Cheese Farmer, with the tagline, "A real farmer making cheese." Why not Argyle Farmstead Cheese? Because, she explained, "people don't know *farmstead*" in upstate New York. At the ACS meeting, Alyce Birchenough said that in Alabama, where she makes cheese on her Sweet Home Farm, people are not impressed by the idea of a farm, thinking, *Where else would you make cheese?* Customers there do not care whether milk comes from "your animals or from down the road." "The farmstead romance," Alyce noted, "is not universal." It would seem to have the strongest appeal in college towns and regions with a heavy urban-rural traffic of recreational vacationers and second-home owners—the same regions most heavily populated by second-career farmstead cheesemakers, New England and the Pacific Northwest.

Summarizing the discussion at the ACS panel, Jennifer Bice concluded: "We know farmstead doesn't necessarily mean size, doesn't necessarily mean quality. We know it means education. It's more a way of life—and a piece of the puzzle of marketing." The language of farmstead production points to a "way of life" through farming, one that, as Jennifer added, may also prevent nonagricultural development in exurban landscapes. Through a strategic romanticization of their own often arduous labor, and by enfranchising nonhuman agents as co-laborers, the farmstead label trades on a pastoral farm idyll in a way that—cheesemakers hope—may help realize a more complex post-pastoral landscape.

Cheesemakers would seem to want both to promote interest in their cheese by marketing the appeal of rural goodness—a pastoral romance to which neither they are nor I am fully immune—and also to challenge consumers' naive assumptions about the economic and practical realities of farming and craft food-making. This tension is embodied in what I have called a post-pastoral ethos. I turn in the next chapter to identify the sentiments that brought people to take up cheesemaking in the first place and to analyze how cheesemakers negotiate principle and pragmatism as they confront constraint and contingency through economies of sentiment.

3

Economies of Sentiment

Here is the thorny paradox: how do I . . . find that point of balance that
gives me accolades and accomplishment while also preserving what I love:
foraging for dinner in the garden, nurturing my animals and transforming
the gift of their milk into cheese?

—LISA SCHWARTZ, *OVER THE RAINBEAU: LIVING THE DREAM*
OF SUSTAINABLE FARMING

Sampling a fresh, clean-tasting chèvre at a New England farmers' market, I asked the trim woman behind the table if she made the cheese. "I'm the farmer," she replied. She went on to describe herself as "a farmer who makes cheese," by which she meant that cheesemaking was "for earning money," while dairy farming was her love.

Speaking with me early on in my research, this farmer predicted that I would find two groups of people involved in cheesemaking: people like herself, who were primarily farmers and made cheese as a way to make their farm viable; and people who wanted to handcraft cheese and left some other occupation to do so. In a later interview, she elaborated:

> I grew up on a dairy farm. . . . We sold milk [by bulk tank to a processing plant]. I've spent my whole life in agriculture. You have to understand, my heart and soul is working with the animals, and this—the cheesemaking to me is just an extension of that. And I don't want to romanticize any part of it; it's somewhat matter-of-fact for me. That's my background.
>
> And then the other side—I don't want to put down the other side—but you have people who made money in another career. And I give them a lot of credit because they have given up that secure sense of income to take on a challenge that they have gathered information about, but don't have necessarily experience or, you know, that gut knowledge [from growing up on a working farm]. And [for them] it's like a dream thing: "This is what I want to do." And in many ways they're more educated and aware of new items, or the trends, because that's what they did in another career path. There's a difference. I don't want to put one above the other, there's just a different attitude.

In contrasting gut knowledge of working with farm animals to an educated awareness of consumer trends, this farmer called my attention to how people bring to cheesemaking not only unequal economic means but also different attitudes. Such attitudes manifest as skills, tastes, and other embodied elements of class disposition, but also as sentiment, including emotional attachment to vocational aspects of farming and cheesemaking. Heterogeneity in what making cheese means to those who make it underscores one way in which artisanal cheese is an unfinished commodity: because artisanal cheesemaking is ripe with possibility for realizing numerous values and sentiments—and because such sentiments help configure ecologies of production—it remains to be seen which values "artisanal cheese" comes to represent on the market. Tied to shifting class dynamics in rural America, the cultural and economic status of artisanal cheese production is neither uniform nor settled.

Producers who distance themselves from the artisan label by insisting that they are "farmers who make cheese" may be responding to a perception that artisanship, in an industrial society, must surely reflect the privilege of those who do not need to earn a living through work. Unlike artisans, farmers are not assumed to be elites. To be sure, a handful of wealthy businesspeople have retired early, bought land, and started million-dollar cheese businesses. When white-collar scandals involving Enron, Wall Street bonuses, and the mortgage-backed securities debacle of the banking industry strengthen an understanding that crafting a tangible product with one's own hands is "good, honest work," the CEO-turned-artisan may appear as a vexing figure. But the majority of today's artisan cheesemakers are operators of modest businesses. Many urban transplants are becoming farmers in their own right, reporting on average a sixty-six-hour work week during their busiest season and becoming emotionally and economically invested in land and rural communities.[1] David Major's path from Harvard undergraduate to Vermont shepherd, sketched in the previous chapter, has been different from that of the farmer I met at the New England farmers' market, but David also considers himself "a farmer who makes cheese." Both are part of an emergent post-pastoral form of life.

In struggling to get by—and in deriving value from that struggle—the smallholder farmer is more representative of American artisan cheesemakers than is the retired CEO. At the same time, the craft production of a good that must be marketed to consumers importantly differentiates "farmers who make cheese" from commodity dairy farmers who ship milk by bulk tank to processing plants. Having argued that one way producers derive value from farmstead ecologies of production is through representing livestock and microorganisms as laborers, in this chapter I show how producers invest their own labor with the potential to satisfy the question of how to live a good life. For some, this revolves around the ecological sustainability of farmland and the well-being of farm animals, while others derive primary satisfaction and pride from the tactile job of transforming milk into cheese.

I call these projects of multiple value-making *economies of sentiment*.[2] Economic activity is social activity, and so it is not surprising that craft farmers and artisan food-makers are simultaneously "motivated by social fulfillment, curiosity, and the pleasure of mastery, as well as instrumental purpose, competition, and the accumulation of gains," as Stephen Gudeman writes.[3] Market rationality is one organizing principle of economic activity, but not the only one.[4] Each of us in a market society "makes a living" through competitive exchange as well as through the cooperative projects by which we also maintain relationships with others and "make a life."[5] Likewise, the embodied human capacities—knowledge, skills, dispositions—that are harnessed to produce commodities (what Marx called "forces of production") are simultaneously cultural forces that are shaped by and give meaning to people's self-identity.[6] By recognizing that market relations already include nonmarket relations we can better grasp people's simultaneous projects of making a good life and a good living.[7]

The first half of this chapter identifies the motivations by which people arrive at making cheese. Through exploring stories of why people have taken up commercial cheesemaking, I maintain that the industry cannot be reduced to a division between those who make decisions of economic necessity and those who pursue lifestyle choices of desire.[8] After all, farmers who make cheese care about lifestyle, too: they are willing to acquire new skills and assume new responsibilities so that they might maintain an agricultural way of living. Nevertheless, while farmer-cheesemakers share moral regard for their enterprise, their particular values—as well as their strategies for prioritizing or reconciling apparently competing values—vary. That variation is rooted in personal history, in political commitment, and in unequal economic opportunity. Implicitly if not explicitly, cheesemakers may judge one another as makers of good and not-so-good cheese, and also as being good artisans, farmers, and, perhaps, good persons.

In the second half of this chapter I investigate how cheesemakers grapple with the tension of artisanship in its dual capacity as commercial business and personal vocation.[9] This tension is particularly apparent in farm-based operations, which are at once profit-oriented enterprises catering to external markets and also household-based enterprises comprising affective, mutual relations.[10] Through exploring how cheesemakers identify and confront their own particular challenges, we gain a better sense of how the economy of farmstead cheesemaking is guided by a mix of qualitative and quantitative values, of moral sentiment and business sense. Sited in and around spaces of domesticity, this economy entails a division of paid and unpaid labor through which gender and kinship are realized.[11] A farmstead operation might participate in direct retail trade at a farmers' market and also sell wholesale through a distributor; might pay cash wages to an underage family member to staff the farmers' market stand while also paying an office manager formal wages, Social Security, and benefits; might buy milk for making cheese at market price from one neighbor, but barter cheese for eggs with another.[12] Rather than try to pigeonhole artisan enterprise as one economic form or another, I consider particular instances of business decision-making and economic activity and how people reflect on and draw meaning from those actions. Striving daily to reconcile principle and pragmatism, cheesemakers engage in a kind of "value-work" through which they continually assess and reorder their commitments.[13]

Because consumers expect artisans to sell their story and trade on what they most value about their work, these producers are made keenly aware of how economic relations are simultaneously competitive and affective.[14] Ethnographic exploration of cheesemaking—considering not just what economic and ethical decisions cheesemakers make, but how they *think and feel* about those decisions—sheds light on how culture works to reproduce and also to transform such social structures as the market.[15]

ARRIVING AT CHEESEMAKING THROUGH SENTIMENT

Economies of sentiment point to the cultural, emotional, ethical, and political dispositions that motivate people, in this case, to assume the economic risk and backbreaking labor of making cheese in small batches using minimal technology. These sentiments are multifaceted. In responding to my survey, one cheesemaker described her initial goals as "to make money and keep our goat dairy alive. To educate the public about goat cheese and its value to the health of your body. To sell our cheese to restaurants. And have a safe environment for foster care."[16] For this producer, what it means to be an artisan cheesemaker will be influenced by also being a goat farmer, educator, salesperson-marketer, and foster mother. She will approach business decisions not only with the aim of producing a salable high-end consumer good, but with these other goals and sentiments in view as well. This is the shape of an economy of sentiment.

There is no typical profile of the American artisan cheesemaker; even so, a few themes stand out. An open-ended survey question, "What were your original goals in becoming a commercial cheesemaker?" elicited the responses shown in table 1.[17] When reported goals are aligned with respondents' year of entry into the commercial market, a pattern emerges. Those who took up commercial cheesemaking early in the current revival (1980s into the early 1990s) report initial goals skewing toward "lifestyle" objectives, such as seeking a way of making a living in a rural area or wanting to defray the upkeep of an existing herd of goats. Inspired by the environmental and cultural politics of the 1970s, this wave of farmstead

TABLE 1   Goals motivating people to go into commercial artisan cheesemaking,
from survey conducted February 2009

Original Goals	No. Respondents (n = 146) Citing This Goal	Percentage Respondents Citing This Goal
To produce high-quality artisanal food; provision local markets	37	25
To make a value-added product to support or save a dairy farm	33	23
To have fun and make money; doing a job I love	22	15
To find a means of making a living in rural area, on a small farm (for the "lifestyle")	20	14
To pay existing mortgage; create a sustainable business for future generations	6	4
To spend time with and pay for the care of animals (goats were most frequently mentioned)	12	8
To seek independence, self-sufficiency	7	5
Other:		
Retirement occupation/supplemental income	4	3
Work with and support family, including foster kids	4	3
Support local farmers and participate in community	4	3
Respond to consumer demand	3	2
Preserve land in agriculture	1	0.5
For money/profit	5	3

cheesemaking reflected people's search for an engaged, relatively independent mode of rural living and working. These pioneering artisans are baby boomers, members of the generation born during the post–World War II demographic rise in births (between 1946 and about 1960) associated in cultural terms, at least among the middle classes, with a rejection of traditional authority as represented by the patriarchal families and paternalistic ideals of industrial capitalism dominant during the 1950s of their childhoods. In the 1960s and 1970s, such persons sought self-realization through the counterculture; in the 1980s they came to seek self-fulfillment through self-employment.[18]

A later wave of second-career neo-farmers, beginning in the mid 1990s and carrying into the 2000s, coalesces around other historical and cultural landmarks: the dot-com bust, 9/11, the Wall Street crash, a general disillusionment with the fractured promise of easy money. Like their hippie homesteader predecessors, these lifestyle migrants moved to rural areas and bought farmland, often intending to make a living by working the land, but they tended to be a bit older and better capitalized at the start. Among them exist a range of sentiments: joy in hands-on productive labor and self-employment, desire to work outdoors with animals, concern to fit into an adopted rural community, commitment to producing (and eating) good food.[19] Reflecting the exponential growth of artisan cheesemaking in recent years, those who set out specifically to handcraft high-quality cheese for local markets opened their businesses in 2005 or later.[20] Running somewhat parallel to this generational tale and engaging sentiments of their own, dairy farmers are also taking up cheesemaking to add economic value to milk they were already producing.

With this overview in place, I turn now to characterize the sentiments that people bring to their craft and work, and that have brought them to participate in reinventing American cheese.

Getting "Back to the Land"

Mary Keehn, founder of Cypress Grove Chevre, known for its Humboldt Fog cheese, acquired her first goats in 1970. She did so out of maternal sentiment. She was weaning her first daughter and "just wanted good milk" to give her.[21] Mary and her husband were living on a dairy farm in Sonoma, California, where goats were kept to control brush. When Mary asked if she could buy a goat to milk for her daughter, the farmer laughed and said, "'Honey, if you can catch one, you can have it.'" Mary caught two, "and that was the beginning of it."

Soon the family moved to Humboldt County and bought an eighty-acre parcel of land with Mary's sister and a couple of friends, envisioning it as a communal vacation place. They "built a house with logs that we drug down from the woods with our horse. It was very, very primitive. I mean, our hot water was from a black pipe that we laid in the sun, or you would heat it on a wood cook stove. That was back-to-the-land time." Mary remembers reading such countercultural staples as *Mother Jones,* tracts on organic gardening by Rodale Press, and the *Whole Earth Catalog,* publications whose antiestablishment, ecologically minded, can-do sentiment—in no way antithetical to entrepreneurial capitalism—is part of the story of artisanal cheese's commercial development.[22] Mary grew vegetables and kept chickens for eggs, even making her own ketchup. She taught herself from books how to make fresh cheese from her goats' milk. After a few years, "we had two other daughters and pretty soon we were looking at . . . school, so we moved to town. That was the beginning of moving away from the 'back-to-the-land' time to 'this is the real world now.'"

Mary kept her goats. Viewing breeding as a form of aesthetic creation, she "got into the genetics of goats and how you can use goats as an art form." She crisscrossed the country to goat shows, pulling her animals in a trailer and stopping to milk them at rest areas or in vacant lots. She "made a small living" selling breed stock, "but then, of course, you have too much milk, and that's how the cheese started." A friend who was opening a restaurant told her, "If you start a cheese factory, I'll buy your cheese."

Mary's story, however, is more densely plotted than what at first hearing might seem a quintessential entrepreneurial tale of opportunity taken. By then she had divorced. "I was single, I had four kids, I had goats, so what else are you going to do? I'll start making cheese." She had no business training, and no formal training in making cheese. What she had was a close network of female friends, goat's milk, a need to make money, and confidence in her own ability. Mary's confidence was nurtured by a middle-class upbringing (her father was a naval attorney and Mary attended college, majoring in biology), but Mary herself points to the role played by feminism. Reflecting on the emergence of domestic goat cheese in the early 1980s and that it was women—baby boomers like herself (including Laura Chenel, Allison Hooper, Letty Kilmoyer, Judy Schad, Jennifer Bice, Barbara Backus, Anne Topham)—who brought it into being and to the market, Mary said: "I think it was a change in the sixties, that we all felt like we could do what we wanted. I mean, really, birth control, which—it was all happening then. We women really felt that we could do what we wanted. You didn't have to meet some guy and marry well, which was what most of us learned [one was supposed to do]. This was a harder degree [than the 'Mrs. degree'], for sure. A lot of us had serious problems along the way."

The feminist movement of the 1970s deserves significant credit for reviving farmstead cheese. Not only did consciousness-raising boost (in particular) white, middle-class women's self-confidence, throughout the 1970s, beginning with California, states across the nation adopted unilateral "no-fault" divorce laws that contributed to the frequency and social acceptability of women living—and making a living—on their own, even as farmers.[23] The social capital of women's networks also translated into economic opportunity as female chefs, Berkeley's Alice Waters most famously, bought cheese and produce produced by women. Mary and the rest were not just eating counterculturally; they made independent livings from producing foods that countercultural peers purchased at food co-ops and farmers' markets.[24] For these women capitalizing on their ostensibly domestic labor, pursuing the craft of food-making "reasserted female competence and control" in a modern economy dominated by men, as Warren Belasco has noted.[25]

Marjorie Susman and Marian Pollack, of Orb Weaver Farm (fig. 8), met in the 1970s in western Massachusetts, where Marian worked as a therapist and Marjorie attended community college. Wanting to make a living together, emboldened by the feminist movement, and inspired by the creative outlet of friends (Marian's supervisor raised goats and made cheese in her kitchen), the couple set out to farm. Their goals were modest. "We didn't have any family money," Marjorie told me, "and we thought that if we did a variety of stuff we could do it." "We were sorta still in the 'back-to-the-land' mind-set," Marian added. "Not like you needed to make money, just you needed to make enough" to get by.

FIG. 8. Marjorie Susman, at left, and Marian Pollack of Orb Weaver Farm outside their cheese cave. Photo by author.

Marjorie enrolled in a two-year program in animal science at an agriculture school, motivated by a no-interest loan to encourage students to take up farming. Their initial plan was to raise and milk goats, "because that seemed to be what girls could do." In Vermont they found a job milking cows and raising heifers (young cows yet to be bred) that came with accommodation in a "beyond dilapidated" farmhouse. A year later the owners offered to sell them the farm, its crumbling buildings set on beautiful rolling hills edged by woodland. "We gave up goats when we realized we couldn't in Vermont because that would have been too cosmopolitan"; "We didn't think anybody would buy goat cheese," they explained. Vermont was cow country.

They bought a small herd of Jersey cows (women *can* handle cows, a fact to which the Cowgirl Creamery in Marin County, California, pays winking homage) and experimented with milk in the kitchen. "We wanted to make just regular cheese, you know, nothing fancy. . . . Our number-one thing has been to be able to sell our cheese locally, and affordably." Setting out to make a living by working the land rather than to produce a high-end specialty food, they developed a farmhouse cheese, their own recipe. The cheese carries the same name as the farm, Orb Weaver, after a spider that spins an elaborate circular web. Commenting on the name in 1986, Marjorie said, "A spider's web is its universe. They build their world around them. We want to make our farm—our web—to be a self-contained unit."[26]

Early on, they made cheese every third day, year-round, in addition to selling milk. They also had four acres of land in vegetables. Finding they could not sustain the pace of year-round cheesemaking, they shifted to a cycle of making cheese for a few months until they needed a break; then they would exclusively ship milk before returning to cheesemaking when they felt ready. Customers would run up to them on the street clamoring, "Where's the cheese?" After a couple of years of forgoing cheesemaking altogether, they "sat back one day and thought, *We're off track here*." "We forgot what we wanted to do when we started." Also, they were so poor they "couldn't afford tuna fish."[27]

In the mid 1990s they downsized their herd from thirty to seven cows and returned to cheesemaking, but only during the winter months. "It's fabulous," Marjorie observed. "Our quality of life now—we don't work in the summer!" "We don't make the cheese in the summer," Marian corrected. Instead they garden intensively and preserve food for winter, lining their pantry with fire-roasted salsa, canned tomatoes, and strawberry jam, and filling their freezer with corn and Swiss chard. In summer they sell organic produce fertilized with composted manure to local food co-ops and restaurants. This feels less "like work" than does making cheese.

Milking seven cows, they make seven thousand pounds of cheese a year in an intricate choreography of working and living. During cheese season, mornings begin at 6:00 A.M. when they pump milk into the cheese vat. Marian goes off to milk the cows while Marjorie sanitizes the cheese molds and washes the bulk tank. While Marjorie is raising the temperature of the chilled milk to begin cheesemaking, Marian has finished milking and returns to the house to start breakfast. Marjorie dashes back to join Marian for breakfast, making sure she returns to the cheese house before the milk has reached 90°F, at which point she adds the rennet. Marian "is doing cow stuff," readying the animals to go outside, but when the curd is cut and ready to be drained from the whey Marian returns to the cheese house. Together they "work the curd" by hand, crumbling it between their fingers before salting and pressing it into Gouda-shaped molds. Together they clean up. This routine, honed day in and day out from nearly thirty years of practice, not only has come to produce consistently excellent cheese, it is integral to the intimate relationship of this couple.

Twenty-seven years after they licensed their creamery, Marjorie and Marian have nearly paid off their mortgages and manage to pay their bills. "I feel like we make a good living here, you know, a good life here. But as far as disposable income, anytime we've ever had any money, we put it into the house." They do not keep an individual retirement account or have any other savings. At the time of our interview, Marian was about to turn sixty and Marjorie was in her early fifties. They pay more than seven hundred dollars a month for private health insurance. "We would qualify, without a doubt, for the poor people's thing"—for Medicaid—Marjorie said, except that to qualify "you have to be without insurance for a year. I had breast cancer in '99. I can't be without health insurance." Marian pointed out that a universal (single-payer) low-cost public health insurance program would really help small farmers (and artisans) like themselves who manage to buy insurance but at great cost: "It kills us, every friggin' month." They keep it up because the thought of Marjorie suffering a relapse without insurance is too frightening.

Marjorie and Marian acknowledge that keeping their business small is "a choice we made. We could be bigger. We could make cheese year-round. We could hire people." But they have held on to their goal of being as self-sufficient as possible. What they did not choose was to be poor. All too frequently, assumptions that American poverty results from personal failing or volition obscures the policies—such as Medicaid qualification—and economic structures that generate economic inequality.[28] However modest, Orb Weaver Farm's infrastructure requires serious capital to maintain. Marjorie described their barn as "falling in, pretty much." They asked their repairman what they should do about it. He suggested, "How about retire?" The women are unable and, frankly, unwilling to take out a significant loan at this point in their lives to fix the barn properly. Marjorie and Marian love their life. "We don't ever want to have to move," they told me. But the cheesemaking is so physically demanding that they anticipate a time when they will have to phase it out. It remains to be seen which will go first: the barn or their bodies.

Engaged Labor

Among the next wave of people to get into farmstead cheesemaking are those who identify more closely as artisans or entrepreneurs than as farmers.[29] As craftspeople, they care about quality work, not simply to maximize the market value of what they create, but because their identity and sense of self-worth are tied up in doing a job well.[30] Greg Bernhardt and Hannah Sessions used to host a gallery of their oil paintings (for sale) on their Blue Ledge Farm Web site. Greg told an audience at the 2007 American Cheese Society (ACS) meetings that he and Hannah set out to pursue goals that were not "just about farming but about life. We went into this wanting to do something creative with our life, something interesting. We didn't want to ship milk [to a processing plant]. . . . Creating cheese, we felt like, would be interesting."[31] Artisans make decisions about aesthetic design and process. They direct much of what they do on the job. In general, if not every single day, they do not feel alienated from the process of production.

John Putnam, a former commercial litigator, left Boston and bought a deteriorating Vermont farm with his wife, Janine, in 1986; the couple started selling Tarentaise cheese in 2002. John barely paused in his daily routine of making cheese, taking orders, and running a farm when I visited in 2007, but when I managed to ask him about his favorite part of the entire enterprise he replied, "It's making something that's yours. And I mean the big We, Us," meaning also his wife and teenage children, who help on the farm in summer. "When you're making mistakes, they're yours. When you're making decisions, they're yours." He spoke about lawyering. He was good, he told me. Never lost a significant case. But a lawyer, he explained, works for a client, and "clients have no idea what you did for them. . . . Now I feel that we're working for us. We own everything. We own the successes. We own the failures." The experience of being recognized for doing skilled work has itself become meaningful. "We don't have any illusions about being the best cheesemakers in the world, about having the best farm in the world, about making the best cheese in the world—but we're trying. And that's what matters." Such artisan-entrepreneurs take pride not only in the quality of their workmanship but also in their ability to manage economies of sentiment.

Bob Stetson, who left a career in shipping to buy a farmstead goat cheese operation, Westfield Farm, in central Massachusetts, said similarly:

> I spent just about all of my life since [age] eighteen, nineteen in freight forwarding, customs brokerage. And I had gotten really tired of that . . . I kind of missed the purpose of everything. But [when] I had been in the shipping business I did a bit of sales, and I always envied people who were selling *things,* selling tangible items. It didn't matter what it was. I just wished I had a sample case that I could go in [with] and say, "Do you like it? Fine, this is what we'll do. If you don't like it, fine. I'll leave." But selling this intangible future [in customs brokerage], you end up selling B.S., because that's what people are buying. And it just got to be *depressing. . . .* This had always been my ideal: to have a product that I could sell that I could be proud of.

Bob, by no means a foodie, found that product in goat cheese. He purchased Westfield Farm, goats, equipment, recipe, brand, and all, after founders Bob and Letty Kilmoyer, wanting to retire to Florida, placed an ad in the *Boston Globe.* Westfield farm and cheese continued from one owner-operator to the next because they shared an entrepreneurial sentiment.

Others spoke of the tactile, even sensual experience of transforming milk into cheese. Brenda Jensen, a former executive manager who makes sheep's-milk cheese in Wisconsin, said appreciatively of the engaged focus it demands, "It makes you lose your senses, your common senses." Laini Fondiller told me that cheesemaking *is* her life: "Without this it's hard for me to focus. I have ADD. It helps me to settle down. It's medicinal, for me." A friend wonders how it is that Laini never gets bored. Boredom might be averted because in artisanship there is always a new element of skill to perfect. Laini herself likens making cheese to running a marathon: "an adrenaline builds up, you have to be constantly aware of time." The pressure of this, for Laini, heads off boredom. Like Brenda, she gets a rush from the "flow" of engaged consciousness and focused attention that cheesemaking demands.[32]

Although a few second-careerists turned to cheese after being laid off from previous jobs, most chose to change pursuits. The attacks on the Twin Towers and Pentagon on September 11, 2001, serve as one narrative turning point.[33] "All of us have a 9/11 memory," Steve Getz told an audience at the 2007 ACS meetings.[34] His is from that evening, in the backyard of the Pennsylvania home he shared with his wife Karen and their children, when he was not traveling on business as a software consultant: "I looked at the sky—and there in eastern Pennsylvania we were under the flight path from Newark, La Guardia, Kennedy—the sky was *empty*. And, just sitting, . . . looking at the sky, I said: 'We're done. No traveling. We're going to do something else.' Life is short, and I've got two daughters who are growing very quickly, and that's when we decided to move." In 2003 the Getzes bought a Vermont farm with the intention of making organic-milk cheese.[35]

In these narratives, cheesemaking is portrayed as a rustic "no-collar" job, neither stuffy office work nor alienated wage labor—a rural counterpart to the "new economy" jobs in media technologies that flourished briefly in the 1990s by capitalizing on a self-sacrificing work ethic and trading on the casual aesthetic of the bohemian artist.[36] Tumalo Farms in Oregon is the second career project for a cofounder of the Internet start-up WebMD, who left his position there after realizing he had lost track of who the company's six hundred employees were, just five years after having known all the employees and their children by name.[37] The no-collar sentiment may be particularly powerful for those who have come to cheesemaking from confining white-collar occupations—or, on the other hand, from farming.

Among the "agrarian values" that anthropologist Peggy Barlett identified in her 1980s study of farm life in Georgia as contrasting with "industrial values" of material gain are "freedom from supervision, flexibility of work pace, and daily independence from supervision"—sentiments echoed by former white-collar workers seeking a more satisfying way of life through crafting cheese.[38] "Traditional" dairy farmers may make cheese "for money," more out of a feeling of necessity than a desire to make cheese for its own sake (as the farmer quoted at the beginning of the chapter suggested), but necessity and desire are not mutually exclusive. As will be elaborated below, when heritage dairy farmers turn to cheesemaking, they do so to carry on a farming way of life. The perception that "traditional" dairy farmers exercise less choice when they go into cheesemaking compared to those who are new to farming repeats a familiar, and flawed, modernist narrative that pitches "tradition" (in this case, heritage dairy farming) as static and given, in contrast to modernity's demand that, in Anthony Giddens's phrasing, "we have no choice but to choose."[39] As Jane Collier has argued, however, people in supposedly traditional agricultural societies are not so duty-bound that they have no choices to make, just as in modern capitalist societies people are not as free to choose their own destiny as they might like to think.[40] To be sure, heritage farmers may have less disposable income with which to realize their values than the typical second-career rural in-migrant, but farmers are just as committed to "lifestyle" and to engaged labor—in farming, if not in artisanship—as anyone else.[41]

From Pastoral Dream to Rural Economic Revitalization

If the new farmstead cheesemakers in the 1980s framed their enterprise as an independent exercise in getting back to the land, people who bought rural properties with an eye toward artisanal agriculture in the 2000s are apt to speak of building vital rural communities.[42] Many of these people spent childhood summers in rural areas, often on a working farm.[43] Many are the college-educated children or grandchildren of farmers who are not so much returning to their roots as bringing urban sensibilities and, often, business acumen to reinvent what it means to farm in the United States.

Marcia Barinaga was just starting up a farmstead sheep dairy in Marin County, California, when we met. A former *Science* writer with a doctorate in biology, Marcia was breeding sheep to develop a strong dairy flock while experimenting with cheese recipes in her kitchen. She and her husband, a research scientist, had spent weekends on the Marin coast since 1993 and purchased a hilltop ranch in anticipation of building a house for their retirement. However, as they spent more time in Marin and got to know local ranchers and farmers, they started thinking twice about their new property. She told me in an interview:

> We decided that we really wanted to do something that would make our ranch fully sustainable—I mean sustainable as a business, as a ranch, but also that would contribute to the sustainability of the community. Every ranch out here that gets bought by somebody who just wants to build a house on it and doesn't really care about doing agriculture weakens the whole community. It was very important to us to pull our weight, to be active members of the community, to be employers in the community, to be doing all the things that strengthen the community. And so we were thinking, *What can we do as something value-added?*

Cooperative extension agents suggested organic strawberries, but raising produce did not engage Marcia's interest. Then her father, whose Basque family "is

FIG. 9. Marcia Barinaga with her sheep on Barinaga Ranch in Marshall, California.
Photo by author.

in the sheep business," wondered whether Marcia might put sheep on the ranch,
noting, "Back in Spain, everybody who has sheep milks them and makes cheese."
When Marcia mentioned cheese to the county extension people, they assured her,
"That's viable. The market is bottomless." Marcia—PhD, daughter of a Basque
American engineer who had grown up on a sheep ranch in Idaho, "a range operation with thousands of sheep" where "the notion of bringing them into the parlor
every night and milking them is completely foreign"—began a sheep ranch in
order to craft Basque-style sheep's-milk cheese (fig. 9).[44] Marcia's enterprise is not
a return to the past but a decidedly modern agricultural model—a twenty-first-
century artisan post-pastoral.

Second-career farmstead cheesemakers raised by parents who had themselves
"escaped" the farm communities of their childhoods often discover a new vocabulary through which to communicate with their parents. One told me, "Both my
parents desperately wanted to get away from farm backgrounds," but when she
began raising goats, her father started telephoning to ask of a doe, "How did she
freshen?"—posing questions related to animal husbandry that her closest friends
do not know to ask. The woman marveled, "This is my father? Who worked
for DuPont?" For her, an unexpected dividend from raising goats has been the
emergence of a new basis for relationship with her father.

Making Good Food Well

As the Rodale Press and *Whole Earth Catalog* did a generation earlier for the baby boomers, a spate of popular books and films about food politics at the turn of the millennium, by Gary Nabhan, Michael Pollan, and Barbara Kingsolver, among others, inspired many middle-class Americans to draw new connections between everyday eating and the political economy of agricultural and industrial food production.[45] Such texts emerged apace with interest in the Slow Food movement, the rise of locavorism, and the intensification of organic agriculture. Cheesemakers reporting via my survey primary goals of "wanting to make great cheese," especially "for local markets," generally got their start after 2005, in the wake of such publications. In 2005, with two milking does and a licensed creamery, Lisa Schwartz started a farmstead cheese operation, Rainbeau Ridge, in suburban Westchester County, New York. In a 2009 self-published book, *Over the Rainbeau: Living the Dream of Sustainable Farming,* Lisa recounts her efforts to begin farming land she and her husband began buying in 1988 out of a desire to "restore and protect" the original holdings of a nineteenth-century gentleman farmer. "I just knew I wanted to get closer to nature and my food sources and produce something of value with my own hands," she writes.[46] She has turned her restored farmhouse into an education center, offering workshops on gardening and cooking to children and adults.

Lisa Schwartz's narrative is reminiscent of *The Perils and Pleasures of Domesticating Goat Cheese,* Miles Cahn's tale of starting up Coach Farm in New York's Hudson River Valley, in which he writes: "You know how nice it is when you stop in a restaurant in one of those little villages in Provence and the *patron* brings out a platter of fresh goat cheeses that a local farmer had brought in that very morning. Well, we were going to be the local farmer, and we were going to bring our cheese, direct from our farm, to the restaurants in New York."[47] Cahn maps a circulating path of upscale, well-traveled urban consumers and rural producers, suggesting a translation of the family farm into a sustainable retirement project. In addition to vast economic capital, the Cahns brought to Coach Farm the cultural capital associated with upper-middle-class lifestyles, including classy consumer tastes. But not all makers of artisanal cheese dine in restaurants serving cheese platters, let alone vacation in Provence. In wanting to make good food, not all artisanal makers of cheese strive to create products with classed distinction.

The sentiments I have sketched—making a living from the land, being attached to small livestock, appreciating the mental-manual engagement of practical labor, valuing good food—map onto a range of economic realities and sensibilities. Diana Murphy of Dreamfarm in Wisconsin was born on a conventional Wisconsin (cow) dairy farm, following six older siblings and preceding four younger ones. Six of the eleven children continued their education beyond high school, self-financing their studies through work-study in the Wisconsin public university system. Diana studied graphic arts, but after bouts with debilitating headaches she wanted to return to farming life. Diana and her husband bought a twenty-five-acre farm in 2002 from an investor who had purchased it from an elderly couple who were no longer able to work it. Diana's two older daughters learned about pygmy goats and wanted to raise a pair to show in 4-H. "They loved them, and they loved showing them, and they did a good job—but as I see it," Diana told me, "if we're going to have these animals, let's add something that will give back a little bit." It is wonderful to have fun living with livestock, in other words, but a farm should be productive, too. They added dairy goats to their small herd.

From the start, the Murphys have farmed organically. "I don't think we need to be putting all this [chemical] stuff into the system," she told me. "I know way too many people—and a lot of farmers—who have died from cancer, and . . . if we don't change the way we live, I think we're gonna wipe ourselves out eventually, and I—it's just what I believe in. I don't want any additives put into the stuff I eat and drink, and my animals don't need any, because, you know, I eat the cheese and drink the milk." Diana is not pronouncing on organics as an abstract ethical imperative. She is speaking from the situated knowledge of a daughter of a farming community and as a mother of teenage children.[48] Good food—healthy, tasty, well-made, organic—is not the exclusive purview of elite foodies.

SURVIVING WITH SENTIMENT

Once people arrive at cheesemaking, they face the question of how to survive as a business. One cheesemaker who was readying to ramp up production (to one hundred thousand pounds) said, "To really have a commercially viable enterprise, the reality is you've got to put out a lot of cheese." A central challenge is to grow big enough to be economically viable without undermining the sentiments—daily, hands-on work with land and animals, joy in transforming milk into cheese, time with one's family, and so on—that inspired them to get into farming or take up cheesemaking in the first place. How might they turn *qualities* of good living into *quantities* that sustain their business, without selling out those very qualities?

In entrepreneurialism no less than consumerism, rational evaluation is always tangled up in emotions, desires, and aspirations.[49] Which strategies people adopt and how their economies of sentiment play out is not strictly a matter of choice—neither the dispassionate maximization of rational choice theory nor the romantic desire of lifestyle choice. All calculative action entails qualification: calculative terms must "qualify" in order to "count" in one's calculations, and qualitative judgment based often in sentiment enters into calculative reason.[50] I turn now to consider how cheesemakers make *qualitative calculations* as they work to build successful businesses in ways that will not undermine the multiple values they seek to realize. I take up three arenas for qualitative calculation—sustainability, accounting for pricing, and value-added dairying—to show how these calculations vary and are subject to moral judgment. There is no consensus among cheesemakers on how appropriately to translate qualities into quantities and back again.

Scaling Up for Sustainability: How Big Is Big Enough (without Getting Too Big)?

Sustainability is a term of qualitative calculation that often refers to the simultaneous, long-term realization of economic, environmental, and moral values. It is of recent vintage, having been coined in the 1980s (coincident with the revival of on-farm cheesemaking) in discussions of international development. Sustainability assumes market capitalism to be the inevitable frame for economic action. Karen Weinberg, who with her husband bought a hundred-acre farm in eastern New York in the late 1980s and began working it commercially a decade later, acknowledged that what it takes "to make the farm financially and economically sustainable" changes as her business and the market change. This "is a big issue," she emphasized, because however wonderful ideas about environmental sustainability are, "if you can't survive, then it's all sort of out the window."[51] Beyond the success of a business, both financially and in terms of personal fulfillment, at stake in approaches to scaling up for sustainability are also what kinds of artisans, parents, neighbors, and business owners these farmer-cheesemakers are and might become. It is one thing to figure out an economic calculus for business growth and profit, but as one cheesemaker put it, "if it puts distance or borders between you and your children and your partner—your wife or husband—then what's the point?"

A panel session at the 2007 meeting of the ACS in Burlington, Vermont, titled "How Big Is Big Enough? Getting at Size for Farmstead Sustainability," provided a platform for community discussion of these issues. The organizer of the panel, a small ruminant dairy specialist at the Center for Sustainable Agriculture at the University of Vermont, introduced the session by noting, "There's no such thing as sustainable growth. In biology, it plateaus. The only thing that is sustainable is change and adaptation, so that's what these farmers have to do."[52] Greg Bernhardt, a panelist at the session, presented a frank account of how he and his wife and partner, Hannah Sessions, continue to adapt their life-business strategy.[53] His account reveals the inherent tension of artisanship in a capitalist society, in many ways indicative of any self-employment enterprise and reminiscent of Dorinne

Kondo's reflection on small family-owned Japanese firms: "with their long hours, pressing deadlines and the feeling of being constantly 'squeezed,' one wonders how much 'independence' they really have."[54]

In 2000 Greg and Hannah, recently graduated from college, took out a personal loan to buy 130 acres and an abandoned cow dairy barn, assorted outhouses, and a farmhouse in central Vermont.[55] In 2003 Blue Ledge Farm became licensed for commercial cheesemaking. By the end of the decade, an average investment of eighty thousand to one hundred thousand dollars was required to build and equip a certifiable commercial cheese plant.[56] To approach this average, some enterprises build from the ground up but purchase used equipment, while others retrofit old buildings and invest in a new cheese vat or bulk tank. After expenses, by 2007 Blue Ledge Farm was turning a modest profit, which they reinvested in expanding the business.

Capital investment requirements are rising because dairy inspectors, having become accustomed to on-farm cheese plants, expect them to be up to code from the beginning. In the past, operations like Orb Weaver were able to grandfather in cobbled-together buildings and makeshift equipment, but today states may require new cement floors, special walling material, and automated capping machines for packaging yogurt.[57] One-size-fits-all requirements designed for large industrial factories set financial obstacles for artisan producers. Of the seventy thousand dollars that Steve and Karen Getz spent to build a cheese house on their Vermont farm in 2005, seven thousand reportedly went for a requisite incinerating toilet for the use of state inspectors; Steve has described it as "a seven-thousand-dollar storage closet for boxes."[58] A New York producer complained to me of a change in regulations that required her to buy a newly designed sink, one that "didn't exist used." Food production is highly, and not always sensibly, regulated. "There are so many stupid, little, teeny, bitty regulations that cost money," she said. "It's enough to make me a Republican," joked a Vermont cheesemaker who knew his leftist politics were apparent to me.

Without supplemental earnings from an off-farm job, Greg and Hannah are raising two children on the income generated by Blue Ledge Farm. Since becoming incorporated as a limited liability corporation (LLC) in 2007, they have paid themselves an annual salary of eighteen thousand dollars each. Greg and Hannah were working nine hours a day, seven days a week. A central theme of Greg's presentation was their ongoing struggle to find an optimal production level at which they could afford to pay waged employees and thus cut back on their own hours. Might an annual production volume of twenty-two thousand pounds of cheese be their "magic number"? Every operation has "a different number," Greg acknowledged, since cheesemakers have "different goals." The trick, he said, is to figure out "what you want to be," not only as a cheesemaker or business owner, but also as a parent, spouse, neighbor, creative individual.[59] He and Hannah are artists, "so that is one of our goals—we have to balance how we find time for this other aspect of ourselves." They were hoping that full-time employees would provide the solution.

For others, to take on full-time employees would be to compromise sentiments of independence and engaged labor. Mark Fischer explained, "There's a limited volume you can get to in farmstead production because of the amount of work to do with both the animals and the cheesemaking. To get beyond that point you have to start hiring people, and once you start hiring people you move away from the actual work itself and become more of an administrator." A significant portion of farm-based cheesemaking enterprises remain small enough to be nearly self-sufficient in terms of labor.[60] Labor issues themselves are shot through with qualitative calculations. Some farmstead businesses make it a priority to pay a small, central staff a living wage to ensure employee continuity and because they believe it is important to do. Others augment part-time wages with farm produce or other indirect benefits. Jon Wright's employees are welcome to bring their children and dogs to work, which is one reason why people "want to work here," as Jon told me, even when they could earn twice as much per hour cleaning vacation houses. Blue Ledge Farm was relying on unpaid seasonal interns, working forty hours a week for room (in a barn apartment) and partial board (including access to the vegetable garden), as well as the unremunerated labor of Hannah's parents, who hand-wrap cheeses and tend a farmers' market stall on weekends. Unpaid interns, often college students or recent graduates, are cheap, but time must be set aside each season to train them.[61]

Within farm households, labor tends to divide according to preference, personal history, skill, and inclination, rather than follow a customary gender division.[62] This does not preclude gender narratives from being called upon to explain or legitimate the assignment of tasks, or for these to break down along traditional gender lines.[63] Two or three years after one family started a farmstead business, the wife went back to teaching full-time because, the farmer-cheesemaker husband told me, "Quite literally, it was better for us personally" not to work together all the time. I was told a story about one farm couple who, unlike many who farm organically, maintain organic certification of their dairy because it helps settle domestic disputes. The cheesemaking wife apparently feels that the dairying husband could keep his milking parlor tidier, but she cannot rightly complain when routine test results show his milk to be the cleanest in the state. The inspector, she admits to friends, serves as a "marriage counselor," validating the efficacy of their separate yet collaborative labor. At the same time, when one owns and operates a business with one's spouse, divorce can mean losing a job, perhaps even a vocation.[64] One reason why artisan businesses fail is that marriages fail.

Four years into their business, Greg and Hannah were milking about sixty goats, turning all their milk into cheese, and selling all their cheese—and still they were not turning a profit.[65] Because of the additional costs of farming, farmstead cheese businesses report a lower profitability rate than off-farm creameries.[66] Bearing out a view that livestock contribute value-generating labor, one farmstead producer estimated to me her overall debt per cow, and another told me she expects each of her goats to bring in a certain income (calculated in milk yield) per year.[67] Consultant Peter Dixon advises that new cheese businesses should expect not to earn a profit for the first three to five years while initial capital investments are paid off, sales markets are secured, and production is gradually ramped up.[68] Greg and Hannah were growing nervous because they were already hitting the upper limit of their farmstead ecology of production, milking as many goats as their barn and property could sustain.[69]

To increase cheese production without increasing their herd, Greg and Hannah decided to buy milk from a neighboring goat farm to augment their own. From 2005 to 2006 their cheese production doubled. The next year they started buying cow's milk as well. Although about one-fourth of farm-based cheesemakers buy milk to supplement their own farm's production, this practice, for some, undermines the value of self-sufficiency that farmstead production is often said to embody.[70] Buying milk also introduces the moral calculation of how much a farmer, who well knows how difficult it is to sustain a small farm through selling fluid milk, will pay for someone else's milk.[71] In 2007, Laini Fondiller in northern Vermont paid her friend and neighbor who was "having hard times" well over the going commodity price for his cow's milk (thirty-eight dollars per hundredweight), commenting, "I've been there, so I know what it's like to be freakin' broke!" Her business is "allowing him to stay alive" farming.

In light of such considerations, how do cheesemakers approach scaling up for sustainability? Rather than pursue growth and profit for their own sakes, many describe a calculus of sufficiency. Speaking of the farmstead business he runs with his wife, one explained:

> I think realistically, we *should* be able to pay the bills and afford to go out once in awhile . . . and put a little bit in savings. That's the goal. But let me make it clear, we also hear people say, "This is really great cheese; what do you do to turn this into making a lot of money?" And the answer is, "You don't!" You put yourself in that mind-set, then it's really ramping up on manufacturing and distribution and travel—all kinds of things that defeat the purpose of what you wanted to do in the first place![72]

The principle of sufficiency, like making cheese for commercial trade, is nothing new to American farm families. Popular among eighteenth- and nineteenth-century American dairy farmers and their British counterparts was the notion of *competency,* signaling "a degree of well-being that was both desirable and morally legitimate."[73] Webster's 1852 edition of the *American Dictionary* defined *compe-*

tency as "such a quantity as is sufficient; property or means of subsistence sufficient to furnish the necessaries and conveniences of life, without superfluity."[74] As Sally McMurry points out in her history of American dairying, "one family's competency might conceivably be another's poverty"—or luxury, for that matter.[75] In California, one second-career cheesemaker told me he had read about the notion of a competency and was taken with it. He and his partner were raising twenty-five goats and making cheese on an inherited seven-acre parcel of land. "We can make a living if we can sell our cheese," he said. "We don't see the thing as a business, where you build a brand and sell it."[76] The couple aimed to take home thirty-five thousand dollars a year in profit, the figure they set as sufficient to make a living (three years in they had yet to break even and were living off savings). On the day I visited we drove to a nearby winery for a picnic lunch and opened a bottle of Viognier to enjoy with a homegrown tomato salad with goat cheese curd, their homemade goat *rillettes,* pickled mushrooms and preserved figs they bartered for cheese with a friend, purchased bread and olives, and, of course, their own cheeses. In eschewing superfluity, these artisans were after sufficiency, not asceticism.[77]

Sufficiency, sustainability, viability—these are all relative, situated values. A cheese business augmented with a spouse's off-farm income may have a lower economic threshold of viability than one expected to support a household (about a quarter of producers rely for all or most of their household income on cheese and other farm sales).[78] Blue Ledge's viability is predicated on Greg and Hannah deeming a household income of fifty-four thousand dollars (salary plus rent paid by the business, out of which they are paying off multiple mortgages) as sufficient for their family of four. Given Vermont's relatively high cost of living, this represents a comfortable but not extravagant income. As Greg put it, "It pays for our lifestyle . . . everything that we need." Cheesemakers are not getting rich on their labor; they are getting by—or they are relying on wealth generated through other means.

Pushing back against structural features of the market that seem to eat away at their self-expectations, cheesemakers such as Greg and Hannah embrace the qualitative calculus of sufficiency as a means of realizing the value they place on pursuing a creative vocation. Their practical yet sentimental reasoning belies the capitalist compartmentalization of values that many of us rehearse in our own daily lives (that is, while acquiescing to the pursuit of individualist values to get ahead "at work," many of us strive to cultivate relational values at home, in our religious communities, and in other domains perceived as sequestered from the market).[79] When cheesemakers articulate a tension between principle and pragmatism, "dream" and "necessity," this does not demonstrate the selling-out of their values but indicates instead how aware they are of the ethical and political stakes of their economic practice. Nevertheless, lack of economic flexibility may throw off their qualitative calculations.

Accounting for Pricing

Every cheesemaker has heard the complaint, "Why is your cheese so expensive?" The question is often accusatory, implying, "You must be raking in the money" or "Can it really cost so much to make?" or even "What do you think 'cheese' is, anyway?" Having previously noted the role of government subsidies in creating the imbalance between prices of artisanal and supermarket cheeses (and between domestic and European prices), here I consider how cheesemakers account for their own marketing and pricing practices. Deciding on a market price to ask for one's cheese can be a daunting prospect, particularly for dairy farmers accustomed to accepting the commodity price set for their milk.[80] *Accounting*, referring both to bookkeeping and to storytelling, is a form of qualitative calculation.[81]

Cheesemakers were often reluctant to give me a detailed account of their financial accounting, partly as a competitive stance regarding other producers, and partly because Americans are often uncomfortable talking about money on account of its moral connotations—if the accounts are too marginal, this may be taken as personal failure, while there is also a risk of making too much money, which can index the moral failure of receiving more than is deserved. Because the qualities that characterize the value of artisanal cheeses are still being hammered out (they are unfinished commodities), it may be unclear, even to producers, what constitutes a good value when artisanal cheese is bought and sold. When cheesemakers did talk with me about money, they also spoke of moral decision-making and compromise. As Karen Weinberg said, "It's one thing to make a cheese you love; it's another to make a cheese you can sell. And so to try and manage both of those demands—certainly to waste something you've produced because it doesn't sell, to throw it away, is a sin, given how much work goes into getting milk in the first place and taking care of the animals."

I first met Mark Fischer at the Londonderry, Vermont, farmers' market. As I nibbled on free cheese samples (accounted for as a marketing expense), Mark told me ("I hate to say it after five years") that he felt they were still doing a pilot study of whether farmstead sheep's-milk cheese is an economically viable thing to do with one's life. Echoing the mantra of dairy farmers, the Fischers felt they had to "get bigger or get out" of the cheese business. In that summer of 2007, Mark and his wife, Gari, were expanding their cheese aging facilities and installing a new pasteurizer. Investing in an expensive pasteurizer would enable them to market younger cheeses, but their reasoning also had to do with the ecology of sheep's-milk cheese production: "It'll allow us to reach *this* market," Mark said, indicating the farmers' market where he sells the bulk of their inventory. The seasonality of sheep's-milk cheese, peaking in the fall, does not fit well with the seasonality of Vermont farmers' markets. Mark's table on this June day was pretty bare. He and Gari were clearly nervous about whether their expansion would pay off.[82]

Sheep's-milk cheese is the most expensive to produce because sheep, per animal, yield less milk than either cows or goats, and as sheep feed on pasture they are seasonal milk producers. Fresh or vacuum-packed cheeses made from pasteurized milk can be packaged and sold soon after production, whereas natural-rind cheeses require labor-intensive nurturing in an aging facility.[83] Not only does the time required to age cheese tie up inventory and delay income necessary to pay bills, but regulating the temperature and humidity of an aging room is also a significant drain on utilities. Some cheeses are simply more expensive to make than others, a fact that is not always obvious to the consumer.

Artisan producers sell cheese in one or more of four ways: direct retail to consumers (at farmstands or farmers' markets, through mail order); direct wholesale to retailers (specialty shops, food co-ops, restaurants); indirect wholesale through distributors (to supermarkets, retail shops, and restaurants); and, least frequently, through private labeling. When cheese is "private-labeled," producers sell wholesale to a major retailer such as Trader Joe's or Whole Foods, or to a mail-order operation such as Swiss Colony, which company puts its own brand label on the cheese. Many cheesemakers try to find a balance between retail and wholesale marketing, as wholesale ties up less labor than retail while retail generates better return and quicker cash flow. However, contingency and personality also figure in such qualitative calculations.

Producers get the highest financial return on direct retail. While cheesemakers like Mark Fischer look forward to their weekly farmers' markets as an opportunity to witness customers tasting and appreciating the fruits of their labor, others much prefer to sell to an anonymous distributor. For a market stand to generate a decent income, producers must offer a variety of goods; customers buy more when they can select from a variety of offerings. This might be a diverse mix of cheeses, a line of flavored chèvre spreads, or a range of agricultural products from a diversified farm. Cheesemakers who specialize in a single cheese are less likely to rely on farmers' markets. Vermont Shepherd relies almost entirely on direct wholesale and mail order, though an honor-system farmstand, where customers can select wedges of cheese from a cooler and leave cash in a box, brings in a couple hundred dollars a week. On-farm direct retail works best when farms are situated in proximity to residential or tourist areas, and not all cheesemakers enjoy such proximity. Then again, this benefit may become a burden; Mark Fischer explained, "we need the advantage of being in an affluent area to market our product, but that pushes the real estate value usually way above the actual business value." The Fischers are in a position where they would not be able to sell their cheese business while also holding on to their property, which has been home for many years. This raises the stakes of business sustainability.[84]

Producers set different "price points" for retail, direct wholesale, and indirect wholesale. I once heard a farmstead cheesemaker (married to a banker) share with a colleague (married to a hedge fund manager) her pricing strategy of not selling wholesale for less than two-thirds of what she can get retail at an afflu-ent urban farmers' market (many producers accept one-half). This may sound straightforward, but assertive self-confidence may be required to negotiate with an experienced retailer. Not every cheesemaker has the nerve to ask $24 retail or $15 wholesale (which would be marked up for resale in a shop at $30) for a pound of cheese, even if it costs more than $10 to make. To a producer who thinks about market relations in terms of social bonds, this may seem greedy or arrogant. For that matter, some cheesemakers are morally committed to producing high-quality cheese for people who cannot or will not pay $20 or $30 a pound. But as a retailer said to me of artisan cheesemakers, "If you think you're competing against the supermarket, you will never make enough money."

In Sonoma County, California, the owners of Pugs Leap Farm, a seven-acre goat dairy, priced boldly from their costs, calculated in 2007 at $16.50 per pound of cheese marketed. The owner-operators, Pascal Destandau and Eric Smith, factored into this a significant amount of wastage (they were still learning their craft), but still, coming to artisan production as former consumers of artisanal food, they were driven to make the best-tasting cheese they could; frugality did not figure significantly in their qualitative calculus. They bought organic feed for their goats because they buy organic food for themselves, and Pascal, going after the flavors he recalled from his native France, did not stint on expensive adjunct bacterial cultures. Priced per pound, theirs was perhaps the most expen-sive domestic cheese on the market. In 2010, they sold their farm and business to a young couple they trained to make Pugs Leap cheese.[85]

Other producers, equally committed to organic methods, choose to make economizing compromises in their qualitative calculations because they do not want to price their cheese out of the market—or into an even more exclusive market. As a Massachusetts producer put it to me, "the cost of organic grain isn't worth it" because "it's not enough of a value-added that it matters to consum-ers"; in other words, the added expense of buying organic grain would not be recouped by higher retail value. For the high-end retail market, as with wine (but not milk), organic labeling does not add exchange value to a handmade cheese; taste and style are what sell cheese in gourmet markets. Cheesemakers who pro-vision these markets and also farm organically do so because they believe it is the right thing to do for the land, for their animals, and for the health of people who eat their food.

Class disposition affects the degree of confidence that cheesemakers bring to the marketplace. This is evident not only in the aesthetics of product design and display, and in pricing based on costs rather than what the market might bear, but also in whether producers start out paying themselves a salary. Some imagine their personal income as coming out of "profit," as a sort of bonus; in a poor year they may earn nothing beyond what goes back into the business. In some cases, cheesemakers do not need to pay themselves a salary, but in others this reflects nonmarket values overshadowing market logic. Linda Dimmick, who puts in full work weeks at Neighborly Farms, described paying herself a salary as something of a luxury: "I think I paid myself like ten thousand dollars the first year, and maybe five thousand dollars the second year. But after that, I stopped paying myself" until 2006, when she began receiving a full salary; "it's like thirty thousand a year."[86] At what point do cheesemakers value their own labor enough that they make financial reward a priority?

One energetic young cheesemaker suggested that dairy farmers selling milk by bulk tank and living below the poverty level in his region were too "conservative" in their business decision-making; they would benefit from "thinking more entrepreneurially," which, to him, means learning to become more "comfortable" with risk-taking, more confident in investing today for a better tomorrow. He described this as a matter of "class difference." But there are limits to this conventional thinking. First, farming is inherently one of the riskiest occupations there is (weather, commodity pricing, blight). Dairy farmers Linda and Rob Dimmick have certainly been willing to take risks to redefine their dairy, if out of a sense more of desperation than of adventure. In Linda's words:

> In '04 we took a gamble and stopped shipping milk, and it's not that we had all that cheese marketed. . . . My husband, the risk taker, was all for it. . . . So, our gamble has paid off a couple of times. In '05 and again in '06, we were able to sell off huge shipments of raw-milk cheddar that had been aged. A one-time sale to a huge company [to be sold under private label]. And it was really great, because we could pay some bills with that. But again, it's risk-taking.[87]

Furthermore, the successful businesspeople moving into artisanal cheese are decidedly not risk-tolerant; they are risk managers. Before Karen Weinberg began farming, her husband, a financial adviser, said, "'Okay, we have to pay off our mortgage so that's not hanging over our heads.'" In the beginning, they were careful not to buy on credit, though now they are able to forecast earnings with sufficient confidence to take out short-term loans. Just as the American farmers who survived the crisis of industrialization in the 1980s were often the cautious ones who resisted the pressure to adopt an "entrepreneurial style" of risk-taking, successful entrepreneurs do not, for the most part, take excessive risks.[88] Quite the opposite: they do their homework and work to engineer as much of a sure bet as possible.[89]

Rethinking the Value in Value-Added Dairying

Linda Dimmick's story reveals how the very concept of "value-added" agriculture is a qualitative calculation whose conversions are not adequately captured by the misleadingly straightforward notion that market value is added to a commodity (milk) through the labor of processing (cheesemaking). Labor, however, does not magically "add value" to a niche product. Taking up "value-added" agriculture means acquiring not only new processing skills of cheesemaking but also what Cristina Grasseni calls the "packaging skills" of marketing.[90] By telling and selling a selective story of a cheese's coming into being, cheesemakers work to translate the qualitative values that make its production good to undertake into the perceived quality of the cheese thereby produced, in such a way that it might generate through market exchange the quantitative value of added income. There is nothing straightforward about it.

"My mother in Michigan thinks we're nuts," Linda Dimmick told me in 2004 when I first visited her at Neighborly Farms in Randolph, Vermont (fig. 10). "Normal" people, she suggested, would not cash out their life savings to put into a failing business. But that is essentially what Linda and her husband, Rob, did. They sold a business that made money (industrial septic system design) to inject capital into a business that had previously failed. That business was a dairy farm, the same farm where Rob had spent a happy childhood. Encouraged by strong milk prices in the 1970s, Rob's parents expanded the barn and increased the herd to 180 cows, a size that "burnt out the family." Depressingly low milk prices spurred Rob's father to start a cattle-trailer sales business; in 1986, the family sold the herd while Rob was at college. Linda, a dental hygienist originally from Michigan, married Rob in 1989. When she became pregnant with their first child, Rob declared his determination to raise his kids on a farm—an announcement that came as some surprise to his young bride.

In 1990, two weeks before their first son was born, Rob and Linda bought fifty cows. Three years later milk prices had fallen from sixteen dollars to eleven dollars per hundred pounds of milk, and they almost reached bankruptcy. Heartbroken, the Dimmicks sold the cows to help pay off mounting debt. Rob started the waste treatment business and Linda had two more babies, but they never gave up the dream of farming. In 1999 they bought a second herd of Holsteins. Rob renamed the place Neighborly Farms, in recognition of crucial help they received from the family next door. This time, they were going to add value to their milk by making cheese.

Adding value to milk through on-farm processing seems an appealing prospect to dairy farmers for a couple of reasons. First, it adds commercial value to milk they are already producing. Generally speaking, it takes ten pounds of milk to produce one pound of cheese, but cheese, by weight, sells for considerably more than ten times the price that dairy farmers get for their milk, which has fluctuated over the past several years between eleven and nineteen cents per pound. Second, retail markets are more stable than the volatile commodity milk market, which is set by federal mandate and applied uniformly across the coun-

FIG. 10. Neighborly Farms in Randolph, Vermont. The farm features a store with glass windows through which visitors can watch cheese being made. Photo by author.

try through the milk market order. Prices are based on supply and demand in international commodity markets, not so much for fluid milk as for tons of non-fat dry milk powder, whey protein concentrate used in processed foods such as protein bars, and blocks of commodity cheese.[91] Dairy farmers responding to my survey described both added income and increased fiscal stability as motivations for getting into the cheese business.[92] In clarifying the intricacies of commodity pricing to me, Bob Wills, who owns and operates the Cedar Grove Cheese factory in Plains, Wisconsin, commented, "The artisan cheese business has come about by necessity, not merely because of opportunity. Innovating to find new markets was not optional." Artisanal cheese is not only a consumer-driven market.

Federal and state legislative support for value-added agricultural initiatives proliferated in the early 2000s.[93] After discouragingly low prices in 2006 (down to $11.60 per hundredweight that July), 2007 and 2008 saw a huge jump in on-farm milk prices as U.S. exports rose to meet increased demand in China and other new markets, simultaneously with reduced competition from Australia (which was suffering a drought) and Europe.[94] To take advantage of higher prices, U.S. dairy farmers added cows and increased production. But in early 2009, while feed prices remained high, milk prices plummeted as competition rose on the supply side and demand fell amid global recession and the melamine contamination of milk in China. American farmers in the summer of 2009 spent twice as much to produce milk as they got from selling it.[95] The U.S. Commodity Credit Corporation bought vast quantities of nonfat dry milk as well as block cheese in the hope of stabilizing price drops, turning commodity surplus into food aid distributed internationally as well as domestically through food pantries and school lunch programs.[96] In such an uncertain economic climate, value-added processing would appear to be an attractive alternative, especially when the consumer market for specialty and niche food products looks only to be expanding.[97]

"The thing with agriculture," one farmer explained, "is that it's the one business where you buy all your materials at a retail price and sell your product at wholesale. You don't need an MBA to figure out that that makes for tough living. So by going into the value-added product—which was the buzzword for a couple of years—converting your raw material or your wholesale material into something you can get a retail price for, makes all the difference." A couple of years ago, this farmer, who makes cheese, looked into selling her raw milk to another cheesemaker, but the difference in income was too great. Even reduced labor and equipment costs would not make up for the income loss. Then again, she commented as she strung heavy, whey-logged bags of fresh curd high over her head to drain, "I didn't include the wear and tear on my body" in the calculations.

When I first met Linda Dimmick in 2004, she and Rob had owned their farm for fourteen years, not one of which had been profitable (by 2007 they were breaking even). But for Linda's husband, giving up on farming "was not an option." As Linda and I talked, it became clear to me that what differentiates the market value of artisanal cheese from commodity milk—or from commodity cheese, for that matter—is not so much the additional physical labor of processing one into the other, but the qualitative work of adding symbolic distinction to a product such that consumers will notice and prefer it to another label or type of cheese. It's selling the story.

When the Dimmicks started over farming a second time, they not only invested in cheesemaking, but also converted to organic production. Linda described this as a "business decision." Prices for organic milk are about twice as high as for conventional milk, so were the Dimmicks to ship fluid milk (which they did in 2003) it would be worth more at the farm gate. Here is how Linda figured the numbers: Shipping organic milk brings in about thirty dollars per hundred pounds. In 2007, Linda wholesaled her cheese at six dollars a pound. Since ten pounds of milk yield one pound of cheese, she figured the cheese to bring in sixty dollars per hundred pounds of milk. "So by producing your cheese you can double your income on the farm. But you really have doubled the problems," too, she added.

Having approached farmstead cheese as a pragmatic means to make their farm economically viable, Linda was initially unprepared to think of cheese as a fundamentally different object of value than the milk they had long produced. Jerry Heimerl, who makes Saxon Creamery cheese on the Wisconsin dairy farm his wife's family has worked for five generations, spoke to the same experience: "We had no idea what the marketplace was. Our marketplace was somebody came in and told us the price they would pay for our milk and they'll pay us forty-five days after delivery at whatever [price] they wanted." Coming from this experience of the market, Linda said, "I kind of just thought, *If I make the cheese, they will buy it.* Like 'if you build it, they will come.' It's just naive. . . . If I could go back, I'd spend that thirty to forty thousand dollars a year for a full-time marketing person."[98] Insufficiently bold marketing is one reason why a value-added product is "no panacea" for already struggling small dairy farmers.[99]

Linda's accounting to me of how she "did the numbers" reveals how agricultural processing is often presented as merely a calculation, a set of numbers to crunch. Eventually, Linda learned to "tell and sell" the story of her husband's farm family and the ecology of cheese production; as Cindy Major would have advised, cheese sells more easily when Linda introduces herself to a buyer as "the farmer and I'm making cheese and it comes from our farm." It is not so easy to sell it as simply "cheese" that just happens to be made in small batches, by hand, from organic milk—qualities that account for why it must be priced higher than industrially produced commodity cheese.

Value-added, like sustainability, is a complicated form of qualitative calculation in which not only are qualities presented as quantifiable, but quantities are discovered to have qualitative value. Since their conversion to organic farming as a quantitative measure of increasing their milk's commercial value, Linda has seen such a change in the animals—and such a reduction in veterinary bills—that she is now a "convert" to organic principles of well-being. Organic milk does not, in fact, generate much added economic value when processed into cheese, but organic production has been "good for the cows and good for us," Linda said, explaining that she now gives more thought to what she and her family eat.

The acquisition of packaging skills—the ability to tell one's story in a way that sells one's cheese—requires a certain comfort in making the personal marketable. Another Vermont cheesemaker described how the farm family with whom she worked was initially "reluctant" to put their family name and the label "third-generation family farm" on their cheese. The artisan worked to convince the farmers of the value of advertising their cheese using old family photos taken on the farm—"There are cows whose maternal lineage would go back fifty years; people need to know that." Eventually the family consented to putting their name "out there" on the market. As the artisan told me the story, not only did marketing the family name and story add symbolic value for consumers that translated into economic value for the producers, it also generated for the family the inalienable value of pride. She described the thrill of the farmers' children seeing "their name on their pizza" at a local restaurant. The adults were stopped in the street by fans exclaiming, "Oh, you make that wonderful cheese!"—recognition that they had never received when they were selling milk to a processing plant. In this cheesemaker's analysis, the "value-added" of turning milk into cheese included "cultural value, financial value—then also, I think, it's being part of a community."

ETHICS OF EVERYDAY LIVING

To conclude this chapter, I return to Greg Bernhardt's suggestion that the "trick" of turning cheesemaking into a viable family business is to figure out "what do you want to become?" In the daily economy of commercial artisans, sufficiency vies with superfluity, and quantity is evaluated in terms of quality. Economies of sentiment that make a virtue of thrift (by, say, buying secondhand equipment and doing one's own repairs) may generate savings that can be passed on to customers.[100] But when cheesemakers such as Laini Fondiller pay well over commodity prices for their neighbors' milk, or, like Pascal and Eric, insist on "the best" feed for their animals, those increased costs translate into higher retail prices and narrower consumer markets. Sticker price alone is not a reliable moral guide to an economy of sentiment. Nevertheless, when cheesemakers evaluate the quality of other products, producers, and businesses (as they often did off the record in conversations with me) they make moral judgments, just as when talking about their own business plans and work routines they do so by describing their own moral decision-making.

How is it that artisanal cheese can serve as a node through which so many different sentiments might be realized? I have suggested that the unfinished character of artisanal cheese as a commodity enhances its potential on this score. But it is also the case that as cheesemakers go about their daily and seasonal routines, they experience the pull of multiple goals and sentiments. They do not feel themselves to be operating under the weight of an overarching ideology.

Trying to do the best they can from one day to the next within economic and other constraints, artisan food-makers challenge the moral criticism that is common in American food politics today. Where moral points of view are not shared or circumstances are not well understood, it is not unusual to find people making ad hominem arguments criticizing others for moral inconsistency, particularly when the speaker rejects the moral principles attributed to those criticized. Witness the disdain that a vegetarian can receive from carnivores if she ingests so much as a bite of bacon. Whether that vegetarian's action is inconsistent with her moral principles would depend on what those principles happen to be; avoidance of meat may be motivated by a set of beliefs about animal welfare, good health, prudent use of resources, thrift—as well as gustatory preferences.[101] Increasingly,

I see such a tendency for presumptuous moral criticism in agricultural politics. At a farm open house I attended in Vermont, dairywoman Lisa Kaiman (who supplies milk to the cheesemaker at Consider Bardwell Farm) had to defend nearly all her farming practices to a consumer audience that, despite its appreciation for the product of her labor, second-guessed her at every turn ("Where do you get your hay? Is it local?").[102] While the audience spoke in terms of normative standards for what they imagined as "good" agricultural practice, the farmer grounded her moral decisions in the specific, productive ecologies of her farm. She buys hay from across the state because that is where she can get the deal she wants on the quality and type of hay she deems best for her Jersey cows. She uses a pour-on insecticide because she does not want her cows to suffer welts from fly bites (one reason she refuses to go fully organic). Similarly—from her perspective—she does not feed silage (fermented corn) because "it changes the rumen" of the cow's digestive system and thus, to her mind, is unnatural; besides, she hates the taste of silage milk, "And I don't like the way the poo smells." From the abstract, idealistic perspective of consumers, purity in organic production might seem to demand refusing insecticide as well as silage (one attendee was adamant that pour-on insecticides were in part responsible for the alarming disappearance of honeybees). From the perspective of farmers, the moral calculus is more complicated.

It is not surprising to encounter consumer expectations of moral purity when artisanal foods are marketed on ethical grounds. Part of the story that sells cheese and other value-added farm products, after all, is a narrative of moral consistency: healthy foods are said to emerge from practices that also safeguard the environment; nonalienated labor is imagined to generate particularly tasty foods. With their celebrated work ethic, artisans may be asked to embody the moral aspirations of a society; this can put them in a position of guarding against charges of hypocrisy. I think of Mark Fischer, who conceded that buying a pasteurizer and moving away from the exclusive production of raw-milk cheese is for some people "taboo." I think of a family, doing well selling raw milk from their farm, being argued out of their plan to make cheese from pasteurized milk for fear that this would dilute their message of healthy and happy cows supposedly conveyed by their trade in raw milk. Exposé critiques of industrial organic farming often fall into similar all-or-nothing thinking, as if the negative aspects of industrial-scale farming canceled out the environmental and health benefits for fieldworkers and consumers of produce grown without carcinogenic pesticides and herbicides, even or especially at an industrial scale.[103] And so Lisa Kaiman could not simply say that her farm is not organic but had to justify every aspect of her practical reasoning in terms of sentiments consistent with her audience's ideal of a grass-based dairy selling raw milk.

Purity of practice need not be a moral imperative—indeed, moral ambiguity is captured in the notion of economies of sentiment. Buying "local" hay might appear to benefit the immediate community financially, but Lisa feels she is more directly responsible for and to her cows; for them, hay from farther afield is better than local—and besides, buying hay from across the state is financially good for that farmer on the other side of the state. The Kehler brothers, by contrast, prioritized their commitment to "keeping the money in town," and so they have bought hay from a neighbor and wooden packing crates from a local carpenter instead of "getting on the Internet" to find a source of organic hay or the cheapest prices. The Kehlers' economy of sentiment does not aim to produce cheese as cheaply as possible. As we will see more fully in chapter 7, their accounting is less concerned to expand their consumer base beyond urban affluent eaters than it is motivated to revitalize the productive economy of northern Vermont. To criticize their high retail prices as exclusionary, while accurate, might also miss the point of what they are intending their practice to accomplish.

Morality need not be viewed as adherence to fixed, predetermined criteria; indeed, to do so risks overrationalizing human behavior, forgetting how people's actions respond to the contingencies of experience.[104] When artisan entrepreneurs account for their decisions in terms of sustainability or sufficiency, and when they think about what it means to add value to a good through processing and packaging, they do so within a particular economic and agricultural system. Economies of sentiment may be experienced as personal commitments, but they nonetheless reflect the historical moments in which they were forged and to which they must continue to adapt.

4

Traditions of Invention

It is obvious beyond stating that cheese is part of the soul of Wisconsin.
—JAMES NORTON AND BECCA DILLEY,
THE MASTER CHEESEMAKERS OF WISCONSIN

Housed in an old rail depot, the Green County Historic Cheesemaking Center in Monroe, Wisconsin, displays a host of early industrial cheesemaking artifacts including old-fashioned milk cans, wooden curd rakes, and huge copper kettles once used in Emmenthaler production (fig. 11).[1] During the first half of the twentieth century, Green County, just north of the Illinois border, was known as the Swiss Cheese Capital of the United States.[2] Its earliest cheese factory opened in 1868, and by 1910 more than two hundred factories producing Swiss-style and Limburger cheeses accounted for the county's prosperity.[3] Only in the 1950s were copper kettles replaced by rectangular stainless steel vats and generic "Swiss" cheeses molded into forty-pound blocks, better suited to deli slicing machines than unwieldy Emmenthaler wheels. Today just eleven cheese factories remain in operation in Green County, including the sole domestic producer of Limburger. Still, Monroe's high school football team remains the Cheesemakers.

I visited the historic cheesemaking center in July 2008. A docent, a gray-haired woman named Janet, described to me how, fifty years ago, her husband would reach into a copper kettle and gather a handful of curd in his hand, squeeze, and "flake it off" with his thumb; from the curd's "grip" he would determine when it was time to pull it up in a cheesecloth, removing curd from whey.[4] At one factory, her husband tended six kettles simultaneously, each yielding a single 180-pound wheel of Emmenthaler. Sometimes, Janet explained, the first kettle he got going might not be ready to "dip" after fifteen minutes—that is, the curd might not be ready to drain—but the second one would; he would know from the feel of the curd. "There was an art to it," she said. Janet was proud of her husband's specialist know-how. She pointed to a photograph of him gathering up curd using a

FIG. 11. The Historic Cheesemaking Center in Monroe, Wisconsin. Photo by author.

strenuously manual technique of "dipping" a square of cheesecloth beneath a hot mass of curd (120°F), holding two corners in his teeth to keep it from falling in, and hooking his feet around the crossbar of a metal T, something like a tire iron sunk into a block of concrete (fig. 12). The photo fascinated me, in part because it depicted almost precisely a technique I had seen demonstrated the previous summer in Vermont (fig. 13).

In 2002, John Putnam learned to "dip" curd from a French consultant he and his wife and partner, Janine, brought to their newly licensed creamery on the Vermont farm they purchased in 1986, located fifteen miles from where John grew up. After a few weeks' work alongside the European artisan, the Putnams launched an Alpine-style cheese they named Tarentaise. Putnam's eight-hundred-liter copper vat was custom-made in Switzerland. And here I was in Wisconsin, speaking to a woman who decades ago had hemmed her husband's cheesecloth so that it closely resembled what Putnam uses today. In Vermont, history seemed to be folding in on itself as the obsolete was being reintroduced as the novel.

As the Historic Cheesemaking Center reminds us, handcrafted cheese did not suddenly appear on the American landscape in the 1980s. For decades men such as Janet's husband plied their craft over open kettles and in moldy aging rooms using artisanal techniques and sensibilities to coax the desired fermentation of milk. When the current efflorescence of artisan cheesemaking in the United

FIG. 12. *(left)* Exhibit at the Historic Cheesemaking Center showing a nineteenth-century cheese vat with a metal *T* used to make Emmenthaler. Photo by author.

FIG. 13. *(below)* John Putnam, aided by a summer intern, dips curd for Thistle Hill Farm Tarentaise in North Pomfret, Vermont. Photo by author.

States is heralded as a "renaissance," a rebirth, this implies the death of an earlier era of artisan cheesemaking, brought about by the machines of industrialization.[5] In fact, alongside the history of American industrialization lies a submerged yet continuous history of small-batch, hands-on manufacture by artisans of European-derived cheeses including Cheddar, Emmenthaler, Limburger—even Brie and Camembert. Artisan cheesemaking never died in the United States. Concentrated in but by no means restricted to Wisconsin, second- and third-generation cheesemakers still run family-owned creameries, making cheese in much the same way as did their fathers and uncles and grandfathers before them.

Viewing the nineteenth-century factory consolidation and scaling up of cheesemaking as the first wave of artisan professionalization, I reframe the "renaissance" of the past thirty years as a second wave of American artisan innovation. I argue that continuity in artisans' *know-how* and fabrication methods—over time and across factory and farmstead practices—is obscured by changes in artisanal *production* over the past century. After being introduced as a farm chore whose responsibility fell to colonial and pioneer women, making cheese by hand in the United States was transformed into a blue-collar factory job, a rural alternative for men to farming. It shifted again in the twentieth century to a lifestyle choice pursued, among others, by professionals escaping office-bound careers and urban or suburban backgrounds. The meaning of making cheese by hand has moved from being a chore to a skilled trade to an expressive endeavor.

American cheesemaking past and present is linked not only by continuities in artisanal method, but also by a broader cultural commitment to valuing entrepreneurial innovation and invention. Often heralded in the media as "pioneers," the farmstead cheesemakers profiled in the previous chapter are just as committed to the idea that what they are doing is innovative as were the nineteenth-century founders of cheese factories. In both periods, American cheesemakers have worked to build a *tradition of invention* in cheese recipes and in marketing strategies. A tradition of valorizing innovation differs in content, if not in form, from Europe's "invented traditions," meant to legitimate present practices by claiming continuity with the past.[6] Jim Boyce, CEO of the Marin French Cheese Company, founded in California in the nineteenth century, remarked that the early 1890s saw a flourishing of cheesemaking activity in the upper Midwest and also in port cities up and down the Pacific coast; among the more successful was Oregon's Tillamook, dating back to 1894. In 2010, the Oregon Cheese Guild, founded in 2006, boasted fourteen members including Tillamook.[7] Both eras—the late-nineteenth-century rise of artisan factories and the millennial surge of farmstead creameries—have been periods, Boyce told me, "of innovation in local cheese."

It is an irony that the tradition of American cheese innovation, itself committed to continuous change as a mark of progress, obscures its own historical continuity, a continuity that, today, might help us recognize an affinity between second- and third-generation artisan cheesemakers working in heritage factories that resisted automation, and freshly minted cheesemakers working in backyard facilities. When continuities in artisanal fabrication are masked, this shores up a class distinction between factory and farmstead producers, one that carries over into the commercial market to grant some cheeses "boutique" status while others are deemed everyday fare, and priced accordingly. Recognizing that Brick and Limburger, no less than Vermont Shepherd or Constant Bliss, can be made artisanally rumples common assumptions about the elite status of artisanal foods and their makers.

In what follows, I examine the historicity of American artisanal cheese, taking this—the ideologically conditioned manner in which people "make sense of the past, while anticipating the future"—to be itself an object for ethnographic inquiry.[8] To begin, I present a historical overview of commercial cheesemaking in the United States, reaching back to the seventeenth century and up to the artisan factories still operating today. Rhetorical and practical disconnections between current farmstead activity and an enduring cheesemaking tradition reproduce class hierarchies even as they reflect growing equality in gendered occupational opportunities. After assessing the tension between a relative continuity of artisanal practice and changing cultural evaluation of that practice, I consider how two seasoned Wisconsin cheesemakers resist and accommodate the tendency among new cheesemakers to look to Europe, rather than to America's enduring artisan factories, for inspiration in creating new cheesemaking traditions. The first critiques the American inclination to romanticize European production as quaintly traditional when the reality is that much European cheesemaking has also become industrialized; the second adapts to and capitalizes on the new domestic artisanal market. Bringing regional cheese factories into the contemporary picture of American artisanal cheese highlights how differences in class, including dispositions and tastes, help to shape the landscape of artisanal food production in the United States.

A HISTORY OF CHEESEMAKING IN
THE "LAND OF OPPORTUNITY"

Nearly four hundred years ago, Puritans from East Anglia brought dairy cows, methods of handcrafting hard cheeses, and a gendered division of farmstead labor to the New England colonies. On colonial farms, men practiced animal husbandry while women took charge of dairying, milking cows and processing milk into butter and cheese. Cheese is a means of preserving milk, dramatically increasing the geographic reach of its market while reducing transportation weight tenfold. For generations, practicing a mode of agriculture that has been called composite farming, New England farmwives made cheese for household subsistence and also for commercial trade.[9] New England exported "farm-dairy cheese"—cheese made on dairy farms by farmwomen, akin to what is now called farmstead—to the West Indies and the southern American colonies throughout the seventeenth and eighteenth centuries.[10] This was hard, English-style cheese known through trade by its town of origin—Litchfield cheese, Cheshire cheese.[11] In the early 1800s, Braintree cheese enjoyed quite a following (Braintree, Massachusetts, is better known today as a terminus on Boston's subway system).[12]

In addition to moving cheese, New Englanders themselves moved, taking dairy cows and cheesemaking techniques with them. Yankee dairy farmers began resettling in New York in the mid-seventeenth century; in the wake of the Revolutionary War, numerous New Englanders headed west, into New York and on into Ohio, and also north into Vermont. New York led the country in farmhouse cheesemaking by the early 1800s.[13]

The number of milk cows in a family's herd set production volume. For generations the average was a manageable size of about five to six cows, but by the 1830s a New York dairy might have grown to the more daunting number of forty cows.[14] A farm family made and stored cheeses over the course of the dairying season and, in the fall, marketed their surplus beyond what the household could consume in a year. Initially farmers marketed their own cheese, but in New York state by 1830, on-farm cheese production had grown sufficiently to warrant specialty brokers, called factors, who toured dairying regions in the fall, sampling cheeses and securing contracts to buy a farm's entire production the subsequent year. The factor would sell farmhouse cheese to urban retailers, with a portion going to exporters.[15] The nineteenth-century cheese factors were not unlike today's distributors and were often similarly regarded with suspicion by producers concerned, then as now, with whether the tradesmen's profit motive could comport with their own aims of attaining a competency.

The first specialized cheese factory set up to process milk pooled from multiple dairy farms was established in Rome, New York, in 1851. The story of Jesse Williams's cheese factory comes down through oral tradition. While accounts vary, historian Sally McMurry notes that all revolve around intergenerational tensions within the Williams family. Jesse Williams, born in Rome, New York, to a family of Connecticut Yankees, grew up to become a dedicated farmer. By 1850 he was raising more than sixty-five cows, and the farm, thanks also to the labor of his wife, Amanda Wells Williams, was turning out 25,000 pounds of cheese in a year (note that in 2008, on-farm cheesemaking operations produced an average of 8,000 to 14,000 pounds per year).[16] That year, 1850, Jesse and Amanda's eldest son took a wife. According to McMurry, some accounts blame the bride's stubbornness while others blame the son's deficient skills, but in any event, Jesse Williams did not set up the young couple with a farm-dairy cheese operation

of their own. Instead, to ensure that his son's cheese fetched the same advanta-
geous price as his and his wife's, he consolidated their efforts.[17] Jesse Williams
persuaded his factor to contract for the cheese produced by both farms and built
a central cheesemaking facility in which to process the pooled milk.[18] Within a
few years, he was processing the milk of other area farmers as well.

All around New York's dairying regions, cheese factories began to be built at
rural crossroads to serve as central nodes to which farmers could bring their milk
each morning, first by horse-drawn wagon or sled and later by pickup truck. Built
as long, low structures, factories were ideally dug into a hillside so that the cellar
portion provided a cool, humid environment for cheese ripening. The cheesemaker and his family often lived in quarters above the factory.[19] By the mid 1870s,
cheese factories had virtually supplanted home cheesemaking in New York, and
New York émigrés began opening factories in Wisconsin (the first in 1864) and
Ontario, Canada.[20] Dealers preferred handling factory-made cheese over farm-
made when uniformity was achieved through standardized production.[21]

McMurry's analysis of the rapid ascent of the cheese factory system turns on
what I have called economies of sentiment. Still operating within the logic of a
competency, farmers did not start selling their milk to specialist cheesemakers
in order to make more money.[22] Instead, desire to reduce increasingly strained
social relations within families and households "moved thousands of farm families to dispatch their cheese presses to the attic with alacrity and harness up the
milk-cart team."[23] In short, women coming of age in the wake of the Civil War
began to view the heavy labor of their mothers' cheesemaking as a drudgery
they would as soon do without. In 1875 Mrs. E. P. Allerton addressed the third
annual Wisconsin Dairymen's Association on the topic, "Dairy Factory System—
A Blessing to the Farmer's Wife": "In many farm houses the dairy work loomed
up every year, a mountain that it took all summer to scale. But the mountain is
removed; it has been handed over to the cheese factory, and let us be thankful
time does not hang heavy on the hands of the farmer's wife now that it is gone.
She does not need the dairy work for recreation."[24] The composite farm strategy
of producing simultaneously for family and for market was being worn down,
Richard Bushman suggests, "by demands from the consumer culture"—as home-
spun cloth gave way to the wonders of the Sears Roebuck catalog, "farmers had to
maximize their cash returns in order to purchase the desired goods."[25]

Cheese factories were not invented out of whole cloth; rather, neighboring
farmers pooled milk and appointed the most skilled or willing among them
to carry out the cheesemaking on behalf of the collective. This is an important
point. The early factories were established to extend the skill of particularly
proficient cheesemakers, not to supplant artisan skill (as did later automation).
Since, as Lauren Briggs Arnold wrote in her 1876 manual for farmhouse cheesemakers, "An occasional expert may be found in family dairying, but it is not

possible to find one in every family," this innovation undoubtedly led to wider enjoyment of well-made cheese.[26] Professional cheesemakers would eventually be hired by farmer cooperatives (in Wisconsin these were often skilled immigrants from Switzerland or Germany), but initially the designated cheesemakers simply scaled up their farm-dairy recipes and techniques for larger quantities of milk. Crowley Cheese in Vermont still embodies this tradition. It got its start in 1824 as the farm-dairy cheese of the Crowley family, dairy farmers in the Green Mountains of Vermont. In 1882 Winfield Crowley built a cheese factory for processing his neighbors' milk.[27] The rustic, hand-waxed cheese is still made today using unpasteurized milk and (purportedly) the same procedures developed by Crowley women and men across generations.[28]

Nevertheless, the shift from household to factory production ushered in a number of changes in how cheese was made and marketed. Not least of these was a masculinization of cheesemaking labor, as women trained men to join them in or to take over their craft. Quoting a newspaperman reporting on an 1863 visit to a New York state cheese factory—"'it does one good to witness the difference between the order and cleanliness of this model institute, and the suspicious and slatternly surroundings of some home dairies'"—McMurry reminds us that as an epithet, *slatternly* (unkempt, "dirty through habitual neglect") is pointedly gender-specific.[29] The gender transition of professionalization contributed to an image makeover for cheesemaking, transforming it from a farm-based craft, not immediately into an art, but into a modern science. Factories, after all, were exemplary sites of nineteenth-century scientific rationalization and modern efficiency, introducing into rural areas the industrial principles that would come, in the early twentieth century, to inform agricultural production itself.[30] Empirical method in cheesemaking—tracking temperature, careful measuring, strict hygiene—would generate a standardized, widely marketable commodity. Such methods were often described as antithetical to women's customary ways of knowing. In England, too, "the role of women as producers [of farmhouse cheese] came under attack, as commentaries on labour described their agency as incompatible with systematic and profit-oriented methods. . . . Profitable industry became joined to a model of organization and productivity associated specifically with men," notes historian Deborah Valenze. Women's dairying, she continues, "was seen as an art rather than a science; as a consequence of its reliance upon apparently incalculable procedures, as well as its irregular results, dairying belonged to an occult branch of husbandry."[31]

As production scaled up, new equipment was invented to handle larger quantities of milk: cheese vats lined with steam-heated jackets whose temperature could be held constant, sloped curd sinks to facilitate draining, steel curd knives, and a variety of cheese presses.[32] In addition, wheels of cheese were no longer held until the end of the cheesemaking season, but instead marketed "twenty to forty days from the hoop."[33] While this innovation was thought to be an improvement, note that under the previous custom of holding cheese until the end of the season, those cheeses were not simply sitting in the basement but were "maturing," ripening and quite possibly (though not necessarily) improving in flavor. In 1885, a Wisconsin cheesemaker offered the following comment to Mr. T. H. Curtis, a dairy consultant from Syracuse, New York: "I found myself, as winter was coming on, with about forty or fifty boxes of cheese stored in the cellar one year, and I was very happily surprised in the spring to find it the finest cheese I ever sold."[34] At the time, not even Louis Pasteur fully understood the role of bacterial and fungal activity in cheese maturation. Mr. Curtis had no reply for the Wisconsinite, choosing instead to speak to "the subject of coloring" cheeses. Curtis advised regional producers to standardize their coloring "so that it will come out, not a pale or high colored cheese, but medium straw color, that is what the buyers want in the market."[35] Coloring cheese, initially with annatto seed, obscured evidence of milk seasonality.[36] The perceived need to color cheese indicates that the unpasteurized milk with which factory employees worked did vary seasonally. Factory men made cheese from raw milk (without the benefit of laboratory-isolated starter cultures) using the same practical techniques as the farmwomen of previous generations. This is artisanal production.

New York dominated the early years of factory cheese production, but by 1890 the state's market dominance was eroding. For one thing, the bottom dropped out of the British export market. While exports grew rapidly beginning in 1860 as British tariffs were lifted just as the American factory system was getting under way, in a few decades Canadian cheese was outcompeting New York for the British market, in no small part because American cheese developed a reputation for lacking "keeping quality."[37] It turned out that some New York cheesemakers had been skimming the cheese milk (so as to make butter on the side) and "filling" cheese with lard. While such cheese looked fine initially, over time it turned rancid. There was nothing legally prohibiting the practice; in fact, patents were issued on the "filled cheese" processes, which spread to Illinois and Wisconsin.[38] In 1884 the New York legislature cracked down, and in 1889 a newly formed Dairy and Food Commission followed suit in Wisconsin.[39] But by then the damage to the American cheese industry had been done. A contemporary commentator noted, "the English know Canadian cheese to be genuine, while all the United States product is more or less suspected."[40]

If the product that first gave American cheese a bad name in Europe was tainted English-style hard cheese, indigenous cheese types emerged from the melting-pot cultures of the upper Midwest and, later, California. Over the centuries, the descendants of New England Puritans and Yankees who fanned westward across the continent were joined by Dutch, Swiss, German, and eventually Spanish and Mexican immigrants with cheese cultures of their own. German settlers were making cheese in Pennsylvania as early as 1800.[41]

After wheat crops failed in the upper Midwest, Wisconsin took over from New York as the predominant cheese-producing state.[42] The number of cross-roads cheese factories in rural Wisconsin reached a height of 2,807 in 1922.[43] The majority of cheese produced in these factories was labeled "American cheddar," but roughly one-fourth of Wisconsin cheese was classed as "foreign," including Limburger, German Brick, and great wheels of Emmenthaler Swiss.[44]

Brick cheese, along with Colby, Monterey Jack, and Teleme, are considered American originals, cheeses that began as new-world regional takes on European standards. Colby, named after a town in Wisconsin in 1874, is similar to Cheddar but omits the labor-intensive cheddaring process, which entails the repeated stacking of heavy blocks of curd to remove whey. Brick, also originating in Wisconsin, is a sort of mild, drier Limburger developed in 1877 by a Swiss immigrant catering to the tastes of his German-born neighbors.

The California story of Dry Jack—an important chapter in the tradition of artisanal cheese inventions in the United States—is also set within a diverse European immigrant population at the turn of the twentieth century. While factories such as Marin French and Sonoma Jack, near the San Francisco Bay, were supplying domestic markets with fresh cheeses (including the semisoft Monterey Jack, which dates to eighteenth-century Spanish Franciscan monks who settled in what was then New Spain), hard-aged cheeses most commonly came from Italy. As the late Ig Vella explained when I interviewed him at his small factory in Sonoma, "the hard-type cheeses they wanted from the Old Country." Italian wholesalers imported Parmigiano, Asiago, Reggiano. But then necessity became the mother of invention—at least according to Dry Jack's origin story. In 1914, D. F. DeBernardi, a cheese factor, bought up all the fresh cheese he had contracted for in the Sonoma area, but as Ig Vella, who knew DeBernardi as a child, narrates:

> All of a sudden there was no market for it. What the hell happened? My Uncle Joe told me about going down to see DeBernardi... pleading... "Can I sell you some cheese?" And DeBernardi said, "Giuseppe, if you can climb a rack [in his warehouse] that has empty spaces, count those empty spaces and I will buy the cheese from you" [to fill them]. So my uncle claimed he went from the basement to the third story and could not find an empty rack. And so that's where it stood. And so all of a sudden, 1915—in '14 World War I started—1915, Italy entered the war on the side of the Allies. No more [imported cheeses]! So in the meantime, DeBernardi had taken that Jack cheese [that he could not sell] and he put it in his basement ... and every week he had his crew go down there and turn the cheese and rub in the salt. ... And all of a sudden when there were no more imports of the dry types of

cheese, it was great! So he'd been watching it [the market, but also the cheese in his basement] and he'd go to the sales meeting and he'd say, "Take this out and sample it because I think we've got something here." And so they did, and naturally—then everybody *else* got in the Dry Jack business, too. . . . The fact is we supplied the hard cheese, let's call it that, back East as well. We had a hell of a business going!

Dry Jack, whose cocoa-rubbed wheels are puckered at the top from having been formed by a tightly tied piece of cheesecloth, embodies the invented tradition of American entrepreneurial innovation.

At one time, Vella said, as many as sixty factories crafted Jack cheese in open vats along the Northern California coast. Today there are two. What happened to the artisan factories, here as in Wisconsin? Some failed to make it through the Great Depression; others survived the 1930s only to fold in the 1980s as their milk supply dried up during that decade's farm crisis. A few factories burned to the ground. Most important, improved roads and the introduction of the refrigerator truck, which eased farmers' ability to transport milk greater distances, led to the consolidation of smaller plants into larger ones. Twentieth-century researchers invented new technoscientific methods of testing and standardizing milk butterfat, new automated technologies for obviating the strenuous labor of cheddaring, and new materials for vacuum-packaging cheeses to bypass the manual turning and washing of wheels formerly necessary to nurture rind development. Kraft, Borden, and other growing giants bought out, consolidated, and industrialized the small artisan factories (fig. 14).

James L. Kraft, who began his career in 1903 as a wholesale distributor (or factor) supplying Wisconsin cheese to the Chicago market, opened his first cheese factory in 1914 and began experimenting with pasteurization and emulsification to create a more stable product. Kraft took out the first patent on process cheese in 1916; the process entails grinding together a mix of cheddar-style cheeses, pasteurizing the slurry, adding emulsifying salt, and reheating the mixture. In 1917 Kraft supplied the U.S. armed forces with tinned process cheese.[45] When Kraft came out with grated Parmesan (in 1945), Ig Vella told me, "the Dry Jack business went to hell, and that's when a lot of those factories closed."

Beginning in the mid-twentieth century, cheese production was scaled up and automated to the point that factory laborers were demoted to machine operators "pushing buttons."[46] Published in 1964, *The Cheese Book* bemoaned the rise in Green County, Wisconsin, of industrial plants "in which the rindless block Swisses come off the assembly line like endless yellow dominoes."[47] In 2000 Randy Krahenbuhl dipped curd from a kettle for one final 180-pound wheel of Emmenthaler. A second-generation Wisconsin cheesemaker, Krahenbuhl owned, operated, and shut down the last of the old-style Swiss cheese factories, selling the copper kettles to pay off debts.

FIG. 14. Salting cheeses floating in a brining basin, Kraft-Phenix Cheese Corporation. Where flavor development begins, ca. 1933. Industrial Life Photograph Collection, Baker Library Historical Collections, Harvard Business School, olvwork355015.

And yet, scattered across the country, second- and third-generation cheesemakers working in eighty- to one-hundred-year-old factories still turn out blocks of Brick and Limburger and wheels of Crowley and Dry Jack, using open vats and cutting curd and wrapping cheeses by hand. Although it may be difficult today to imagine for those to whom the phrase "artisan factory" comes across as an oxymoron, these cheese factories are staffed by skilled craftspeople applying artisanal techniques and sensibilities learned through apprenticeship. After our conversation in his office, Ig Vella, who took over his father's factory in 1981, introduced me to cheesemakers Charlie Malkassian and Jeffrey Catrambone, who spoke to me as they cleaned the cheese room about how they adjust their process in response to milk's seasonality by feeling the curd. In both early and postindustrial eras—in factories as well as on farms—artisanal practice (detailed in the next chapter) is recognizable in a cheesemaker's tacit, sensory evaluation of milk and curd through such means as testing the curd's "grip," a state of readiness that antebellum farmwomen judged by a telltale "squeak between the teeth" and that Janet's husband, reaching deep into his copper kettles in Wisconsin, assessed with the motion of his thumb.[48] Charlie Malkassian, Vella's head cheesemaker, who began as an apprentice thirty years ago, knows the curd is ready to cut just from the look of its surface appearance, though he confirms this with a manual "clean-break" test to ascertain whether the curd, as an 1876 cheesemaking manual describes it, will "cleave before the finger when passed through it."[49] Many of the artisanal techniques and technologies that the new farmstead cheesemakers I interviewed said would ensure a product superior to commodity cheese—such as gravity-fed cheese vats, which obviate the industrial method of pumping milk, said to break up the delicate chemistry of nonhomogenized milk—would have been found in nineteenth-century factories.[50]

In 2005 Bruce Workman, the son of a preacher and a home economics teacher who had her son cooking in the kitchen from age three, reintroduced "big-wheel" Swiss to Green County, Wisconsin. Bruce gutted Randy Krahenbuhl's recently shuttered factory (built as a cooperative in the 1890s) and refitted it with a 10,500-pound-capacity copper-lined vat bought used from a Swiss cheesemaking school that was closing. Bruce's twelve full-time employees do not hand-dip curd from kettles, but they do lift, turn, and rub the natural rinds of 180-pound wheels of Emmenthaler. Bruce told me he was "looking to make true, authentic Emmenthaler, because I'm not the kind of guy who says, 'Every day I'm going to make Muenster.' You can make Muenster in your sleep." Back in high school, Bruce worked the 4:30 A.M. shift at a local cheese plant before heading to class, returning in the afternoon to wash the forms for molding Brick and Muenster before zooming back to school for sports practice. Bruce wanted to make bigwheel Swiss, he told me, because "That's what Green County is all about."

CONTINUITY, CHANGE, AND CLASS
IN ARTISANAL PRODUCTION

Considering the history sketched above, why is it common to hear cheesemakers—especially outside Wisconsin—claim that the United States lacks an artisanal cheesemaking tradition? (A related question might be to wonder why Wisconsinites like Janet, at the Green County Historic Cheesemaking Center, are unaware of new artisan activity.) For one thing, the history of cheesemaking in the United States is often narrated as the triumph of industrialization over artisanship. For more than a century, industrialization has been the predominant form of innovation in American cheesemaking, to the point that "American cheese" has popularly and even legally come to name pasteurized process cheese sold in plastic-encased blocks or individually wrapped slices (introduced by Kraft in 1950).[51] In such a market, the few tenacious holdouts among the old artisan factories may well be hidden behind the avalanche of "pizza cheese," an industrial invention that arrived to top the "pizza pie" in the 1950s and now accounts for the majority of cheese produced in the United States.[52]

Changes in the social organization of artisanal production as well as a cultural shift in what it has meant to make cheese by hand further obscure historical continuities in artisanal practice. Although nineteenth-century cheese factories were neither mechanized nor automated, early factory workers "possessed the same skills that their home-cheesemaking counterparts had wielded," and "the work was not divided into smaller, less skilled tasks"; as McMurry writes, the factories were clearly organized through a capitalist mode of production.[53] People worked for hourly wages, selling their labor power to the factory owner (who often served as manager). They learned their skill through formal apprenticeship, followed procedures approved by management (increasingly directed by scientific expertise), and may have felt a commonality with tradesmen in nonagricultural fields. In contrast, as the previous chapter detailed, to speak of artisan cheesemakers in the United States today is overwhelmingly to refer to small, owner-operated family businesses. As home-based craft enterprises, today's farmstead operations would seem to resemble antebellum farm dairies—"Farm families owned the land and their tools; they commanded specialized skills and controlled the work process from start to finish"[54]—more than contemporary factories, although on farms today men are nearly as likely as women to assume cheesemaking duties.

Those who made cheese from raw milk using manual technology in nineteenth- and early twentieth-century factories were then and are now considered laborers, tradesmen—artisans but not artists—understood to work more directly with their bodies than with their minds. Compared to cheesemakers of a century ago, the persons acquiring artisan skills and developing practical cheesemaking knowledge today are coming from different socioeconomic worlds. For artisan cheesemakers who are likely to have college degrees and former professional careers, cheesemaking is not a job like any other for which one receives a paycheck, nor is it a family business one stumbles into. It is a chosen way of life. For them, perceived differences in the lived experience of working in a factory as compared to a farmstead setting seem to overshadow commonalities shared in the crafting of cheese, such as evaluating the "grip" of the curd or perfecting the technique of hand-waxing fresh wheels.

The masculinization of factory cheesemaking—significant in shoring up the masculinity of male cheesemakers as they took over what had been a predominantly feminine enterprise—carries into the present to divide factory and farmstead producers.[55] In the early 1990s, Wisconsin's Center for Dairy Research and the state's Milk Marketing Board established a Master Cheesemaker certification program to recognize the expertise of its veteran producers; of the forty-nine cheesemakers to have obtained Master certification by 2009, just one,

Carie Wagner, is a woman.[56] While women led the resurgence of domestic craft production, artisan factories remain the province of men.

And so when Marjorie Susman and Marian Pollack started Orb Weaver Farm in 1982, they taught themselves how to make cheese. "We just started making mistakes in our kitchen, feeding it to the dogs," they told me. "We never traveled to Europe; we haven't been, you know. And we didn't go to any other cheesemakers, because there *weren't* any." In fact, less than two hours' drive away, the Crowley Cheese Factory has been making Crowley Cheese "in the same manner, from the same recipe" developed in the Crowley family's kitchen "since 1824."[57] The factory, when in operation, is virtually silent; no motorized machines help to create Crowley from raw milk and calf rennet. An American original, Crowley cheese is classified by the FDA as a Colby, despite the fact that the Crowley family had been making the cheese for sixty years before Colby was invented in the Wisconsin town for which it was named. Asked to describe Orb Weaver cheese, Marjorie said to me: "Well, it's our own recipe, so somewhere in between a Havarti and a Colby. I don't know if that's really true, but somebody once said that and I thought, *Oh, okay. That works!*" Orb Weaver and Crowley resemble each other as cheeses—both are mild, creamy wheels of hand-waxed cow's-milk cheese—but they emerged in different eras from parallel histories. During my three-hour interview and lunch with Marjorie and Marian, Crowley never came up.

In a follow-up e-mail, I asked Marjorie whether she and Marian had visited the Crowley factory when they were starting out. It turned out that they had, a few years before launching Orb Weaver. When prompted, Marjorie recollected the Crowley factory's extensive use of wooden shelving in the cheese room, writing that although "it took some time to remember it . . . I think we took away a good amount of knowledge from them." Marjorie and Marian know a number of cheesemakers across the state, but those they keep up with tend to be small farmstead producers like themselves. Crowley's scaled-up factory operation, staffed by paid workers who learned to make an established cheese using milk pooled from multiple dairy farms, feels categorically different from producers who milk their six or seven cows before breakfast and make cheese together using a method they developed themselves.

A central theme of this book is that artisans working curd in open vats and curing natural-rind cheeses are producing more than artisanal cheese; they are producing themselves as food makers, artisans, and farmers. It matters more to the identity of the makers of Orb Weaver and Crowley than to the quality characteristics of the cheeses that Orb Weaver is made on a woman-owned and -operated farm and Crowley in a factory that dates back to the nineteenth century. Anthropologist Robert Ulin urges us to think of labor as more than the instrumental (and exploitable) appropriation of and transformation of raw materials into commodity goods; labor is a far-reaching mode of cultural production.[58] In his ethnography of winegrowers in the southwest of France, Ulin demonstrates that the differentiated cultural status of an agricultural-based product like wine—with both high and low status labels—affects grape growers' attitudes about their own work as producers of an agricultural commodity that is transformed into a culturally mediated good. Although the work of growing grapes is essentially the same whether it takes place in the Médoc or Dordogne, Médoc grapes may go into celebrated Bordeaux wines while those from the Dordogne are fated to become everyday table wine—not, Ulin explains, because Médoc grapes are inherently superior but because Bordeaux wineries have successfully traded on favorable historical contingencies, have labeled their wines by year of production to establish the distinction of vintage, and employ more sophisticated marketing. Invested in helping to produce the superior "distinction" or "cultural capital" of Bordeaux wine, Médoc grape growers talk differently about their labor than do their counterparts working in less-celebrated regions, claiming "to recognize their labour as being embodied in a final product whose taste and quality bore witness to the distinction of the region and thus a source of identity."[59] Thus, Ulin argues, the meaning of work is fully caught up in the cultural and symbolic values it embodies.[60]

So it is with artisanal cheese. Another reason post-pastoral artisans may not seek counsel from or community with factory artisans is that they may implicitly believe in, or even consciously wish to create, a firm sense of differentiation between their cheese—sold in gourmet shops and restaurants—and anything that might be found at a supermarket.[61] Many among the new generation of cheesemakers come to cheese production with experience as discerning cheese consumers. Their tastes, like everyone else's, are influenced by the social conditions of their upbringing and by the social circles in which they have lived and worked. This is what Bourdieu writes of as "cultural capital." Similar again to what Ulin has argued of French winegrowers able to trade on the cultural cachet associated with elite winegrowing regions (compared with their neighbors on less-celebrated terrains), the elevated cultural capital of novel, even whimsical cheeses made to be served in the European style, on their own, perhaps with an accompaniment of preserved fruit or toasted nuts—rather than as a sandwich element or casserole ingredient—produces distinction not only for the consumers but also for the producers of such commodities.[62] A raft of recent consumer-oriented books on American artisanal cheese featuring professional food photography, producer profiles, recipes, and wine pairing suggestions (not to mention television appearances with Martha Stewart) contributes to this culinary economy.[63]

Liz Thorpe, vice-president of Murray's Cheese in Manhattan, confesses in her 2009 book, *Cheese Chronicles,* that she had once been one of "the sophisticates" who "liked to mock" the waxed Goudas and Pepper Jack turned out by small domestic factories. Having been thoroughly industrialized by industry giants, Brick and Colby—as cheese types—have undergone the status loss that can accompany product extensification, almost regardless of where and how a product is made.[64] It is with a touch of rueful surprise that, in a chapter symptomatically titled, "When Did 'Factory' Become a Dirty Word?" Thorpe reports on a tasting tour of Wisconsin factory cheeses and comes to realize that cheesemakers working on bucolic Vermont farms and in hundred-year-old midwestern factories are in fact connected by shared skills, techniques, and artisan sensibilities. What had concealed this from her—and she is not alone—is not only a culinary and cultural distinction between a Pepper Jack and a Pecorino—but also a categorical distinction, staked out by romantic Pastoralism, between a factory and a farm. After spending time with the old-timers (including the indomitable Ig Vella) and seeing firsthand just how low-tech some of these factories really are, Thorpe was able to see beyond her taste.

REINVENTING AN AMERICAN
TRADITION OF INVENTION

It is a cliché that Europe outshines the world in culinary taste and customary technique in cheesemaking. I lost count of how many times over the course of researching this book I heard repeated General Charles de Gaulle's complaint, "How can you govern a country which has 246 varieties of cheese?"[65] (The number of cheeses changed with each recitation.)[66] De Gaulle's quip can help us rethink what is meant by cheesemaking tradition. His 246 (or so) varieties of cheese work as a symbol of national unruliness only if we imagine each of those cheeses emerging from a politically entrenched patchwork of customarily distinct regions; de Gaulle's task was to unify a people loyally committed not to the excellence of "French" cheese but to 246 regional cheeses and the invented traditions for which they stand.

One of France's most elaborate and successful invented cheese traditions concerns Camembert, said to have originated when a Norman farmwoman named Marie Harel followed a "secret" recipe for Brie using a smaller Livarot cheese mold (practicing the sort of improvisational tinkering found among contemporary American artisans) and trained her children and grandchildren to carry on making the cheese as family patrimony. As Pierre Boisard details in *Camembert: A National Myth*, the cheese's story begins to transcend Norman regionalism and to take on the significance of a national myth because the tale is set in the early years of the French Revolution (1791) and because the secret Brie recipe is said to have been given to Mme. Harel by a priest who sought refuge with the Harel family while fleeing persecution by the revolutionaries (and thus stands as a representative of the Ancien Régime). Thanks to Mme. Harel's entrepreneurial industry, writes Boisard, "a bit of old France, of pre-Revolutionary France, will survive" into the future in a new form.[67]

The myth of Camembert fits precisely Eric Hobsbawm's formula for "invented traditions," described as "responses to novel situations which take the form of reference to old situations, or which establish their own past by quasi-obligatory repetition."[68] No surprise, then, to learn from Boisard that Marie Harel's mythological fame does not date back to the Revolution. Instead, it was 130 years later that Joseph Knirim turned up in the town of Camembert (population 300) to venerate the memory of Mme. Harel and her "veritable Norman Camembert" by erecting a statue in her honor. Knirim, an American physician, adulated Marie Harel's cheese not for its taste and sumptuousness, but for its "digestibility."[69] Only once her statue had been erected by a visiting American did Marie Harel's name begin to stand for the essential contribution that peasant agriculture has made to the French nation. Camembert's iconic Frenchness seems little tarnished by having become one of the nation's most industrialized cheeses. Long seeded with laboratory-isolated strains of *Penicillium candidum* to produce a pure white coat of mold and now most often made from pasteurized milk, Camembert's contemporary materiality is only a shadow of what once cured Knirim's indigestion. In hopes of recuperating at least a hint of that past, Norman dairy farmers and cheesemakers have secured *appellation d'origine contrôlée* (AOC) status not for Camembert per se, but for Camembert de Normandie. For a cheese to qualify for the site-specific name, production must occur within geographically limited areas and comply with a voluminous set of regulatory standards.[70] For now, Norman Camembert and French Camembert vie for consumer sentiment and market position. In Normandy as throughout Europe, what "traditional" food will look like in the future is a contentious matter of politics and policy, to be worked out through the legal instruments of geographical indications.[71]

Such well-cultured European cheeses as Camembert, Comté, and Taleggio are usefully analyzed as embodying and preserving the "invented traditions" of country idylls populated by an immemorial peasantry.[72] When members of a new wave of American cheesemakers travel to France to learn how to make "real" cheese, they reinforce European inventions of culinary tradition as authentic and gastronomically superior. Without a doubt, many excellent cheeses are made in France and throughout Europe—but so, too, are boring supermarket cheeses. It is a testament to the success of France's invented cheese traditions and to the branding of French cheeses as fundamentally authentic and traditional—even when most Camembert today is, in fact, made from pasteurized milk and ladled by robots—that foil-wrapped, processed wedges of Laughing Cow (La Vache Qui Rit, in its native tongue) are never metonymically dubbed "French cheese."[73] Invention of tradition is a particularly useful concept in a European context,

where "the traditional" and "the modern" continue to be potent, mutually constitutive tropes through which people stake moral claims of belonging, authenticity,
and progress.[74] But in the United States, where progress is valued over patrimony
and, today, pastoral ideologies of pristine nature have given way to post-pastoral
recognition that nature does not stand apart from human cultural activity, what
is invented as tradition—what is enshrined as a matter of cultural heritage—is
continual change, not continuity. In the New World, continuity in practice, in
know-how, and in form risks being labeled old-fashioned or, worse, boring; continuity is thus often obscured in narratives of innovation.

Americans, ever impatient for a brighter future, are continually remaking and
marketing their traditions as new, fresh, and exciting. Moreover, a "tradition"
of innovative cheesemaking seems to be in continual need of creation. As illustrated by Ig Vella's story of Dry Jack, in the United States, cheesemaking origin
stories celebrate entrepreneurial innovation. Compare to the story of Camembert
outlined above that of Marin French Cheese, the oldest continuously operating
cheese factory in the United States, located in Petaluma, California. In 1865, with
Lincoln in the White House and the Civil War just coming to an end, the Marin
French Cheese Company (originally the Thompson Brothers Cheese Company)
began making cheese after Jefferson Thompson, a dairy farmer, recognized an
emergent market niche in the port town of San Francisco. The late Jim Boyce,
who in 1998 purchased the company from Thompson's descendants, told me the
story as he had learned it from an employee who had recently retired after sixty
years with the company.[75]

During the California gold rush (1849–1855), the story goes, European steve-
dores (deckhands) who sailed into Yerba Buena harbor (later, San Francisco Bay)
delivering goods to support the mining enterprises got "caught up in the fever"
and abandoned ship to seek their own fortunes in the mines. After the gold rush
went bust, workers returned to the Bay to make a living at the dockyards. Boyce
continued:

> Now, in any workman's bar or inn . . . you work hard, you get dehydrated, you go
> to the bar for hydration and energy—most typically that's given to you by beer
> so you can quickly restabilize yourself. . . . The beer gives them hydration and
> carbohydrate but no protein. And most typically in a workman's bar there's a jar of
> pickled eggs or something like that, pig knuckles, sausage. [But here] there weren't
> any eggs; no chickens—nothing had been developed. . . . Well, Jefferson Thompson,
> the dairyman on this farm [the site of the present-day factory] says to himself in
> a moment of marketing brilliance, "I wonder if they'd eat cheese instead?" So he
> starts making these little cheeses, three-ounce cheeses, more or less. And he hauls
> them off to the docks, and they put them on the table in a bowl, and they were an
> immediate hit! Why? Because these are European stevedores: they knew cheese.
> They ate it breakfast, lunch, and dinner. And that was the origin of the company.

Whereas Europe's invented food traditions mean to legitimate present practices by claiming continuity with the past, American ones mark decisive breaks with the past: Marin French's Breakfast Cheese celebrates the creation of new markets; the story of Dry Jack embodies entrepreneurial opportunism. The story of Laura Chenel's chèvre is often told to establish recent interest in artisanal cheese as a "renaissance." In David Kamp's *The United States of Arugula,* Chenel is credited with single-handedly introducing goat cheese to America by becoming its first domestic commercial producer.[76] Chenel's story, in his telling, contains two mythologically significant features: she traveled to France to perfect her art, and she famously got her commercial break in 1980 when she drove to Berkeley from her Sonoma County goat farm and walked into Chez Panisse. Alice Waters put the chèvre in a salad, named Chenel on the menu, and the rest is an invented tradition of entrepreneurial innovation. A few of Chenel's goat-breeding, cheese-making friends from that time told me a more collective, collaborative story about the "birth" of goat's-milk cheesemaking in California.

A tradition of invention is enshrined in the American Cheese Society (ACS) designation of American Originals as a classificatory category singling out varieties invented on American soil (Colby, Brick, Teleme, Jack, etc.) for its annual judging and competition. In recent years, the ACS has added "original recipe" subcategories of American Originals; 2011 award winners include Mt. Tam, Cocoa Cardona, Flagsheep. The theme—"Creating Tradition"—of the twenty-second annual ACS meeting in 2005 in Louisville, Kentucky, did not so much offer a self-conscious look at how American traditions had been invented as it set out to create tradition from this point onward, into the future. The call for Americans to create a cheesemaking tradition largely arises from a feeling among farmstead cheesemakers, like Orb Weaver, that they are starting from scratch.

Allison Hooper, cofounder of the twenty-five-year-old Vermont Butter & Cheese Company, writes in her foreword to Jeffrey Roberts's *Atlas of American Artisan Cheese,* "Without the burden of tradition we are free to be innovative and take risks," suggesting that a lack of tradition in regional cheese types and fabrication method is a virtue rather than a deficit because it opens up possibilities for experimentation.[77] Dancing Cow's Sarabande, a raw cow's-milk cheese with a washed rind, is molded in a truncated pyramid form, the kind used in France for Valençay, a charcoal-dusted goat's-milk cheese from the province of Berry (legend has it that the cheese was once made in a perfect pyramid until Napoleon, passing through Valençay town following a failed military campaign in Egypt, was so enraged by the cheese's taunting shape that he lopped off the top with his sword, leaving the form that survives today). In a presentation at the 2007 ACS meetings, Steve Getz, then co-owner and operator of Dancing Cow, delighted in announcing that it had been recently declared illegal in France to make a cow's-milk cheese in a truncated pyramid form (the shape is reserved for goat's-milk cheese).[78] And Flavio de Castilhos, who started a farmstead cheese operation after leaving a successful Internet start-up, described the reaction of a Dutch cheese-making consultant he brought to Oregon to develop a line of Gouda-style cheeses for his Tumalo Farms:

> I had this really interesting idea that I wanted to make this cheese—I want to have this hoppy flavor, I want to put beer in it. So Kase turns to me and says, "I can't help you."
> I said, "Why not?"
> "Well, in Holland, we drink the darn beer. You're on your own."
> So I had to go and figure it out myself. But that's how the Pondhopper was born.[79]

Cheesemakers develop original product lines by tinkering with established recipes and bestowing novel names on resulting cheeses: use goat's milk rather than cow's in a Gouda recipe, wash it with a local microbrew beer, and call the cheese Pondhopper; or start with a Havarti recipe but blend sheep's and cow's milk to come up with Timberdoodle.[80] These cheeses exemplify how American artisans, unconstrained by expectations of fidelity to a customary form, seek to redefine "American cheese" by creating a tradition of invention.

But again, this sentiment has a history. Marin French, Jim Boyce told me, "survived wars, it survived depressions, it survived dot-coms, it survived what I call the Cheese Depression, which was in the early eighties—it was discovered that cheese had fat and . . . if you had fat in your food, it was no good." While Marin French's success has been made possible by the strong cheese market of San Francisco, that market has had to be marketed *to*. Innovation is not to be romantically imagined as a craftsperson's singular artistic creativity. Successful entrepreneurial innovation responds to customer tastes, which transform along-side demographic shifts (immigration, urbanization, class mobility) and broader culinary trends. As sociologist Howard Becker points out, craft's defining utility implies that its objects and activities must be useful to *others*: "If a person defines his work as done to meet someone else's practical needs, then function, defined externally to the intrinsic character of the work, is an important ideological and aesthetic consideration."[81] As will be further discussed in the next chapter, consumer desire helps to constitute craft not only by providing necessary markets, but also through informing aesthetic standards.

Having got its start selling small rounds of Breakfast Cheese to European deckhands to accompany their morning ale, by the turn of the twentieth century Marin French had introduced an Austrian-style, smear-ripened (or washed-rind) cheese called Schloss (German for "castle"). In the early 1900s it launched Thompson Brothers Camembert: hand-molded Camembert was produced in Marin County prior to the great San Francisco earthquake. In 1907, the year after the quake, Thompson renamed the Camembert Yellow Buck. Jim speculated that Yellow Buck was named after the buck elk that were at one time plentiful in the area and that are now being reintroduced in a sanctuary on the Point Reyes peninsula. At the same time, Yellow Buck is "a symbol of strength" that he interpreted as speaking to the rugged beauty of the Marin landscape, as well as being "sort of masculine." A company that got its start selling cheese in saloons seems consciously to have worked to sustain a masculine image in marketing its cheese with male as well as female consumers in mind. Masculine appeal, like any other culturally meaningful symbolic marker, is not a static quality. The Yellow Buck label was retired in the teens or twenties and replaced by the regal-sounding, Frenchified brand name Rouge et Noir.

Describing to me how the Thompson brothers once transported fresh cheeses by horse and wagon to the Petaluma River and then by steamer across the Bay, Jim offered this analysis: "It's putting a product together with a very receptive group of people who understood and could enjoy the product. It's pure marketing—it's marketing at its greatest! It's the individual who's saying, 'What if?' . . . I also think that it is part of the foundation of why today San Francisco is the strongest cheese market in the country. I think you can take its roots right back to the day cheese was delivered to the docks of San Francisco, to the workers."

In locating the authenticity of a food in its history of "pure marketing," Jim offers a savvy cultural analysis. Getting a product to market at a viable price is essential to any commercial enterprise. Eighteenth-century cheesemakers "made adjustments for seasonal fluctuations as well as for the marketplace."[82] One Massachusetts farmwoman, Elizabeth Porter Phelps, innovated a recipe for full-fat cheese after her husband, who marketed the cheese in Boston, reported that it would command a higher price than the usual skimmed-milk cheese.[83] In the early 1800s, Elizabeth Porter Phelps, like Thompson a hundred years later—and like Swiss immigrant John Jossi, developing Brick cheese for German settlers in Wisconsin—was a cheese innovator driven by commercial possibility.

Considering the depth of Wisconsin's tradition of invention, it is fitting that in the "open" categories of American Originals, in which compete new cheeses given fanciful names made exclusively by a single producer, ACS awards have been dominated not by fledgling newcomers working in home-based creameries but by Wisconsinites working in artisan factories.[84] Between 2004 and 2009, twenty-one ribbons in all three open categories of American Originals have been awarded to Sid Cook, third-generation Wisconsin cheesemaker and owner of Carr Valley Cheese. Cook inherited the cheese factory in which he grew up and which he has since expanded by buying up small factories in southern Wisconsin and turning out inventive artisanal varieties—Cocoa Cardona, Mobay, Canaria, Menage—alongside the forty-pound blocks of commodity cheddar and Colby that were made by his predecessors.

Although American cheesemakers may not be burdened by the constraints of Europe's government-protected "traditional" recipes, neither are they start-ing from scratch. When cheesemakers dream up new cheeses, they inevitably modify old ones. A recently minted Wisconsin cheesemaker, adding value to his German American wife's 160-year-old family dairy farm by making Italian-style cheeses, acknowledged that "the technical part of making cheese . . . we're grab-bing, stealing, borrowing" from European models. Pondhopper, on this view, is not so much an American Original as a fancy Gouda. While Europe's traditions may not be as old as some imagine, so too may America's inventions not be as innovative.[85]

In suggesting, then, that in the United States artisanal cheese is better char-acterized as a tradition of invention (albeit invented as such) than as the inven-tion of tradition, I mean to point out the ideological influence of the American celebration of entrepreneurial innovation. The pioneering ideal and quest for newness that are the hallmarks of both the industrial ideal and also today's artisan renaissance contribute to the collective neglect of an ongoing tradition of domestic artisan cheesemaking. Temporalizing artisan factories as relics of a preindustrial past—lagging behind modern industry on the one hand, and of a different, older era compared to the postindustrial newcomers on the other—helps account for a lack of communication between factory and farmstead.[86]

WHAT'S NEW ABOUT AMERICAN ARTISANAL CHEESE?

What do a couple of veteran Wisconsin factory cheesemakers make of the artisanal cheese "rebirth" happening around them, as young upstarts receive high-profile media attention for their newly acquired craft? While one indi-rectly critiqued the Eurocentrism lurking in dominant narratives of America's cheesemaking "renaissance" by pointing out how industrialized European cheesemaking has become, the other has worked to promote the artisanal status of his traditional American cheese, invented three or four generations ago by European immigrants. Both responses point to something I observed elsewhere: while people in this country may like to eat European cheeses, domestic produc-ers want to make American ones.

Limburger and the Tradition of American Modernity

Myron Olson, a congenial, mustachioed man, manages the Chalet Cheese Co-op, situated near the Green County crossroads of N and C and begun in 1885 as a cooperative creamery (the Weiss Cheese Factory) owned by five Green County dairy farmers. Still operating as a co-op, today it is owned by twenty-four farm families. Together with a sibling factory, Chalet transforms one hundred thou-sand pounds of milk a day into smear-ripened Brick, Baby Swiss, deli Swiss,

Cheddar, and the factory's signature Limburger. Chalet, which for about seventy years supplied Limburger to Kraft, is the only remaining Limburger-producing plant in the United States.

A few years ago, Olson traveled to Switzerland to serve as a judge in a cheese competition. The visiting judges toured a modern factory, dispelling any romantic notion of European production happening exclusively in tiny creameries:

> All this cheese is being made, kinda like the Wizard of Oz—"Don't look behind the curtain! Don't look behind the curtain!" They're making all this Brie and Camembert, and it's all machine. . . . In comparison, they took us to a multimillion-dollar museum that they had just built. . . . We went through it and one of the first things was—[speaks in announcer voice] "Back in the old days they had these metal racks, and wooden boards, and they'd take the cheese from the forms, put it in a box of salt, and roll 'em, and put 'em onto the boards." And I'm standing there thinking, You know, today's Friday, and I did that Tuesday! We've still got the salt box, we've still got the boards, we still have the rack. And that's in their museum of "How we used to do it."

Olson was floored. But considering that today nearly 90 percent of Camembert cheeses are industrially produced, the European fate of Limburger is not so surprising.[87] Bowing to regulatory demands of the European Union, more and more of Europe's cheeses are made from pasteurized milk, and even raw-milk cheeses are changing as stricter standards for dairy hygiene mean that European cheesemakers are working with fundamentally different milk than they did in the past—"cleaner," with less microbial diversity and activity.[88] As Grasseni writes of Taleggio producers, "the celebration of tradition in a natural environment happens while manual skills are being transformed by mechanization and standardization."[89] From this visit (and after touring other factories across Europe) Olson gained renewed appreciation for the tradition of the cheesemaker's art that he inherited from his mentor, Albert Deppeler, a second-generation Swiss maker of Limburger who managed Chalet from 1939 until he handed things over to Olson in the early 1990s.

Chalet's Limburger has been smeared day in and day out for nearly one hundred years with a continuously renewed ecology of the same *Brevibacterium linens* cultures; it is as if sourdough bread had been made continuously from the same starter for a hundred years. As a form of culture, the bacterium whose cultivation Olson inherited from Deppeler is metonymic of the dynamic tension between change and continuity that constitutes artisan tradition. In 1947, the Kraft brothers, who had been distributing Chalet's Limburger since the 1920s and who in the mid 1930s helped develop a method for producing the cheese from pasteurized milk, invested in capital expansion of the facility.[90] Norman Kraft's goal was to build the world's most modern Limburger cheese plant, and construction of a new facility up the hill from the original plant proceeded. Kraft, Olson told me,

> brought in new smear boards, they brought in new cultures. They made cheese, took it into the cellars, and put their new cultures on it. And the first month all they could make was moldy green Limburger. And [Deppeler] had the idea of going back down to the old factory and bringing up the smear boards that had the bacteria already on the boards. They brought them up and then that was the start of getting it going, because they were inoculated with the combinations of bacteria. So when you put the cheese on it, then they picked up the bacteria and then your smear started to grow. And . . . then they were able to make Limburger.

The irony is not lost on Olson that, sixty years later, Norman Kraft's "most modern" Limburger factory in the world resembles a museum exhibit in Europe. What Boisard writes of Camembert applies equally here: "The modernity of today can become the tradition of tomorrow, much as the most established tradition can give rise to an unanticipated modernity."[91] The story also demonstrates that continuity of artisan know-how is essential even to industrial invention.[92]

Myron Olson's acquired cheese culture also manifests in terms of taste and consumption. Myron grew up on a nearby farm. As a child, he refused to eat cheese because his family "got whey from the cheese factory and we made hog slop out of it"—his earliest association with cheese was agricultural rather than culinary. "And then I heard this rumor that they use calves' stomachs to make cheese, which is the rennet, and I was like, 'No way!' I mean, I haven't missed too many meals in my life, but there's no way I was gonna eat cheese." When he started working in the cheese plant as a senior in high school, he wondered at coworkers who nibbled trimmings as they cut and packaged cheese, or popped warm curds into their mouths "like candy." Eventually, Myron tried it himself—and liked it, gradually moving from milder cheeses up to Limburger.

Aversion to Limburger, a notoriously pungent cheese, is a cliché. I had never seen, smelled, or tasted Limburger before visiting the Chalet plant. It was strong, yes, but no more so than smear-ripened Époisses or a really good Taleggio. There was some lingering bitterness but certainly no hint of old socks. I wondered whether the recent excitement surrounding artisanal cheeses had rubbed off on Limburger. Myron noted that the expanded palate of increasing numbers of American consumers has likely induced more people to put a piece in their mouth (free samples are available at the factory).

> Everybody's got their connotation of what Limburger is, their thought in their mind that *No way am I gonna try it*. But if you give that same style cheese a fancy French name, then people will try it. Then it's "Oh, that's not bad! That's kinda good. It smells, it stinks, but, yeah, it's not bad. I think I'll try another piece." But if you told them "Limburger," that's it. . . . Two years back we had people asking

us, "Could you make Taleggio, could you make this, could you make that?" . . . We experimented. . . . But I reached the conclusion I'm just gonna stay on Limburger because it's stinky cheese against stinky cheese. I'm not really gonna gain sales [by adding Taleggio]. I'm just gonna do Limburger the best I can, make the best Limburger, and sell Limburger as Limburger. That way there's room for the artisan cheesemakers to make these other ones, which will bring people to Limburger. So it's no use buying extra labels, no use trying to market something. Just keep yourself out there, knowing that the public can [be] aware that Limburger, the old-time standby that grandma and grandpa used to make, is still available.

In his 2008 book *American Cheeses,* Clark Wolf, a food consultant and early manager of San Francisco's Oakville Grocery, good-naturedly recounts visiting Chalet Cheese and suggesting to Myron Olson that he "ought to make up special batches, wrap them in some fancy paper, call them 'select,' and sell them for three times the price. He blushed."[93] But Limburger's last American producer makes no apologies. The cheese, which retails at the factory store (as of summer 2010) at \$4.77 for a one-pound brick (down from \$4.82 in 2008), is not a fancy cheese. It does not belong on an after-dinner tray paired with quince paste but instead is comfortably at home between thick slices of rye, sandwiched with onions and mustard. "Traditional around this area," Myron told me, "is also to put Limburger on top of boiled potatoes." It is a farmer's cheese, a worker's cheese. At Baumgartner's Tavern (est. 1931) in Monroe, patrons wash down a \$2.95 sandwich made with Myron Olson's Limburger and onions with a pint of locally brewed beer.

Capitalizing on Cultural Capital

I first met Wisconsin cheesemaker Joe Widmer at a "meet the cheesemaker" event at the 2007 ACS meetings in Burlington, Vermont. Sampling a piquant cube of his ten-year-aged Cheddar, I invited Widmer to give me the short spiel on his cheese. He began with his grandfather's emigration from Switzerland in 1905; as a condition of entry, he was set up as an apprentice in a Swiss-owned cheese factory in Wisconsin. When John Widmer purchased his own factory in 1922, "he was surrounded by Germans," so he made smear-ripened Brick—the cheese, also known as German Brick, developed about 1875 by John Jossi, another Swiss-born Wisconsin cheesemaker catering to a German-born community.[94] Much as John Putnam and Mike Gingrich, in the 1990s, tinkered with the recipe for Beaufort d'Alpage in Vermont and Wisconsin to come up with Tarentaise and Pleasant Ridge Reserve, Jossi's Brick emerged from tinkering with the recipe for Limburger (itself a cheese that predates the German nation-state, having been developed in Liège and marketed in the city of Limburg, then part of the Duchy of Limburg and now located in Belgium). The symbols and resources of class, though, separate enterprising travel from the United States to Europe to acquire artisanal techniques from the immigrant's arrival with little more than the embodied skills of a craftsperson or, as in John Widmer's case, ethnic-based artisan networks.

Third-generation Swiss American owner-cheesemaker Joe Widmer, who grew up in an apartment above the factory, still makes Brick using his grandfather's techniques: bucketing curd to fill the cheese molds, turning each cheese the first day three times by hand, even pressing the individual blocks of cheese with the same masonry bricks used by his grandfather (figs. 15 and 16). Joe is intently conscious and proud of the artisan traditions of American cheesemaking, embracing them as family patrimony. In a promotional video shown to visitors as part of a factory tour, he says, "All of our products are authentic and traditional, and we make it all the old-fashioned way, which we believe makes it a better cheese." This is not to say that Joe has refrained from introducing changes since he took over the family business in the early 1990s. He added rooms for aging and packaging, allowing him to expand the mail-order business. He opened the factory to tours, promoting cheesemaking, and his cheese in particular, as Wisconsin heritage. He commissioned an extensive Web site that retells through archival photos the history of the family business and of Brick cheese. And he introduced a new logo. Previously, there had been no unifying label tying the cheeses they produced (Cheddar, Colby, Brick) into a single brand. Joe has successfully branded the name Widmer's Cheese Cellars and the logo, "A Family Tradition of Excellence. Producing Quality Handcrafted Cheese since 1922," embellished with a Swiss cross and Joe's personal signature. Success in craft production entails, in part, the successful selling of sentiment. Just as bucolic images of a family farm can help sell handmade cheese, so too can a photo-documented story of transgenerational family patrimony help convey that a cheese is, in fact, handmade.

Joe's innovations have helped him place cheese in "more upscale markets, fancier chains of stores [e.g., Whole Foods], and even individual stores." This was his goal: "When you're in this size of business, it's not how much cheese you make, it's how much [money] you make per pound. That tells you if you can stay in business." Annual meetings of the ACS, an organization Joe joined about the time he took the company's helm, have been instrumental in cultivating contacts with upmarket distributors and retailers.

Joe Widmer embraces the new artisan movement as an opportunity to enhance the value—both symbolic and economic—of the same cheese that he, with his uncles and father, following their father, have produced for eighty years. Like Myron Olson, Joe makes recognizable varieties of everyday, affordable cheese (as is traditional in Wisconsin, most of Widmer's Cheddar is colored bright orange, though he makes a limited amount of white Cheddar for select markets). Unlike Myron (whose handmade cheese was until recently sold under the Kraft label), he has taken steps to ensure that his product is not confused with industrially

FIG. 15. *(top)* Widmer's Cheese Factory in Theresa, Wisconsin. Photo by author.

FIG. 16. *(bottom)* Eighty-year-old masonry bricks pressing Widmer's Brick cheese. Photo by author.

produced commodity cheese. As Joe said: "One of the things that made some-body like me an artisan wasn't inventing new cheeses, it was sticking with what I did. Then a lot of people, their companies evolved into a giant where it was all machine-made stuff and it turns into a commodity type of thing. By sticking to tradition, it made us winners."

Cristina Grasseni explains of Italian producers, "the commercialization of cheese as a traditional product entail[s] not only a transformation of traditional skills but also the acquisition of new skills for managing one's image."[95] Although Joe insists the cheese itself has not changed—he follows the same recipe, buys milk from the same farmers, pasteurizes the milk because that is what his pre-decessors did, even uses those same bricks to press the cheeses—the *quality* of the cheese, understood in symbolic as well as economic terms, has changed. It is winning awards. It is fetching higher prices. His cheese is what Marilyn Strathern would call "quality-enhanced"—"Quality is not there to be discovered: those attributes which define things are made explicit, even superadded, in the course of the marketing process."[96]

What Grasseni calls "packaging skills" are, in Italy, hidden behind appeal to heritage, but in the United States they are as likely to be announced as evidence of authentic entrepreneurial acumen. Jim Boyce, who reintroduced the Yellow Buck label in 2000 to commemorate the Camembert's centennial, took over Marin French Cheese Company amid a fiscal slump. To turn things around, not only did he diversify the product line by introducing blue-veined, flavored, and goat's-milk varieties, like Joe Widmer he revised the company's marketing strategy. Marin French was making Brie and Camembert in small batches from hand-cut, manually bucketed curd and individually wrapping each wheel by hand—and it was all sold in the deli dairy section. As Jim schooled me, commercial dairy products are sold in supermarkets as either deli dairy or service deli. Deli dairy refers to the large refrigerated cases along the back wall of a supermarket contain-ing butter, milk, and yogurt in addition to cheese. Today, while Marin French still owns deli dairy shelf space (SKUs) in regional stores, most of its product is instead directed to the service dairy and displayed as a specialty item—in a center island near the produce, say—rather than as a "grab and go" staple food slotted alongside milk and butter. Like Joe, Jim marketed cheese in a way that calls atten-tion to its method of production, bestowing the cultural cachet of "artisan" fabri-cation on a label that has been around for more than a century but must now be "discovered" by an emergent base of discriminating consumers. Jim Boyce was energetic in entering Marin French cheeses in competitions, dominating many of the fresh and soft-ripened awards categories at ACS competitions. In 2005 Marin French staged something of a coup by winning a gold medal in the soft-ripened category at the World Cheese Awards in London—beating the French at Brie in a blind tasting, a feat reminiscent of the 1976 surprise triumph of California wines in a blind taste test memorialized in *The Judgment of Paris*.[97]

The change that is predicated on continuity in these cases is accomplished, as Strathern writes, by collapsing "the difference between what is taken for granted in the nature of the product and what is perceived to be the result of extra human effort."[98] In marketing established cheeses to capitalize on newer artisan enterprises, Joe Widmer and Jim Boyce are not just "sticking with" what they and their companies were already doing, but compelling a discriminating consumer culture to discover the twenty-first-century value of artisanship as a quality inherent in old-fashioned cheeses, cheeses whose recipes and flavor profiles were developed when the symbolic value of their manufacture and taste meant something else entirely: Swiss German, immigrant, working-class, local tavern.

CHEESE OF MODERATE SPEED

As this chapter has demonstrated, today's artisan factories and farmstead operations seem to operate along parallel historical tracks, with old-school factories periodized as early industrial while newer farmstead endeavors are not only postindustrial but, more pointedly, counterindustrial. That each type of enterprise seems to belong to a different era, a different time, inhibits communication between them.[99] Consumption follows much the same pattern, since even when households consume both factory and farmstead cheeses these may not be eaten at the same meal. The cultural capital of taste contributes to how cheeses are understood in time, further separating producers who cater to "old-fashioned" (read: working-class, small-town) tastes and those who strive to tickle the fancy of highbrow eaters ever on the lookout for the novel, the unexpected, the latest cheese sensation. When cheesemongers in the United States are asked, "What's new?" (rather than, say, "What's especially good today?"), the answer may literally be a new cheese emerging from a just-licensed domestic creamery. In such manner America's tradition of invention is continuously invented anew.

The time of artisanal cheese is not just the time of history but also of tempo. In the United States, it is ironic that cheeses that are celebrated by Slow Food, a movement that valorizes Europhilic food-making traditions imagined as embodying the virtues of patience and leisured conviviality, are among the most recent on the scene. Slow Food means to reverse the sped-up tempo and efficiency measures associated with Taylorist manufacture and the consumption as well as production of fast food.[100] But while the temporality of Slow Food is intended to recapture the slow-moving time of transgenerational tradition, its tempo is often astonishingly quick, particularly in the United States.

Originating in Italy as a movement for inventing tradition, on this side of the Atlantic the Slow Food movement has been repurposed as a marketing machine to accelerate a reinvented tradition of artisan invention. The Slow Food USA Presidium of American Raw Milk Cheeses "protects" cheeses as young as two years old, created by artisans who are still learning their craft.[101] Compared with the *longue durée* of European recipes and food-related customs that Slow Food was invented to protect (in part through narrating them as traditional), Slow Food USA would seem to telescope the collective history of a people into the biographical experience of an individual. Many of the cheeses promoted by Slow Food have been quick off the mark getting on the World Wide Web and their producers are efficient networkers, participating in ACS meetings and Slow Food events, often to the bemusement of those who have been making cheese day in and day out for an adult lifetime. I heard one longtime cheesemaker disparage a newcomer from the same state: "He started making cheese last year and now he's the expert giving workshops? Who *is* this guy?" However long it takes to make a single batch of cheese, some of the new artisans are undoubtedly participants in today's hyperfast production regime.

How did this happen? How can Slow Food be so fast? Again, it has to do with the cultural capital of taste. Slow cheeses are not exclusively defined by method and mode of production—small-batch, with little mechanization—they also represent styles of cheese to be savored with a crusty baguette and a glass of wine. As Alison Leitch writes of Carlo Petrini's vision, Slow Food is not just anti–fast food, Slowness "is linked to pleasure, conviviality and corporeal memory."[102] "Slow" cheeses are thus unlikely to be sent to school in a child's lunchbox or tossed into a macaroni and cheese casserole. But why not? Why privilege the special treat food over the high-quality staple? Whose "corporeal memory" should be honored here? Sidney Mintz suggests, "Why not make our goal good and healthy food, produced locally, for everybody? Perhaps that would be food at moderate speeds."[103] Cheese at moderate speeds would be Joe Widmer's Brick, Myron Olson's Limburger, Marjorie Susman and Marian Pollack's waxed Orb Weaver, and Ig Vella's high-moisture Jack.

"If you're talking about artisan cheese in general," Ig Vella said to me, "you're talking about quality and consistency and, whether you like it or not, filling a niche." The toughest niche to find in the cheese world is the niche of moderate speed, enjoying neither commodity economies of scale nor special-treat retail pricing. Bruce Workman, who reintroduced natural-rind, big-wheel Swiss because "That's what Green County is all about," had a warehouse full of 180-pound wheels of cheese that he had yet to sell, an inventory that requires continuous attention and care (i.e., labor costs).[104] He is working to recultivate a niche market: "I'm producing a piece of cheese that nobody's handled for a long time. I'm not going into the deli to say, 'Gee, I got 180 pounds of Swiss, wanna take it?' They're going to go, 'How am I going to cut it? How am I going to move it around?' So . . . we're struggling in training people at the storefront with how they're going to handle it."[105] Success in craft production includes educating appreciative users about craft objects, a point to which I will return in the next chapter.

Visiting Bruce reminded me of Vermont farmers Linda and Rob Dimmick, who also produce cheese of moderate speed that they have struggled to sell. Just as the number of "mom and pop" delis still able and willing to handle wedges of Bruce Workman's 180-pound wheel Emmenthalers is limited, Neighborly Farms lacks sufficient volume to get into the service deli of regional supermarket chains.[106] Not even opening their picturesque farm to agritourism has ushered them into sufficient niche markets for their cheese. Why? The Dimmicks make cheese on the farm Rob grew up on using the organic milk of their own cows— and they turn that milk into flavored Cheddar, Monterey Jack, and Colby. "We're an everyday cheese," Linda said to me. Although her husband tells her she is "selling herself short" when she says that, Linda embraces the idea of an everyday cheese. She does not want people to have to wait for the holidays to buy her cheese. To some consumers—though not to the Dimmicks—the moral sentiment of their production and the everyday distinction of their cheese creates cultural-capital dissonance that makes the cheese difficult to place. This is a downside to producing an unfinished commodity, one that has more to do with the cultural politics of food, ethics, and class than with entrepreneurial savvy.

Since the nineteenth century, American originals have been hybrid cheeses: a reduced-moisture Limburger (Brick); a cow's-milk cheese in a Valençay mold (Sarabande). Looking ahead to the twenty-first century, we are beginning to see hybrid cheesemaking enterprises carving out a syncopated—though moderately paced?—temporality. Reminding us, "The extremes of slow and fast, local and global, artisanal and industrial, are ideal types," Richard Wilk suggests, "all the real action takes place *in between*."[107] This is where I locate the majority of American artisan cheesemaking enterprises.

Fayette Creamery, situated at the crossroads of County G and F in Wisconsin's Lafayette County just west of Green County, is becoming one of these in-between space-times. Fayette is a new label added to an old business, Brunkow cheese. Brunkow was established in 1899 as a farmer-owned cooperative and the factory, like most that endured the past century, transitioned from big-wheel Swiss to industrial cheesemaking, turning out commodity cheddar, Jack, and Colby. After California's huge dairies entered the commodity cheese business in the 1980s and 1990s, Brunkow upped its production, cranking out two vats of cheese in the morning and two in the afternoon. In a move reminiscent of medium-size dairy farms turning to value-added agricultural products, the company shifted gears in 2005 by moving into artisanal production. The third generation of Geissbuhlers to make cheese at the plant (the family now owns the former co-op) hired a new cheesemaker, Joe Burns, to introduce a line of English-style artisanal cheeses under the Fayette label. Before making cheese for the Geissbuhlers, Joe was selling wine in Chicago. Though a novice cheesemaker, Joe brought to the partnership a taste for the sort of cheeses the Geissbuhlers wanted to add to their product line.

At Fayette Creamery, artisanal cheese is reinvented as the future in parallel—in the same room even—with the continuation of an industrial tradition. Joe's 2,400-pound-capacity vat, in which he makes curd for Little Darling and Avondale Truckle, stands crammed into a corner of the cheese make room. When I arrived for an interview, Joe was needling columns of an experimental batch of blue cheeses, poking deep holes, one by one, using an ice pick; the artisan end of the plant was decidedly low-tech. Meanwhile, working in the long open vats that dominate the room, Karl Geissbuhler was down to making two vats of commodity cheese three days a week. Might labor-intensive cheese made using the artisanal techniques and sensibilities that their grandparents' generation overcame with automated technologies enable a fourth generation of Geissbuhlers to carry on the family factory? The hope that it will do so represents a factory version of the farm story others tell of "going back to the future." However much the obsolete is reintroduced as the novel, the practice as well as the meaning of artisan cheesemaking is ever-changing; regulations, bacterial cultures, tastes, and sentiments all evolve. The next chapter examines how change and continuity play out in the practice of artisanal technique and sensibility.

The Art and Science of Craft

Cheesemaking is not a thing which comes of itself. It is a mystery which one must pay to be allowed to learn; or it is an art, based on science, which one must pay to be instructed in, as in the other arts of life.
—HARRIET MARTINEAU, 1863, IN THE POPULAR VICTORIAN
ILLUSTRATED MAGAZINE *ONCE A WEEK*

What makes artisanal cheese *artisanal*? More than a decade after the organization was founded, the American Cheese Society (ACS) offered the following definition: "The word 'artisan' or 'artisanal' implies that a cheese is produced primarily by hand, in small batches, with particular attention paid to the tradition of the cheesemaker's art, and thus using as little mechanization as possible in the production of the cheese."[1]

Artisanal cheese is inescapably defined against the industrial: it is made more by hand than by machine, in small batches compared to industrial scales of production, using recipes and techniques developed through the practical knowledge of previous artisans rather than via the technical knowledge of dairy scientists and industrial engineers. Indeed, the question of what counts as artisanal cheese only becomes significant in an era of industrial processing. Artisans are increasingly compelled to articulate what distinguishes their product from that used as an ingredient in, for example, Nabisco Artisan Cheese Crackers, a line of Wheat Thins available in Wisconsin Colby and Vermont White Cheddar varieties that was launched in 2009 by one of Kraft Foods' largest brands. Today "industrial cheesemaking" refers to the large-scale, fully automated process of computer-aided manufacturing; recipes are programmed into computers and cheesemaking proceeds according to a prescripted plan in closed vats that restrict milk and curd from view (let alone smell, feel, or taste). Factory workers attend the transformation of milk into cheese at a hygienic remove while cheesemaking knowledge and skill materialize away from the factory floor, in research and design and in quality control. The ACS definition of artisanal cheese implies that attention to a tradition of cheesemaking art promises to diminish reliance on mechanization. Yet at the same time, the open-ended qualifiers in that articulation—*primarily* (not exclusively) by hand, in *small* (how small?) batches—acknowledge that artisan cheesemaking is not strictly artistic.

Like other artisanal foods today, cheese relies on elements of "technoscience," a modern arena of practice that "transcends the conventional association of science with knowledge and technology with manual production," as Heath and Meneley write.[2] Very few cheesemakers eschew the enhanced predictability of seeding milk with freeze-dried, laboratory-isolated strains of known bacterial cultures or employing standardized, commercial rennet. Empirical observation, scientific testing, and meticulous record-keeping all aid in cheesemakers' mastery of *consistency,* an important criterion in evaluating artisan skill. Microbiological assessment of pathogenic risk also guides scrupulous hygienic practice in milking parlors and cheese rooms.

Artisan and *artisanal* emerge as terms of convention, not objective properties. Yesterday's specialty cheese might be today's artisanal—or the precursor to today's industrial. Artisanal cheesemaking is a form of craft practice in that it is defined by a particular material (milk) and by methods invented for transforming it (into cheese); it is made substantially by hand; it produces objects of utilitarian value (to be eaten); and it draws on a prior tradition of practice (a new cheese is never sui generis).[3]

Nonetheless, cheesemakers rarely if ever speak of what they do as craft. This chapter investigates how and why artisan cheesemakers consistently describe what they do, instead, as a balance of art and science. In this formulation, *art* stands for creative expression as well as an intuitively interpretive grasp of one's materials, while *science* refers to empirical observation and measurement, disciplined attention to record-keeping, and steps taken to ensure product safety.

In contemporary American thought, *art* connotes creative expression as well as manual fabrication; art gains rhetorical appeal over craft through signaling greater distance from industrial production.[4] We can understand this historically. Throughout the European Middle Ages, being a painter and being a potter were analogous trades learned through apprenticeship and organized through guilds, but eighteenth-century philosophical discussions of aesthetics and nineteenth-century industrialism came to frame painters of decorative canvas and potters of utilitarian stoneware as categorically and qualitatively different professions. Not only did the modern period see art elevated to a mode of personal expression, but craft, made obsolete by industrial fabrication, was demoted to mere hobby or derided as anti-modern.[5] Today, the "cheesemaker's art" might refer simultaneously to creative, individual expression and to the practical knowledge required to make something of value by hand: art stands in opposition to the rational efficiency, mechanical standardization, and hygienic regulation that gave the world mass-produced, sandwich-ready, prepackaged slices of American cheese.

At the same time, post-pastoral thinking regards scientific knowledge—of milk chemistry, acidification, microbial succession in rind development—as a crucial means of understanding how "nature" behaves in a way that can complement the customary "tradition of the cheesemaker's art." As I demonstrate below, some artisans embrace scientific vocabulary and principles of technique as aids for gaining practical knowledge of milk's transubstantiation into cheese—and intimate knowledge of the local conditions of their own farm or creamery—that will enable them to tweak a recipe and guide milk's fermentation, coagulation, and ripening to craft a particular cheese successfully, over and over again. Tom Gilbert, a Vermont cheesemaker with more than a dozen years' experience, articulated to me the arts and sciences of cheesemaking craft in this way:

> I like solving problems . . . and rescuing cheese. The main job of a cheesemaker is to be looking for perfection, to understand what it is that you're trying to do, in your own mind—how this cheese should be produced. And then day after day after day to try to achieve that. Any cheesemaker's going to tell you that none of it just happens by itself, that the most subtle variations of everything that goes into it—from the milk to the weather—are going to make your cheese different. So . . . the cheese *wants* to be different all the time, and you're fighting that, against the perfect cheese you're trying to produce. So that's where the cheesemaker steps in and says, "I'm going do this a little bit differently today. I'm going to try to compensate for something I see happening." You try to make an adjustment and try to bring [back] a cheese that you feel is running away from you, getting outside of the parameters that you're trying to look for—and I love doing that. You can take notes on everything that you do, every day's production, and then you make notes on the adjustments, and then you have to wait for a long time to see the results—but I'm always anxious to see.

Tom derives joy from "solving problems" and "rescuing cheese," and he is "anxious to see" how his tinkering and adjustments play out not only because he would hate to waste a batch of cheese but because he is genuinely curious: perfecting his skill entails learning how the organic processes of fermentation and ripening unfold under the guidance of his mindful hand. When contemporary cheesemakers describe their craft as a balance between art and science, this is neither incidental nor mere posturing; it is indicative of the complex and ambivalent status of craft (or artisanship) in an industrial yet post-pastoral era.

To better understand for myself what makes artisanal cheese artisanal today, I signed up for a couple of two-day workshops run by Vermont cheesemaker and consultant Peter Dixon for beginners interested in commercial production.[6] I gained an appreciation for how artisans employ human-scale machinery in light of scientific understandings and technological modifications of cheese's natural ingredients (milk, bacterial cultures, enzymes that facilitate coagulation). For cheesemakers like Peter Dixon, scientific knowledge is a tool to be employed in the service of craft. At the same time, objectivist accountings to track what happened when and with what outcome to particular milks, microorganisms, and cheeses results in improved practice and product only if the cheesemaker *interprets* his or her data successfully, a feat described repeatedly as an "art." Contemporary craft in cheesemaking, as I have come to understand it, joins subjective sensory apprehension and tactile, bodily knowledge with the rational objectivism required to make and record careful observations of how milk and curd behave under specific circumstances.

As I discuss what practitioners mean by the art and science of cheesemaking I work toward an outline of an anthropological theory of craft practice.[7] Located at the nexus of art and science, I suggest, craft operates through *synesthetic reason*. Synesthesia refers to the cross-registering of sensory experience; in clinical terms, it describes cognitive conditions whereby people may see letters or numbers as inherently colored, or may register color through sound. But synesthesia can refer more broadly to cross-sensory experience, to the way that particular tastes might evoke memories of place, or to how hearing a familiar song might trigger a flood of tears.[8] I extend this notion to get at how artisans "understand" milk and curd by allowing their sight, touch, smell, and taste to register through one another. In craft practice, synesthetic reason engages cross-sensory as well as objective analysis and places value on personal expression as well as consistency of form.

To begin this chapter I demonstrate how sensory apperceptions and conceptual understandings of nature come together in craft by working through key elements of artisanal cheesemaking: assessing milk; gaining a feel for the curd; and working with one's hands. Turning next to an ethnographic account of Peter Dixon's workshop, I explore how beginning cheesemakers seek, in part through scientific vocabulary and technique, to acquire the embodied knowledge of the "cheesemaker's art." Although cheesemakers speak of their own and their colleagues' inclinations toward either the art or the science end of things as a personal matter, artisan subjects are inescapably formed within regulatory and market contexts. I conclude by analyzing craft as a form of work organization and as an aesthetic form to consider how a counterindustrial marketplace helps to shape contemporary craft practice.[9] For commercial cheesemakers, improved practice and evaluative standards are keyed to consumer expectation and preference. For this reason, taste education—of producers and consumers alike—is an important aspect of artisanal cheesemaking.

MILK

Artisanal cheese begins with minimally modified milk. Just as woodworking begins with selecting a piece of wood amenable to being turned into a bowl or planed into a tabletop, artisanal cheesemaking begins with clean yet distinctive milk that might carry traces of its ecology of production.[10] Milk is notoriously variable, its material composition (protein, fat, minerals, microbiota) affected by animal species, breed, feed, and health as well as by climatic and weather conditions. Artisan cheesemakers not only embrace milk's variability, they locate an artisanal cheese's value in that variability when it is appropriately expressed—shepherded into the taste and feel of a distinctive cheese—through skilled practice.

Furniture designer David Pye draws a useful distinction between craftsmanship and ordinary (that is, industrial) manufacture. Whereas industrial manufacture ensures a certain, standardized outcome by following a "workmanship of certainty," according to Pye, in craftsmanship, "the quality of the result is not predetermined, but depends on the judgment, dexterity and care which the maker exercises as he works."[11] Craftsmanship entails a "workmanship of risk" in which product quality remains "continually at risk" throughout the manufacturing process. In the words of Myron Olson, "There's more room for error because you're doing it yourself instead of being mechanized. That, to me, I think is one of the biggest factors of being artisanal." Risk can be introduced from human error or from flaws occurring in the raw materials.

Industrial manufacturing seeks to obviate both sets of errors by deskilling production and standardizing materials. Based on a "workmanship of certainty" to ensure a known, standardized outcome, industrial processing filters out organic variables by denaturing milk: pasteurizing it to kill off microorganisms, standardizing butterfat content, and homogenizing the size of fat globules by forcing milk through fine-gauge filters—and before that, by breeding animals year-round to blend early- and late-lactation milk.[12] Industrial cheese looks, feels, and tastes the same from one batch to the next because a great deal of techno-scientific work goes into standardizing the milk used from one batch to the next, and because quality control imposes uniformity on the finished product. Inconsistent batches are melted down to be reconstituted as processed products.

Milk used in artisanal cheesemaking may be pasteurized (heat-treated to kill off bacteria), but generally the milk is neither homogenized nor standardized and is often produced by seasonally bred herds. As Jill Giacomini Basch and I set out on a walking tour of the family dairy and creamery at Point Reyes Farmstead Cheese Company, which she and her sisters manage, she explained that one of the primary benefits of being a farmstead operation "is that we don't have to manipulate or agitate our raw ingredient, the milk, to the degree that other, urban-based cheese manufacturers have to do because they're heating and cooling and transporting their primary raw ingredient. . . . Everything that we do in our process is done specifically to minimize the stress on that raw ingredient, on the milk. Ultimately, this allows us to produce a finished product that is more representative of the flavors found at the source—the milk our cows produce." In some farmstead operations, I have seen milk flow from udders through tubing attached to the milking apparatus directly into the cheese vat located in an adjacent room.

As milk composition changes throughout a season, artisan cheesemakers adjust their method. Rather than standardize ingredients as a first, essential step in standardizing their product, they work with variations that affect milk's fermentation and coagulation, as well as the eventual taste and texture of cheese.[13] To do so, proficient cheesemakers develop an intimate understanding of their milk—not so much milk chemistry in the abstract, but, as Diana Murphy of Dreamfarm said to me, "Part of the artisan feel of it is knowing your milk, knowing what cultures complement your milk, what rennet complements your milk, how to manipulate that."[14] It is similar to a potter's knowledge of clay, a knowledge that guides the modification of even the most carefully selected material through adding grog or moisture and by extracting air through wedging and kneading. Howard Risatti writes, "when irregularities are encountered in material, for instance discolorations or knots, say in pieces of wood or in fibers, the hand of the craftsman can negotiate around these natural occurrences or work with them and incorporate them into the finished piece. In this way, rather than liabilities, irregularities become positive factors that contribute to the creative process."[15] Working with irregularities, even turning them into virtues of design, generates the diversity of form that Pye identifies as the chief value of craftsmanship in an industrial age.[16] In this way craft resists the steady creep of standardization in a global market.

Yet, as I will discuss at the end of the chapter, returning to the notion of an unfinished commodity, material flaws are made virtues only if the resulting form is recognizable within a particular social context—a market niche, for instance, or a cheese competition category. Unlike clay or wood or fiber, cheese is intended for human consumption; some flaws are not merely ugly or inconvenient, they may be harmful to human health. When a public-health perspective on milk's variability is brought into view, as we will see in the next chapter, the workmanship of risk takes on entirely new meaning.

CURD

Making cheese "by hand" is a tricky, uncertain business. Inherent to artisanal cheesemaking is a tension between allowing natural variation to flourish and maintaining sufficient control over fermentation and ripening that the result is a safe, recognizable, tasty food. Dairy scientist Paul Kindstedt, who helped found the Vermont Institute for Artisan Cheese at the University of Vermont, puts it this way: "The challenge for the farmstead cheesemaker is to strike the right balance between art and science. The goal should be to achieve the appropriate level of control to ensure safety and consistently high quality while at the same time giving nature enough free rein to encourage the diversity and uniqueness of character that make artisanal cheeses special."[17] On this view, crafting cheese entails calibrating one's intervention in fermentation and coagulation at a delicate midpoint between total control and domination—Pye's "workmanship of certainty"—and letting bacteria run wild, risking a possible biohazard or unpalatable, unmarketable cheese.

To strike this balance, artisans learn how to work *with,* rather than against, such variations as may be introduced by seasonality, ambient temperature and humidity, herd health, and inconsistent human practice. In an interview, Kindstedt elaborated, "What the traditional cheesemakers have always done is to learn how to work with nature—and they did have to learn, you know, from past experience and past generations, what worked and what didn't work." As with other heritage foods, contemporary artisanship turns yesterday's necessity into today's virtue.[18] Kindstedt continued, "And I think what strikes the heartstrings of a lot of folks who really believe in artisan cheese, and the traditional crafts— not just in cheese, but in brewing and wines and so forth—is that nature is your partner, not to be abused or dominated, but worked with." In keeping with a post-pastoral vision of nature's collaborative role in human productive projects (or, seen otherwise, of humans' supportive role in ostensibly natural processes), artisanship approaches the "nature" and "culture" of turning milk into cheese as mutually constitutive aspects of each other; nature is not simply given as the raw material for cultural transformation.

In order to respond artisanally to desirable organic variation, the first order of cheesemaking is observation. In the words of a Wisconsin cheesemaker, "Observe what happened today and predict it may happen tomorrow, and from those predictions you may make adjustments." First, make and record empirical observations of milk, curd, environmental conditions, and how the process of a particular batch unfolded; second, know how to interpret and evaluate or judge one's observations; and third, know how to translate one's evaluations into practical interventions in the organic processes of fermentation and coagulation in order to make good cheese consistently, given fluctuating materials and conditions. Objective assessment of carefully observed environmental and material conditions (temperature, humidity, milk acidity, curd pH, etc.) and meticulous record-keeping (e.g., how much time the curd took to set before being ready to drain from the whey) are important because the idea is that one can and will return to these notes to compare observed phenomena from one day to the next, one season to the next, in order to trouble-shoot a failed batch or to reverse-engineer a successful one. Maria Trumpler, who made Vermont Ayr cheese with Crawford Family Farm (and is trained as a historian of science), said to me, "The thing I love about cheesemaking is it's very eighteenth-century, it's extremely empirical. . . . Our batches vary [but] we at least try to keep really good notes and then at least correlate in our heads: this batch was great, here's what we did to get it. This batch was less good, here's how we did it, what's going on?" Understanding the craft of cheesemaking means stepping back to consider what a cheesemaker does, not just in making a single batch of cheese, but over the course of a season and from one year to the next. Experience counts.

Instead of following a set recipe, cheesemakers speak of developing "a feel" for their milk and curd. Patty Karlin said in an interview:

> Cheesemaking is a funny thing because any person who is a good cook [can make cheese]—one time. So you heat the milk up, you pasteurize it, cool it down, add culture and rennet—that is not a hard recipe if you're an experienced cook. So what goes wrong? The weather changes, the humidity changes. You have to be able to smell, taste, and feel the cheese. Every batch of cheese, I put it into my hands, I squeeze it, and I know [i.e., recognize] by the imprint of my fingers if that's going to be an aged cheese, or a fresh cheese, or a soft cheese. . . . The *curd* for those different cheeses is different. So having that *feeling* is something that is hard to teach.

That feel is metonymic for knowledge generated through nearly all the senses— sight, smell, touch, taste. Skilled artisans engage their senses to interpret and evaluate empirical data in order to execute a batch of cheese successfully: this is synesthetic reason. Subjective, sensory knowledge is required to make objective knowledge work in practice, which is why excellence in craft skill is described in terms of virtuosity rather than expertise.[19]

In the terminology of today's practitioners, the ability to gather and interpret sensory data and apply it practically is the *art* of making cheese. This art captures a seemingly subjective, even intuitive (rather than consciously reasoned) interpretation of empirical conditions. Craft practice moves between what is *sensed* (apprehended through sensory input and subjective evaluation) and what is *being* sensed (the empirical conditions and materials that are manipulated by "tweaking" a recipe and through prior orchestration of the ecologies of milk production). Art and science represent the subjective and objective angles from which cheesemakers triangulate on the moving target of a particular batch of milk's transubstantiation into cheese on a particular day. Jerry Heimerl said of the process of learning to read the objective data—temperature, pH, time it takes for curd to set, and so on—that he faithfully collects throughout the making of each batch of cheese, "It becomes an art when you're sensing with your senses and trying to predict changes in that cheese based on history. And you've taken it from raw data to sensory: the eyes, the nose, the taste, the feel. All of your senses, and then there's probably the sixth sense . . . just intuition." Joe Widmer, who not only apprenticed with his family but also took classes at the University of

Wisconsin toward a Master Cheesemaker's certification, explained how he knows when to cut the curd:

> Most guys use a pH meter, and I learned in school the isoelectric points—4.5 to 5.2—where it's the perfect biochemical pH, and that's when it's time to cut [the curd]. But growing up with my father and uncles, I just learned that when you sanitize your hand and put your finger in and lift it, and if you put your thumb right here and it looks just right, then you know it's ready to cut. That's what we do [i.e., the clean break test]. For certain cheeses, you want to hold it longer or shorter—then you can feel that. If I walk by a batch of cheese that's in the cottage cheese-curd type form and I pick it up, if there's something wrong I can feel it right away. . . . Or I can taste it and see that something's wrong.

The synesthetically mixed metaphor in Joe's final sentence is telling: the language used to describe the empirical observation required to correlate cause and effect, condition and intervention and outcome, conveys a multisensory dimension to the artisan's apprehension and interpretation.[20] Joe can "taste it and see."

What makes artisan cheesemaking artisanal is a reflexive, anticipatory practice guided by synesthetic evaluation of how the materials (milk, curd, cheese) are behaving and developing in a particular instance, as understood in light of past experience.[21] Bodily knowledge emerges from a particular cultivation of the senses—sight, hearing, smell, taste, touch/tactility, temporality—and from learning to act through employing that trained sensory apparatus. It is a sensory reason. As proficiency is gained, watching and seeing become habituated—not by virtue of repetition but by acquiring a reflexive feel for strategic action under contingent circumstances. When one knows *how* to look, one starts *seeing* and *feeling* things differently. Cheesemakers who go by feel may after years of practice no longer be able to articulate what it is that tells them it is time to cut the curd or drain the whey. Their knowledge has become tacit.[22] In her work on skill and standardization in cattle breeding, Grasseni describes how Italian breeders acquire the discernment to see high-quality cattle through what she calls "skilled vision."[23] Such ability, she writes, constitutes a "gestalt shift": once one learns how to see quality (that is, to rapidly evaluate objective conditions in a consistent and legible way) one can hardly fail to see quality from then on. It is akin to developing an acquired taste; once one learns to appreciate the taste of fine wine, it may be hard to return to three-dollar plonk.

Historically speaking, the "tradition of the cheesemaker's art" referred to in the ACS definition quoted at the start of this chapter reaches back further than the factory artisans with whom Joe Widmer apprenticed to the preindustrial practice of farmwomen who transformed their cows' perishable milk into cheese, regardless of whether they enjoyed proficiency in feeling the curd.[24] Highly particular, even idiosyncratic, their art was deemed unscientific.[25] While its apparent arbitrariness was precisely what the nineteenth-century advent of cheese factories meant to overcome, its efficacy in the hands of an especially skilled cheesemaker is what nineteenth-century reformers strove to capture through scientific means. In an 1865 address at the Rhode Island Cattle Show, the Honorable Geo. B. Loring, president of the New England Agricultural Society, acknowledged that the "best agricultural colleges . . . are the farms of intelligent and successful cultivators" and marveled, "The shrewd, observing youth who never read an essay on cattle—how, as it were, by magic, will he read the capacity and quality of the animals with which he is to stock his farm. . . . The tillage of the fathers, and the household management of the mothers—we may still study these with advantage to ourselves." By way of illustration, he continued:

> There is the effort of a wealthy capitalist in eastern Massachusetts, who . . . laid out and conducted one of the most ample and imposing farms in all that section. . . . His stock could be traced to the best blood in England. His dairy-room was of the most approved plan. But still he failed in one important item. His neighbor, less pretentious and more skillful, a tidy and industrious matron, always outstripped him in the products of her dairy. It was her cheese, and not his, which always took the premium at the county fair. He bore this as long as was possible, and then applied to her for knowledge. She gave it to him; but his cheese failed still. . . . At last it occurred to him that he had not used a thermometer. . . . The thermometer was bought, and with an air of triumph our capitalist waited upon his practical teacher, to inform her that he had at last obtained an instrument for ascertaining the temperature of the milk . . . a thermometer.
>
> "A 'mometer," said the good matron, "what is a 'mometer?" "Why" said he, "a thermometer is an instrument by which we ascertain the temperature of air, water, &c. How do you ascertain how warm the milk is, which you are converting into cheese?"
>
> The dairy-woman looked puzzled and astonished for a moment, and then exclaimed, with genuine simplicity—"why I use my finger."
>
> The capitalist was beaten. The science of practical farming was suddenly unfolded to him, and he retired a wiser man, and we hope a better farmer. At any rate he knew the difference between science and practice.[26]

That almost mystical understanding of milk and curd can still be found. One Wisconsin cheesemaker, who works on a family farm, told me the following story:

> An old German cheesemaker . . . came in here, and he looked at the milk and said, "Ah, that's beautiful milk!" He smelled it and he said, "You've a pump back at the farm that's damaging fat." And I'm going, "Where'd that come from?" And he said, "I can smell some oxidation of butterfat in here." [laughing] Oh geez, are you jivin' me!? He says, "No, you can smell that." And I can't distinguish those things, but that's the art. . . . He knew that . . . we had a pump back on the farm that beats up butterfat, and we put that pump in because it was cheaper. But we didn't know the difference [it made to butterfat]. And he's saying, "It would pay to change it out someday."

Simply by evaluating milk and curd, proficient cheesemakers can learn what a colleague is or is not doing. David Major told me that when they took Vermont Shepherd's precursor to the Pyrenees, a Basque cheesemaker knew simply by feel and taste that David and Cindy were mixing milks of different temperatures and adding rennet before bringing the milk to a uniform temperature.

Among today's post-pastoral entrepreneurs who are new to cheesemaking, the empirical science of the modest witness intent on observation represents a tool that might aid in obtaining the practical wisdom of the proficient farmer and craftsperson; it could never substitute for it.

HANDS AND OTHER TOOLS

The ACS indicates that artisanal cheese is "hands-on," but making cheese by hand does not mean making it with nothing but one's hands. Tools are required: vats or kettles in which to heat milk and cook curd; paddles or ladles for stirring; knives or other devices with which to cut curd; tools for removing curds from whey; forms or molds for shaping wheels of cheese; weights or presses for expelling more whey; fans and refrigeration to regulate the aging environment. In these tools a range of technological sophistication can be found in artisan creameries. Understanding the centrality of synesthetic reason to artisan cheesemaking helps to adjudicate a contentious question among cheesemakers: How much technology may a cheesemaker adopt and still work "by hand"?[27] Does it matter whether a pneumatic press, or free weights picked up at a yard sale, or lengths of PVC tube filled with food-grade salt are used to express whey from curd? (See fig. 17.) Matter to what—to the resulting taste and texture of the cheese? (Probably not.) To the operation's start-up costs? (Decidedly.) To the self-identity of the cheesemaker as an artisan? (Likely.)

Consider the mechanical stirring device (fig. 18). For those who have adopted this labor-saving technology, there is no turning back. Commenting on the sixteen-amp battery that powers a stirring arm over his vat, a Vermont cheesemaker told me, "I'm not going to be out here stirring curd for forty-five minutes. That's my chance to open mail." Keeping one eye on the thermometer, he can turn his attention to cheese orders, bills, and payments. For those who have experienced years of manual labor, the technological promise of alleviating bodily strain may also look increasingly appealing. Mary Keehn, founder of Cypress Grove Chevre, has introduced a number of automated technologies out of concern for her employees' physical well-being as well as a business owner's imperative to cut costs (including worker's compensation). Looking at artisanship as a mode of production—a business enterprise entailing many tasks beyond the making of cheese—puts craft practice in broader perspective.

Some who stir by hand recognize the appeal of automation. Jon Wright, who

FIG. 17. *(top)* Two means of pressing curd in Vermont, low- and high-tech. At left, free weights. At right, pneumatic press. Photos by author.

FIG. 18. *(bottom)* Mechanical stirring arm affixed to a 130-gallon vat. Photo by author.

makes Gouda on Taylor Farm in Vermont, was looking to upgrade to a mechanized agitator, explaining that hand-stirring curd in his four-thousand-pound-capacity vat (which holds up to 465 gallons of milk) ties up an hour and a half of labor each day: "While you're stirring, you're thinking about all the things that need to get done" but cannot get to while tied to the vat. Yet "one thing I really like about [hand-stirring] is that I can really watch the curd, can adjust the rate of stirring. I like it, but I could get over it!" Diana Murphy, of Dreamfarm in Wisconsin, said:

> When I make my Feta or aged cheeses, I have to be at the vat . . . and I have to get up on a stool to get in there, and I have to stir it [using a handheld paddle], sometimes for hours. And I set the stirrer down, and I go get a cup of coffee sometimes, and then you come back and the curd is kinda stuck together. So I would *like* to have a [mechanized] stirrer. But on the other hand, I see part of the beauty of what I'm doing is—everything is by hand. I don't need all this special equipment to do it. And I can still come out with a good cheese. . . . You know, if I had more milk I'd have less time, so I'd probably consider some of that equipment.

Jon and Diana appreciate stirring with a handheld paddle because it offers constant, direct engagement with the material being transformed, affording opportunity for reflexive adjustment of speed, vigor, and depth. For Diana, there is also a certain beauty in creating "a good cheese" without resorting to fancy equipment. Working "by hand" connects the mind and body; the hand represents an artisan's skill and practical knowledge. But Diana is not a romantic. There are days when she would just as soon grab a cup of coffee, but the curd will not pause with her. A thoroughly ruined batch ends up on the manure pile, representing a significant loss of capital. She realizes that the beauty of her quiet, rhythmic practice is a luxury afforded to her because her business is small. She does not wish for more milk so as to afford to invest in mechanized equipment. Rather, having more milk would mean more work in caring for more animals, resulting in less time to make cheese—thus necessitating a costly equipment upgrade. Would this compromise the beauty of what she is doing? Perhaps—though if the size of her batches or the scale of her operation grew, her aesthetic appreciation might shift to alight on another aspect of her craft.

Karen Weinberg's single favorite part of making cheese is stirring curd:

> I love to do that. I put on a tank top, so I can go up to here [tapping her upper arm]. I just love it. Sheep's milk makes really dense, soapy curd, and it's like folding in egg whites: you have to be really gentle in the beginning, and you really get a sense how the curd changes as the temperature rises and as the whey gets expelled from it. It's just a great learning experience, to get to do that. But you can't be doing anything else while you're doing that, so for the twenty minutes or forty minutes, that's it. I find it sort of therapeutic. You know, I can't answer the phone.

Karen enjoys the sensuous feel of the warm, foamy curd on her arms, an experience augmented by the custardy smell of sheep's milk. The rhythmic motion and focused attention can generate a therapeutic absorption or "flow." But Karen also regards hand-stirring as a learning experience. When artisan hands touch and feel the curd, it is as empirical as it is manipulative.

In determining artisanship, it is less important what a cheesemaker uses to stir the curd—a bare arm or a plastic paddle or a mechanical device—than how a cheesemaker determines when to begin cutting the curd and when to stop stirring it. Does one go strictly by the clock, according to a recipe? Or does one plunge hands into the vat to feel the "grip" of the curd? When "hands are in the vat, feeling the curd"—one cheesemaker's simple definition of *artisanal*—they are not just accomplishing the manipulations that industrial manufacture effects with robotic machines. Hands are evaluating the curd through touch, feel—grasping in the metaphorical sense of apprehension as well as in the physical sense of holding in one's hand.

Artisanal tools afford synesthetic evaluation of materials and reflexive response to contingent conditions—tools that afford a workmanship of risk.[28] When guided by the craftsperson's experienced assessment of material conditions, the use of mechanical equipment might count as artisanal practice. Art critic Peter Dormer writes, "Craftspeople can be defined generally as people engaged in a practical activity where they are seen to be in control of their work. They are in control by virtue of possessing personal know-how that allows them to be masters or mistresses of the available technology. . . . It is not craft as 'handcraft' that defines contemporary craftsmanship: it is craft as knowledge that empowers a maker to take charge of technology."[29] The enskillment of artisan producers includes learning to use tools in a way that extends the artisan's body into the environment.[30] Such tools include not only cheese knives or harps for cutting curd and various implements to aid in stirring, but also devices to enhance one's understanding of the contingent materiality of milk, curd, and cheese: thermometers, acidity titrators and pH meters, computerized spreadsheets for data collection. Arms, hands, and noses are other such tools that must be trained. Harry West and Nuno Domingos describe a previous generation of Portuguese cheesemakers as "folk meteorologists" who, in order to age their cheeses successfully, had to read correctly changes in the direction and humidity of prevailing winds.[31] Calling to mind Loring's tale of the nineteenth-century farmwoman, one cheesemaker said to me admiringly of an Italian colleague who could feel when milk was ready for starter cultures to be added, "His hands are [as] accurate as a thermometer."

Taking me on a tour of the Wisconsin factory he recently retrofitted to make big-wheel Emmenthaler, Bruce Workman pointed out the control panel of a computerized system that regulates milk flow and the addition of bacterial cultures. He has programmed the computer to alert him when sufficient time may have passed for milk to curdle or the curd to "cook" sufficiently—and then to pause. Nothing further happens until Bruce gets his hands in the vat and feels, smells, evaluates the curd. Once he has determined that it is time for the next step, he pushes a button and things proceed.[32] As if to head off potential complaints that the computer system might cross a line beyond artisanal fabrication into industrial, Bruce stressed that he purchased the equipment, used, from a school in Switzerland. Indeed, the handful of cheesemakers I visited who use computer-programmed equipment legitimated it by explaining, "This is what everyone in Europe uses," the implicit claim being that Europeanness itself confers artisanal authenticity on a method of manufacture.[33] Such domestic producers (including Cypress Grove Chevre) are among those most widely recognized as making artisanal cheese; the production volume that warrants and enables the purchase of imported, high-tech equipment is also what gets cheese into restaurants and specialty supermarkets nationwide.

Using a patchwork of used and new equipment, American cheesemakers are *bricoleurs,* cobbling together pieces of preindustrial and cutting-edge technologies in often surprising ways. John Putnam uses a mechanical stirrer and powerful pneumatic press, but labors to maintain a "mother" culture (similar to a sourdough starter) in lieu of buying commercial cultures and preprepared rennet. Peter Dixon uses a mechanized stirrer but a jerry-rigged weighted lever-arm (beam) press weight consisting of a plastic bottle filled with water. The ethos of the contemporary artisan is not a throwback to the past; it is a modern pastiche.[34]

Cheesemakers regard hands-on manufacture as what Loraine Daston and Peter Galison call an "epistemic virtue," a standard for practice that is embraced by a community insofar as it is understood to be an effective means of obtaining knowledge and is consistent with shared ethical values.[35] The empirical work of the hands establishes the artisanal character of a cheesemaker no less than of a cheese. The epistemic virtue of hands-on fabrication is poised to become a culinary virtue if a business is sufficiently small to pose minimal technology as a virtue of necessity, rather than as a marketing gimmick.

LEARNING THE UNTEACHABLE

With experience, the ability to move from observation through evaluation to contingent, reflexive practice—the ability to make cheese artisanally—becomes an ineffable matter of tacit knowledge. Patty Karlin told me:

> I have had any number of apprentices. Three years ago I had a lovely girl; she was nineteen years old. And for whatever reason, that girl had a feeling for the cheese, and she made the cheese perfectly all year, and she gave me the deceptive illusion that it was easy to teach cheesemaking. Wrong. Five people that followed her made *disastrous* results.... Now I have a lovely young lady who is a breadmaker. And guess what? She is number two with feeling for the cheese.... So what is that? That's artisanal. And you can't teach it. You can teach the recipes, you can teach the procedures, the molds, the cultures, all of that, and you can stand over a person and they *still* can't do it.

Nevertheless, two-thirds of commercial artisan cheesemakers report having taken a formal cheesemaking workshop.[36] What are aspiring cheesemakers hoping to get from an instructional class in something that everyone agrees is fundamentally unteachable? What are instructors hoping to give them?

"In our country," Peter Dixon lamented in a workshop I attended in 2007, "we've lost the heritage of farmstead cheesemaking, we've lost the techniques that Europeans have." They have been eroded by industrialization. However, Peter enthused, "we're regaining them" by building new communities of practice and inventing new traditions of invention. "For the less experienced cheesemakers," Dixon writes in his essay, "The Art of Cheesemaking," "traditional methods should be supported by scientific principles to the extent necessary to make consistently high-quality cheese."[37] This is what Peter teaches in his workshops: not only craft techniques—such as how much of what kind of bacterial culture to add to the milk to create a particular type of cheese—but also the scientific principles (of acidification and so forth) behind the techniques. Through such principles, he suggests, cheesemakers might gain a deeper understanding, a better grasp, not only of what is going on in the vat and in the cheese, but of why. Such knowledge might provide rationales for developing new traditions of practice and thus jump-start the craft know-how of tomorrow's artisans. For Peter, scientific knowledge of biochemical reactions, in addition to technoscience (e.g., defined-strain starter cultures, acidity testing, hygienic practice), can enhance craft practice—not, as in industrial production, substitute for it.

The 2007 workshop was hosted at Woodcock Farm, owned by Mark and Gari Fischer, who had been making farmstead cheese in Vermont for ten years. Most of my classmates had some home cheesemaking experience. They included a middle-aged farmhand working for a dairy farm that was considering on-site cheese processing; a resident of a farm cooperative in Tennessee interested specifically in raw-milk cheese; a woman who had recently moved from city to farm to give her four daughters an "alternative way of life" and was looking to be as self-sufficient as possible; two friends planning to go into the cheesemaking business together on Cape Cod; and a goat-keeping novelist. The workshop combined a morning lecture sitting around the Fischers' dining table with an overhead projector and afternoon hands-on experience in the cheese house. Peter distributed a packet of recipes and spent two days teaching us rough guidelines for interpreting and adjusting them for our own contingent conditions.

Peter's workshops do not convey the specific, situated knowledge of apprenticeship—how to make this particular cheese from the milk of this particular herd grazing a particular plot of land—so much as they aim to develop a practical understanding of how to make cheese based on reasoning grounded in technical knowledge. Artisan cheesemaking, after all, is fully embedded in an entire ecology of productive agency (though one that is itself subject to evaluation and adjustment), and Peter was well aware that he was teaching students who would go off and work in different ecologies of production.[38] Unlike the working knowledge of nineteenth-century farmwomen, the modern craft of today's cheesemakers offers an account of itself: what Paul Kindstedt advocates as a "balance between art and science."[39] Peter's task in the workshop, then, was to present scientific instruments and measures as tools akin to cheese harps and even milk and curd; to use each of these well under fluctuating conditions, one must develop a feel for them. His premise was that by gaining a more intimate understanding of what is happening in the milk and curd at the molecular level, people may more quickly learn how to read from objective data (temperature, acidity, time) suggestions for how to work with a particular day's milk. One of the first tools we were given in the workshop was a blank manufacturing record or "make sheet" for recording daily observations (and to help us remember what to observe).

Throughout the workshop, Peter imparted to us what might be understood as two forms of knowledge: theoretical or abstract scientific knowledge, or *knowing why*, and practical craft knowledge, or *knowing how*.[40] My fieldnotes summarized the knowing why: "cheesemaking basically entails developing acidity and dehydrating milk." But beyond that simple overview, my classmates and I struggled to determine what we were being told as a fixed rule, based on knowledge of why milk in general behaves in particular ways, or as a contingent strategy of knowing how to work with a particular batch of milk on a particular day. To illustrate, we spent a good bit of time discussing a chart, reproduced in table 2, differentiating types of curd.

Rennet (we learned) causes milk to coagulate at a high pH (low acidity).[41] Without the addition of rennet, soft cheeses coagulate at a lower pH, once the milk sours (low pH = high acidity; acidity = souring). This is why cottage cheese and chèvre are called acid curd cheeses; coagulation occurs when bacterial cultures produce sufficient lactic acid to lower pH to 4.6, the (isoelectric) point at which casein (milk protein) molecules change their electrical charge and aggregate with calcium ions to form a network that produces the gel-like substance that can be separated into curds and whey.

Peter's chart also conveys the message that harder cheeses (in the left-hand column) require more rennet than softer cheeses (for which the curd is "cooked" at lower temperatures to retain more water). Rennet, Peter explained, contains a proteolytic enzyme that "digests" proteins, causing them to shrink. As proteins contract, whey is expelled (this is syneresis). Despite my shaky performance in high school chemistry, I could follow: the more rennet added, the more coagulation occurs; the more coagulation, the more water is expelled; the less watery the curd, the faster it firms up and the harder the resulting cheese will be. (Note that soft-ripened cheeses such as Brie and Camembert contain less fat per ounce

TABLE 2 Differentiating types of curd

86°F–90°F		68°F–72°F
Rennet Curd	*Lactic Curd*	*Acid Curd (no or little rennet)*
	Use ½ amount of rennet "hybrid types"	
Cheddar Alpine types	Chaource, Époisses, aged chèvre	Cottage, farmers, chèvre, fromage blanc + yogurt and sour cream
Workable, durable curd		Fragile curd, holds water well

than a hard cheese like Cheddar because soft cheese contains more water than fat solids.)[42] Fine. Use rennet when making harder, aged cheeses.

But then Peter introduced another variable: ruminant species. In general, we were told, goat's and cow's milk require a similar amount of rennet, but sheep's milk requires less. This is where *milk composition* comes in. Fresh milk coming from the bodies of sheep tends to contain more casein (milk protein) and calcium (on which the enzyme acts) than either cow's or goat's milk. Hence, Peter told us, if you are milking sheep, use less rennet than a recipe (likely written with cow's milk in mind) calls for. This was an important tip for the American cheesemakers who, unfettered by artisan customs, let alone bureaucratically regulated regional recipes, may "pick and choose among traditional methods," as one cheesemaker put it to me, and tend to experiment with cross-milk hybrids: a Camembert made from sheep's rather than cow's milk, or a fresh-ripened pyramid of cow's-milk cheese in a French goat-cheese style. Okay, Peter was saying. *But you may need to adjust the recipe.* "Oh!" one of my classmates breathed audibly, apparently gaining a fresh understanding of a past mishap. Knowing *why* can thus inform knowing *how*.

Another key variable is the time at which curd is cut into pieces: sooner after initial coagulation (while softer) or later (while firmer). Many of us in North America tend to think of time as an objective measure. Bake for 35 minutes, a brownie recipe will say. We might remove the pan from the oven a minute or two before or a minute or two after the 35-minute mark, but that 35 minutes is an objective guide; we interpret variation either as a matter of how well calibrated our oven thermostat is, or as a matter of taste (aiming for fudgy or cakelike brownies?). And so it might seem with cheese. After allowing bacterial cultures to dissolve for 20 minutes (a recipe might say), add the rennet; 50 minutes after adding rennet, cut the curd to release whey. But Peter described *playing* with time—with the timing of various steps in the cheesemaking process—as if time were a subjective rather than an objective tool. Peter taught us to create a temporal instrument particular to a specific batch of cheese, calibrated from the initial pH of the milk—which, Peter instructed, one should always ascertain at the beginning of each batch using a pH meter ("easily purchased from a scientific supply company"). Milk pH from the same herd can fluctuate from one day or week to the next owing to pasture conditions or herd health. If you start with a lower-acid (high-pH) milk than you usually work with, Peter suggested, to balance things out you might add more bacterial culture than usual or wait a longer time before adding the rennet, or both. He thus posed the craft of cheesemaking not only as knowing *how* to intervene in (without overdetermining) organic processes, but also as knowing *when* to proceed from one intervention to the next. Gaining a feel for the curd engages a sense of temporality as much as tactility.

My classmates began to look worried. How much more culture? How much longer to wait? This seemed to be a matter of knowing-how for which one must develop a feel; it is another kind of qualitative calculation. Scientific language and technique are put in the service of craft: the reasoned, skilled ability to work with natural variation under fluctuating conditions toward a predetermined goal. It is one thing to make cheese when it is 40°F outside in April, and another thing when it is 90°F and humid in July: the milk responds differently to cultures and rennet and touch. As Peter described it, the objective measure of pH can suggest to the cheesemaker how to play with variables—time, temperature, size into which the curd is cut—to forestall potential problems. He presented this technique as one that scientific knowing-why might successfully guide in the place of lost traditions of knowing-how.

This became clearer in the afternoon when the class moved to the cheese room to make four wheels of Appenzeller, a hard rennet-curd cheese. As instructed, we duly noted the time at which the rennet was added, set aside the paddle stirrer, and waited for flocculation to occur, that instant when milk suddenly solidifies into curd. Gently, Peter rested a plastic scoop atop the warm milk. Periodically someone gave the scoop a spin. At some point, Peter instructed, the scoop would no longer spin freely—a sign that the milk had reached the flocculation point. It is pretty cool to think about milk shape-shifting from liquid to solid, as if magically, and we were excited to identify the precise moment. Once we agreed that there was sufficient resistance against the scoop, many fingers were thrust into the curd as we all wanted to produce a clean break for ourselves (see fig. 19). The time was again noted. It turns out that this interval we had just clocked, the flocculation time, was to become a unit of measure specific only to this batch to determine how long the curd should continue to set before being cut. Rather than go by a standard recipe (e.g., add rennet and wait thirty minutes before cutting), we had just customized the procedure to suit this milk on this day by applying a general algorithm. For this cheese (and other Alpine-style hard cheeses) the set time is three times the flocculation time. With a soft-ripened cheese such

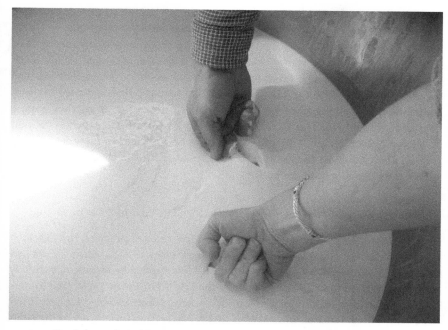

FIG. 19. Checking to feel whether the curd has set. Photo by author.

as Camembert, for which the curd would not be cut at all but gently ladled into molds, the wait would be six times the flocculation time.[43]

However, on the second day of the workshop, when we reconvened to make Saint-Paulin, a semisoft cheese, Peter made an adjustment to his adjustment of the recipe. Although this recipe gave a fixed time to allow the curd to set—thirty-five minutes after flocculation—Peter went again with his customizing algorithm. But today he added more rennet proportionate to milk volume than he did the day before because, he explained, it had taken longer to reach flocculation *than is usually to be expected.* Peter commented with a wry smile (and to the consternation of some students), "It's a subjective thing. It's just a recipe. I can do what I want!" Subjectivity and objectivity are revealed to be as figure to ground; which comes into focus as relevant is a matter of the epistemic commitment of the knower.[44] The trick (my classmates were increasingly realizing) is to know what one wants to do. How the cheesemaker decides on variations in wait time or amount of rennet or size of curd cut results not simply from repeat practice but from reasoning based on intimate, even intuitive knowledge of one's milk in the context of its ecology of production.

For the beginning cheesemaker, hearing what is entailed in tacit knowledge so explicitly articulated—or, from another angle, having the seemingly objective revealed to be largely subjective—can be daunting. My fellow students, who may have hoped to come away with some tried-and-true recipes, perhaps a formula or two, appeared a bit unnerved by Peter's seemingly cavalier approach. At one level, Peter was displaying the relaxed mien of a craftsperson, a stance that Michael Herzfeld associates with the "nonchalant skill of one who does not need to think about what he is doing in order to do it successfully."[45] But at another level, a couple of students seemed to have come with an unrealistic expectation that acquiring proven recipes and a few tips might be sufficient to move seamlessly from kitchen hobbyist to commercial cheesemaker. In the cheese room, I witnessed the following quiet exchange:

> *Danielle to Nathan:* "So he followed the recipe?"
> *Nathan to Danielle:* raised brows and wobbled hand to indicate, "kind of, sort of."

If by *recipe* Danielle and Nathan had in mind rules of practice, in craft such guides are better understood as what Michael Polanyi calls "rules of art" or maxims: "Maxims cannot be understood, still less applied by anyone not already possessing a good practical knowledge of the art."[46] For Peter, a scientific understanding of acidity is more of a maxim for practice than an objective condition to be confronted. It is not the case that the skilled artisan has mastered the rules of practice (the recipe); instead he has become comfortable with the rules of art. As Patty Karlin said to me, "My definition of *artisanal* would be loving attention to detail. I think that when you oversee every step of the production, that's when love develops."[47] On this view, making cheese artisanally entails thinking and feeling like an artisan, working with a confidence born of personal commitment as well as experience.

That experience emerges as much from accident as from design. Each afternoon in the cheese room, Peter tested four times for pH, beginning with the milk as it was poured into the vat and ending with a piece of curd trimmed from a freshly pressed wheel of cheese, recording the numbers on the make sheet that we were given (fig. 20). To do the tests he borrowed Mark's digital pH probe. When Peter first tested the fresh milk he had picked up from Lisa Kaiman's farm, it gave a reading of 6.83. That morning, Peter had told us that if the initial pH of a vat of milk reads at 6.8 or higher, this indicates something is wrong with an animal in the dairy herd, *or*—he amended in the afternoon—something is wrong with the probe. Mark recalibrated the temperamental probe and got a reading of 6.73. "That's the one I like!" exclaimed Peter, who *now* tells us, in probable hyperbole, "I recalibrate my pH meter about six times a day." So much for the seemingly objective numbers that we had taken to be the scientific basis of beginning an artisanal batch of cheese. My classmates exchanged more worried looks. Peter recommended washing the probe in distilled water.

FIG. 20. Peter Dixon holding a vial of indicator solution in preparation for conducting an acid test using the acidometer on the right. Photo by author.

In the end, I discerned in the workshop a kind of *technical intimacy* with scientific instruments and principles. Herzfeld introduced the notion of "cultural intimacy" to describe the sometimes rueful self-awareness a people may share among themselves, but deny to outsiders, about the idiosyncrasies of their own cultural sensibilities.[48] Behind the presentation of authoritative knowledge conveyed in Dixon's classes and academic-sounding manuals is a shared, tacit understanding among practitioners (one that may be denied to safety inspectors or licensing regulators or other outsiders) that scientific testing (of pH or temperature) in artisanal cheesemaking may be more suggestive than definitive. Marcia Barinaga, a fledgling cheesemaker with a professional science background, explained that sometimes when taking a pH reading, "you look at it and say, 'I think there's something wrong with the pH meter. My gut tells me this cheese is right and I don't trust my pH meter.' You have to be *ready* to not trust your pH meter." Measuring pH is as tacit and embodied as is feeling the grip of the curd. Thus do science and art come together in craft.

Artisan cheesemaking turns out to have much in common with running a series of laboratory-based scientific experiments. After all, the bench work of scientific experimentation relies not only on principles of scientific method but also on the sort of practical knowing (e.g., how to measure a fluid, use a pipette, read the contents of a Petri dish or a microscope slide) more commonly associated with craft.[49] For this reason, it is insufficient for one scientist to write down the recipe of an experiment to enable another to verify her results by replicating the work.[50] Tacit knowledge is required to do any work that is difficult to convey via a formulaic set of instructions. "But this scares some cheesemakers," Marcia conceded, mentioning her friend Barbara, who taught herself to make cheese from a book that a friend translated from French. Barbara (whom I also interviewed) is skeptical of pH readings—not just the devices that take readings—and thinks of what she does as an art and not at all as a science. People who are not trained in scientific practice, who are excluded from scientists' technical intimacy, tend to be committed to the idea of science as totally rational, objective—untainted by the subjective inclinations of the scientist. When it is revealed to them that scientific work is not sealed off from subjective experience and interpretation (or in other contexts, from political influence), laypersons may dismiss scientific expertise as useless or irrelevant. Here the epistemic virtue of art, presented as the alternative to technoscience, is in announcing that we are on subjective ground.

In fact, a scientific understanding of milk chemistry is not requisite to making cheese well. Nor does knowing more science lead seamlessly to new and improved ways of making cheese. Most commercial artisan cheesemakers do not understand much of the scientific information presented in Peter Dixon's workshops. In 2007, Laini Fondiller characterized herself as a cheesemaker to me by declaring, "I'm a hack." When I asked why, she replied, "I don't use a pH meter. I'm always fiddling." She was working on being more consistent, she told me, but even without acidity testing she generally makes cheese successfully because "I know my curd." A while earlier she had bought a pH meter. "I took a reading," she said. "It didn't mean anything to me." A young cheesemaker friend explained that using the pH meter requires practice, and that if she began using it she would figure out what it was telling her. In the years since, that has turned out to be the case. By 2012, Laini had purchased a new pH meter and taken classes on understanding pH values. "I still observe the curd," she wrote to me in an e-mail, "but the pH meter now makes me feel more confident and I enjoy watching the consistency of the batches and taking the time to make more notes." After more than twenty years at her craft, Laini is acquiring a new sort of tacit knowledge.[51]

What, then, might aspiring artisans get from formal workshops? Tracking pH readings and exercising a working knowledge of milk chemistry might shave off months, even years, from the process of acquiring and incorporating synesthetic reason. But something more ineffable is to be gained here as well.

Learning the science of crafting cheese can appeal to cheesemakers' sense of wonder. *Magic* is a word I heard often to describe the transformation of milk into cheese. Heat some milk, add a little of this, a pinch of that, stir it around—"and the magic happens," said one of my classmates. And Patty told me, "What happens in the aging process that I find thrilling—oh, I find a lot of things thrilling about the aging process! To me it's pure sorcery and witchcraft and everything else." Since today's science offers authoritative knowledge on the workings of nature, scientific tools promise craftspeople a window onto that magic, not to gain technological mastery over it but so they might gain another level of appreciation for the ecologies of production of which they are but a part. For some American cheesemakers, science seems less an instrument to deploy than a post-pastoral medium through which to experience the wonder of nature.

When artisans take pride in working with forces of nature, the epistemic virtue of scientific knowledge contributes to the making of a craftsperson driven by a desire not only to perform better but also to know better. For post-pastoral artisans, science would seem to tap into a folk theory of magic; it enhances a sense of wonder about the natural world in an era that has moved from the counterculture of back to the land to the cyberculture of tracking data using computerized spreadsheets to get back to nature.

A TASTE FOR CRAFT: THE CHALLENGE OF AN UNFINISHED COMMODITY

Thus far this chapter has demonstrated how "cheese is made in the vat," a maxim Peter Dixon uses to call attention to how a recipe must be adapted to fit contingencies. But cheese is made not only in the vat. Having begun on dairy farms, cheesemaking extends beyond the make room and aging facilities into the marketplace. Taking the market into account is essential to a general theory of craft. Extrapolating from cheesemaking, I regard craft as

- beginning with technical knowledge of and direct engagement with raw materials;
- hands-on in an empirical as well as a manipulative sense;
- engaging synesthetic reason;
- expressing appreciation for the process of workmanship;
- engaging social as well as practical knowledge embedded in traditions of practice (a craftsperson is not an auteur);
- producing well-functioning objects with utilitarian value;
- producing nonstandardized objects whose natural variation adds aesthetic and commercial value to the objects, yet that conform recognizably to a pre-imagined form.

To grasp how running an artisan business contributes to the crafting of cheese, it is useful to consider how neither practice is ever fully rational, playing out a premeditated script, but nor are the actions of artisanship and economies of sentiment universally instinctual. Instead, artisanship is guided by a third field of action: the habituated.[52] Artisan cheesemaking's synesthetic, integrated way of thinking-doing is akin to what French theorists have called *habitus:* an embodied set of habituated dispositions required for social proficiency in a culturally (or professionally) specific field of relations.[53] An artisan habitus is less a matter of ability than of sensibility. It combines a synesthetic grasp of the materials with an ethic of doing a job well for its own sake.

In developing Marcel Mauss's notion of habitus as culturally acquired faculty, Pierre Bourdieu borrowed craft-related terms—tact, dexterity, savoir-faire—to make sense of how the world of social relations permeates an individual's sense of self-identity and possibility.[54] That is, Bourdieu worked to understand how social norms could be embodied, incorporated into worldviews that may be experienced as objective reality but are in fact "sedimented history." For Bourdieu, individuals are socially conditioned but not in a cookie-cutter fashion; there is room for individual improvisation in our actions and self-presentations. In his interpretation, *habitus* names a reflexive feel for strategic action under contingent circumstance. The practice of everyday life sounds a lot like the artisanal making of cheese.

Moving away from cheesemakers' own terminology—art, science—I suggest that an understanding of craft practice can further benefit from Bourdieu's social theory because, in regarding everyday life as a kind of craft, his theory asks us to consider the influence of artisans' lives outside the cheese room on their embodied practice within it. Because artisanal proficiency develops from a habituated, practical knowing-how that entails social as well as technical knowledge, in order to understand *techne* (the practical knowledge of making or doing), we must understand the technologist (craftsperson, artist, designer, engineer) as a person engaged in relationships and embedded in social hierarchies. Artisanship, after all, emerges in an industrial society through struggles with values.

This perspective sheds light on an interesting paradox in the construction of artisanal quality in American cheese. From the ACS definition at the beginning of this chapter, it might seem that the less technology and technoscience used, the greater the claim of a cheese to artisanal status and the higher its cultural capital. But cheeses requiring the least technology—fresh cheeses that can be made in one's kitchen such as chèvre, mozzarella, and farmers' cheese—do not enjoy the cultural status of, say, Tarentaise, John Putnam's Alpine-style cheese made using a mechanical stirrer and pneumatic press, or the Pawlet that Peter Dixon makes for Consider Bardwell Farm using a mechanized cheese harp to finish cutting the curd. There are a few reasons for this. Use of mechanized technologies is not readily apparent to the average consumer from the taste or appearance of a naturally aged cheese; neither do producers advertise it. Moreover, since fresh cheeses require less labor, they are priced more affordably, making them available to a wider consuming public.

Meanwhile, higher-status cheeses that might seem more artisanal are not necessarily made by the most experienced and proficient artisans. Among cheesemakers I interviewed who seemed most thoroughly to embody the artisan habitus described in this chapter were several who make the most everyday styles of cheese. They include second- and third-generation cheesemakers, such as Joe Widmer, who inherited their craft from first-generation American artisans who worked in a different culinary landscape.

Consider Michael Scheps. The setting for our interview—his corner office in the aluminum-siding warehouse that houses Maplebrook Farm Mozzarella in Bennington, Vermont—could not have been more different from the picturesque farmstead operations I visited elsewhere in the state. Michael took me into the windowless room where he and his staff stretch mozzarella. To hand-stretch one-pound balls of cheese, Michael's equipment consists of a commercial sink, a stainless steel bowl atop a milk crate, a wooden spatula, and a tap from which 165°F water runs. That is it. When Michael gets going, he can stretch more than a hundred balls of cheese in an hour. To a casual observer, it might seem like rote activity. Even Michael, who called mozzarella a "mainstream cheese," seemed a little unsure of whether he was part of an American artisanal cheese movement.[55] But listen to Michael—who learned to stretch cheese from his father (a former cheese factory owner who, when Michael was growing up, molded mozzarella at home for domestic consumption), who in turn had learned from his father (who ran a cheese factory in New Jersey)—offer an impassioned, firsthand account:

I really enjoy making cheese. You learn a lot through making mistakes, and sometimes you agonize over why something's not coming out right or consistent. And when you solve it, it really means a lot. When you figure it out and you really work hard—you put your heart into it. Everybody that makes cheese wants it to be the best, not only for themselves but for other people. . . . When you put a piece of cheese down, you put a piece of yourself down. . . .

Sometimes you agonize over milk and the time of the year and solids and fats. And the more you learn, the more you learn how technical it is and that milk's not just milk. Milk comes from an animal and animals get stressed in high heat and how is it affecting your product and what can you do to your formulation to adjust to what's happening with the milk?

I can remember my father. He was taught by my grandfather, an old-timer. My father's facility was high-tech and had like three lab techs [and] a certified lab. My father would be tasting the milk, like a wine. And I was young, I said, "Dad, why don't you just do like everybody else, bring samples to the lab, get a reading of what it is?" He wouldn't buy that lot. He's like, "You need to know. You need to know your milk tanks—smell the milk, *smell* it!" [Michael inhales deeply] You can tell— you get that instinct in you. When you're young, you don't buy that—but [now] I do. I am constantly with my nose. Even when I'm molding cheese or stretching it. I'm always bringing it up [he draws his hands up to his face, sniffing]—you get a flavor, you get a feel. And then you don't know it until all of a sudden something's not right, something smells different—the thing that's gonna trigger it off. It becomes an art, I guess.

Just as I was about to ask Michael to walk me through how he takes a lump of curd and transforms it into a silky ball of mozzarella, Al Scheps walked in, stopping by to visit his son. Al agreed to demo. "That's beautiful stuff, Michael," he said appreciatively as he worked the steamy *pasta filata* with his callused bare hands.[56] Part of an artisan's sensibility, as another cheesemaker put it to me, is that "you *want* to have your hands on every batch, in some form. You *want* to be sensorially involved in each batch." Al and Michael Scheps revealed to me the emotional element of craft habitus that Patty Karlin articulated above, helping to explain how the most engaged and experienced artisan may make the humblest variety of cheese.[57]

Consumers are willing to pay upwards of thirty dollars per pound for an aged cheese, and cheesemakers can dream of making a viable business from hand-crafting it, because people are not simply buying a source of nutrition for thirty dollars per pound; they are buying the adventure and pleasure of taste, the status of connoisseurship, the pride of supporting a local business or the institution of small-scale farming. As a corollary, producers are not just making and selling cheese, either. In Michael's words—"When you put a piece of cheese down, you put a piece of yourself down"—I hear him drawing a parallel between crafting cheese for commercial trade and crafting social relations through feeding someone. It *means* something to make and share food. Cheesemakers such as Michael want to extend into the commercial realm food's capacity to serve as a medium for social relations, relations in which affection and power are tightly braided.

As Bourdieu's work suggests, artisan habitus is shaped by institutional structures, including economic ones.[58] Craft forms and artisans' dispositions are forged in relation to a dynamic consumer market. (The regulatory frameworks concerning the health and safety of commercial cheese will be considered in the next chapter.) Noting that craft objects are commonly contrasted to art objects by virtue of their utility, Howard Becker urges us to explore how utility—that is, usefulness to some particular person or persons—is never self-evident but, like craft skill, emerges from customary aesthetic and evaluative standards that are spoken of in terms of taste.[59] With artisanal foods, this is taste both in the sense of *having* taste (social distinction) and also what is *tasted* (organoleptic, sensory experience).[60] Informed by social conventions embedded in a shared political economy, craft and taste help shape each other.

The successful commercial practice of a craft includes educating a consuming public to discern and appreciate the variation (within reason) produced by a workmanship of risk.[61] John Putnam spoke to this when I asked what he wished consumers better understood about his Vermont farmstead cheese:

> It's a natural, organic process. . . . If it's a cold but wet week, or a hot but dry week, the flavor changes, the texture changes—the cheese changes. Many people, in this country, anyway, think that everything out there should be Kraft Singles, it should all taste the same way, be the same thing every day. But that's not the way life is. Do you wake up in a good mood every morning? Do you love your husband every single day? . . . Some people have an appreciation—they want an "October" cheese, or a "September" cheese, or a cheese that's aged eight months. They've learned the difference and what they like. It's like the old ladies in France [shopping for produce], picking out "this one, and that one, but not that one" [he points with his finger at an imaginary stall]—because they see a difference! It's not all the same stuff to them.

American consumers, he suggested, need to be trained to see (and taste) the difference that seasonal dairying and artisanal production make. Only then can they develop preferences that are true to their own palate and pleasure.

This sort of taste education helps to cultivate regular consumers of artisanal goods, but as I witnessed at Peter Dixon's workshop, it is also crucial in training producers. Back at the Fischers' (our workshop hosts') house, Peter extolled the virtues of raw-milk cheese and natural variation among batches, saying, "That's what consumers value." In "The Art of Cheesemaking," he writes: "In the same way that the set of six mugs our neighborhood potter made for us are slightly different in form and appearance, my wheels of cheese are different in size and coloring of the rinds. I believe that it is precisely this quality that distinguishes artisanal cheese from its industrial, mass-produced counterpart."[62] One of my classmates, bearing out John Putnam's complaint, interjected that she had heard the opposite, that what consumers are looking for is consistency. Peter backpedaled to acknowledge that thanks to industrialization, consistency is expected of most American cheese, but "not twenty-dollar cheese."

At this point, Mark Fischer called out from the next room that variation stemming from material or environmental conditions is one thing, but "not variations from poor skills, which is what most American variation is." He expressed annoyance with cheesemakers trying to pass off genuine mistakes as variations caused by seasonality or *terroir*, the notion that elements of the place of food production can materially influence its taste (see chapter 7).[63] A workmanship of risk, he was reminding us, does not mean that anything goes; artisans are still after a consistent, recognizable product. Artisanal method—hands-on, minimal technology, attention to the tradition of the cheesemaker's art, having a synesthetic feel for the material—does not in itself guarantee quality.

Tom Gilbert, quoted at the beginning of this chapter, described "the main job of a cheesemaker" as "to be looking for perfection," to produce a batch of cheese that matches the vision "in your own mind" of what it can and should be.[64] Such a vision aids craft when it draws on collective, social knowledge. During lunch at the workshop, we sampled and discussed cheeses made by class participants. One of my classmates unwrapped a slouchy pile of wet, bloomy-rind cheese she had made in her kitchen. It was presented as "Chaource." This did not look like Chaource, a cylindrical, densely fluffy cheese from the Champagne region of France. Peter helpfully diagnosed a moisture problem and suggested strategies for overcoming it. Then Mark asked whether the maker had ever had (tasted, seen, cut into) "a real Chaource." She had not. Sometime later, Mark made a speech about how important it is to seek out real instances of the cheese one is interested in making. Want to make an Asiago? Go to a good cheese shop and buy all the Asiago they carry. Although none of us would or could replicate precisely another Asiago, he advised us to have a clear picture in our minds (and taste on our tongues) of what we wanted to make. The beginning cheesemaker is not simply following a recipe, after all, but tinkering with a recipe to generate as consistent a form as possible. Not incidentally, the Italian word for cheese, *formaggio*, like the French *fromage*, comes from the Latin *forma*, meaning "form."[65]

In craft, the image of perfection is not a platonic form but a customary form. A trained palate helps in grasping the customary form of a cheese type or style. The tradition of the cheesemaker's art is a sedimented social history that, in the United States, allows for improvisation but does not escape the structuring structure (or the formative form) of the retail marketplace. If a cheese is named or described as a Chaource, it should not more closely resemble a Robiola. Then again, cheesemakers trade in different marketplaces. I once bought cheese labeled "Feta" at a farmers' market in rural Maine; the soft balls of fresh, pepper-coated goat's-milk cheese suspended in olive oil spread nicely on crackers, but the cheese might not have fared well in a retail shop as "Feta," by which name consumers might expect a firmer, even crumbly cheese with a piquant bite from being aged in salty brine. Vendors at farmers' markets enjoy the latitude to offer samples of cheese gone slightly (but not harmfully) awry; customers who like the taste can buy it—it hardly matters if the cheese only vaguely meets the promise of its label. In my local cheese shop I have sampled unusually colored or shaped batches of otherwise familiar cheese (the outcome of unanticipated mold growth or an error in manufacturing) labeled as a one-off with a play on the name of the intended though not-quite-realized cheese. Producers who lack close relations with their retail clients or who sell through third-party distributors are less able to market imperfect batches and thus are particularly pressured to maintain consistency from batch to batch. Consistency is the most difficult skill to master in artisanship.

The structured disposition of taste shapes artisanship in several ways. Exposure (through foreign travel or dining in high-end restaurants) to a variety of European cheeses, served at their peak condition, can contribute to the formation of an artisan habitus—as would growing up in a family where mozzarella was made in the kitchen alongside pasta. In this way, people who come to cheesemaking from previous professional careers (and higher standards of living) might have an advantage over farmers who turn to cheesemaking in knowing what the market wants. But the funkiest cheeses have a select market. While cheesemakers might wish to play with mixed-species milk or let grow whatever fungi want to grow on a mold-ripened cheese, income needs may require a more conservative approach. Some of the most experimental cheesemakers, such as Laini Fondiller, maintain quite a modest living standard. Scaling up to reach larger markets means producing quantities of cheese with consistent quality, in familiar varieties with broad market appeal—not the cheeses, perhaps, that artisans might in an ideal world prefer to make. But at the same time, there are cheesemakers such as Linda Dimmick who remain committed to making "everyday" cheese of more moderate speed. Charlie Parant, who makes (for different markets) both natural-rind and block cheese (such as Jack) at his family-run West River Creamery in Vermont, put this sentiment in terms of the craft/art divide, telling me in an interview:

> I don't feel that only people that can afford twenty-dollar-a-pound cheese should be able to eat well. I like making the Jack for that reason. It's a simple cheese, it's very mild, but you know it's good, whole milk—raw milk. And that's quite different from a lot of the cheesemakers. I don't consider what I do an art, I guess probably because I have a science background [teaching high-school biology], and if I were going to make art I'd make it out of something that lasts longer than cheese! . . . I'm making a product for somebody to eat; I don't want them to hang it on the wall.

When, as Paul Kindstedt suggests, the artisan cheesemaker works to "strike the right balance" between domination of and collaboration with the organic agencies of fermentation and mold development, finding this equilibrium poses a particular challenge when, as in the United States, the scale must be calibrated to a consumer market that is taken with artisanal exceptionalism while it also demands a reliably consistent and safe product.[66] When cheesemakers invite consumers to visit their farms, technical intimacy with pH meters and computer databases is not likely to be displayed on the tour. However, even when a cheese's artistic merits and artisanal mode of manufacture are marketed as defining features, its scientific basis remains. It is to the regulatory and practical constraints on craft practice, aimed at ensuring the health and safety of artisanal cheese, that I turn in the next chapter.

6

Microbiopolitics

"It is an irony of cheesemaking that bacteria are both your best friends and your worst enemies."
—HENRY TEWKSBURY, *THE CHEESES OF VERMONT*

"A fair amount of learning about cheese involves embracing the desirability of mold."
—GORDON EDGAR, *CHEESEMONGER: LIFE ON THE WEDGE*

Cheese is fermented and ripened by the metabolic action of microorganisms—bacteria, yeasts, and molds—on the proteins, carbohydrates, and fats in milk. To make cheese is to cultivate a microbial ecosystem, or, as microbiologist Rachel Dutton views it, "every cheese is an experiment in microbial ecology."[1] Working in her Harvard laboratory, Dutton, a Bauer fellow in systems biology, is sampling and sequencing the genetic material embedded in the rinds of naturally ripened cheeses (including several made by people in this book) with the aim of developing a new taxonomy of cheese types based on their bacterial and fungal populations. In studying the surface rind of cheese, her goal is to generate general knowledge about the behavior of microbes in complex communities.

When I visited her lab, Dutton acknowledged that when she first invited domestic cheesemakers to participate in her study, she did so nervously. As a microbiologist, she is accustomed to encountering a public squeamish about microorganisms, even addicted to hand sanitizer, so she was pleased to find cheesemakers curious to learn what she would find on their cheeses. "They've been very open to new information," she said—for example, that what is happening on the surface of ripening cheeses "is more complicated than what they've been told." That sticky, pungently smelly surface of a smear-ripened cheese results from more complex interactions than the singular presence of the well-known *Brevibacterium linens*. Dutton said that cheesemakers appreciate microbial complexity "because of all the trouble-shooting they have to do" in working from one batch or season to the next. Artisans' interest in cheese microbiology makes sense in light of a post-pastoral desire to collaborate with the organic agencies of nature.

Consumers are also showing an interest in cheese microbes. The spring 2011 issue of *Culture: The Word on Cheese* featured an eight-page photo spread of highly magnified, aestheticized images of bacteria and fungi that Dutton had sampled from cheese rinds and cultured in petri dishes. A caption explained, "Bacteria and fungi growing together make up a microbial ecosystem, and as the microbes grow they contribute to the flavor, smell, and texture of the ripening cheese."[2] How might we understand the apparent uncanny thrill in recognizing, as one journalist puts it, that "When you eat such a cheese, you are eating an evolving ecosystem. There are billions of bugs in every bite"?[3]

After all, the microbial life within a cheese—indeed, the microbial life that *constitutes* a cheese—may harbor peril as well as gustatory promise. The magazine's celebration of cheese microbes is all the more striking considering that the issue was published just months after federal agents, on October 21, 2010, locked down the Estrella Family Creamery in Washington State, suspending trade of Kelli Estrella's award-winning, raw-milk cheeses. A federal judge ordered the seizure after the Estrellas refused to initiate a total recall of their cheese, a recall the U.S. Food and Drug Administration (FDA) deemed warranted in light of the "persisting presence" of the potentially pathogenic bacterium *Listeria monocytogenes* in one of their aging rooms. Two months later, in December 2010, federal officials in eastern Washington demanded that Sally Jackson upgrade the well-worn cheesemaking equipment she had been using on her farm for thirty years. Unable to afford the required modifications, Jackson retired after the U.S. Centers for Disease Control and Prevention (CDC) demonstrated a link between her raw-milk cheese and eight cases of illness caused by enterohemolytic *Escherichia coli* infection.

For the FDA, such cases (and there have been others) provide a warrant for revisiting cheese safety and the regulation of cheese made from raw, unpasteurized milk.[4] The very quality that gives food-safety officials pause about raw-milk cheese—it is teeming with an uncharacterized diversity of microbial life—makes handcrafting it a rewarding challenge for artisan producers and consuming it particularly desirable for some eaters. Whereas the FDA views raw-milk cheese as a biohazard, potentially riddled with "bad" bugs, fans see it as the inverse: a tasty, traditional food made safe by the activity of "good" microorganisms. (In microbiological terms, the potential for benign microbes to outcompete pathogens for access to proteins and fats in milk is based on the principle of competitive exclusion.)

Why is the raw-milk cheese debate so often framed as an all-or-nothing proposition? How can raw-milk cheese be declared one of the most beautiful and perfect foods that humans have known, and *also* an inherently dangerous threat to public health? Eating raw-milk products, says FDA director John Sheehan, is "like playing Russian roulette with your health," while a cheesemonger in Rhode Island has blogged, "There is a *je ne sais quoi* about raw milk cheese. The flavors . . . are more pastoral, have a touch more earthiness to them, more nuanced in flavor profiles and just, seemingly, more vibrant."[5] Others celebrate raw milk's potential to convey health benefits through its supposed "probiotic" aspect.[6] The polarization of the raw-milk cheese debate hinges, I argue, on contrasting ideas about what our relations as humans should be to the ubiquitous activity of microorganisms that inhabit our social worlds.

In this chapter I analyze contemporary debates over food quality through the lens of *microbiopolitics,* a term I introduce to make sense of governmental and grassroots efforts to recognize and manage human encounters with the organic agencies of bacteria, yeasts, fungi, and viruses. Extending Michel Foucault's theory of biopolitics to describe the modern exercise of governmental power over a citizenry through indirect control over sexual and reproductive behaviors within a population, *microbiopolitics* characterizes means of social regulation carried out through control of microbial life.[7] It entails creating and popularizing categories of microscopic biological agents (*Penicillium, E. coli, L. monocytogenes,* HIV, etc.); evaluating such agents through an anthropocentric lens (are particular microbes "good" or "bad" for humans?); and promulgating appropriate human behaviors and practices in view of our interrelationships with microorganisms that enable (or possibly derail) human digestion, infection, and inoculation.[8] Cheese, like milk, is a thoroughly microbiopolitical artifact.[9]

In the wake of the Estrella seizure, the American Cheese Society (ACS) issued a position statement "On the Importance of Artisan, Farmstead, and Specialty Cheese," declaring, "Dairy farmers deserve the right to make cheese from raw or pasteurized milk as a viable way to protect their livelihood, support local economies, add diversity to the nation's diet, and preserve long-standing methods and traditions."[10] With that right comes an obligation to make cheese as safely as possible. A significant repercussion of the Estrella case and others like it is that it casts a shadow on one of the perceptions of the local food movement: that food produced artisanally by small-scale producers is (or should be) inherently healthier and safer than industrial food. However, as this chapter will demonstrate, when it comes to food safety, nothing is inherent.

For one thing, food safety is political. Just as unprecedented numbers of new artisan creameries were opening for business, funding was drained from the FDA budget during the first decade of this century when the Bush administration dismantled much of the nation's regulatory infrastructure, from oil to banking to food safety. According to one Vermont cheesemaker, his state's FDA office closed, leaving just one understaffed office to inspect all of Maine, upper New Hampshire and Vermont, and upstate New York. Under President Obama, the FDA has stepped up its inspection and enforcement regimen in line with legislative work to pass the 2010 Food Safety Modernization Act, which increases the frequency of routine federal inspections and gives the FDA new authority to mandate the sort of recall that the Estrellas refused to initiate. In April 2010, the FDA launched a nationwide effort to inspect more than one hundred cheesemaking facilities, of all types and sizes, with emphasis on microbiological testing for *Listeria monocytogenes* (about which more below).[11] Systemic regulatory disinterest has given way to intense scrutiny, an attention that some small-scale food producers interpret as reflecting the current Administration's political will to demonstrate efficacy through prosecuting violations of codes that during the Bush administration had been virtually ignored.[12] While cheesemakers are not generally opposed to regulation per se—no one is more concerned to avoid sickening consumers than artisanal commercial food producers—many are nervous that the push to reform food safety may exacerbate the burden placed on small-scale producers by one-size-fits-all regulations designed for industrial scales and methods.

The recent shuttering of artisan creameries in light of safety concerns does more than signal renewed political will for federal regulation of commerce; it brings into focus how post-pastoral politics operate at a microscopic level. Taking shape within regulatory frames of action, ecologies of production are populated by microbial agents that both challenge and enable human intentions. Care of the cheese, care of the animals, care of the land, and care of the consuming human self—all must consider the microbe.

Cheese microbiopolitics extends beyond the negotiation of government policy and its impact on a handful of food producers to frame the (polarizing) terms through which American producers and consumers think about risk and seek to minimize it. The revival of artisanal cheesemaking in the United States reveals a clash between a regulatory order bent on taming nature through forceful eradication of microbial contaminants—a *Pasteurian* microbiopolitics—and a *post-Pasteurian,* post-pastoral alternative committed to working in selective partnership with microscopic organisms, figured as agents of a nature that is not fully objectified and never fully separate from human enterprise. Whereas a Pasteurian approach treats the natural world as dangerously unruly and in need of human control, a post-Pasteurian view emphasizes the potential for cooperation among agencies of nature and culture, microbes and humans. And while a Pasteurian assessment of cheese quality harnesses technoscience to achieve predictability and standardization, post-Pasteurian investments in quality accept some degree of variability in embracing the potential of a raw-milk cheese to express exceptional, distinctive flavors.

After reviewing the history of cheese safety and its regulation in the United States, I demonstrate how a conceptual opposition between "nature" and "culture" has informed food safety regulation, including the rule that requires all raw-milk cheese to be aged a minimum of sixty days, while showing how cheese's organic variability defies easy categorization. In the second half of the chapter, I return to the practice of making cheese to consider what cheesemakers do—or could do—to manage microbes through managing the cheesemaking environment. Reporting from a workshop on risk-reduction practices I attended at the Vermont Institute of Artisan Cheese (VIAC), I discuss how consultants aim to impart to cheesemakers a scientific understanding of microbial activity that might better enable them to make cheese *safely* as well as *artisanally*. Their hygiene is not the sterile Pasteurian dream of safety regulators bent on attaining "no-germ" food.[13] Their post-Pasteurian approach follows Pasteurianism in recognizing risk and guarding against microbial infection, but it moves beyond Pasteurianism in recruiting "good" microbes (including those present in raw milk) as friends and allies in this effort. To conclude, I return to Dutton's exploratory microbiology to comment on how cheesemakers work, within legal regulations, to cultivate microbial environments conducive to fermenting what they believe to be tasty, healthy, locally expressive—and safe—cheese.

PASTEURIAN AND POST-PASTEURIAN VISIONS: WHAT IS THE NATURE OF CHEESE?

In *The Pasteurization of France,* Bruno Latour tracks the social and regulatory repercussions of Louis Pasteur's discovery of microorganisms' role in food spoilage.[14] Latour argues that once microbes were revealed in the laboratory, scientists believed their control would revolutionize social relations; butchers, for example, would be able to sell meat without *Salmonella* hitching a ride. Hygienists, government officials, and economists laid the groundwork for what they believed to be "pure" social relations, relations that would not be derailed by microbial disruption and therefore could be predicted and rationally ordered. By the end of the nineteenth century, markets and medicine were to be modernized through Pasteurian hygiene.

Scientists at the Pasteur Institute in France, meanwhile, established that the seemingly magical process of curdling and cheese ripening is not (as had been previously thought) "spontaneous" but, rather, the outcome of microbial activity. Researchers isolated and cultivated strains of lactic acid bacteria responsible for acidifying milk as well as members of the *Penicillium* genus responsible for the formation of snowy-white edible mold atop Brie and Camembert. By the end of the nineteenth century, Pasteurian researchers had convinced French cheesemakers to impose technoscientific control over the fate of their cheeses by seeding them with laboratory-made bacterial cultures. These Pasteurians, according to Pierre Boisard, aimed not to displace artisans but rather to aid them in their work of turning out a reliable product that could travel into a distributed market.[15] Bacteriology's applications in hygiene and food safety are at their foundation market-oriented and political.

When laboratory scientists first cultivated and propagated lactic acid bacteria, all cheese was made from what is today designated as "raw" milk. In an 1892 issue of *Science,* biologist Herbert Conn predicted that microbial seeding would lead to a larger, safer cheese supply. Describing the occasional invasion of cheese by poison-producing bacteria, Conn spoke in optimistically Pasteurian terms: "The cheese manufacturer is entirely innocent. . . . But occasionally [these 'tyrotoxicons'] get in and his cheese is ripened then under the agency of these injurious bacteria. . . . The evil is done. Now, when our cheese-makers have learned to apply to the manufacture of cheese the processes which our brewers have learned in the manufacture of beer, these troubles can be prevented."[16] When pasteurization was introduced for milk intended for drinking in the United States beginning in the 1890s, the primary public-health concern was the bacillus that Robert Koch had recently linked to tuberculosis; but the "evil" microorganisms that thwart human intent during cheesemaking are not restricted to disease-causing pathogens. As in the making of Vermont Shepherd, when cheesemakers alternate strain mixtures of starter cultures—a technique learned from brewers—they do this to outwit bacteriophages, bacteria-infecting viruses that are injurious to fermentation and desired cheese development, but not to human health.

With the expansion of the regional factory system of cheesemaking, milk traveled farther from farm to creamery and larger quantities were pooled from more numerous and bigger farms; all of this increased the risk of introducing injurious bacteria into cheesemaking. By the 1930s, cheese factories across the United States began pasteurizing the milk they received. Because pasteurization, a time- and temperature-calibrated heat treatment, kills 95 percent of all bacteria in fresh milk including the naturally occurring *Lactobacilli* that sour milk and start the fermentation process, pasteurized milk must be reseeded with lactic acid starter cultures to initiate acidification. More than a century ago, Conn anticipated two industry advantages from the use of pure starter cultures: safety and variety. Noting that each of 400 or 500 known species of bacteria produce "different sorts of decomposition . . . odors and . . . flavors," he speculated that microbial seeding could lead to 400 or 500 varieties of cheese: "Perhaps fifty years from now . . . a man may go to the store and order a particular kind of cheese . . . made by a peculiar kind of bacteria."[17] The story of twentieth-century industrialization, however, is that it produced uniformity rather than the gastronomic variety of which Conn dreamed. As with fluid milk, the cheese industry adopted routine pasteurization and commercial starter cultures to promote consistency and standardization along with safety.[18] Pasteurizing milk and reculturing it with commercial strains was essential in transforming cheesemaking from an artisanal workmanship of risk to an industrial workmanship of certainty.[19] Treating cheesemaking as an industrial biotechnology, a mode of harnessing living organisms and biological processes to engineer new products, dairy science has developed hand in glove with industrialization.

For dairy scientists trained to optimize the safety and standardization of industrially made cheese, the benefits of pasteurization are obvious and incontrovertible. Colin Sage, who has studied artisan cheesemaking in Ireland, suggests, "Pasteurization has taken on the characteristics of a 'black box' for many scientists for which it is simply unimaginable that it would be circumvented."[20] An assemblage of equipment, technique, and technician is considered to have become a "black box" when all elements "act as one" to generate an outcome that is tacitly and widely accepted as factual.[21] Put another way, once a hypothesis has been established as accepted result, that result may be black-boxed as a utilitarian device having unquestionable efficacy. According to food regulators and scientists, heating milk at 72°C for fifteen seconds or at 63°C for thirty minutes *kills* pathogens that may be present; that is what pasteurization *is*—therefore, pasteurization is legally confirmed by recording time and temperature treatments, not by testing milk for residual microbial vitality. (The high price tag for a vat pasteurizer is partly attributable to a federal law requiring that it be fitted with a mechanism that automatically records correlations between time and temperature so as to leave an auditable demonstration of proper pasteurization.)

There is more to the black-boxing of pasteurization as the essential means of producing dairy products safe for human consumption. Milk must first be defined as essentially in need of purification. To support his claim that pasteurization has been black-boxed by the dairy industry, Sage quotes a U.S. food safety scientist saying, "There is no mystery about why raw milk is a common vehicle for salmonellosis and other enteric infections; after all, dairy milk is essentially a suspension of fecal and other microorganisms in a nutrient broth."[22] On this view, contamination of milk is unavoidable, but eradicable through pasteurization.

Pasteurians take the position that raw milk is by its very nature hazardous to human health. On drinking the stuff, the FDA is unequivocal: "Raw milk is inherently dangerous and it should not be consumed by anyone at any time for any purpose."[23] I once toured the research lab of a state university food sciences department that produces dairy products served on campus. Standing before a glass wall overlooking the automated processing plant gleaming with high-tech equipment, the lab manager answered the raw-milk question with a weary shake of his head. People get sick, he said. They die. Between 1998 and 2009, 93 outbreaks of infection resulting from consuming raw milk or raw-milk products, totaling 1,837 illnesses, 195 hospitalizations, and 2 deaths, were reported to the CDC.[24] He seemed genuinely puzzled that anyone would risk drinking raw milk and said, "We've done all this science over the last century. Why would you want to take a step backwards into the past? You take antibiotics, you get better. That's science." Why, he wondered, would anyone in this day and age ignore scientific knowledge and reject technoscientific progress? One answer is that although the FDA says that drinking raw milk may kill you, you may have grown up knowing a farm family that thrived on the raw milk of their own cows or witnessed a child's dairy allergy disappear after switching to raw milk (a claim frequently made). The contraindication of experiential knowledge may lead laypeople to dismiss the authoritative knowledge of scientific experts as overreaching, or even beholden to industry interests.[25]

Post-Pasteurians are not immune to all-or-nothing thinking about cheese or milk, either. Some claim that raw milk, being "more" natural than pasteurized milk (taken here to be a good thing), makes for an inherently good food. One Washington state dairy farmer who sells raw milk refuted public-health officials' claims that his farm had been traced to three cases of *E. coli* poisoning, saying to a reporter, "God designed raw milk; man messed with it. . . . You draw your own conclusions."[26] Espousing a more secular romanticism, Steven Jenkins, author of the *Cheese Primer* and cheesemonger for Fairway supermarkets in New York, said to a *New York Times* reporter after an early indication that the FDA may be considering a ban on raw-milk cheese, "This whole thing is crazy. . . . It's going to wipe out one of the most beautiful and romantic links between human beings and the earth that we will ever know, and we are going to be the lesser for it."[27]

To be clear, fluid milk and fermented cheese are fundamentally different substances, with very different risk profiles. Cheese, after all, is a means of *preserving* milk (though not indefinitely). My point is that the microbiopolitical sentiments of raw milk spill over into regulatory debates about raw-milk cheese. Consequently, the FDA treats raw-milk cheese as inherently different from pasteurized-milk cheese, to the point that this distinction overshadows any other meaningful classificatory scheme that could differentiate cheese types. As is most notably evident in the sixty-day aging rule for raw-milk cheese, cheese safety standards in the United States are defined by a binary distinction, one that I as an anthropologist cannot help but see as a Pasteurian dualism between "nature" (not us) and "culture" (us):

RAW MILK   PASTEURIZED MILK
NATURE   CULTURE

This structural principle implies that pasteurization civilizes raw ruminant milk, making it safe and, indeed, appropriate for human consumption.

In the eyes of Pasteurian dairy scientists, to eschew this unquestionable good is (at best) to behave irresponsibly. In 2011, I attended the annual meeting of the International Association for Food Protection, a gathering of food-safety scientists, regulators, lawyers, and industry representatives. The meetings were held in Milwaukee, Wisconsin, and at the gala dinner, Wisconsin-made raw-milk cheeses were almost reluctantly served; sequestered in a corner, they were marked by a sign that served as a warning label. When I asked one attendee whether she had tasted any of the raw-milk cheeses, she looked at me as if I had come from another planet. Pasteurization has become a key symbol of modernity's techno-scientific ability to dominate nature for human ends.

This book, however, demonstrates that industrial ecologies of cheese pro-duction are no more or less "natural" than farmstead ecologies; they are dif-ferently cultured. Industrial-scale dairying and the black-boxing of pasteuri-zation as sound technoscience developed in conjunction with one another. Post-Pasteurians challenge Pasteurianism's founding assumption by arguing that fecal matter is not natural to milk; it gets into milk only if humans are less than scrupulous in their dairying practices (I would not describe the milk produced at Major Farm and other cheesemaking dairies I have visited as "a suspension of fecal and other microorganisms in a nutrient broth."). If raw milk is polluted and polluting, the post-Pasteurian view holds, it is because of culture, not nature. It therefore can be avoided.

In our interview Paul Kindstedt put the contrast to me this way: "The mental-ity of much of the food industry, and food scientists—of which I am one, and this was my mentality for many years—is, 'I will deconstruct nature, I will figure out how it works, and I'll remake it in my image, and I will make nature do what I want it to do.' And that's a different attitude, or philosophy, versus, 'I'm not going to mess with nature, I'm going to work with it.'" In contrast to the hyper-hygienic ethos that brought us the limitless shelf life of Velveeta, a post-Pasteurian under-standing embraces the idea that "real" cheese, as a fermented food, is teeming with living bacteria and molds.

If blandly predictable supermarket cheese is the industrial legacy of a Pas-teurian ethos of microbial domination, Vermont Shepherd, made from unpas-teurized milk and microbially cultivated to develop a natural rind, exemplifies post-Pasteurian cheese. David and Cindy Major, after encountering problems in the 1980s trying to develop a protective natural rind on the Shepherd's Sharp cheese they were aging, sought the advice of dairy consultants at the Univer-sity of Wisconsin. The scientists knew only industrial cheesemaking—working with vast quantities of milk pooled from multiple farms, in automated factories, fabricating plastic-encased blocks of cheese that would mature, unattended, in refrigerated warehouses. The experts suggested that the Majors dip their cheeses in an antiseptic mold inhibitor. On their advice, the Majors let off chlorine bombs in their aging room to keep it sanitized! Not surprisingly, this hyper-hygienic strategy did not facilitate the successful development of natural rinds, which are the outcome of successive waves of bacteria and fungi colonizing the surface of a cheese. Eventually, as a colleague of theirs recalled to me, David drew an analogy between the cheese wheels and his sheep pastures, an analogy that suggested to him, "Rather than sanitize, maybe we need to cultivate in the cave." After their encounter with "anti-mold" scientists, whom Cindy described to me as teaching "fear and cheesemaking," Cindy wrote to British cheese expert Patrick Rance about their "crust problems," which opened their way to the Pyrenees and the eventual success of Vermont Shepherd.

Anthropologists have long argued that nature and culture are meaningfully categorized in opposition to each other only if and when people insist on it; there is no essential, fundamental division between the two domains. What nature "is," materially and symbolically, relies fundamentally on human engagement with organic processes; recognition of this—a fundamental tenet of post-pastoral thinking—suggests that humans can decide, to some extent, what kind of nature to insist upon. Microbiopolitics fully pervades post-pastoral endeavors. Ruminant milk is no more essentially a healthy and safe food for humans than it is a harmful one. Hygienic milking practices applied to healthy herds can produce clean milk—most of the time.[28] More broadly, food safety is itself largely relative and "not an inherent biological characteristic of a food," writes nutritionist Marion Nestle.[29] A food may be healthy and safe for some individuals but not others (think of allergies as well as immunities—and with milk, lactose intolerance), in small quantities but not large, or at one point in time but not another. Such contingency poses a challenge for food-safety regulators and food producers alike.

In 2011, the *New York Times* described Kelli Estrella and her battle with the FDA as "a potent symbol in a contentious national debate over the safety of food produced by small farmers and how much the government should regulate it."[30] Sidney Mintz has named the question a fundamental conundrum of democratic capitalist societies: "how to provide protection to the citizenry on one hand, yet maintain freedom of [consumer] choice on [the] other."[31] A safe food supply is not to be underestimated. The question is how best to ensure it.

FOOD SAFETY REGULATION AND PROBLEMS OF CLASSIFICATION

In the United States, safety in cheese production is promoted through pasteurization, with random product testing as a safeguard. Raw-milk cheese is a regulatory exception. Absent pasteurization, a minimum aging period is required for a raw-milk cheese to make it to market. The FDA requires that cheese made from unpasteurized milk be aged at least sixty days prior to being sold, at a temperature no less than 1.7°C (35°F). The sixty-day rule is part of FDA standards of definition for cheese and applies equally to domestically produced and imported cheeses.[32] There is no such aging rule for raw-milk cheese in France or Italy. In Canada, domestic producers must follow a similar sixty-day rule with a 2°C minimum temperature, but since 2001 the Canadian Food Inspection Agency has permitted the importing of French-made unpasteurized cheeses without mandatory aging, and since 2008, Quebec has gone its own way in permitting the sale of young domestic raw-milk cheeses, provided that guidelines to mitigate risk are followed.

The mandatory aging period for raw-milk cheese means to offer protection against pathogenic microbes that could thrive in the moist environment of a softer cheese. The idea is that as a cheese ages it loses moisture and may gain acidity, thus becoming increasingly inhospitable to many pathogenic germs. Introduced in 1949 as a guideline for industrial manufacturing, the sixty-day rule represents a regulatory response to an outbreak of typhoid fever traced to heat-treated (but unpasteurized) Cheddar contaminated with *Salmonella typhimurium* shipped overseas to U.S. servicemen during World War II. Following the typhoid outbreak, a government-sponsored study found that aging Cheddar made from unpasteurized milk for sixty days proved sufficient to knock out *Salmonella*. Hence the sixty-day aging rule.

Since the late 1990s, the FDA's agenda has included reevaluation of the sixty-day aging period for raw-milk cheese "to determine if this process criterion is adequate to protect public health."[33] Initially this alarmed people in the world of artisanal cheese. A total ban on raw-milk cheesemaking, they feared, could compromise the futures of raw-milk cheeses and of cheesemakers who, even if they could afford a pasteurizer (many cannot), have developed market reputations for cheeses whose flavor and texture might be altered by pasteurization. It is becoming increasingly clear, however, that the sixty-day rule may be made obsolete by changes in the gastronomic, agricultural, and microbiological landscape of America—changes that have produced new cheeses, as well as newly virulent pathogens.

The Shiga toxin–producing O157:H7 mutation of *E. coli,* an intestinal bacterium, was first characterized in 1982 and may not have existed when the FDA introduced the sixty-day rule. *E. coli* O157:H7 appears on the CDC list of bioterrorism agents and in recent years has been in the news by way of bagged spinach (grown on land leased by a cattle ranch) and ground beef. (A 2011 bean-sprout scare in Germany was caused by a newly characterized mutation of enterohemorrhagic *E. coli,* O104:H4). Review of the sixty-day aging rule was introduced to the FDA's agenda after a South Dakota State University study, reported in the *Journal of Food Protection,* detailed the persistence of *E. coli* O157:H7 in a cheese matrix beyond sixty days in a controlled laboratory experiment.[34] In reviewing the study for the Cheese of Choice Coalition, Catherine Donnelly, a microbiologist in the food sciences department at the University of Vermont, reported that the study used far less salt (an antibacterial agent) than would be added to Cheddar intended for consumption, and it inoculated one of its test batches with a larger concentration of *E. coli* (1,000 cfu/ml)—which originates in cow intestines and spreads through manure—than could have slipped into artisanal cheesemaking undetected.[35] Despite the study's flaws, it called attention to the presence and persistence of a relatively new pathogen of concern.[36]

From a microbiological perspective, the trouble with the universal sixty-day rule for raw-milk cheeses is that not all cheeses are constituted like Cheddar and not all pathogens behave like *Salmonella*. O157:H7 is not your average tummy-bug *E. coli*. More significantly, perhaps, hard, dry, sharp Cheddar and soft, moist, low-acidity, bloomy-rind cheeses such as Camembert represent fundamentally different substances when it comes to pathogenic vulnerability. Undermining the premise of the sixty-day rule, the longer a bloomy-rind cheese ages, the more hazardous, not less, it becomes, because—quite unlike Cheddar—as it ages its acidity declines (pH level rises), thus making it more hospitable to *Listeria*.[37] *Listeria monocytogenes*, the bacterium chased after by the FDA in 2010, can cause listeriosis, an infection that may manifest as septicemia, meningitis, or an intrauterine infection that sometimes results in spontaneous abortion or stillbirth.[38] *Listeria* in combination with soft-ripened cheese offers a scientific counterindication for aging a raw-milk cheese for sixty days to reduce risk. In recent decades, the sixty-day rule has confronted a growing number of cheesemakers who wish to work with raw milk and also make varieties of soft-ripened cheeses that are usually considered ripe well before sixty days of aging.

Further complicating the microbiopolitical field, unlike the tubercular bacillus, which can be carried from sickened cow to human through milk, or *E. coli*, which originates in manure and can enter the milk supply through unsanitary milking conditions, *Listeria* is a ubiquitous environmental contaminant found in soil, silage, foliage, and manure. You may have it on your shoes. For this reason, *Listeria* is most likely to contaminate a cheese during manufacture, aging, or packaging. Pasteurizing milk prior to cheesemaking is no barrier to this sort of environmental contamination. In fact, Catherine Donnelly, whose research team helped pioneer methods of detecting *Listeria* in foods, suggests that cheese made from pasteurized milk may even be more conducive to *Listeria* growth because it lacks the microbial diversity of a raw-milk cheese that can facilitate "good" microbes outcompeting "bad" ones; "Mandatory pasteurization of milk may increase the susceptibility of cheese to growth of pathogens introduced via postprocessing contamination," she writes.[39]

Listeria's simultaneous ubiquity and uneven pathogenicity complicates regulatory action aimed at promoting public health. The FDA has zero tolerance for *Listeria monocytogenes* (requiring its absence in a twenty-five-gram sample of food) because, though rare, listeriosis has a 20 percent fatality rate and accounts for roughly a quarter of deaths attributed to food-borne illness in the United States.[40] This is the pathogen that led to the shutdown of Estrella Family Creamery, even though no epidemiological link emerged between their cheese and human infection. Kelli and Anthony Estrella's problems with sanitation emerged in early 2010 when routine testing by the Washington State Department of Agriculture turned up *Listeria monocytogenes* in samples of cheese, a brine bath, and one of the creamery's aging rooms. Working with state officials, the Estrellas initiated three recalls of soft-ripened varieties and endeavored to improve sanitation.[41] But when subsequent FDA inspections reported evidence of *Listeria*'s "persistent presence," federal officials requested a total recall of their marketed product.[42] The Estrellas' refusal instigated the court-ordered seizure.[43] Producers such as the Estrellas chafe against the zero tolerance policy because, although listeriosis can be lethal, not all species of *Listeria* cause listeriosis. France, Germany, and the Netherlands tolerate trace amounts of *Listeria monocytogenes* in foods at point of consumption.[44]

It does not help that popular cheese books continue to repeat the myth of pasteurization's infallibility while also overstating the protective function of a sixty-day aging period for raw-milk cheese. One author writes that raw-milk cheese must be aged in the United States "as the FDA has determined that beyond sixty days potentially harmful pathogens such as *Listeria, E. coli,* staphylococcus, tuberculosis, and brucellosis cannot survive," although as I have demonstrated, the scientific evidence is far more complicated than such language allows.[45] A book showcasing Vermont cheese declares, "Cheesemakers need to choose between making raw-milk cheese, which must be aged for a minimum of sixty days to destroy the bacteria in it, or pasteurized cheese, which requires heating the milk to destroy bacteria beforehand."[46] That statement is misleading on two counts. First, as evidenced by *Listeria,* aging cheeses for sixty days does not "destroy the bacteria in it" in any absolute sense. Second, cheeses themselves do not fall into discrete, essential categories of being either "raw-milk" or "requiring" pasteurization—technically (if not legally), any cheese can be made from either raw or pasteurized milk.

Some of the confusion over raw-milk cheese safety stems from the inconsistent application of categories in standards for production and in standards for consumption. As noted above, with the exception of the sixty-day rule for raw-milk cheeses, the FDA regulates the production of all cheeses equally, resulting in a binary classification:

RAW MILK   PASTEURIZED MILK

However, when it comes to FDA guidelines for the safe *consumption* of cheese, the agency introduces an additional category: *softness.* Softness is meant to represent an indirect measure of moisture, high moisture being conducive to the growth of pathogens including *Listeria monocytogenes.* But to toss in softness alongside raw milk and pasteurized milk as a fundamental cheese category is rather like adding to the categories of raw and cooked one like "sort of yellow." It introduces semantic confusion. When I was pregnant in 2005, the FDA advised me not to eat "soft cheeses" such as "Brie, Camembert, feta, blue-veined cheese, or Mexican-style cheeses such as queso blanco fresco." But other cheeses are also soft. The first question I asked the nurse practitioner once my pregnancy was confirmed was, "What about fresh mozzarella?" She had no idea, so I went online. I found quite a lot of confusion and some erroneous information on pregnancy Web sites. Many women interpret the FDA warning as a binary classification quite different from the raw/pasteurized dichotomy governing safe production:

SOFT	HARD
BAD	OKAY

But how is one to identify a "soft" cheese when one sees and feels it? On Babycenter .com, one woman asked, "Does anyone know if those little Laughing Cow wedges are considered a soft cheese?"[47] Laughing Cow, a pasteurized, process cheese whose bite-size wedges are individually machine-wrapped in foil, is undoubtedly soft but almost certainly free of pathogens.[48] In emphasizing a cheese's softness in its dietary guide for pregnant women, the FDA inadvertently drew attention away from the protective function of pasteurization.

At the same time, in introducing the category of softness the FDA importantly acknowledged that eaters are not identical; they embody different risk profiles for food-borne illness. Pregnant women, the elderly, and the immunocompromised are particularly susceptible to listeriosis, and *Listeria monocytogenes,* as noted, takes particularly well to bloomy-rind cheeses with low acidity, such as Brie and Camembert. The actual occurrence of food safety—that is, the avoidance of food poisoning (though not of food allergies)—calibrates to a direct relation between a particular food substance (*this* food, in this condition, right now) and the bodily capacity of an individual eater to incorporate that substance, hitchhiking microbes and all. The regulatory promotion of food safety works differently. It operates by setting production standards calibrated to broad categories of food substance, not to particular substances of food. Those standards are set by antici- pating possible encounters between types of foods and types of eaters. Inevitably, regulatory categories cast a wider net than might catch all those interrelation- ships in which food poisoning would occur; the resulting gap may be viewed as either an abundance of caution or overregulation. Producers shoulder the burden in promoting food safety because the government cannot prevent individual con- sumers—women who are pregnant, or persons living with AIDS—from ingesting particular food substances. Consumers can only be warned; producers can be shut down.

Food-safety officials regulate from the exception—from the exceptional consumer, but also from the exceptional producer. "Mexican-style" cheeses, for instance (to use the FDA's term), are prominent on the FDA warning list of foods that pregnant women should avoid, not because of their pH or inherent susceptibility but because a couple of food-borne illness outbreaks have been traced to cheese made by immigrants in unlicensed facilities. The largest outbreak of cheese-related listeriosis in the United States was linked to *queso fresco* made in a bathtub and sold door-to-door.[49] The problem imagined here is not so much "Mexican-style cheese" but instead the unruliness of a local microbial ecology that might flourish in the shadow economy of unlicensed commercial food production. The deployment of broad classificatory categories obscures the specificities—or exceptions—on which regulation is often based.

In August 2005, the FDA reasserted its faith in pasteurization by revising its warning, now advising pregnant women to avoid eating "soft cheeses such as feta, Brie, and Camembert . . . unless they have labels that clearly state they are made from pasteurized milk."[50] Continuing to build on the structural categorizations I have begun to develop, the FDA's revised recommendation gives us a classificatory grid rather than a binary opposition (see table 3).

This should take care of the Laughing Cow question, but it leaves unaddressed the status of a "hard" cheese made from raw milk, even beyond the classificatory question of where the line between "hard" and "soft" cheese should be drawn in the first place—at Fontina? Gouda? Cheddar? And, of course, it suggests that a bloomy-rind (or mold-ripened) soft cheese is perfectly safe when it is made from pasteurized milk, which—owing to the risk of postprocessing contamination—it is not.

Taking acidity into account, the local ecology of Camembert, whose pH increases to 7.5 with ripening, is far more hospitable to *Listeria* than Feta (pH 4.4). Having learned this, when I was pregnant I tried to employ my own classificatory guide to avoid encountering *Listeria* (see table 4). However, because I was unfamiliar with the pH of many cheese types, this scheme had limited utility. It started to make more sense to me why the FDA was sticking with the language of simple oppositions (raw versus pasteurized; soft versus hard) rather than more complex classificatory grids. Indeed, to address my earlier mozzarella question we would have to differentiate among "soft" cheeses to recognize yet another category: freshness. A fresh cheese such as mozzarella (not pizza cheese, but the kind served in salads with tomatoes and basil) or *queso fresco* is best eaten just days after fabrication—by *best*, I mean both tastiest and safest. Environmental contamination (e.g., *Listeria* infection) is less of a concern for these short-lived cheeses, but pasteurizing—ensuring that the cheese is made from pathogen-free milk—is advisable, and legally required in the United States (see table 5).

Microbiopolitics relies on classification. Government regulators, inspectors, producers, retailers, and consumers (highbrow, low-income, pregnant, parental) may be talking about the same material objects but using different classificatory

TABLE 3 Classificatory grid for cheese based on August 2005
FDA warnings for pregnant women to avoid encountering *Listeria*

	Soft	Hard
Raw Milk	Avoid	?
Pasteurized Milk	Okay	Okay

TABLE 4 My own classificatory guide, taking acidity into account,
to avoid encountering *Listeria* while pregnant

	Soft	Hard
High Acidity	Okay (Feta)	Okay (Cheddar)
Low Acidity	Avoid (Brie)	Avoid (blue-veined)

TABLE 5 Yet another unofficial classificatory guide to avoiding *Listeria*,
taking freshness (very young age) into account

	Fresh	Soft-Ripened	Hard
Raw Milk	Avoid	Avoid	Probably okay
Pasteurized Milk	Okay	Risky	Okay

systems, at times shifting their frame of reference in speaking to different audiences. Cheesemakers, for instance, may understand the role of acidity in cheese safety, but to avoid misunderstanding, they may speak to retailers and consumers only in terms of softness.

It may seem that to oversimplify is to err on the safe side—better to be overly broad in one's recommendation than to allow anyone to get sick. The trouble is, overgeneralizing does not always promote safety. When I interviewed Catherine Donnelly in her office at the University of Vermont, where she codirects the Vermont Institute of Artisan Cheese (VIAC) with Paul Kindstedt, she said of the sixty-day rule, "What's sad is, there are cheesemakers who read the letter of the law [and think] 'Great! For a [raw-milk] bloomy-rind cheese, I'll just hold it for sixty days.' And it's like, Oh, my God! We've got an accident waiting to happen. And they're perfectly within legal bounds to do that." In fact, it is what the law requires of them.

I thought of this conversation in spring 2009 when I went on a dairy tour in a mid-Atlantic state. The tour took a group of visiting scholars to visit a cheesemaking dairy farmer, whom I will call Dave, who has ventured far from his conventional dairying roots to pasture a couple dozen cows, which he milks once a day. He does not own a pasteurizer. On Mondays he makes cheese using a Camembert recipe. As the group stood in his cheese room sampling his Cheddar, Colby, and Camembert-style cheeses, Dave explained of the latter that it took him a year and a half of tinkering with the recipe "just so it could stand up like that." When asked whether he had "any problems with making raw-milk cheese," Dave answered in technocratic rather than technical terms: "I get along really well with my [state] inspector. I only see him once a year." Question: "Are all the cheeses aged for sixty days?" Answer: "We're going to lie about this one a little bit," indicating the Camembert, a cheese that in France is considered ripe and ready to eat after twenty-one to twenty-eight days. Having discovered that the raw-milk cheese ripens more quickly when made from early-season milk compared with milk from later in the year, Dave delays producing Camembert until several weeks into the cheesemaking season to avoid really rapid ripening. Still, by sixty days even a later-season Camembert may become too ripe—runny and ammoniated—to market and enjoy.

Since his state's regulations do not specify a protocol for making Camembert, his inspector "didn't know what to do with it" and, in the end, they simply classified the cheese as "soft." "Camembert" did not leap out at his inspector as a type of cheese that is difficult to hold for sixty days. In a state such as Vermont or California where artisan cheesemaking is better established, inspectors would be apt to question the viability of a raw-milk Camembert-style cheese. Two Vermont producers I know worked hard to engineer bloomy-rind, raw-milk cheeses that they could hold for sixty days, but in the end both bought pasteurizers and readjusted their recipes accordingly. It was simply too difficult to hold these cheeses for sixty days and maintain consumer desirability, while their cognizant inspectors were increasingly watchful to see that they did.

I doubt that many on the tour were aware that Dave's Camembert-style cheese grew microbiologically riskier the longer it aged (and so it was to our benefit that we were offered it underage); regardless, they seemed unworried by any question of legality. No one declined to sample the younger-than-sixty-day raw-milk Camembert. Several bought wheels. In fact, the cheese's illicitness, produced by the sixty-day rule, might well add to its consumer appeal. Forbidden, potentially risky—it is a sexy cheese.

As the basis of cheese safety regulation, the sixty-day rule is imperfect. The law homogenizes cheeses as belonging to the same class of food, treating them as microbiopolitically equivalent, when different families of cheese embody quite different microbial ecosystems (based on acidity and moisture as well as microbial populations) and thus constitute different risks for human eaters. When current regulations would seem irrational or, worse, ill-advised—and as there is clearly a consumer market for raw-milk products—some producers are tempted to operate at the edges of the law by, for example, selling a raw-milk cheese at farmers' markets as "pet food" or "fish bait" rather than (wink-wink) for human consumption.⁵¹ This discomforts many in the industry.⁵² At a cheese festival I attended in Seattle, Jeff Roberts addressed a comment about underage raw-milk cheese marketed "as cat kibbles" by saying, "I'd rather not see that. . . . When there were only a handful of cheesemakers scattered around the country and you did something like that and you got busted, it would affect only you. That's no longer the case." Selling illegal cheese poses potential economic harm to the industry as a whole.

Of greater concern than licensed cheesemakers who may on occasion sell underage cheese, Jeff continued, are people who make and sell cheese without a commercial license at all—and recent immigrants are not alone in doing this. Catherine Donnelly told me about a recall of Vermont goat cheese in the early 1990s. Made by an unlicensed producer, the cheese had nonetheless been sold at a farmers' market and caused several people to develop salmonellosis, an intestinal infection; because the contaminated cheese was produced and sold illegally, this food-borne illness outbreak attracted heightened media attention. The message sent was simply, "Vermont goat cheese is making people ill!" As a result, Donnelly said, "Everybody selling goat cheese in Vermont was affected." While praising an "esprit de corps" running throughout the community, Donnelly cautioned, "That's the fear, as this industry grows—will everyone be conscientious about protecting the name and image of the industry?"

Artisan cheesemakers—particularly those who make cheese from raw milk or cultivate natural rinds—want to stake out responsible relationships with and through microorganisms, relationships that run counter to the Pasteurian orthodoxy of industrial technoscience, which would introduce chlorine bombs into cheese aging facilities. In no way does a post-Pasteurian perspective suggest a cavalier attitude about microbial agencies. Precisely what a post-Pasteurian microbiopolitics of artisanal cheese can and should look like is being discussed by cheesemakers, retailers, and sympathetic dairy scientists. The ACS, no less than the FDA, has become interested in exploring the possibility of setting new production standards to promote safety.

In 2011, the ACS invited Jack Mowbray, the regulatory policy analyst at the FDA tasked with reevaluating the rules for raw-milk cheese production in light of the 2011 Food Safety Modernization Act, to speak at their annual meeting (also by invitation, at the same meeting held in Montreal, I gave a presentation on the cultural history of raw-milk cheese). The ultimate responsibility for producing safe food, Mowbray told cheesemakers, lies with them, with the food industry; the responsibility of government is verification. While this may be accurate in legal terms, Mowbray's division of labor failed to recognize the productive role of government in setting the standards that its agents then subject to verification. Nevertheless, Mowbray reassured cheesemakers that the agency would not arbitrarily extend the mandatory aging period for raw-milk cheese to 120 days (which many had feared), acknowledging that the FDA can no longer take the "one-size-fits-all approach" of the sixty-day rule. Instead, he announced, the agency has "decided to develop a comprehensive risk profile" for artisanal cheeses with respect to current scientific knowledge. In theory, this suggests that bloomy-rind cheeses and hard-aged cheeses may yet be asked to meet production standards tailored to their respective vital materialities. Such a move would, of course, bring on an entirely new set of classificatory woes. How far might the FDA carry the proliferation of legally meaningful cheese categories? Mowbray was unable to discuss what regulatory options his agency is actually considering. It is, after all, a political and budgetary question as much as a technoscientific one.

DO-IT-YOURSELF REGULATION

Not waiting for government solutions, American cheesemakers are beginning to develop their own Hazard Analysis and Critical Control Point (HACCP, pronounced *HAS-sip*) plans. Initially developed in the 1970s to ensure the safety of space food for NASA astronauts, HACCP is mandated by the U.S. Department of Agriculture for the meat and seafood industries, but not dairy. The system works to identify and cut off what Bruno Latour might call "obligatory points of passage" for microbial contamination as well as chemical and physical hazards to food safety (residue from overly concentrated sanitizer counts as a chemical hazard; an embedded bit of ground glass or metal constitutes a physical hazard).[53] HACCP plans use flow charts to track areas of hazard throughout the production process, punctuated by "critical control points" (CCPs), instances when control can and (it is deemed) must be asserted to prevent or minimize identified hazards. HACCP regulates process rather than product. Since bloomy-rind cheese made from pasteurized milk presents somewhat different hazards from those of raw-milk Cheddar, distinct HACCP plans would need to be drawn up for each. The customizable, preventive approach marks a potential departure from current one-size-fits-all dairy standards reliant on spot inspections, random product sampling, and "pasteurizing or irradiating products that may have been produced with varying attention to quality and safety."[54] Posed as an alternative to mandatory pasteurization, reliance on HACCP as a food safety system presupposes that raw-milk cheese can be made safely.

While HACCP's customizability offers an advantage in thinking about the microbiological safety of various cheese types, as a legal system of food protection it introduces a new set of complications. To serve as a legal measure of protection, as in the seafood and meat industries, HACCP operates through audit.[55] Compliance with CCPs as well as "prerequisite programs," such as correct temperatures for bulk tanks and coolers, is verified through inspection of paperwork recording satisfactory measures taken at every step of production for each batch of cheese. Cheesemakers who are responsible for milking, cleaning, packaging, and shipping might be overwhelmed by the addition to their already busy schedules of moment-to-moment monitoring and daily record keeping.[56] A need for verification implies, further, that the preventive measures that constitute CCPs must indeed be measurable. Since each industry that employs HACCP is responsible for defining acceptable practices that may constitute CCPs, what measures could and should count as legitimate CCPs within a legally binding HACCP program for cheesemaking is an important question. When HACCP is used as a regulatory tool, industries tend to maintain minimal numbers of CCPs. It has been suggested for cheesemaking that these may be limited to "metal detection, pasteurization and aging."[57] In this case, the sole CCP for raw-milk artisanal cheese would be aging, thus begging the question of how long an aging period for any particular cheese type is sufficient to constitute a critical control. The FDA would need to accept a range of aging periods for a variety of cheese types to enable raw-milk cheesemakers to overcome the limitations of the sixty-day rule through a HACCP-style alternative system of verification.

HACCP is designed to ensure safety rather than quality, meaning that a perfectly safe cheese may not meet a producer's own aesthetic standards for taste, texture, or appearance, and vice versa. Nonetheless, other potential CCPs—fermentation at the proper acidity (though we have seen how difficult accurate measuring of pH can be) or salting or meeting standards for initial milk quality—also track variables that contribute to good-tasting cheese.[58] "You can't make good cheese from poor-quality milk," Donnelly assured me. "You can't make good cheese if you don't manage your cheesemaking environment. And all the measures you put in place to combat bacteriophages—which are the viruses that infect starter cultures—those measures can curb all pathogens. So cheesemaking's a pretty safe kind of activity—unless you're aging the bloomy-rind cheese for sixty days!" We laughed ruefully as Donnelly reiterated, "I don't recommend that." There is much confusion among cheesemakers as to which "good manufacturing practices" might also count as CCPs. Regular and thorough handwashing, proper sanitation of equipment, proper milk storage temperature, and appropriate acid development of curd are all crucial to making good cheese (cheese that is both edible and safe), but they do not count as CCPs. Clearing up such confusion is important because the potential of any HACCP system to control risk is only as great as its design and protocol.

"If you really want to control risk," Donnelly told me, "you've got to manage the environment." The principle of managing the microbial environment as a means of preventing opportunities for contamination sounds promising, especially when considered as an alternative to heat-treating or irradiating filthy milk. But in practice, as any artisan knows, environmental management is not so straightforward, which is one reason artisan cheesemaking entails a workman-ship of risk. As a regime of environmental management, HACCP operates at a remove: fundamentally, it is a regime of monitoring regular practices that should ensure environmental management of microorganisms. Beyond regulating tem-perature and humidity, it is one thing to manage one's own actions—by constant and thorough hand-washing, changing footwear upon entering a cheesemaking space, and so on—and another to manage the activity of employees, visitors, animals, and, not least, microorganisms. "By creating categories of actions that 'count,'" Elizabeth Dunn writes of HACCP and other systems of audit, "they also create residual categories of actions that become invisible, seemingly unimport-ant and uncounted."[59] Dunn reports, as the U.S. meatpacking industry learned in fulfilling its USDA mandate to implement HACCP, that the more a food proces-sor looks to find spaces for microbial containment, the more risk areas—and the more *E. coli,* in the case of meatpacking—turn up. I once heard a cheesemaker at an ACS meeting acknowledge similarly of unwanted microorganisms in the cheese room, "If you look for it, you will find it." And so environmental manage-ment of microorganisms might be better approached as a mode of practice than as a final goal. There is no definitive end point when it comes to microbiopolitics.

Still, increasing numbers of cheesemakers intent on preventing pathogenic contamination are thinking through CCPs in designing their facilities and in developing their own safety protocols.[60] In the wake of the Estrella Creamery seizure, the Vermont Cheese Council sponsored HACCP workshops and the ACS applauded those cheesemakers who "voluntarily exceed current require-ments" by following HACCP plans.[61] An ACS survey of its cheesemaker members conducted in November 2010 found that 52 percent reported following HACCP plans.[62] The ACS has suggested to members that HACCP may become a sought-after stamp of safety assurance for retailers and consumers. With this goal in mind, the ACS recommends that cheesemakers contract third-party audits to monitor the monitoring systems so that the authoritative basis of HACCP as a label of safety assurance is not undermined by the fact that producers write up their own HACCP protocols.[63] To prepare producers for third-party audit, a new industry of preaudit consultation is springing up. All of this, of course, costs producers money—one factor behind a noticeable rise in the price of domestic farmstead cheese in recent years.

Finally, we must remember that once a cheese leaves the producer's premises, its "life" and its vulnerability continue. Cheese may be a means of preserving milk, but it remains perishable. As the popularity of artisanal cheese rises and more grocery stores are stocking it, more people are handling cheese without clear knowledge of the risk they are taking on. Brenda Jensen, a sheep dairy farmer and cheesemaker in Wisconsin, told me about visiting a grocer who was interested in carrying her cheese. The conversation went well until she asked,

"So where are you going to keep her?" "Keep who?" replied the perplexed grocer. "My cheese!" Brenda explained, engaging in the personification that is common among cheesemakers. "You know, she's real finicky, she likes it to be cool." They laughed, but Brenda insisted on seeing his storeroom, asking at what tempera- ture it is kept. "Where's the thermometer? I don't see a thermometer," Brenda asked, worried. The storekeeper rooted around, muttering, "Oh, where did that thing go?" Brenda was not reassured. Again, the ACS is taking it upon itself to establish and verify standards for practice, launching in 2012 a Certified Cheese Professional Exam for cheese retailers "to encourage improved standards of comprehensive cheese knowledge and service."[64] The exam will cover areas of knowledge from the practices of cheese ripening and storage to cheese nutrition and regulation.

"KNOWLEDGE IS POWER": POST-PASTEURIAN RISK MANAGEMENT

"Cheese is a potentially hazardous food." This sentiment, projected onto the screen at the front of a University of Vermont classroom, welcomed cheesemakers attending a January 2008 workshop at VIAC titled "Risk Reduction Practices." The institute is housed at the University of Vermont's Department of Nutrition and Food Sciences within a new glass building fronted by a dramatic egg-shaped entrance. ("The egg," explains text on an interior wall, "is not only a source of food, but a source of life.") Established in 2004, VIAC views handcrafted cheese as potentially hazardous food, and also as a means of maintaining rural liveli- hoods and the dairy landscape that is important to Vermont's tourist economy and self-image. VIAC programming, including this daylong seminar led by Senior Research Scientist Dennis (D. J.) D'Amico, is designed to help small-scale artisanal food producers succeed; ensuring food safety is one key to success. Researchers at VIAC, not unlike their early counterparts at the Pasteur Institute, endeavor to promote artisan manufacture by equipping makers with scientific knowledge of cheese chemistry and microbiology for working effectively "with nature," as Paul Kindstedt has said, in transforming milk into cheese. Codirector Catherine Donnelly explained in our interview, "We believe by putting people through classes that illustrate, firsthand, 'Here are the risks, here is how to man- age them, here's what you have to pay attention to'—knowledge is power, right? It's a much better approach than sending out an inspector to tell people what they're doing wrong all the time." Instead of reprimanding producers, VIAC wants to inculcate in them a scientifically sound microbiopolitical ethos that considers food safety to be an aspect of artisanal proficiency.[65]

D'Amico's workshop on risk-reduction practices encourages cheesemakers to approach hygiene as constitutive of craft practice. On this snowy day, my classmates included three well-established farmstead cheesemakers (one brought along a couple of interns), a novice (now award-winning) cheesemaker, a food distributor, a woman who aspired to open a cheese shop in the Midwest, and a former dairy farmer. For hours, we followed D'Amico's detailed PowerPoint presentation and took copious notes in three-ring binders provided by VIAC. The atmosphere was somber as well as studious, as the tenuous legal viability of raw-milk cheese cast a long shadow over D'Amico's presentation.

D'Amico systematically demonstrated that cheesemaking microbiopolitics extends far beyond the sixty-day rule to feature in producers' decision-making at every turn (note that my ethnographic report is presented to highlight this dimension and does not necessarily represent D'Amico's priorities). Design of facilities, whether and how to open facilities to public viewing, choice of coagulant, selection of cheese styles, hiring practices, and, most centrally, whether to make cheese from raw or pasteurized milk all raise microbiopolitical questions.[66] Risk, he lectured, is inherent in cheesemaking and in cheese. Gesturing toward his first PowerPoint slide picturing a surfer riding a wave, he commented that people often think of risk in positive terms as being about "daring, fearlessness, adventure"—a matter of individual character. "But this is not my message!" Instead, he urged us to realize that, as cheesemakers, "when you take risks you're putting others at risk, too."

D'Amico began by reviewing the twentieth-century history of milk-borne illness. With the exception of *Salmonella,* which has demonstrated remarkable durability, the major culprits between 1900 and 1940 were germs we no longer hear about—*Corynebacteria diphtheriae, Mycobacterium tuberculosis, Streptococcus pyogenes* (associated with scarlet fever). D'Amico reviewed such bugs, rendered obsolete thanks to Pasteurian practices of mandatory vaccination and improved public hygiene, because "they can come back." Another instance of post-Pasteurianism, after all, is resistance to routine vaccination, most notably by those convinced that thimerosal, a mercury-based preservative previously used in vaccines, might cause autism—or even, drawing a parallel with antibiotics resistance, that "overvaccination" might undermine a child's natural immune system.[67] "Because not everybody is doing vaccinations anymore, I might want to be sure everyone working in my plant has been vaccinated for diphtheria," D'Amico said, adding that migrant workers might not be vaccinated, and "in Mexico typhoid is endemic."

This is microbiopolitics: acting on recognition that human social relations are frequently threaded through microbial bodies. D'Amico encouraged cheesemakers to institute sick-day policies to ensure that employees who fall ill will stay home from work or be reassigned to tasks that will not bring them into contact with milk or cheese. In response, one cheesemaker at the workshop reported having learned (after the fact) about employees coming to work with diarrhea.

Her voice became pinched in frustration as she explained that she cannot afford to pay people not to come to work, as she put it, and her employees do not want to lose their pay. She depicted it as an impossible situation. D'Amico was sympathetic, but unbending. He related several dairy-related illness outbreaks in which ill persons handling milk and cheese by hand were implicated, commenting as an aside, "employee health is a bigger issue than I'd considered." [68]

Managing the microbial environment—what Catherine Donnelly, D'Amico's former thesis adviser, also advocates—begins with farm ecologies of production. Avoid feeding dairy animals silage (fermented grain and hay) because it is notorious for harboring *Listeria*. Keep feed bins covered and protected from bird and other animal poop. Control fly populations. Test water quality more frequently than the annual testing of cheese plants performed by state inspectors.[69] One seemingly commonsense piece of advice—keep deer out of sheep pastures—reveals how microbiopolitical management of the environment can challenge environmentalist attitudes, which are generally in sync with post-pastoralism. *Mycobacterium bovis* can cross species boundaries and cause tuberculosis in humans, which is a major reason why milk came to be pasteurized in the first place.[70] D'Amico advised that deer be kept out of pastures because farms and cheesemaking facilities can be infected by *Mycobacterium* species (*bovis, tuberculosis*, etc.) carried by wild animals and deposited on the ground in fecal material. A farmstead cheesemaker in the class countered that it is impossible in Vermont to keep deer out of sheep pastures—without a gun, anyway. If it takes hunting to keep down the deer population around sheep pastures, a cautious microbiopolitics might suggest removing the no-hunting signs.

In a series of slides, D'Amico walked us through the most serious pathogens for cheesemakers to consider and what may be tested for in routine FDA samples of cheese products. These were *Listeria monocytogenes,* various *Salmonella* species, *Escherichia coli,* enterohemorrhagic *E. coli* (O157:H7), and *Staphylococcus aureus.* The FDA has "zero tolerance" for *Salmonella* and *E. coli* O157:H7 as well as *L. monocytogenes,* meaning (as the Estrellas learned) that the agency can seize product if these bacteria are detected in any amount in a twenty-five-gram sample.[71] *Staphylococcus aureus* produces a heat-resistant toxin that survives pasteurization and is held accountable for 85.5 percent of food-borne illness outbreaks related to milk and dairy products in France.[72] *Staph* may be present in raw milk.[73] It is also carried by people via the nose, throat, and groin and transmitted through contact. Hand-washing during food production and service helps to prevent the food poisoning caused by *Staph* infection, whose symptoms include vomiting as well as diarrhea. At great expense to small producers (such as Major Farm), voluntary recalls have followed outbreaks of non-life-threatening but undoubtedly unpleasant *Staph*-consistent symptoms traced to the consumption of artisanal cheese.

I had some difficulty listening to this part of D'Amico's presentation. Following dinner with classmates from a VIAC workshop on recall procedures I had taken the previous day, I had been up most of the night contending with *Staph*-consistent symptoms in the en suite bathroom of my bed-and-breakfast room. It was the first serious attack of food poisoning I had suffered (I was professionally grateful that cheese had not featured as part of my dinner). Without doubt, the experience gave me renewed appreciation for food safety.

Two issues are involved in producing food safely: knowing what the potential hazards are and how risk can be minimized, and consistently acting on that knowledge through routine practice. A responsible cheesemaker—a "good" one in microbiopolitical terms—is a thoroughly modern subject who internalizes hygiene as part of cheesemaking. And yet a study of safety practices among farmstead cheesemakers in the Northeast conducted by the University of Connecticut Cooperative Extension Service concluded, "Among farmstead cheese makers who claim to be knowledgeable in the area of food safety, it is evident that the knowledge does not always translate into good food safety practices in their operations."[74] Insanitary conditions observed and identified included

> lack of testing of sanitizer strength; no concern about sanitizer being overly
> strong
> use of deteriorating "raw wood" boards as shelving for aging cheeses
> infrequent and improper hand washing
> unclean storage of cheesemaking equipment
> moving from farm work or working with children to working in cheese room
> "without changing outer clothing"
> handling curd with bare hands
> dogs in cheese room.[75]

In my own visits to artisan creameries, I have witnessed wide variation in protective clothing worn (e.g., hairnets or caps, lab coats or street clothes), in policies regarding visitor entry into cheesemaking facilities while processing is taking place, and in strategies for keeping environmental contaminants out of cheese facilities—something of particular concern on farms, where livestock live in proximity to food processing. How can we account for risk-taking behavior among knowledgeable and conscientious persons?

Risk "is always assessed from a specific, experiential location," Rayna Rapp observes.[76] Among cheesemakers, that location may be informed by prior occupational and educational experience, by histories of personal and family health, and by gender, among other things.[77] Cleaning and sanitizing is productive of high-quality cheese because it helps enable the good microbes, the bacterial agents of fermentation and the flavor-producing molds, to win out over the harmful. For generations American women have been targeted by lessons in good hygiene through home economics classes, how-to manuals, and household product advertising; they have been socialized to think hygienically.[78] In my interviews, female cheesemakers frequently spoke authoritatively about sanitation while, in comparison, a few men admitted to shocked surprise at discovering, in the words of one, that "80 percent of quality cheese is cleaning up." One man in Massachusetts said to me about cleaning cheesemaking equipment, "I always thought about it as a chore. I'd give as little attention to it as I could, but it's really a science unto itself. If you want to properly clean a certain surface, you need so much percentage of soap and so many minutes—if you approach it like that, it's not so much cleaning up, it's doing something necessary and productive."

At VIAC, at the University of California, Davis, and across Europe, microbiologists are beginning to study cheese development, not to contribute to industrial efficiency, but to gain a better sense of what is happening in less-standardized and less-sterile cheesemaking facilities with the aim of fortifying artisanal methods. Not only are their questions different from the applied science of industry; their methods differ as well. While in his controlled experiment the South Dakota researcher neglected to add the amount of salt that would be used in cheese for human consumption, when D'Amico makes a test vat of cheese he takes pains to replicate (in miniature) the conditions of a real food. In addition to experimental science, D'Amico also conducts field science, driving to cheesemaking farms across Vermont to collect environmental and cheese samples for testing that will give him, along with the farmer-cheesemakers, an empirical snapshot of actual conditions, rather than a hypothetical worst-case scenario. Experimental sciences and field sciences operate differently. "Laboratory workers eliminate the element of place from their experiments," writes Robert Kohler, while field biologists "use places actively in their work as tools; they do not just work *in* a place, as lab biologists do, but *on* it. Places are as much the object of their work as the creatures that live in them."[79] D'Amico is not only studying *Listeria monocytogenes;* he is studying, say, Laini's and Jon's and Linda's particular ecologies of production. The bacteria connect D'Amico the scientist to the farmer-cheesemakers who produce the food he not only studies, but also eats. As Kohler puts it, "nature connects field biologists to other social worlds."[80]

Returning to the field study conducted by the University of Connecticut Extension, it is worth noting that while some of the observed insanitary practices would seem to violate common sense (dogs!), others may in fact be considered proper artisanal practice. It would be difficult to gain a proper feel for the curd while wearing rubber gloves, for example. And as Albert Deppeler learned when he worked with Norman Kraft to modernize Limburger production in Wisconsin in the 1930s, wooden boards—if properly maintained—contribute a microbial environment conducive to developing a proper smear of *B. linens* on a washed rind. The affidavit filed by an FDA compliance officer as part of the seizure order against Estrella Creamery castigated as insanitary what sounds like routine practice in *affinage:* "Most significantly, the owner was observed tasting the cheese and placing the uneaten portion back into the cheese wheel."[81] While the FDA officer (who did not carry out the inspection) makes this sound sinister, it is standard practice in curing cheese to pull a core sample from a wheel using a specially designed tool called a trier, break off a bit of the sample, taste it to determine how long to age the wheel, and then plug up the hole with a remnant of the sampled cheese; microbial activity will bind the cheese back together. If the U.S. government wants to support the artisanal cheese industry rather than undermine it, inspectors, extension agents, and third-party auditors might be better familiarized with basic artisanal production methods.

At the same time, some of the risk-reduction techniques that artisan cheese-makers employ may not be as effective as they believe. "One of the riskiest practices in a dairy plant in regards to *Listeria*," said D'Amico, is the improper use of high-pressure water hoses to clean drains, floors, and equipment. I have seen such equipment used in countless facilities and have even been handed the high-pressure hose to "help" out myself. In the workshop, we learned that the water splashed up on walls and equipment might harbor pathogens, that pooled water and floor drains are the most likely environmental homes for *Listeria* growth, and that hose nozzles, floor squeegees, and wheels that carry carts between rooms are all likely agents of contamination if not regularly sanitized.[82] Although my classmates seemed to find paid sick leaves impractical, I suspected from their diligent note-taking that many would rethink their cleaning routines.

Environmental management is effective in inhibiting pathogens, but it is not failsafe. D'Amico recommended routine environmental swabbing and testing for pathogens in cheese making and aging facilities, which is largely how European regulations promote food safety (though heat treatment is increasingly embraced). The only true safeguard of consumer health would be to test every cheese of every batch for the presence of pathogens prior to marketing, but at sixty-five dollars plus shipping to send each sample to a lab, universal product testing is a prohibitive expense. In other words, there is no true safeguard. In a post-Pasteurian world, there is only risk reduction.[83]

"WHAT'S OUT THERE?"

There is, however, more to cheese microbiology than developing methods of pathogen risk-reduction. Wanting to study, through cheese, how communities of bacteria and fungi interact with one another, Rachel Dutton is engaged in natural science research aimed at learning, as she puts it, "what's out there" on the rinds of cheese. This is more Darwinian field exploration than technoscience.

Rachel wants to understand what a cheese is and how it got that way; she is not professionally interested in improving its market stability. Her early sequencing has turned up a few surprises. When Dutton cultured and sequenced the rind of Winnimere, Jasper Hill's raw-milk, salt-brined cheese washed with a local lambic beer, she found that the predominant bacterium was not, as might be expected from an orange-colored washed-rind cheese, *Brevibacterium linens*. It was *Halomonas variabilis,* a salt-loving bacterium that does not appear in cheese science textbooks. It is associated with hypersaline ponds, Arctic sea ice, and deep-sea hydrothermal vents. How did these extremophilic bacteria end up on Jasper Hill cheese? And what might that tell us about cheese rinds—and environmental microbiology—more generally?

Mateo and Andy Kehler were particularly excited to learn about another bacterium that Dutton found on their Winnimere: *Brachybacterium,* an unusual microbe that has been found in Arctic sea ice, on human skin, and in an Etruscan tomb. It was the tomb that captured the Kehlers' fancy. While Dutton is interested in generalizing from cheese, cheesemakers like the Kehlers are more interested in specificity. Might there be, they wonder, a microorganism indigenous and unique to their farm and their cheese? On the wall of Jasper Hill's complex of cheese caves, cheesemaker and microbiologist Noella Marcellino has scrawled, "The world of cheese awaits wonderful cheeses aged in these beautiful caves. And I await learning more about the fungi grown here that are uniquely yours!"[84] Post-pastoral, post-Pasteurian cheesemakers such as the Kehlers seek to rescue indigenous microbial cultures from industrial homogeneity. Not only do they spy marketing potential for distinguishing their product, they also are drawn to the possibility of isolating a tangible, material connection between their cheese and the place, the environment, the land on which it comes into being.[85] Might unique or indigenous microorganisms offer a living emblem of their particular ecology of production?

As this chapter has shown, microbiopolitics produces new categories of food, new zones of regulation, and new alliances among farmers, artisans, research scientists, merchants, and foodies, as well as expanded notions of nutrition and health. It also brings into view new materials—microbes—for imagining post-pastoral relations among humans and other living things.[86] The appearance of full-color magnified images of Rachel Dutton's bacterial colonies in the spring 2011 issue of *Culture* magazine reflects an expanded awareness that our human bodies, like wheels of cheese, are largely made up of microbial bodies. If microbes are us, then the fact that microbes are cheese not only makes sense, it can make cheese, naturally "probiotic," appear to be an even more valuable and desirable food.

However, while scientific tools would seem to bring the invisible forces of fermentation and cheese-rind development into visibility and hence legibility, as those scientific tools are employed more thoroughly it may become less clear, not more, what meanings we should draw from the "good" microbes that are cheese. While the Kehlers were most taken with the strain of halophilic bacteria that matched some found in an Etruscan tomb, Winnimere's halophiles are also similar to ones that colonize human skin. According to Dutton, this likely reflects the shared environmental characteristics, from a microbial perspective, of soft salty cheese, seawater, and sweaty human skin. *Brevibacterium linens* not only gives smear-ripened cheeses their pungent orange rind, it is closely related to *Brevibacterium epidermis,* native to the "warm, humid clefts between human toes."[87] As material symbols of the distinctiveness of place-based taste, the Etruscan tomb is far more romantic, though no more representative, than sweaty armpits.

The next chapter will consider how the French notion of *terroir,* glossed as "the taste of place," is being taken up in the United States as a way of framing self-consciously cultivated relations between cultural practice and agrarian landscapes. Microbiopolitically, *terroir* talk champions raw-milk cheese as a biotechnology for regionalism (biotechnology being a technology derived from the scientific use of living organisms or parts of organisms)—or, in more contemporary argot, as a biotechnology for localism, the expression of a people's connection to a piece of land. But yet again, as we will see, microbes defy the boundaries humans attempt to shore up, whether material or classificatory. Place may be better tasted in other ways.

7

Place, Taste, and the Promise of *Terroir*

Every raw-milk cheese is an artifact of the land; it carries the imprint of the earth from which it came. A cheese—even a fresh chèvre—is never just a thing to put in your mouth. It's a living piece of geography. A sense of place.
—BRAD KESSLER, *GOAT SONG*

Each place at the table was set with two glasses of wine, white and red, flanking a dinner plate arrayed with wedges of seven cheeses surrounding a small dish of an eighth, soft cheese in the center. As I took a chair at the front of the conference room at the Petaluma Sheraton, I noted baskets of crispy flat breads and cups of water close at hand for us amateur tasters, attendees of the third annual California Artisan Cheese Festival, to cleanse our palates between cheeses.[1] Having attended many such recreational tastings, I knew we would first sample the fresh cheese and then proceed in a clockwise fashion from the soft-ripened cheese positioned at twelve o'clock. I also knew to wait to begin nibbling until prompted by the hosts of the session, titled "Go Local-Global with the Cowgirls." In their cheerful introduction, Sue Conley and Peggy Smith of Cowgirl Creamery in Point Reyes Station, California, explained that they had selected the cheeses on our plates, French and domestic, to "address the *terroir* topic." They would "talk about cheeses in terms of the place they're made in, and how place contributes to the cheese."

Terroir is a French term dating back to the thirteenth century, used primarily to describe the influence of the material conditions of a vineyard locale (particularly soil quality and sun exposure) on the sensory character of a wine.[2] By the eighteenth century, *terroir* and the expression *goût du terroir,* "flavor of the terrain," had been elaborated to offer an agrarian model for how people and place, cultural tradition and landscape ecology, could develop in relation to one another over time.[3] Wine writer Hugh Johnson defines *terroir* as "the whole ecology of the vineyard: every aspect of its surroundings from bedrock to late frosts to autumn mists, not excluding the way the vineyard is tended, nor even the soul of the vigneron."[4] Since the productive ecology behind artisanal cheese encompasses a similarly heterogeneous mix of material and symbolic forces, it is no surprise that in recent years the notion of *terroir* has taken hold in cheese worlds on both sides of the Atlantic.

Amy Trubek writes that *terroir* is best understood as a conceptual category "for framing and explaining people's relationship to the land, be it sensual, practical, or habitual."[5] Wine and foods understood to embody and express the unique typicity of a place help to define and reproduce such relationships. In France, that notion of place refers not only to the material conditions of a locale— soil, topography, microclimate—but also to the collective, cultural know-how behind agricultural products that helps to constitute place as a locus of shared tradition and affective belonging. When the consortium of Comté cheese producers claims a thousand-year history for Comté, a product distinguishable by a characteristic sensory profile said to emerge from a place-based tradition of dairying and cheesemaking, they root a people as well as a food product in the soil of the French Alps; the connections are figured to be, as Trubek puts it, "as timeless as the earth itself."[6]

In the United States, cheesemakers are test-driving *terroir* as a vehicle for conveying the value of their craft practice and products. They do so both *descriptively* and *prescriptively*. As a value-adding marketing label, descriptive claims to "*terroir* taste" may boost a cheese's price per pound, its exchange value, by promoting place-based distinction. Cypress Grove Chevre's Web site illustrates: "We like to think that the softness and mystery of the fog infuses our cheese. A Humboldt Fog made in Peoria just wouldn't be the same!" The suggestion that the physical characteristics of a place—here, coastal fog and salty Pacific breezes— leave an indelible mark on a cheese implies that the cheese is so special it could not be replicated elsewhere.[7]

In France, the idea that *terroir* delineates the typicity of a place underpins the bureaucratically regulated system of *appellation d'origine contrôlée* (AOC), or geographic origin labeling. Under this system, certain agricultural products may be manufactured and sold under registered place-names—Champagne, say, or Camembert de Normandie—only if production occurs within designated geographical areas and complies with specified methods. AOC cheese rules may regulate the breed of animal (not only species) milked, stipulate whether animals graze on alpine slopes or valleys, determine whether heat treatment of milk is permissible, and set the recipe for how a particular cheese is made.[8] The idea is that AOC rules might protect through regulation the sort of collective enterprise that David and Cindy Major witnessed during their 1993 trip to the French Pyrenees, when they visited shepherds who worked in mountain huts to make cheeses that were distributed equally among families.[9]

Inspired by that cooperative activity, in the late 1990s David and Cindy secured a Sustainable Agriculture Research and Education (SARE) grant to train other Vermont families to milk sheep on their own farms, craft Vermont Shepherd, and send the green wheels to Major Farm to be collectively ripened, labeled, and marketed.[10] The Vermont Shepherd guild lasted only a few years, though its influence on Vermont cheesemaking endures. Once members got the hang of sheep dairying, they moved on to develop their own labels and cheeses, adapting techniques from Vermont Shepherd and milking flocks seeded with the genetic stock of the Majors' lambs.[11] Seeking personal recognition for their creativity and innovation, American artisans do not want to be boxed in by place, constrained by tradition or bureaucracy, or confined to ecological niches.

Acknowledging American individualism, claims to *terroir* taste among U.S. cheesemakers tend to scale down to the privately owned farm, rather than up to encompass a geographical region—more a matter of intellectual property than of collective patrimony. When the Web site of Marin County's Point Reyes Farmstead Cheese joins Cypress Grove Chevre in claiming the influence of Pacific breezes, it proclaims not regional affinity with Humboldt Fog so much as a similar source of distinctiveness: "What makes Farmstead cheese so special? The French have a word for it . . . 'Terroir.' From the land. About the land. Of the land. The terroir of a farm has everything to do with the end product."[12] When used as a descriptive term to promote place-based distinction, *terroir* conveys the intrinsic values of a cheese or other foodstuff, attributing quality in taste to the material, environmental characteristics of a place. But how to draw meaningful borderlines between one *"terroir"* and the next? In Europe, this is largely a political and legal question fought out by producers' unions and bureaucrats; in the United States, at least for cheeses, it is up to the claimant's discretion.

This chapter focuses on how American cheesemakers are translating the concept of *terroir* to argue that the gustatory values that make artisanal cheeses taste good to eat are fundamentally rooted in craft practices that are themselves valuable. In this articulation, *terroir* is not so much about cheese's intrinsic value but instead raises instrumental questions of value: what good might be achieved by making farmstead cheese, not only for those who make it, but also for the agrarian communities and landscapes from which a cheese emerges? The notion that *terroir* may become a model for the instrumental value of artisanal foods was evident at the California Artisan Cheese Festival tasting seminar. Drawing on *terroir*'s holism, artisan entrepreneurs such as Sue Conley and Peggy Smith argue that the commercial value of their cheese derives from the same underlying assets that it protects: unconfined dairy animals, family farms, revitalized rural communities, working landscapes. These assets, many believe, have the potential to revitalize rural places or even to create place anew. The question of *terroir*—like "farmstead," "sustainable," "local," and other quality labels—is less a matter of attributes to be defined than an ethical argument to be made.

This American incarnation of *terroir*, rooted in the Lockean virtue of improving society through improving the land, reframes it as a *prescriptive* category for thoughtful action, for creating from the ground up places where some people wish to live, and others to visit—or at least taste. Such experiments in translating *terroir* raise a number of questions. When people claim that an artisanal cheese tastes of place—or that artisanal cheesemaking might improve the economic or environmental conditions of a place—what sort of place are they talking about? What conditions, and which residents, may be excluded from portraits of place-making?[13] And why presume that "place" is good to eat, or that it tastes good? With these questions in mind, I discuss how cheesemakers' *terroir* talk offers a means for conveying what they view as fundamental connections between the gustatory and instrumental values of artisanal cheese. Rather than derive the value of authenticity from demonstrating continuity with the past (as with Comté), these translations of *terroir* embody more American aspirations invested in place: environmental stewardship, agrarian enterprise, and rural community.

Elaborating on each of these values in turn, I have selected emblematic cases of people addressing the "*terroir* topic" in each of the states where I conducted significant research. First, at stake in the taste education at the California cheese festival is the idea that commercial food-making can be consistent with environmentalist principles and practices. Second, for Wisconsin, I look at state-level efforts to promote regional dairying and cheesemaking. In seeking a material basis for a Wisconsin cheese "*terroir*," whether in geography or local microbial ecology, consultants hope to stake out common ground among cheese factories, multigenerational dairy farmers, and post-pastoral artisans. Third, I return to where this book began, at Jasper Hill Farm in Vermont, to investigate the Kehler brothers' grassroots experiments in reverse-engineering a regionally meaningful "*terroir*" that might boost the rural economy and community of northeastern Vermont. Built into the foundation of an expansive cheese aging facility is the hope that value-added agriculture can bring economic benefits to rural economies without imposing drastic cultural change on rural communities. In each of these cases, people who are inspired by the holistic sensibility of *terroir* also draw on its naturalistic language to legitimate their cultural projects.

Let me acknowledge that the material specificity of agricultural production does influence what we taste when we sip a well-made wine, bite into a home-grown tomato, or savor an artisanal cheese. Indeed, as I have argued, part of what makes artisanal cheese artisanal is that artisans work with, rather than overcome, environmental influences and organic variations in milk that affect the sensory qualities of cheese. However, what people mean in the United States when they talk about *terroir* is still being worked out.[14] Even in France, the concept is not without controversy.[15] My task is not to determine what *terroir* is or is not, but rather to analyze how and why it has come to matter to many American artisan cheesemakers and their boosters. For now, *terroir* offers a conceptual terrain on which artisan entrepreneurs work to negotiate the potentially fraught relation between the ecological and moral values they espouse, and the commercial values they seek.[16]

LEARNING TO TASTE PLACE AT
THE CALIFORNIA ARTISAN CHEESE FESTIVAL

"Go Local-Global with the Cowgirls," the tasting seminar led by Sue Conley and Peggy Smith, was a popular event at the 2009 California Artisan Cheese Festival. Longtime friends, both women moved from the East Coast to the Bay Area in the flower-power 1970s and arrived at cheese by way of the restaurant industry; for seventeen years Peggy cooked at the upstairs café of Chez Panisse, that epicenter of California Cuisine. In guiding our tasting of each cheese on our plate, Conley and Smith drew our attention to numerous principles and practices that might define *terroir*. Throughout, they directed our taste education toward greater understanding of and appreciation for where food comes from, how it is made, and why that matters to how food tastes.[17] The Cowgirls harnessed appreciation for *terroir* taste to give an economic and even moral warrant to counterindustrial methods of farming and food-making.

First up on our plates was Cowgirl Creamery's own *fromage blanc*, a simple, fresh cheese used primarily by chefs ("like cream cheese"), selected "to show the reflection of the milk" from the organic dairy of their neighbor and friend in Point Reyes Station, Albert Straus. As with the second cheese we tasted, Cowgirl Creamery's Mt. Tam, Conley and Smith wanted "to showcase his hard work . . . how he's taken care of the land and his animals." An organic dairy farm, Straus's pastures are free of herbicides and chemical fertilizers; the cows are not treated with hormones or antibiotics. The message conveyed was that the "good, clean" milk we were meant to taste in the fresh cheese was thanks to Straus's environmentally conscious dairying practice. Albert, we learned, inherited his environmentalism from his mother, Ellen, who—inspired by Rachel Carson's *Silent Spring*—cofounded the Marin Agricultural Land Trust to preserve land for agricultural use. The Cowgirls' narrative focuses attention on the role of stewardship in creating the material basis not only of milk (what I have described as ecologies of production), but also on the agricultural *place* said to be typified by a *terroir* cheese. Conley and Smith went on to describe Straus's newly installed methane digester, apparently without worry that we would register suggestive hints of manure in the odor and taste of the cheese. Instead, we were meant to taste the goodness of greenhouse gas mitigation.[18] Something is happening here to taste education.

Combining discernment and cultural distinction, taste education most often refers to *connoisseurship*. Learning to isolate and identify particular flavors, the connoisseur is encouraged to cultivate taste preferences that signal a trained palate. Susan Terrio describes how French consumers of chocolate, exposed to a taste standard adapted from wine connoisseurship, have been educated not only to discern a difference between milk and dark chocolate, but to *prefer* dark. Through an appropriately educated palate, consumers can demonstrate that they are worthy of accruing for themselves the symbolic capital conveyed in a gourmet food.[19] The Cowgirls' cheese tasting conformed to the taste education of connoisseurship, in that we were enjoined to isolate and identify particular flavors in the cheeses through drawing analogies to other, familiar odors and flavors. Mt. Tam, our tasting notes suggested, "is firm, yet buttery with a mellow, early flavor reminiscent of white mushrooms." Once the word *mushroom* was lodged in my mind it was impossible *not* to taste mushroom in the cheese's fungal rind.

However, in contrast to the taste education described by Terrio, at this and many such cheese tastings I have attended, I have never felt my taste preference judged, meaning that I cannot recall an occasion when someone in a position of authority suggested that, say, a hard-aged cheese is inherently and importantly superior to a bloomy-rind one. In the United States, taste education accommodates the individual value of consumer choice: so long as some preference leads to a purchase, few cheesemongers will quibble with what that preference is.[20] Admittedly, I have heard a prominent cheesemonger claim that only cheese made from raw milk qualifies as "real" cheese and that pasteurizing milk would erode any *terroir*-specific flavors originating in pasture grasses. But I have also heard precisely the opposite: that most consumers cannot (and more, need not) taste a difference between raw-milk and pasteurized-milk cheese and that numerous award-winning cheeses are, in fact, made from pasteurized milk.[21] Jeff Roberts, who happily revealed at a blind tasting of raw- and pasteurized-milk cheeses staged in Cambridge, Massachusetts, that Cowgirl Creamery's cheeses are all made from pasteurized milk, also remarked, "The last thing I want to see happen with good cheese is that it takes on the mystique of good wine" through the use of intimidating, jargony descriptors. He would much rather people express their taste in simple terms—"I like the center more than the outside."[22]

For California's winemakers and cheesemakers alike, the vocabulary of *terroir* connects quality in taste to quality in production method.[23] Educational cheese tastings promote counterindustrial food-making indirectly because healthy animals, clean milk, and a diversity of pasture grasses are said to lead to great-tasting cheese. But, as I learned by attending another session at the California cheese festival, "Best Farming Practices Yield Best Artisan Food," taste education can promote counterindustrial farming directly by calling attention to what it can accomplish beyond contributing to tasty food: boosting the fertility and health of pasture soils, contributing to cleaner watersheds by reducing chemical runoff, and keeping land in agricultural use and out of the hands of developers. As befitting a food festival held in Sonoma County, this panel juxtaposed farmstead cheesemaking to the story of organic and biodynamic wine production.

California's wine industry ramped up production volumes after World War II by plying monocropped vineyards with chemical fertilizers, insecticides, and fungicides. By the 1980s, environmentalist concern over water quality came together with winegrowers' dismay over "listless" vines and personal concern for the health of their workers and families to prompt many growers to rethink production methods. Lange Twins Winery in Lodi is one such farm. Speaking as a "Best Farming Practices" panelist at the California cheese festival, fourth-generation Lodi farmer and third-generation grape grower Randy Lange explained that when he and his brother took over the farm, "We looked back to the future," backpedaling from agrochemical inputs to introduce low-tech methods that would have seemed sensible to their great-grandparents, such as fostering the habitat of insect-eating beetles and barn swallows as well as rodent-eating owls, and planting winter cover crops between rows of vines to restore depleted nutrients to the soil. In California, as Amy Trubek writes, "terroir represents a less mechanistic and less invasive philosophy of winemaking."[24]

Many of today's grape growers and dairy farmers, among them baby boomers shaped by the environmentalist ethos of the 1960s and 1970s, insist that agriculture, in the guise of stewardship, can have a positive impact on environmental resources. The Langes farm organically, Randy said, because they believe it is "the right thing to do" for their family's and employees' health and for the sake of generations to come. Some argue further that growing grapes (or producing milk) without chemical inputs enhances the potential for *terroir* taste in wine (and cheese); "Organic growing is the only path of grape growing that leads to optimum quality and expression of the land in wine," says John Williams, owner of Frog's Leap Winery in Napa Valley.[25]

There is little economic incentive, at the retail end, to craft a naturally aged cheese from organic milk or to distill wine from organically grown grapes. Complicating critiques of "green consumerism," which suggest that consumers who are willing to pay a premium for organic and fair-trade goods do so because they want to feel good about their purchasing choices (and so the organic or fair-trade label becomes a new fetish to distinguish a familiar commodity like coffee), organic-labeling has proved to depress wine prices.[26] "Good" wine in connoisseurs' terms could not possibly be organic—this common perception dates back to the 1970s, when organic wine made without stabilizing sulfites developed a reputation for turning quickly to vinegar. Among many wine drinkers, *organic* remains associated with off-flavors (and perhaps hippies). The irony is that many premium wines are in fact made (using sulfites) from organically grown grapes.[27] Organic and biodynamic methods do seem to improve vine health and grape flavor, quality characteristics that carry into wine, and so—despite the fact that wine consumers are unwilling to pay a premium for eco-labels—"certified though unlabeled wine enjoys a significant premium."[28]

When Randy Lange acknowledged at the cheese festival that only one of their seven acres is certified organic since certification costs money, I wondered why they—or, for that matter, farmstead producers of high-end cheeses—would go to the expense and bureaucratic trouble of certifying *any* vineyards or milk-producing ecologies as organic. University of California researchers Magali Delmas and Laura Grant suggest that, in addition to providing consultation on environmental management, eco-certification offers a social capital benefit to growers by boosting their reputation among peers as good stewards of the land.[29] In California, perhaps more than anywhere else, 1970s counterculture merges with 2010s business-class mainstream when "best practice"—management jargon for proven methodology or technique—purports to temper the capitalist virtue of efficiency with the post-pastoral virtue of nurturing nature.

"Stewardship," this reminds us, is more a matter of reputation than a proven methodology. If handmade cheeses, especially when made from raw milk, seem to defy standardization, then to what extent can anyone actually oversee, to the microscopic scale, anything as complex as a vineyard or farmstead ecology of production? Evolutionary biologist Lynn Margulis once dismissed claims of environmental stewardship by saying, "The idea that we are consciously caretaking such a large and mysterious system" as the earth "is ludicrous."[30]

When *terroir* is used as a form of eco-labeling to link high-quality taste to method of production (without the baggage of "organic" labeling), the term runs up against the same problems of reductionism that bedevil organic foods and geographic indications. Although federal certification of organics labeling arguably intended to defetishize food commodities by reinvesting a tomato or a lemon with the value of its social and biological history, when consumers pay a premium for organic produce they may not be getting food grown according to what they imagine to be organic methods and principles.[31] The organic label has come to have a life of its own, detached from the reality of production. Robert Ulin argues much the same of AOC wine, suggesting that, between the bureaucracy of geographical indications and the rhetoric of *terroir*, Bordeaux gains status over a *vin ordinaire* like Médoc "from a process of invention that transforms culturally constructed criteria of authenticity and quality into ones that appear natural."[32] At annual meetings of the American Cheese Society (ACS) and other venues, people repeatedly voice reminders that unreflective claims of cheese *terroir* risk "crossing the line" into mere marketing.[33] Product labeling is a tricky business.

Through the taste education that happens at artisanal food festivals and recreational tastings, talk of *terroir*—when it is gathered together with eco-certification, humane husbandry, and organic farming—can label artisan producers no less than artisanal comestibles as "good"—not only skilled, but moral—in the eyes of the type of consumer who attends wine tastings and food festivals. By suggesting that environmentally sound agriculture is required to convey the *terroir* of a place to the taste of a cheese or wine—and since *terroir* is scaled down to the level of an individual farm—farm families can accrue moral credit (in addition, perhaps, to an economic premium) for the expression of *terroir* taste in their products. In making moral claims, they also open themselves to moral scrutiny.

At the same time, the California Artisan Cheese Festival presented the idea that consumer taste—an eater's gastronomic appreciation as well as cultural distinction—can be enhanced by an eater's knowledge of the instrumental values that an artisanal mode of production affords. Why does cheese taste good? It is not merely because cheese is a food rich in fat and salt, nor even that well-made artisanal cheese reflects the taste of clean milk, healthy animals, and fresh pastures. The festival's taste education suggested that consumer enjoyment of a cheese can be heightened by knowing that the methods of its fabrication helped to accomplish other ends as well—in keeping agricultural land out of the hands of developers, or in the organic remediation of industrially damaged land, or in sustaining the ability of a fourth generation to continue farming as a family. Here, eaters with "good taste" are enjoined to taste the social place of a "good" cheese—or, perhaps, the "goodness" of a place-based cheese.[34]

TRADING ON *TERROIR* TO PROMOTE WISCONSIN CHEESE

In Wisconsin, too, cheese quality, quality of production method, and natural environmental conditions are being bundled together through the language of *terroir*.[35] But in addition to being scaled to the level of an individual farm, here *terroir* is also being adjusted to encompass the political territory of a state. "Wisconsin's rolling hills, limestone-filtered waters, and rich soils have created the perfect *terroir* for producing cheeses second to none," writes James Robson, CEO of the Wisconsin Milk Marketing Board, in his preface to *Wisconsin Cheese: A Cookbook and Guide to the Cheeses of Wisconsin*.[36] Much as Trubek writes of Vermont maple syrup, boosters are investigating whether the "taste of place" embodied by Wisconsin cheese could serve as a brand for promoting the state's dairy sector, as well as its image.[37] One way to scale up *terroir*, they are discovering, is to zoom down to the microscopic scale of bacteria and fungi.

The best thing to happen to Wisconsin's artisanal and farmstead cheese industry may well have been the California Milk Marketing Board's decision to launch the nationwide television broadcast of the "Great Cheese Comes from Happy Cows [and] Happy Cows Come from California" ad campaign during the 2005 Super Bowl. Green Bay Packers fans were not pleased by Californian claims to dairying superiority. Already aware that California's total cheese production was on course to overtake Wisconsin's number one position, and with nothing less than the state's self-image as "America's Dairyland" at stake (the title appears on state license plates and on Wisconsin's commemorative quarter), the Happy Cows ad campaign prompted the Wisconsin Milk Marketing Board to shift strategies. "Where Wisconsin is going to make its mark now is in the quality of the cheese," Jeanne Carpenter, communications director of the state's Dairy Business Innovation Center (DBIC), explained to a *New York Times* reporter in 2006.[38] Reading between the lines: California can keep its Humboldt Fog—midwestern cheeses will be even better.

I visited the DBIC team at their offices, housed in the state Department of Agriculture building, in July 2008. At my mention of California's Happy Cow ads, a staff member left the room to fetch for me a copy of *Milwaukee Magazine;* the September 2005 issue featured a cover story on the "cheese wars," which explains that Wisconsin will "win the battle" by beating California in the artisan and specialty sectors of the market.[39] The DBIC features as the hero of the story for its technical consulting work helping specialty cheese plants to upgrade or open. The center was created in 2004 with support from U.S. Senator Herb Kohl when he became chairperson of the Senate Agriculture Appropriations Committee ("I gather you've figured out we're one of those pork things," is how DBIC's director, Dan Carter, put it to me good-humoredly). Concluding, the article draws an analogy to a different sector of California agriculture, noting that Carr Valley Creamery's owner-cheesemaker, Sid Cook, "talks like a winemaker when he discusses why California will never produce cheese like Wisconsin's: 'In California, the milk is mild and perfect for processed cheese, but it doesn't age out nice. It has a flat flavor. More of a sulfur taste. It doesn't have the same fruitiness and complexity of Wisconsin cheese. . . . The huge advantage we have here is the *terroir.* . . . The beauty of the area is transmitted into the cheese.'"[40] It may veer into hyperbole, but Cook's rhetoric can be considered competitively strategic.

Confronting an increasingly competitive market, Wisconsin's DBIC has sponsored research to explore the potential for adapting *terroir* as a tool to promote regional artisanal and specialty cheesemaking and marketing on the national stage. Drawn to the possibility of isolating a tangible connection between a cheese and the material place—the environment, soil, grasses—from which it originates, in February 2011 the DBIC hosted a symposium proposing the establishment of a *terroir*-inspired designation for an area of southern Wisconsin known as the Driftless region, whose topography is marked by having escaped glaciation at the end of the Pleistocene.[41] In part because the new artisanal and farmstead cheesemakers nationwide imagine themselves as starting from scratch rather than reviving older traditions of craft practice, *terroir* language used in marketing tends to emphasize the influence of natural elements—microclimate, landscape, soil composition—over cultural factors such as customary method or shared culinary tradition. Wisconsin, whose proud regional tradition of cheese-making embraces the progress narrative of industrialization, is no exception.

Seeking an ecological anchor for the taste of place, cheesemakers and their supporters often appeal to the materiality of microbes. A DBIC press release from the *terroir* symposium declared, "The culture, geography and biology of a place give unique flavors to local food products, a concept that could help a group of small Wisconsin cheesemakers in its search to carve out a niche in the crowded marketplace for cheese."[42] The "biology of a place"—a striking phrase!—here refers to ambient microorganisms, whereas in France it might first signal particu-lar breeds of cows, sheep, or goats. Ivan Larcher, a French technical consultant who spoke at the symposium via Skype connection, framed *terroir* as a localized ecology, suggesting that the identity of the dozens of types of bacteria, yeasts, and molds that enter milk before and during the cheesemaking process "is different on different farms, even if they are only one mile apart." Shifting from a descrip-tive to a prescriptive register, Larcher continued, "The dream of every cheese-maker is to develop their own spectrum of bacteria, to make a personal signature. The spectrum is directly related to the place you live, and this is the concept of *terroir,* to make something different based on where you are."[43] Although Larcher, perhaps mindful of an American audience, depicts *terroir* as the personal project of farmstead cheesemakers (or the collaborative project between cheesemaker and dairy farmers), the DBIC workshop expressed clear interest in the possibility of scaling *terroir* back up to the level of a region—inventing, perhaps, a new tradi-tion of innovation. Gersende Cazaux, offering a preview of her DBIC-sponsored master's thesis, "Application of the Concept of Terroir in the American Context: Taste of Place and Wisconsin Unpasteurized Milk Cheeses," joined Larcher in proposing indigenous or ambient microorganisms as an emblem of Wisconsin's "taste of place," emphasizing their power to express the flavors of grass-based milk (especially when unpasteurized).[44]

From a microbial standpoint, however, "place" scales to the environment of a wheel of cheese rather than to the human-scaled environments—farms, counties, regions—that we inhabit. Researchers at the French National Institute for Agricultural Research have found through studies of smear-ripened cheeses that "bacteria isolated from a particular environment are not specific of that environment but are specific of the biochemical conditions (pH, temperature, carbon sources, nutrients requirements) that constitute that environment."[45] Recipe (and resulting cheese type) exerts a stronger selection pressure than does geography (and associated environment) on the microbial species in a particular cheese.[46] And what connoisseurs describe as "complex" flavor in a microbially rich raw-milk cheese derives not from the identity of any particular microbes but instead from the multiplicity of metabolic activity as diverse microbial species and strains break down enzymes and carbohydrates in milk. Microbial claims to cheese *terroir* would then seem to lie not in who microbes *are*, taxonomically speaking, but in what they *do* as organisms. What is it that cheese microbes are imagined to do? In breaking down enzymes in milk, releasing odors and flavors that originated in the fodder digested by ruminants, microbes connect place and taste in a very material way.

In the Driftless region of Wisconsin, I spent an afternoon with Willi Lehner, who took *terroir* into his own hands by inoculating the brine for a Havarti-style raw-milk cheese with soil microbes "harvested" from his backyard. His Earth Schmier cheese originated with an investigatory trip to the British Isles made possible by the DBIC-affiliated Wisconsin Dairy Artisan Research Program. He visited Irish farmhouse cheesemaker Giana Ferguson, known for inoculating her Gubbeen cheese with laboratory-cultured isolates of previously uncharacterized bacteria that a microbiologist discovered on the rinds of her smear-ripened cheese; one bacterium has since been named *Microbacterium gubbeenense*. Ferguson impressed upon Lehner an appreciation for the microbiodiversity all around us and, in particular, on one's own land; "the *terroir* is what's in the soil," Lehner reported having learned from Ferguson. "Don't kill something off until you know what it is," she advised.[47] Back home and outside gardening, Willi "picked up a handful of soil and said, 'This is where our microbes are!'" He strolled into the woods to gather soil samples, soaked clumps of dirt in water to extract the spores ("it's like germinating a seed"), and added the strained solution to light salt brine. "And what grew on the cheese was absolutely magnificent," he marveled. The toothsome cheese, covered with a sticky peach-colored rind inoculated with uncharacterized microbiota harvested from the woodlands surrounding the wood-frame house that Willi himself built in 1992, gives off a woodsy aroma.

Does Earth Schmier taste of the Driftless region or the woods behind Willi's house, or does it simply taste woodsy? How could any of us know? Absent a shared sensory field in which to evaluate such a claim, Earth Schmier works insofar as the idea of it is cool. It appeals to a popular, though demographically specific, understanding that local foods are good foods, and that authentic food should taste of place. The idea of Earth Schmier is not unlike "the message in the bottle" of "sustainable" wines in that it signals a positive correlation between cheese quality and quality of environmental conditions of production—and it is able to do so because the cheese also happens to be delicious, a quality that is not inherent to cheese simply by virtue of being made "by hand" or from raw milk.[48]

In Earth Schmier, as at the DBIC symposium, the microbe is being singled out as an emblem of farmstead or *terroir* ecologies of production. Microbially based *terroir* is compelling because microorganisms, invisible to the naked eye, would seem, as compared to dairy animals' breed or fodder, to be the wildest—and hence, most *natural*—element of a cheese's ecology of production. Whether in terms of "farmstead" designation or the "taste of place," in calling attention to ecologies of production, producers draw an analogy between their own labor practices and such naturally generative forces as decomposition. As I argued in chapter 2, this effectively naturalizes craft production methods, making them seem, as part of "nature," not only legitimate but also moral, in the normalizing sense of "that's how food *should* be made." In seeking to rescue indigenous microbial cultures from industrial homogeneity, post-Pasteurian cheesemakers such as Willi Lehner endeavor to legitimate post-pastoral agricultural practices.

When a place-based food is said to embody its environment, it remains to be asked what might be left out of the frame to make that place seem desirable for humans to ingest through eating.[49] As previously discussed, in no way are post-pastoral environments pristine or pure, and only by defining nature as inclusive of human manipulation—or by thoroughly obscuring the "hands on the land"—may agricultural landscapes be considered "natural."[50] When Steve Getz, as related in chapter 1, tells of digging syringes (for injecting cows with hormones) out of the manure pile on the dairy farm his family bought—the casualty of industrial farm economies—he offers an example of how making and selling cheese enables his family to engage in agricultural remediation. But it is a reminder, too, that in places like Wisconsin, today's grass pastures are yesterday's wheat fields, potentially depleted of soil nutrients and microbial as well as plant biodiversity. Microorganisms are no less cultivated by human activity than are livestock, though human-microbial relations remain less understood. Environmental toxins are one concern; local ecologies can be polluted and polluting.[51] Writing of ocean environments, Becky Mansfield asserts that the nutritional composition of fish today includes heavy metals; mercury has become part of what swordfish *is,* materially. By the same token, toxic *E. coli* is indigenous to livestock farms, while health-threatening *Listeria monocytogenes* is as ubiquitous as flavor-giving *Brevibacterium linens.* When Willi Lehner went microbe-gathering in the woods, he took care to collect a clean sample of dirt from below the surface from which to extract benign microbes. When it comes to the ambient microorganisms that can colonize cheese, not all are equally appealing.

When cultural projects are legitimated, even in part, by leaning on understandings of the natural world, as scientific researchers (such as Rachel Dutton) learn more about that world we might be confronted with knowledge that nature is not quite what many of us imagined it to be. Microbiologists like to say of their object of study that "everything is everywhere," and indeed, claims of grounding cheese *terroir* in local, indigenous microbial ecologies are running up against microbes' mobility—or rather, their ubiquity. More detailed assessments of the microbial populations that form the rinds of cheeses are bringing similarity rather than singularity into view—much as happened to race when molecular genetics revealed uniformity in the DNA sequences of humans from supposedly different populations.[52] A recent study of raw-milk smear-ripened cheese in France turned up trace amounts of Giana Ferguson's *Microbacterium gubbeenense*.[53] The French cheese, like the Winnimere that Dutton examined, was also host to multiple species of salt-loving marine microorganisms.[54]

Ambient microorganisms, unlike land and livestock, cannot be privately owned—this, I believe, is one reason why a microbial basis for *terroir* remains appealing to DBIC staff.[55] Their nonproprietary "nature" positions microbes as culturally neutral when the distinctions that matter in bridging (or dividing) the *people* who make cheese have to do with economic and cultural capital, rather than with artisan skill or whether one works with goat's, sheep's, or cow's milk. In theory, an ecologically based *terroir*, however scaled, could gather together various economies of sentiment and even ecologies of production within a unified geographic indication.

DBIC, I suggest, has turned to *terroir* as a potential "trading zone" to draw together Wisconsin's sociologically diverse cheese community. Peter Galison introduced the notion of the trading zone to analyze how physicists from different traditions of inquiry, experimentalist and theoretical, manage to collaborate, or exchange ideas, "even if they ascribe utterly different significance to the objects being exchanged. . . . Nonetheless, the trading partners can hammer out a *local* coordination despite vast *global* differences."[56] DBIC would seem to aspire to just this sort of pragmatic collaboration among the state's traditional dairying families, specialty cheese factories, and artisan newcomers. Wisconsin's Driftless region includes Anne Topham's one-woman Fantôme Farm, Mike Gingrich's well-capitalized Uplands Dairy, farmer's daughter Diana Murphy's Dreamfarm, the sheep dairy of former corporate manager Brenda Jensen, Willi Lehner's cheese aging facility, and Brunkow cheese factory's foray into artisanal cheeses via Fayette Creamery. Microbes care nothing for the divergent tastes and temporalities among these cheesemaking facilities. Wisconsin's DBIC wants to erect an equally inclusive umbrella under which to promote the distinctiveness and distinction of all types of Wisconsin-made cheese (of course, microbes are oblivious, too, of state borders).

Trading zones may facilitate pragmatic engagement across differential status positions, but they do not erase those differentials. In taking up the language of *terroir*, Sid Cook seems happy to imply a commonality among Wisconsin cheeses (if not cheesemakers) while differentiating them from the Californian competition. Are all members of Wisconsin's diverse cheese world so amenable, or are some dragged into this trading zone? If *"terroir"* were to become the new "artisan" in terms of marketing (though there is no evidence that it will), the stories related in chapter 4 would suggest that some Wisconsin cheesemakers would acquire the new "packaging skills" demanded of them, while others would simply continue to make and sell cheese, much as they always have.

REVERSE-ENGINEERING *TERROIR* AT THE CELLARS AT JASPER HILL IN VERMONT

Taste of place is not the same as taste of proximity. Each Saturday during the month I spent in Londonderry, Vermont, I took home from the West River farmers' market a half-wheel of Woodcock Farm's Summer Snow, knowing that Mark and Gari Fischer sell the seasonal, fragile, bloomy-rind sheep's-milk cheese in just a handful of venues. Summer Snow can be tasted only at certain times and in places not far removed from its site of production. Eaten locally in the sense embraced by the locavore movement, it offers a *taste of proximity*. But does Summer Snow also taste "like" the Fischers' pastures outside the township of Weston? Or the Green Mountains region? Or Vermont? Such questions cannot be answered by the length of a commodity chain. *Terroir* is about being *typical,* rather than about being fresh or simply local.

In Vermont, Mateo and Andy Kehler invest the productive activity of cheese-making with the potential to express place through taste—to typify it—but also to revitalize or even to create place. Whereas in France, as Elizabeth Barham writes, "terroir can . . . designate a rural or provincial region that is considered to have a marked influence on its inhabitants," the Kehlers imagine the inverse: *terroir* in which a region's inhabitants can have an impact on the ecosystem, landscape, and sense of place through rural economic revitalization.[57] Since *taste* is what ultimately sells cheese, to the Kehlers it represents a means to other ends, including the remaking of place. Calling to mind Tim Ingold's proposition that we think of landscapes as "the congealed form" of "taskscapes" where tasks are the connected practices of daily life within an environment, the Kehlers employ the notion of *terroir* to cultivate a regional taskscape of farm-based food-making.[58]

When the brothers spent childhood summers here in the 1970s, they told me, the Greensboro area supported thirty-seven dairy farms; in 2011, just eight remained—including their own. Vermont, like Wisconsin, prides itself on being a dairy state, but in 2008 it contributed only 1.4 percent of the nation's fluid milk. Naming Jasper Hill Farm a critical "response to globalization" and the deterritorializing effects of commodity pricing, which sped the collapse of small farms and their consolidation into huge dairies "out west," the brothers got into farmstead cheesemaking because they saw it as an entry point for *reterritorializing* the food system. Their aim is to reroot food production in local places by drawing freshly meaningful lines of connection among people, culture, and landscape, and by investing rural places anew with affective significance and material relevance. Noting that the region's old barns, like theirs, were built in rolling, rocky valleys to house just twenty-five or thirty cows, the Kehlers argue that this is the scale at which Vermont agriculture should work; "This is what the land was meant to do," Mateo told me.

As the Kehlers know, in France the promotion of traditional "*terroir* products" has been essential to rural economic modernization.[59] While describing their Jasper Hill cheese as "a vehicle to present the land" to people (as discussed in chapter 2), they add to an appreciation for mixed pasture, ambient microbiota, and the digestive power of cows a concern for rural economy.[60] In their farmstead cheese business, rather than import organic grain from further afield they buy conventional hay from a neighboring "old-school Vermont dairy farmer" because, Mateo explains, "We're working here with the concept of *terroir,* and that's local grass."[61] Here *terroir* means local grass not only in the sense that the cheese is said to showcase milk flavored by local pastures, but also, as Mateo noted when I first visited their farm in 2004, because buying local hay "keeps the money in town." For the same reason, at the general store down the road the Kehlers have retailed their cheeses at their usual wholesale prices.

"Conserving Vermont's working landscape is part of our mission as a company," Mateo says. "Cheese is the vehicle to meet our mission."[62] In Vermont—and Vermont alone—the "working landscape" is named as an instrumental value of artisanal cheese: by giving new life to dairy farms, cheese contributes to the preservation of the rolling hills dotted with barns and framed by wooded mountains that sell a postcard image of Vermont and are kept open by hay mowers and grazing livestock.[63] The working landscape that attracts tourists is a dairy taskscape and was named one of the "true values" of dairy farms in a keynote speech given by Robert Wellington, senior vice-president of the Agri-Mark dairy cooperative, at a 2004 Vermont Farm Summit Meeting I attended in Brattleboro with David and Cindy Major.[64] In a 2009 poll conducted for the Council on the Future of Vermont, "the working landscape and its heritage" beat out Vermont's "spirit of independence" and opportunity for privacy as Vermonters' most valued value.[65] Clearly, residents feel this value is under threat. Between 2004 and 2010, Vermont lost 309 dairy farms, translating to a 22.6 percent loss of the 1,364 dairy farms operating when I was at David Major's farm.[66] Calls to protect the "working landscape" from development or reforestation are ubiquitous, from the marketing of artisanal foods to gubernatorial campaign rhetoric. But the working landscape that helps to define the place of Vermont has long been under revision. In the late nineteenth century, 30 percent of Vermont's land was forested and 70 percent kept cleared by grazing livestock; today we see the inverse: 70 percent forested and only 30 percent cleared.[67] It is that 30 percent that many of us today picture when we envision Vermont: gently rolling valleys dotted with farmhouses set against forested hills that turn red-orange in autumn.

As with any landscape portraiture, the postcards frame a selective picture. The maintenance of Vermont's working landscape relies increasingly on the low-wage work of Mexican and Central American immigrants, of whom as many as 90 percent may be undocumented.[68] This feature of the landscape is largely obscured from public view when Latino workers (overwhelmingly men) are assigned indoor jobs in barns and milking parlors and are housed in barracks-style bunkhouses. Older Yankee farmers, too, may feel marginalized by romantic pastoral representations. At the farm summit meeting, a farmwoman from West Brattleboro, featured on the program to offer a "farmer's perspective" in response to Wellington's keynote address, told the following story. While touring Lincoln Center during a recent trip to New York City, she saw a list of patrons engraved on a wall and exclaimed, recognizing a name, "I know him! He's our neighbor!" The tour guide looked her over and drawled dismissively, "I don't think so." The farmwoman insisted, explaining that their Vermont neighbor kept an apartment in the city, too. (He held a prominent position at the Metropolitan Opera.) When the guide remained unconvinced the woman's husband intervened, saying, "We keep the aesthetics for these folks!" The audience at the farm summit erupted in knowing laughter, but it was a touch rueful as well. Vermont's landscape—embodied and enabled by a "taste of place"—is valued by many, but worked only by some. The Kehlers would like to see more residents become active participants in working Vermont's landscapes and, moreover, to receive economic and social reward for so doing.

Thinking beyond Jasper Hill Farm and creamery, the Kehlers, like the Majors before them, hope to "reverse-engineer" a system for collective marketing. They look to European models of centralized distribution and geographic labeling for inspiration, but then work to translate those structures to fit American markets and values. When I first met the brothers in 2004, they were eager to discuss with an anthropologist how they might create a geographical indication for the Northeast Kingdom through which farmstead cheesemakers could collectively benefit from regional branding (as with an AOC) but without conforming to a unified, "traditional" product. Like the DBIC in Wisconsin—and mindful of the cautionary tale of the short-lived Vermont Shepherd guild—Mateo and Andy envisioned rescaling "taste of place" from individual farm back up to region, but in a way that respects local values of independence and entrepreneurialism.

Four years later, the Kehlers launched an ambitious project to operationalize their vision: "22,000 square feet, seven underground vaults and a dream as big as the American cheese movement," the Cellars at Jasper Hill are a 2.3-million-dollar facility for collective cheese ripening and distribution intended to reduce "the barriers of entry" to value-added dairying by relieving regional farmers of the labor of aging and marketing cheeses.[69] The Cellars were designed to move beyond the Vermont Shepherd guild by allowing producers to create their own cheeses under their own labels to sell, unripe, to the Cellars. Built with five different climate-controlled aging environments, the Cellars were designed to "be able to ripen just about any type of cheese that a producer in the Green Mountains could possibly dream up," Mateo has said.[70] (See figs. 21 and 22.) Implicit, too, is the belief that Jasper Hill can capitalize on its own brand to fetch high prices nationally for smaller Vermont makers. "Taste of Place," Amy Trubek's Americanized gloss on *terroir* taken from the title of her book, is the Cellars' tagline.

One year into the project, only a couple of the Cellars' ten cheesemaking partners were heritage dairy farms. Eager to fill the cavernous vaults, the Cellars started out buying unripe cheeses from established artisans across the state who were looking to get into new markets. As the Kehlers tell the story, many of these producers encountered difficulty maintaining consistent quality—that is, replicating a consistent sensory profile in a cheese throughout a season. The variability in sensory characteristics—sharpness of flavor, color of rind and paste, and so forth—that many artisan producers are able to manage through direct sales at farmers' markets became nonviable at the national scale of market distribution on which the Cellars depended. "Quality" cheese means different things in different markets.

As a business enterprise, the Cellars at Jasper Hill is predicated on turning out consistent high-quality cheese by helping producers move rapidly to more "finished" commodity production. In April 2011, I spent a weekend at Jasper Hill (my third visit) touring the caves and updated creamery and talking at length with Mateo and Vince Razionale, a member of the sales and marketing team whom I knew from his former position as domestic cheese buyer for Formaggio Kitchen. "Our business is going away from the artist-as-cheesemaker," Mateo explained to me. "Cheesemaking is not an art, it's a craft." He drew an analogy to a woodworker creating a table; if one leg of a table turns out shorter than the other three, this is not celebrated as unique—it's a problem. In the cheese world, Mateo sees "the ability to celebrate or explain away the short leg" as indicative of "the immaturity of the industry." In fact, he continued, artisanal cheese is not yet a proper industry in this country; "it's a movement." He shook his head in despair at the thought of Americans making and selling cheese—cheese that may even win awards—when they "don't even know their own cheese," meaning they cannot define (or are not interested in defining) the typical flavor and appearance of cheeses they have named and launched on the market. The "artistic" approach of letting natural variability reign and having a somewhat loose idea of what makes, say, a Constant Bliss a Constant Bliss, Vince added, is one thing when a cheesemaker has another source of income to rely on, but "it's no way to grow a business." The Cellars at Jasper Hill must continue to grow to pay off its sizable loans and write monthly paychecks for twenty-four employees.

FIG. 21. *(top)* The Cellars at Jasper Hill. Photo by author.

FIG. 22. *(bottom)* The washed-rind vault in the Cellars at Jasper Hill. Photo by author.

To rectify the problem of consistent quality, the Cellars at Jasper Hill has put in place a detailed audit system that partnering dairies are required to follow and that the Kehlers have implemented in their own cheesemaking. Times, temperatures, and pH readings are recorded at each step of making each batch of cheese that comes in to the Cellars. Spiderweblike graphs of these readings are to be matched to the results of sensory analysis that Vince, Andy, and Mateo conduct on each batch of cheese before it leaves the Cellars. Through cross-analyzing quantitative and qualitative data, they aim to define typicity for each cheese sold under the Cellars label. The idea is that by having defined, quantitative targets (primarily pH levels) to hit at each stage of cheesemaking, producers will be better able to achieve consistent sensory profiles from one batch of cheese to the next. In other words, the Kehlers are looking to scientific measures—other than pasteurization, it is important to note—to help guide craft practice toward more consistent outcomes. To some extent, this goal is at cross-purposes with the principle of *terroir* taste; as Trubek importantly notes, "The presence of terroir also suggests the possibility that there is a limit to our influence on wines"—or on cheeses.[71] Not surprisingly, some cheesemakers the Kehlers initially contracted with chafed at being told to do things differently.[72] In spring 2011, most of the varieties aging in the Cellars were made by relative newcomers to the industry. The Kehlers have found it easier to guide people just starting out than to redirect those who felt they already knew what they were doing.

Terroir here is conceived as "a kind of place marketing," as Barham writes of similar efforts under way in Quebec, "but one that does not simply create a surface association with a place through a product in order to build sales. Instead, it reflects a concerted effort to literally create the social and economic basis for claims of uniqueness and place reputation for quality or high value-added products."[73] The Kehlers have committed themselves, and by extension, those they work with, to growing not just a business but an entire industry. This industry, they believe, holds a key to the future of northern Vermont. What sort of place might the Cellars at Jasper Hill cheese come to typify?

The Kehlers regard the Cellars as an incubator for a twenty-first-century, post-pastoral working landscape, one in which Leo Marx's machine in the garden extends into the infrastructure of a distributed marketplace: pH meters, climate-controlled aging vaults, cold packs, UPS trucks, computer databases, high-speed Internet, a constant stream of visitors from out-of-state cities. This is not the romantic pastoralism that Frank Bryan, author of 1984's *Real Vermonters Don't Milk Goats,* would dismiss as "flatlander" farming ("You show me someone who milks cows by hand and I'll show you a flatlander").[74] At the 2004 Farm Summit Meeting, the speaker from Agri-Mark commented that 2,600 miles of snowmobile tracks stretch across Vermont agricultural land. Without dairy farms, he exclaimed, "we'd lose all that snowmobile tourism!" A state legislator elaborated,

"Southern New Englanders who come here, they own a piece of the rock and they don't want hunters shooting Bambi, and they don't want snowmobilers zooming around all hours of the night," while "real Vermonters don't milk goats and real Vermonters don't post signs" prohibiting hunting or snowmobiling. It might strike urban gastronomes as odd to hear noisy, gas-guzzling snowmobiling named one of the "true values" of dairy farms, integral to the "working landscape" that we are invited to taste in a slice of grass-based, cave-aged cheese. But place, like taste, is a relative, relational category. Creating place does not mean creating unified meanings.

What is the place today of Jasper Hill within Orleans County, Vermont, where the median household income in 2008 hovered just over thirty-nine thousand dollars while the homeownership rate is as high as 74 percent? Does the Kehlers' presence burden less-affluent neighbors by inflating area property taxes? Or is it more accurate to say that the Kehler families contribute significantly to local infrastructure through their own tax payments?[75] Mateo grumbled to me that their property tax rate was inordinately high because one-third of the residences in Orleans County are second-home properties owned (among others) by professors from Harvard, Dartmouth, and Columbia. The Kehlers are not absentee second-home owners. They live and work on their farm and send their children to public schools (Mateo and Angie have two young children and live above the cheese house; Andy and Victoria and their three children live nearby in a house that Andy built).[76] They are mindful of their local image. During an April weekend, I heard Mateo lecture a handful of office employees to take great care, now that the winter's snow had finally thawed, not to speed while driving on the winding roads. Speeding tickets are written up in the local paper and would reflect poorly on what the Kehlers are trying to do.[77] When my family joined Mateo's and Andy's families for dinner at a pizza place in a nearby town, it was clear that the Kehlers were regular patrons. After Mateo took a long time fetching a round of beers from the bar, Angie explained, "He always has to say 'hi' to everyone."

What do longtime residents make of the Kehlers and their cheese caves blasted into a hillside of solid rock? Surely it depends. Do their kids attend school with Kehler kids? Do they know a former Jasper Hill employee? (The Kehlers, one local resident told me, expect notoriously long workdays.) At least one Greensboro native has joined them in the artisanal food business. Over the hill and around the bend from Jasper Hill Farm lives Shaun Hill, whose grandfather was Jasper Hill's first cousin (the Kehlers did not rename the farm when they bought it). Winnimere cheese is washed with Shaun's craft beer. Greensboro is just seven miles from Hardwick, celebrated by writer Ben Hewitt as "The Town that Food Saved."[78] With Pete's Greens, Vermont Soy Company, True Yogurt, and other "agripreneurs" in the neighborhood, the Kehlers' dairy operation is not anomalous.

The Kehlers' business has undergone quite a number of changes since they set out to farm motivated, in part, by a wish for self-sufficient self-employment. In pointing this out I do not mean to suggest that they have sold out their initial values. Instead, I want to call attention to the dynamic tension between being "big enough" and "too big" that is endemic to entrepreneurial economies of sentiment. The Cellars at Jasper Hill has become an "in-between" commercial enterprise—neither industrial nor a cottage industry; not fast but not entirely Slow, either.

From the beginning, a majority of the Cellars' inventory has been held in Cabot Clothbound cheese. Retailing at Whole Foods for about eighteen dollars a pound, Cabot Clothbound is a hybrid-type cheese of moderate speed. Using milk from a single herd of cows and adjunct bacterial cultures imported from England, Cabot Cheese makes cylindrical wheels of Cheddar (called truckles) using automated machinery. The processing plant in the town of Cabot, Vermont, about a fifteen-minute drive from Greensboro, is owned by Agri-Mark, New England's largest dairy-farmer cooperative. Each week green wheels are driven to Jasper Hill, where workers encase the cheeses in cloth, rub them with lard, and stack them high on wooden shelving in what looks like a cavernous cheese library. The cheeses are turned and rubbed and brushed in the Cellars until they are sufficiently mature to send out into the marketplace. In 2010, Cabot sold Jasper Hill two hundred thousand pounds of cheese.

In the spring of 2011, the Cellars were at just one-third capacity and the Kehlers were exploring alternative ways of filling the vaults.[79] The latest plan was to amp up production of their Bayley Hazen Blue and, eventually, to replace Cabot Clothbound by reviving Aspenhurst, an English-style cheese the Kehlers made before partnering with Cabot. To increase volume they were looking into contracting with area dairy farmers to make Jasper Hill's cheeses according to Jasper Hill's specifications. The idea, as they explained it, is that "Jasper Hill Farm" will wither away and be replaced by a well-defined cheese type: Bayley Hazen of northern Vermont. Their company brand will (they envision) be super-seded by an emergent, reverse-engineered *terroir*. Such an arrangement, they acknowledged, would seem more closely to resemble the Vermont Shepherd guild, but with a key difference: which people are involved. The Kehlers are talking with dairy farmers about venturing into cheese by making Bayley Hazen Blue and Aspenhurst; they are not in discussion with urban transplants (like themselves) interested in crafting a product "as an extension of their ego," as one of the brothers put it. Of course, it is their farm's cheese and not someone else's that they envision as becoming *the* cheese of northern Vermont.

The Kehlers aspire to operationalize a model of *terroir* that might mature into what Arturo Escobar calls a grassroots political ecology "concerned with finding new ways of weaving together the biophysical, the cultural, and the technoeconomic for the production of other types of social nature."[80] Reverse-engineering *terroir*, in their current view, requires cultivating a shared economy of sentiment as well as an ecology of production, one that gathers together commitment to a joint project, collective responsibility, and a shared vision of quality expressed in consistent taste. The vision itself is the Kehlers' own, to be sure, more entrepreneurial than grassroots. In that entrepreneurial spirit the Kehlers are willing to improvise as they go. In the midst of agriculture's industrialization, the appropriate tasks of craft dairying and cheesemaking are being worked out experimentally. There is nothing nostalgic here. For all their idealism, Mateo and Andy Kehler are pragmatists. *Terroir* in their project is a placeholder for whatever constellation of values and relations ends up working to inspire the collaborative enterprise they envision.

WHAT MIGHT *TERROIR* BECOME?

Because *terroir* "places" an agricultural product within the conditions of its production, in contrast to "local" foods, which are defined by proximity of consumption—*goût du terroir*, or *terroir* taste, can be meaningfully, if differently, experienced regardless of where a food is consumed. Allison Hooper is quoted in Rebecca Gray's *American Artisanal* saying, "I know I can't truck Vermont to people, but I can truck cheese to them and bring them the character of Vermont."[81] "Vermont cheeses," however, take various forms. Jasper Hill's soft-ripened Constant Bliss or washed-rind Winnimere demand the attention of a special-occasion cheese board, whereas Neighborly Farm's Jack and Colby Cheddar are more at home packed in a lunchbox. Trucked to Cambridge, Massachusetts, or Manhattan, these cheeses carry with them different sorts of Vermont "character." At the same time, "place" may "taste" different in situ and elsewhere—what the taste of any particular Vermont cheese might evoke in Manhattan or Boston is not the same as it will in Vermont's Northeast Kingdom—just as the place of Vermont may mean something different to leaf-season tourists, snowmobilers, and residents whose family roots reach back to the American Revolution.

In Vermont, what we might view through the lens of *terroir* is a palimpsest of the sui generis and the cosmopolitan, of "old-school" and "flatlander," European and American. It tastes of an Alpine-style cheese made from Jersey milk, or a sheep's-milk Camembert, or an organic farmstead jalapeño pepper Jack—novel blends of artisanal and agricultural know-how remixed from culturally diverse, class-inflected sources. What coalesces as the taste of place reflects, above all else, cheesemakers' entrepreneurial creativity and dairy farmers' commitment to making a living by working the land. What gives Vermont cheese *terroir* taste may be an eater's conscious recognition of a relationship—any relationship?— with its ecology of production.

FIG. 23. Anne Topham at the Dane County farmers' market, Madison, Wisconsin. Photo by author.

This is why taste education is so important in the equation between place and taste, though again, that education can convey many lessons. More than a decade ago in Wisconsin, prior to the inauguration of any of today's regional artisanal cheese festivals and before ambient microorganisms came into view, Anne Topham described her vision of *terroir* as a "circle" encompassing her goats, her pastures, herself, and the people who buy and eat her cheese.[82] Anne, who started making goat cheese in Wisconsin before there was a market for goat cheese in Wisconsin, sells nearly all her cheese at the Dane County farmers' market in Madison (fig. 23). At Anne's market stall, taste education works in two directions. She explains to customers that her cheese is "fluffier" when the weather is hot and her goats drink more water, but at the same time, if too much salt has been added to a batch of cheese, her customers let her know and she readjusts her recipe. Surely she seeks customers' appreciation for her labor and skill by training their consciences as well as their palates, but Anne also realizes that as a food-maker she must calibrate the taste of her cheese to the community in which she lives and trades. Anne speaks more passionately about the contribution to the development of her cheese made by her customers at the market, thirty-five miles from her farm, than about the material qualities of her unimproved pastures in the Driftless region. As Anne puts it, through eating her cheese people "have a connection to our farm, to the goats, and to the work of my hands." When speaking at the ACS on the topic "Nurturing *Terroir*," she said self-deprecatingly, "I don't think this fits into the French concept of *terroir*." But it is telling of what *terroir* is becoming in the United States: a coin of value by which artisan food-makers "represent the importance of their own actions to themselves" and to others.[83]

In describing attempts in the United States to translate or to reverse-engineer *terroir*, I have shown that if *terroir* is to have meaningful significance in the United States, it is as a model for practice that has yet to become routinized or standardized, embedded in either landscapes or taskscapes. Cheesemakers' experiments with *terroir* and artisanal practice demonstrate how people create place as they go about the quotidian tasks of agrarian livelihoods that physically shape landscapes and situate people's senses of place.[84] The Cowgirls' cheese tastings, Willi Lehner's microbial harvesting, Jasper Hill's collective *affinage*, and Anne Topham's farmers' market conversations are all "constitutive acts of dwelling" that might constitute the material and affective qualities of place that generate, are expressed in, and are in turn regenerated by artisanal cheese. These enskilled tasks of place-making are also intentional, motivated by ethical commitment. Oriented more toward the future than toward the past, *terroir* is about what American cheese may become and, more, what cheesemakers are trying to be—as rural entrepreneurs, ecological stewards, sustainable developers, and local citizens. Value, then, is not just materially extracted from or discursively inscribed on place; moral values can inspire place-making practices, with potentially durable—and possibly unforeseen—effects.

In calling attention to material and affective relations between food-making and place-making, *terroir* might yet become an American model for the instrumental value of artisanal foods. *Terroir*'s appeal lies precisely in its ideological flexibility; it can be translated to frame various relations between place and production. Sue Conley and Peggy Smith champion agricultural stewardship of coastal pasturelands. Staff at the DBIC want to expand quality values associated with "Wisconsin cheese" to include Anne Topham's goat cheese as well as the squeaky curds beloved as a regional treat. The Kehlers in Vermont, like the Majors before them, look to *terroir* to offer a holistic model for rural economic revitalization consistent with the state's valorization of the "working landscape." Each is well aware that their goals—the instrumental values of cheese—depend on another aspect of cheese's value: its exchange value. *Terroir* and its adjunct, "taste of place," offer cheesemakers a means of accounting for the "spectrum of values" produced by their artisan labor.[85] But as the notion that foods not only can but should taste of place becomes more widespread, and as the word *terroir* is taken up in the marketing of coffee and chocolate in addition to wine and cheese, it becomes less certain that artisan food-makers will have the final say on what *"terroir"* comes to signify in American popular culture. *Terroir,* after all, is not a thing in the world to protect, but an articulation of value that may or may not retain its currency.

8

Bellwether

Although I met novelist and cheesemaker Brad Kessler when we both attended one of Peter Dixon's cheesemaking workshops, I got to know him through reading his book, *Goat Song: A Seasonal Life, A Short History of Herding, and the Art of Making Cheese*. *Goat Song* is an American Pastoral. Opening with the author moving away from society (New York City) toward nature (a seventy-five-acre Vermont farm), it chronicles an experiment in agrarian living. Kessler depicts his developing intimacy with a handful of dairy goats and offers an enviable glimpse of the pastoral good life. Yet he also cautions, "Wherever the notion of paradise exists, so does the idea that it was lost. Paradise is always in the past."[1] The title *Goat Song* is a literal rendering of the Greek word *traghoudhia*, tragedy. Reading it, I was reminded of Leo Marx's analysis of Thoreau's *Walden*. In *The Machine in the Garden*, Marx names Thoreau a tragic, if complex, pastoralist. After failing to make an agrarian living raising beans for commercial trade (although his intent was always more allegorical than pecuniary), Thoreau ends *Walden* by replacing the pastoral ideal where it originated: in literature. Paradise, Marx concludes, is not ultimately to be found at Walden Pond; it is to be found in the pages of *Walden*.

Kessler's book ends with similar wistfulness in reporting his application for a commercial creamery license to be able to sell cheeses to New York City restaurants. "Trade curses everything it touches, wrote Thoreau, and I didn't want trade in cheese to curse what I loved." Making cheese for commercial trade would mean milking more goats. "More goats would require a milking machine and a larger cheese vat, and there'd be more manure and more parasites and everyone would suffer—the animals and us."[2] The tragedy of Kessler's romantic pastoralism is that he cannot quite see scaling up the ecology of production to commercial viability without compromising what he loves: the meditative intimacy of hand-milking his goats, the magical thrill of developing cheese curd by feel rather than pH meter (as Peter Dixon taught him to do). He knows his mode of living with goats is a luxury; the craft of creating with milk is subsidized by his craft of creating with words. As with Thoreau, the pastoral idyll may survive longer in the art of Kessler's profession than in the craft of his vocation.

So where does this leave the fully commercialized cheesemakers I have followed in this book? Is there a post-pastoral way out of the pastoral dilemma shared by Kessler and Thoreau? How might it be possible to convey and reproduce over time what people value in small-scale agrarian enterprise without undermining the character of those values? Reframing the question more broadly, as Jeff Roberts suggests in his *Atlas of American Artisan Cheese,* might handmade cheese be a bellwether that rings in the twenty-first-century arrival of a different kind of food system?[3] A wether is a castrated ram; with bells tied around their necks, "bellwethers" have traditionally been trained to lead flocks of ewes to greener pastures.

Like any food, cheese is a complex cultural artifact saturated with ethics and politics. That complexity is frequently lost in American debates over food politics, which are too often posed in simplistic terms of either-or questions, or with the stakes raised to all-or-nothing propositions. Numerous op-ed pieces and academic publications have called out the self-indulgent short-sightedness of foodies wringing their hands over whether it is morally preferable to buy locally grown conventional strawberries or organic strawberries flown in from Peru when so many Americans are unable to afford fresh strawberries at all, or may never encounter them at the urban markets and big-box stores where they shop for groceries. The point should be not to determine which purchase is the fundamentally superior one—in a complex food system that is always a moving target—but rather to recognize that personal food "choices" not only are constrained by economic ability, access, and cultural appropriateness, but also have consequences for others. The eco-consumerism of a few foodies is no solution to food deserts and the social ills of poverty. But their purchasing power unarguably benefits artisan food-makers, the comfortably well-off and modestly struggling alike. In insisting that personal habit and political action be one and the same, absolutist moralizing limits the possibilities of both.

My hope for this book is that, by conveying a partial sense of what goes into the food we eat—labor, skill, luck, practical knowledge, capital investment, social and interspecies relationships, innumerable qualitative calculations—readers will recognize the limits of absolutist food politics. Again, organic food offers an illustration. The federal certification of "organic" agricultural products, based on inputs more than process or philosophy, reinforces a perception that "going organic" is an all-or-nothing proposition. But many dairy farmers who tend organic pastures refuse to cull animals from their herds rather than administer antibiotics to treat worms or infection. Karen Weinberg is one. Telling me, "The whole issue of organics drives me nuts," Karen explained, "I find that the ones who are the most adamant and pushy about their belief system are the ones who really don't understand how the system runs. Because you can't be that pushy if you really understood it." The complexity of what Karen called the agricultural "system"—and what I have described as ecologies of production, which operate through economies of sentiment—reveals moral or ideological purity to be a naive proposition.

The alternative to moralizing is not, however, absence of moral concern. I have argued that one value of the messy, unpredictable agricultural system to farmers and food makers is precisely the ongoing ethical struggle it engenders. To make food artisanally is to work selectively with organic elements to realize human ends; animal welfare, landscape ecology, and rural community are all implicated. Artisan food-making, as Lisa Heldke argues of home cooking, is a "thoughtful practice" through which practitioners become (to varying degrees) mindful of their local dependencies on individuals and communities, are tuned in to the potential for self-other relations with animals, and come to trust a bodily knowledge in which thought and feeling are merged.[4] Anne Topham's articulation of *terroir* as a "circle" encompassing her goats, her customers, and the labor of her hands might seem to offer a model for a relocalized food system. But Anne's economy of sentiment is not a one-size-fits-all model. Anne's friends at the Dairy Business Innovation Center would love to see her make more cheese for more people to enjoy and to associate with Wisconsin, but they accept that "She's happy. She's comfortable" where she is, as a staff member acknowledged to me. As Kessler's book suggests, something like Anne's model of sufficiency—one shared, in numerous forms, by others across the country—cannot scale up following a self-similar pattern. To get bigger is to change. When about half of all farmstead cheesemakers across the country produce less than ten thousand pounds of cheese annually, "artisanal cheese" is more about making a life than transforming a market.[5]

When businesses do grow, quantitative and qualitative values require reca-libration to each other. Mary Keehn still seems a bit dazed by the evolution of Cypress Grove Chevre, which began in her kitchen after she became a single mom. Having started out as modestly as Anne Topham, today Keehn manages a bustling business with more than forty employees and a nationwide distribution network.[6] Over lunch in downtown Arcata, California, Mary told me, "To me, when money becomes your most important thing, you've failed. People so often think . . . 'I just want to get bigger.' But when *more* is the number, there is no end to it. You're pushing for *more* and you're not pushing for anything that really matters." For Mary, what matters now is offering a good life and a good living to her employees; "I don't think that I can change the world, but I *can* change my corner." In addition to providing health insurance and a matching 401(k) retirement plan to her employees, she instituted profit sharing as a nonoptional employee savings mechanism. She thinks, too, about their children's prospects. "Why are we here? I always go back to that. We're here because I was a mom. So we tell employees, 'Go to your kids' back-to-school days, parent-teacher conferences. You'll make up the time later.'" Through Mary's employment practices and patronage of small-scale goat farms, her business might be regarded as a candidate for what Thomas Lyson calls "civic agriculture," in which "Agriculture is seen as an integral part of rural and urban communities, not merely as the production of commodities."[7] When I drove up to Mary Keehn's newly rebuilt factory on the California coast around noon on a foggy summer day, I encountered a dozen men, some wearing cheesemakers' hygienic hairnets, playing soccer in the parking lot. So integral is this lunch-break tradition to Mary's vision of her company that a photo of soccer-playing cheesemakers appears in a recent brochure for Cypress Grove cheeses. This is one version of how "local" food can create place.[8]

What might American cheese look like in twenty years? Will farmstead cheese sold at local markets be a retro trend, a gourmet reminder of millennial optimism? Or will it be unremarkable for its ubiquity? Will producers' commercial need to differentiate their products on the market lead to divisive competition rather than collective affinity or regional stability? Artisanal cheese is no exception to capitalism's extractive logics; indeed, it can reveal how capitalist systems of value exchange are multiple, ever-shifting, and under constant negotiation. Viewed from the perspective of industrial technoscience, artisanal cheese is unnecessarily labor-intensive, disconcertingly inconsistent, and too risky—in a word, obsolete. A cheesemaker's synesthetic reason, useful only insofar as it is responsive to fluctuating materials and environmental conditions, is valuable today insofar as its epistemic virtue—its virtue as a mode of knowing and making—is shored up by appeals (through the new taste education) to an ecology of production and an economy of sentiment that consumers recognize as generating "good" food. There's nothing essential about it.

Ecologies of production include us all. Gesturing toward this using the language of *terroir,* at the 2008 Seattle Cheese Festival Jeff Roberts spoke to the audience not only as consumers, but also as citizens. He argued that while "we tend to focus on the physical characteristics, where the cows are grazing, for instance," *terroir* is, or should be, more than this. "It's connection to community. These folks don't survive, aren't going to be successful, without us. I don't mean just as consumers, where we spend our dollars. But when the state decides it wants to move in a different direction, if we're there to say, 'By the way, these guys are important' . . . because what [artisanal cheese] does is bring dollars into our local economy." Food citizenship is no more reducible to consumption than it is to production.⁹ We must vote with more than our forks and dollars.

When free-market competition rewards larger enterprises that exploit economies of scale, government support for small-scale agriculture and artisanal food production is crucial. In the United States, this support has been piecemeal and fragile because it has relied on Congressional earmarks. To local communities, earmarks represent public works, jobs, and desired services, but in national political discourse during the Obama administration, earmarks have come to represent the inefficiencies of "big government." Following a decade of waging war without paying for it, earmarks are being evaporated in the name of federal debt reduction. In June 2011, Wisconsin's DBIC announced that its federal funding had been discontinued, its remaining programs will be seriously reduced, and its doors may close for good in a year's time. Initiatives promoting artisanal food in Vermont and elsewhere across the country are similarly vulnerable. Meanwhile, the FDA continues to weigh how best to regulate raw-milk cheesemaking so as to protect the health of a consuming public. Although the ACS remains hopeful that regulators will recognize that artisanal and industrial food producers face overlapping but not identical risks when it comes to food safety, the legal future of raw-milk cheese remains uncertain.

The qualities that characterize and are valued in the unfinished commodity of artisanal cheese are fluid and in flux, in no small part because so too are the politics and economics through which such qualities are evaluated. What is certain is that there is no one-size-fits-all model for artisanal cheese. If civic agriculture is to flourish it will be heterogeneous, with "little guys" and enterprises of moderate speed operating alongside (if in symbolic opposition to) industrial modes of production. Americans will continue to enjoy making and eating artisanal cheese, but artisanal foods (alone) are not going to feed America.

Perhaps artisanal cheese can be a bellwether not for a transformed food system but for a post-pastoral future in which it is no longer possible to imagine food as coming from one of only two sources: either from the belly of the industrial beast, or from a pastoral idyll. Rather than romanticize artisanal labor and family farming, rather than put artisans on a precarious moral pedestal, consumers might imagine the production of food as being similar to the act of its consumption. In shopping for and eating food we all make daily compromises with ourselves: weighing caloric and nutritional value against the immediate gratification of taste; calculating economic cost against convenience. In doing so we are influenced by contingency and affect: are we atoning for a big meal or skipped exercise routine, soothing ourselves after a difficult day, or rewarding ourselves for long hours of dedicated work?¹⁰ Similar complexity is in play in artisanal food-making practice. The life of cheese—as perishable substance, as a vocation—is animated by circumstances both crafted and contingent.

APPENDIX

TABLE 6 Start-up capital initially required to "build, equip, and license" an artisanal creamery (dates range from 1980 to 2008) (n = 141)

Capital Required	Percentage of Creameries Requiring It
Less than $10,000	11
$10,000–24,999	11
$25,000–49,999	11
$50,000–99,999	24
$100,000–249,999	26
$250,000–499,999	6
$500,000–999,999	2
More than $1,000,000	9

TABLE 7 Sources from which creamery start-up capital was acquired (n = 141)

Source of Capital	Percentage of Respondents Obtaining Start-Up Capital from Each Source	Average Percentage of Start-Up Capital Originating from Each Source	
		Overall	Among Only Those Obtaining Start-Up Capital from Each Source
Inheritance	12.77	7.08	55.44 (n = 18)
Savings	59.57	38.19	64.11 (n = 84)
Bank loan	44.68	25.25	56.51 (n = 63)
Loan from family	26.95	9.67	35.89 (n = 38)
State/federal grant	10.64	2.35	22.13 (n = 15)
Selling development rights to land trust	1.42	0.64	45.0 (n = 2)
Other	30.50	16.82	55.14 (n = 43)

TABLE 8 Household income and income from cheese (n = 143)

Household Income of Cheesemaking Business Owners (2008)		Household Income Derived from Cheese	
Annual Household Income	Percentage of Respondents	Percentage of Household's Income Derived from Cheese	Percentage of Respondents
Less than $15,000	8	0–24	39
$15,000–24,999	6	25–49	18
$25,000–34,999	4	50–74	16
$35,000–49,999	13	75–100	27
$50,000–74,999	19		
$75,000–99,999	18		
$100,000–149,999	15		
More than $150,000	17		

NOTES

CHAPTER 1. AMERICAN ARTISANAL

1. Werlin (2000).

2. Kehler (2010: 8).

3. In 2003, the year the Kehlers began farming, 53 dairy farms folded in Vermont, a 3.63 percent decline from the previous year. That year, the state counted 1,459 dairy farms, less than half the number, 3,372, reported in 1980. See "The Number of Dairy Farms in Vermont" on the Vermont Dairy Promotion Council Web site, www.vermontdairy.com/, accessed May 30, 2012.

4. This figure does not account for the Amish cheesemakers who do not belong to professional guilds or organizations.

5. Among respondents to a nationwide survey of artisan cheesemaking businesses I conducted in February 2009, 13 percent became licensed to sell cheese in the 1980s, 17 percent were licensed in the 1990s, and an overwhelming 66 percent had been licensed since 2000. A post-2000 surge in cheesemaking is further evidenced by exponential increases in membership of the American Cheese Society (ACS); membership more than tripled between 2001 and 2007: 426 in 2001, 556 in 2002, 776 in 2003, 810 in 2004, 893 in 2005, 1,069 in 2006, and 1,449 in 2007 (personal communication, ACS administrator). One-third of ACS members are cheese producers, joined by retailers and distributors, academics and technical consultants, food writers and consumer enthusiasts. See "Mission and Values" on the ACS Web site: www.cheesesociety.org/displaycommon.cfm?an=1&subarticlenbr=35, accessed April 21, 2010.

6. See West et al. (2012).

7. Kindstedt (2005: 37). Interested readers should consult this work for a full explanation of the chemistry of cheesemaking.

8. On cheese consumption, see Kenneth MacDonald (2007). On consumption studies more generally, see Miller (1987); on food consumption, Bell and Valentine (1997).

9. Mintz (1985); Kahn (1986); Munn (1986); Meigs (1987); Weiss (1996).

10. Allison (1991); Ohnuki-Tierny (1993); Counihan (1999); Van Esterik (1999); Gillette (2000); Sutton (2001); Farquhar (2002); Rouse and Hoskins (2004); Wilk (2006a); Holtzman (2009); Gewertz and Errington (2010).

11. Appadurai (1981); DeVault (1991). Because food holds the promise of both desired and dreaded social manifestations, Sutton writes, it "provides a key metaphor of social well-being" (2001: 27).

12. Fajans (1988: 143).

13. Although we may feel that our food choices reflect personal tastes and moods, consumer choices are economically constrained by markets that govern the availability of goods from which to choose (e.g., which goods are stocked on what supermarket shelves; Nestle 2002), while a food's seemingly desirable (or undesirable) qualities are culturally influenced.

14. See, respectively, Ulin (1996), Terrio (2000), and Bestor (2004).

15. On alternative agrifood movements in the United States, see DeLind (2002); DeLind and Bingen (2008); Kloppenburg et al. (2000); Chiappe and Flora (1998); Allen et al. (2003); DuPuis and Goodman (2005); Stanford (2006); Guthman (2008); Markowitz (2008).

16. Sonnino and Marsden (2006: 193); Jarosz (2008); Markowitz (2008).

17. Farquhar (2006: 146).

18. Freidberg (2004); Guthman (2004); Striffler (2005).

19. Schlosser (2001); see also Pollan (2006); Patel (2007).

20. On class expectations and disappointments in twentieth-century America, see Walley (2012).

21. The quote is a chapter subtitle from Jenna Woginrich's *Made from Scratch: Discovering the Pleasures of a Handmade Life* (2008). See also Madigan (2009) and Susan Orlean's *New Yorker* article on her adventure in urban chicken-keeping (2009). A masculinist version of this genre can be seen in Matthew B. Crawford's *Shop Class as Soulcraft: An Inquiry into the Value of Work* (2009).

22. The history of British and North American capitalism offers numerous examples of ethically motivated business endeavors; eighteenth- and nineteenth-century Quaker industrialists built iron bridges in lieu of cannonballs and produced "non-slavery" sugar.

23. See Dudley (2000).

24. In Greece, the artisan embodies a sense of subordination felt broadly among Greeks as second-class citizens in the European community (Herzfeld 2004). In Japan, the artisan exemplifies the excellence of skill while chafing at underrecognition of that skill (Kondo 1990: 56–57).

25. Terrio (2000); Herzfeld (2004); Rogers (2008).

26. Terrio (2000: 12–13).

27. Margaret Radin (1996: 106) comments, "complete noncommodification—complete removal from the market—is not the only alternative to complete commodification."

28. The post-pastoral ethos operates as what Michael Fischer, following Wittgenstein, calls an "emergent form of life," or perhaps better, an intended form of life (2003).

29. Petrini (2007: ix).

30. Cheese barrels priced on the Chicago Mercantile Exchange are five-hundred-pound masses of commodity cheddar. Forty-pound blocks of the same cheese are also priced on the CME, at slightly higher prices per pound. Carloads of barrels and blocks vary in weight between 40,000 and 44,000 pounds.

31. Fitzgerald (2003).

32. In 1953, at the time of the first bulk tank, Vermont numbered 10,637 dairy farms with an average herd size of twenty-five milking cows yielding a total production of 1.5 billion pounds of milk. By 1999, Vermont was down to 1,714 dairy farms but had an annual production of 2.6 billion pounds of milk (Albers 2000: 278).

33. James MacDonald et al. (2007).

34. Dudley (2000: 9).

35. Lyson and Gillespie (1995).

36. In 2008, the national average was 9.6 percent; the percentage first dipped below 10 percent in the year 2000. USDA Economic Research Service statistics, www.ers.usda.gov/briefing/cpifoodandexpenditures, accessed May 17, 2010.

37. Mead (1970).

38. See Poppendieck (1998: 88–91).

39. Poppendieck (1998: 148–149). The program was carried out between April 1986 and August 1987.

40. Streeter and Bills (2003a).

41. DuPuis (2002: 202).

42. Streeter and Bills (2003b: 1). The notion that artisanal cheese might "save" family farmers in meaningful numbers has yet to be borne out.

43. On "lifestyle migration" see Benson and O'Reilly (2009); Hoey (2008).

44. Harper (2001: 252).

45. The "true costs" of cheap food—to the environment, to rural communities—are not calculated in its pricing. Schlosser (2001); Nestle (2002); Striffler (2005); Pollan (2006); Patel (2007); Schor (2010).

46. Roberts (2007: xix).

47. Yanagisako (2002).

48. Fitzgerald (2003). This cultural logic has something in common with Quaker economist Kenneth Boulding's (1966) call for a "spaceman economy" as a corrective to the "reckless, exploitative, romantic, and violent behaviour" of the "cowboy economy" that, later, came close to taking down the U.S. economy in 2008 and pumped oil into the Gulf of Mexico in 2010. The "cowboy economy" operates as an "open system" that imagines nature as ever-providential, oil as ever-flowing; there is no tomorrow. This view, cautioned Boulding, is not only naive and destructive, it is immoral. The frontier days are over (if they ever existed) and our world, he writes, has become "closed," like a spaceship; there are no unlimited reserves of anything. Boulding's "spaceship economy" has been taken up as a call for sustainability. But it is also a plea for a more moral economic system. Cowboy economies not only deplete the natural ecology of our planet, Boulding argued; they deplete the psychic well-being of people.

49. I neither propose nor evaluate equivalencies between economic value and moral values such as forwarded in "fair trade" commodity projects (e.g., Fisher 2007). To frame

the issue as one of commensuration is to presume that economic activity, moral activity, and social activity belong to separate spheres that must somehow be brought together. See Graeber (2008) for an extended discussion of anthropological approaches to the value question as well as an argument about why a categorical definition has remained elusive among anthropologists. My discussion is further informed by Munn (1986); Strathern (1988); Appadurai (1986); Boltanski and Thévenot (1991); Myers (2001); Ferry (2002); Callon et al. (2002); Yanagisako (2002); Maurer (2005); and Stark (2009).

50. Stark (2009).

51. Gudeman (2008).

52. See also Rebecca Gould's analysis of American homesteading as a form of spiritual practice (2005).

53. Other scholars have explored similar indeterminacies in commodity relations. In depicting cooperative silver production and its circulation in Mexico as a kind of "inalienable commodity," Elizabeth Ferry writes: "As part of the very process of production and circulation of commodities, those engaged in that process assert multiple forms of value. . . . Commodities can be exchanged within market systems and simultaneously retain a connection to incommensurate and inalienable forms of value. Indeed, these alternate forms of value *are produced within, and depend upon,* a system of commodity exchange" (2002: 351). Margaret Radin introduces the notion of "incomplete commodification" to "describe a situation in which things are sold but the interaction between the participants in the transaction cannot be fully or perspicuously described as the sale of things" (1996: 106–107). In Radin's analysis, many market exchanges turn out to be "incompletely commodified" insofar as a "personal" element is experienced in the interaction despite money changing hands (107). Radin's "incomplete commodification" is similar to Gudeman's notion of "economy's tension." More recently, David Stark has described entrepreneurship as an organizational form devoted to "keeping multiple evaluative principles in play and exploiting the resulting dissonance" (2009: 17). And in the world of food commodities, Deborah Gewertz and Frederick Errington argue that fatty mutton flaps produced in New Zealand and Australia but consumed in Papua New Guinea and Tonga "resist fetishization" as commodities because their rough-hewn materiality calls attention to the means of their production, and because their known undesirability in some settings stigmatizes those who desire them elsewhere (2010). Their value, in other words, is in no way self-evident.

54. Appadurai (1986); Kopytoff (1986).

55. Manning (2010).

56. Marx ([1857–1858] 1978, [1867] 1976). Social scientists have long argued that market exchange produces other sorts of values in addition to economic ones. Values are not fixed once a product leaves the factory floor; the act of exchange itself transforms an object's value. So, for instance, buying a piece of the same variety of cheese made by the same producer may generate for the consumer different social and symbolic values attached to status or moral propriety, depending on whether the act of commercial exchange takes place at a supermarket, a gourmet retail shop, a fancy restaurant, a farmers' market, or the creamery where the cheese was made. "Cultural capital" names the symbolic value that a consumer acquires along with the use value of a good (Bourdieu 1984).

57. See also Meneley (2004: 173). Craft commodities, writes Susan Terrio, "are imbued with and are the bearers of the social identities of their makers and for this reason retain certain inalienable properties" (1996: 71).

58. Arguably, every consumer product is "a sequence of actions, a series of operations that transform it, move it and cause it to change hands, to cross a series of metamorphoses that end up putting it into a form judged useful by an economic agent who pays for it" (Callon, Méadel, and Rabeharisoa 2002: 197). Its qualities are only temporarily stabilized at the moment of exchange. What is significant in the case I am describing is how apparent this is to producers, retailers, and even consumers.

59. Michel Callon and colleagues write, "The characteristics of a good are not properties which already exist and on which information simply has to be produced so that everyone can be aware of them. Their definition or, in other words, their objectification, implies specific metrological work and heavy investments in measuring equipment. The consequence is that agreement on the characteristics is sometimes, in fact often, difficult to achieve" (2002: 198–199). See also Appadurai (1986); Murdoch and Miele (2004).

60. McCalman and Gibbons (2009: 264).

61. See Weiss (1996: 128).

62. Farquhar (2006: 154).

63. Tim Ingold's configuration of landscape as a "congealed taskscape" is here shifted into a future-oriented, promissory register (2000: 195–198).

64. Gifford (1999: 15).

65. Williams (1973: 46).

66. Cahn spoke in spring 2001 at a cheese and wine tasting at the Italian Wine Merchants Store in Manhattan. See also Cahn (2003).

67. Cahn (2003: 6).

68. Marx (1964).

69. Williams (1973: 46).

70. Williams (1973: 46).

71. Mitchell (1996: 83). Sandy Alexandre's *The Properties of Violence: Claims to Ownership in Representations of Lynching* (2012) argues that black agrarian slave labor, black dispossession and lynching violence together constitute a challenge to the kind of pastoral ethics espoused by the often-recurring fantasy that America is a pastoral paradise.

72. Gifford (1999, 2006).

73. "So You Want to Be a Cheesemaker? Stories from Dancing Cow Farm," panel at the meeting of the ACS, Burlington, Vt., August 3, 2007.

74. On other sorts of nature-culture collaborations, see Strathern (1992b); Latour (1993); Haraway (1998); Rabinow (1992); Franklin (2007); and Helmreich (2009).

75. Gifford (1999: 153).

76. Strathern (1992a). See also Escobar (1999).

77. Kohler (2006: 67).

78. Kohler's own Brooklyn-born grandparents were part of this cultural movement, buying a Vermont hill-farm in the mid 1930s; but "Unlike most such 'farms,' this one remains to this day a working dairy farm, making prizewinning artisanal cheeses" (2006: 67). That cheese is Taylor Farm Gouda, made by Jon Wright. Jon also grew up in New York

in a family who had a "summer place" in nearby Londonderry. As part of a high school work-study program, while his prep-school classmates went to Boston to do internships in law offices, Jon went to work on the Taylor dairy farm. The farm closed in the 1980s. Later, after working on a revitalization plan with the Taylor family, Jon leased the barn and farmhouse. Just as he was finishing building a new cheese room, his ninety-six-year-old landlord passed away. Jon thought, "We're done." But then, Jon told me in an interview, "a nephew of his, Rob Kohler, stepped in and bought the entire property. He subsequently sold us the house, barn, and about twenty-two acres of land. And he put the rest of the property into the Vermont Land Trust, which is a conservancy. It's a contingency plan whereby the land and the farmers go together—we and our heirs have lifetime rights to continue to farm here." When Jon was growing up, there were about fifteen small dairy farms in the area; today there are two, and both make cheese.

79. Hamilton (2008). By 2006, Wal-Mart accounted for about 16 percent of the domestic grocery market (Fishman 2006: 4).

80. Cahn (2003: 6).

81. Dudley (2000: 9).

82. Williams (1973: 46).

83. From the Cypress Grove Chevre Web site, www.cypressgrovechevre.com/company/terroir.html, accessed July 5, 2010.

84. Landscapes "embody cultural values" (Kohler 2006: 44); see also Mitchell (1996).

85. Finn (2006).

86. Jarosz and Lawson (2002: 9).

87. Bourdieu (1984).

88. According to my survey, the majority of people who make artisanal cheese grew up favoring run-of-the-mill Cheddar (35 percent) or process cheese—American, Velveeta, or Kraft Singles (21 percent).

89. Ulin (1996).

90. In *Bobos in Paradise*, Brooks writes, "The grand achievement of the educated elites in the 1990s was to create a way of living that lets you be an affluent success and at the same time a free-spirit rebel. . . . Building gourmet companies like Ben & Jerry's or Nantucket Nectars, they've found a way to be dippy hippies and multinational corporate fat cats" (2001: 42). If there are any corporate fat cats in the artisanal cheese world, they did not get there from making and selling cheese.

91. Ross (2003: 124).

92. The assertion also rests on stereotypes about taste, implying that only elites could produce tastes that are appreciated by elites. The corollary that poor people are unlikely to produce frou-frou cheese recapitulates a stereotyping of white rural poverty as culturally "backward" and stemming from lack of industry (Jarosz and Lawson 2002).

93. Florida (2002: 8).

94. Respondents to my survey, distributed primarily to independent business owners, overwhelmingly identified as white (96 percent); out of 174 responses, just 1 person identified (in part) as African American; 1 as Asian; 2 as Latino/a; and 3 as part American Indian. Several artisan creameries, particularly in California and across the South, buy milk from African American and Latino dairy farmers.

95. For example, see Striffler (2005) on the chicken industry. The intersection of labor and immigration is a politically delicate subject in the contemporary United States; one producer named in this book urged me not to discuss the Central American origin of some of his/her employees, in part out of worry that such attention might lead to their being hassled by immigration officials.

96. Russell (2007); Freidberg (2009: 234); Radel, Schmook, and McCandless (2010).

97. Cross (2004). In Amish communities, socioeconomic status is influenced by religious commitments.

98. Herzog (2009).

99. Jeanne Carpenter's Cheese Underground blog, http://cheeseunderground.blog spot.com/2010/07/making-cheese-with-cesar-luis.html, accessed October 3, 2010.

100. In a few instances I interviewed owner-operators formerly engaged in cheese-making who have now turned over the day-to-day process to employees. In one case I interviewed the co-owner of a farmstead operation that has hired a professional cheese-maker. All the people I interviewed are actively making and/or marketing cheese.

101. The following business configurations are characterized as one of two types of artisan enterprise. *Farmstead cheese* is artisanal cheese made on a dairy farm that supplies the milk for the cheese. Among such enterprises: (1) a person or family may buy a farm and animals and make cheese themselves; (2) farm owners may hire a professional to make cheese on their farm; (3) a member of a farming family may learn to make cheese. As the unmarked category, *artisanal cheese* encompasses farmstead cheese but can also refer more specifically to cheese made in an off-farm creamery, which can be characterized as (1) an independent owner-operator buying milk to make cheese; (2) a farmer-owned cooperative cheese factory managed by a professional cheesemaker; (3) a privately owned cheese factory in which the owner may keep his or her hand in the vat.

102. I have visited and interviewed cheesemakers and/or business owners in Massachusetts (5), Vermont (15), New York (1), Wisconsin (11), and California (10). I spent summer 2007 in Vermont, based in Londonderry. In 2008 I spent a month in southern Wisconsin and a month in Sonoma and Marin counties in California.

103. I borrow from Howard Becker's conceptualization and study of "art worlds" (1982).

104. In the first ACS competition in 1985, 30 cheesemakers from 18 states entered a total of 89 cheeses, commercial and homemade (Carroll 1999). In 2009, 197 producers from 32 states, 3 Canadian provinces, and—for the first time—Mexico (the competition was held in Austin, Texas) entered a record number of 1,327 commercially available cheeses.

105. As an incentive, a random 10 percent of survey respondents will receive copies of this book.

106. From my 2009 survey, I estimate domestic production of artisanal cheese for 2008 at roughly 10 million pounds, compared with 429 million pounds of specialty and artisanal cheese (combined) that year in Wisconsin alone. Among my survey respondents, 37 percent produced less than 6,000 pounds of cheese in 2008. Domestic production and sales have risen steadily for a decade, while import figures are falling.

107. Burros (2004). *The Martha Stewart Show,* broadcast Wednesday, December 30, 2009 (available for viewing online at www.marthastewart.com/show/the-martha-stewart-show/the-cheese-show). Hewitt (2008); Goode (2010).

CHAPTER 2. ECOLOGIES OF PRODUCTION

1. In early 2010, Major Farm introduced Queso del Invierno, or "winter cheese," made from a blend of the Majors' sheep's milk and a neighbor's cow's milk.

2. For a related analysis of artisanal foie gras, see Heath and Meneley (2010).

3. Begon, Townsend, and Harper (2006: xi).

4. Kloppenburg (1988: 31).

5. In tracking the contingencies of how a network functions to produce a safe and tasty cheese while sustaining a rural business, I draw on actor-network theory in science and technology studies, which insists on understanding networks of elements and agencies without first segregating them into separate domains of "nature" and "society"; see Callon (1986); Law (1992); Latour (2005). Agro-food studies, devoted to investigating how commodity chains handle the hybrid nature-culture of seed, produce, and livestock, have drawn on political ecology and, more recently, also actor-network theory. See Kloppenburg (1988); Cronon (1991); Murdoch (1997); Goodman (1999); Barndt 2002; Freidberg (2004); Holloway et al. (2007).

6. Locke ([1689] 1982: 26).

7. Yanagisako and Delaney (1995).

8. On political ecology, see Escobar (1999); Watts (2000); Biersack (2006).

9. Aletta Biersack (2006: 24) argues that political ecology's study of the relations of production must more fully "attend to the *culture*" of natural resource access and allocation, and to "the *culture* of the social relations of production and other human-nature articulations" (emphasis in the original).

10. On local-global food ecologies and economies, see Carney (2001); Bestor (2004); Freidberg (2004); Wilk (2006a); Gewertz and Errington (2010).

11. In 2004 it cost David Major $2,000 to have 500 pounds of wool washed in Texas, while for $2,000 an exporter can ship 40,000 pounds of wool and have it processed in China.

12. Carman, Heath, and Minto (1892: 173).

13. Cutts (1869: 287–288); Albers (2000: 145).

14. Albers (2000: 146).

15. Prices fell to just forty cents per pound by 1850 (Barron 1984: 59).

16. Albers (2000: 148).

17. Wool sold for eighty-five cents a pound during the Civil War but dropped to thirty cents by the end of the 1870s, while butter prices held their value after the war. Hal Barron writes, "As the price of butter improved and that of wool deteriorated, the profitability of switching to dairying became increasingly apparent. . . . The cost of feeding one cow for a year was equivalent to keeping eight sheep" (1984: 59).

18. When a couple of days old, the lambs are assigned a number; it is engraved on a strip of metal and clipped to their ears. Singletons are distinguished from twins, and males from females, by the placement of the clip—right ear or left, facing up or facing down.

19. Wooster (2005: 139).

20. Franklin (2007).

21. In contrast, the industrial model of dairy farming is guided by maximizing output; Grasseni (2005: 40) explains, regarding cows:

> The continuous striving for milking traits means that a cow's production is exploited only until the offspring are capable of a production exceeding that of their mothers. "It is a genetic law that the daughters will be better than the mother," explained an agriculturalist friend. Thirty months after a mother's first birth-giving, the calf will have become a heifer, will have been inseminated, will have given birth, and will be lactating. At this point, it becomes an economic imperative for the farmer to maximize production by substituting the mothers with their daughters who carry updated and reliable genetic material. On average, an industrial breeding farm with "use up" a milking cow for three successive suckling cycles and then discard her at about five to six years of age.

22. The economic viability of cheesemaking as a business depends on generating income from the birth of ram lambs, bull calves, and billy kids—male offspring of dairy animals that will not grow to become milk producers themselves.

23. Detachment, Matei Candea (2010) argues of human-animal engagement, should be understood as a possible aspect of relationship, not as its negation. Nigel Clark writes, "A social life that encompasses domesticated animals . . . can be seen to rest more primordially on a kind of mutual *dis*possession than on the possession of animals by human actors; a letting go of customary precautions and boundary maintenance on the part of each participating species" (2007: 57).

24. Haraway (2008).

25. Kehler (2010: 10).

26. This project of commodity defetishization relies on the assumption that "*biological process itself* already *constitutes a form of surplus value production*," a contemporary "form of life" that, Stefan Helmreich argues, naturalizes biotechnology's commoditization of engineered life forms (2007: 293). For a review of the literature on biocapital, see Helmreich (2008). Jack Kloppenburg (1988) has shown how biotechnology's predecessor, scientific hybridization, first had to overcome the "biological barrier to [seed's] commodification"—its natural reproducibility—to convert the surplus value of biology into the surplus value of capital; hybrid seeds cannot be saved and replanted the following season, they must be purchased each year.

27. On the possibility of an ethics of care in artisanal foie gras production, see Heath and Meneley (2010).

28. Mullin (1999).

29. Donna Haraway, writing particularly about dogs, urges that animals "are not here just to think with. They are here to live with" (2003: 5). See also Knight (2005) and Kirksey and Helmreich (2010).

30. Ritvo (1995); Franklin (2007).

31. Anderson (2004: 5).

32. When they bought the property and ran the title, they discovered that the farm had belonged to Judy's husband's great-great grandfather in the 1870s.

33. Each goat then cost her $350 a year to keep; in 2005 Capriole Farm housed 400 goats (only 210 were providing milk).

34. In Mediterranean cultures, in contrast, preference is often expressed for sheep over goats. What is admired as goat "individualism" in the United States is distrusted in Greece as goat greed, disobedience, cunning, and uncontrollable wildness, while "blessed sheep" are appreciated for their peaceful docility (Campbell 1964: 26, 31; Theodossopoulos 2005: 19).

35. Belasco (1989: 64).

36. Goat breeder and dairy farmer Jennifer Bice told me in an interview, "The goats were the favorites of all of us kids because the goats have personalities like dogs. You can teach them tricks, pretend you're having a circus. The cow stands there, and the sheep run away, but the goats are jumping and playing while we dress them up."

37. Wooster (2005: xii).

38. Quoted in Ritvo (1987: 16).

39. Wooster (2005: xvi). Despret writes, "From the point of view of predation, sheep-like behavior, which in our political metaphors seems to be emblematic of their stupidity, could be the foundation of the intelligence of most sheep's social behavior: a strategy of coordination and cohesion that protects them from predators. The closer and more attentive the animals remain to one another's movements, the sooner the enemy will be detected" (2005: 362).

40. Humans regard animals not only anthropocentrically but also culturally. While Americans tend to admire goat cunning as a mark of strong-willed individualism, the Sarakatsani shepherds of northern Greece disparage goats on the basis of this same trait: goats, like women, "are unable to resist pain in silence, they are cunning and insatiate feeders" (Campbell 1964: 31). Ott writes that Basques consider ewes "to be intelligent beasts by virtue of their *asmia,* instinct. They know when a storm or snow shower is imminent and will seek shelter of their own accord. They know instinctively where the trail to the valley, their winter pastures, and the barns lie" (1981: 171). Basque shepherds, like the Sarakatsani, have respected as intelligence what Anglo-Americans belittle as "herd mentality." Cultural prejudice dies hard; in his 1964 ethnography of the Sarakat-sani, English anthropologist John Campbell couldn't resist observing, "The sheep are not as intelligent as the Sarakatsani claim" (1964: 27).

41. Knight (2005); Candea (2010).

42. Nerissa Russell writes, the domestication of animals involves not only "biological processes of alteration to organisms" but also "social and cultural changes in both humans and animals" (2007: 30).

43. Mullin (1999: 215).

44. Clark (2007: 49).

45. Heath and Meneley (2007, 2010).

46. Mateo Kehler, speaking on the panel, "All about Flavor: Aged Raw Milk Cheese Production," at the ACS meetings in Louisville, Ky., July 21, 2005.

47. Percentage of milk butterfat influences the taste and consistency of cheese, and butterfat content, at least in goat's milk, may be influenced by doe maternalism. Peter Dixon, who has a master's degree in dairy science, explained to me that if goats are milked

(by humans) before their kids are weaned, the humans end up with significantly lower fat content in the milk they get because goats who are suckling "hold back for their babies." To ensure higher milk-fat content for cheesemaking, goat farmers can either wean kids immediately after suckling the colostrum, or hold off milking—and delay cheesemaking season—for a few weeks until the kids are weaned. Alternatively, a farmstead cheese-maker might begin the season by making a variety of cheese that works well with low-fat milk, adding higher-fat varieties as the season goes on. In such a way, goats may help to develop cheese product lines.

48. State-mandated testing for antibiotics, even at certified organic farms where anti-biotics use is prohibited, represents a one-size-fits-all response to industrial agriculture's overuse of antibiotics to maintain ruminant animals on grain rather than grass. The routine use of antibiotics has pushed pathogenic bacteria to charge back at us with ever stronger, more resistant strains (cf. Orzech and Nichter 2008).

49. Sheep's milk averages about 7.4 percent fat, whereas cow's milk averages about 3.7 percent and goat's milk a comparable 3.6 percent (Kindstedt 2005: 38).

50. Using whey as fertilizer is legally prohibited in the United Kingdom (Joby Wil-liams, personal communication).

51. For example, see Angela Miller's *Hay Fever* (2010).

52. This is not to suggest that only natural-rind cheeses may be considered "artisanal," as chapter 4 will clarify.

53. West and Domingos (2012: 126).

54. Mol (2008).

55. Lévi-Strauss (1969).

56. Ott (1979).

57. Ott (1981: 185).

58. Ott (1979: 703–704).

59. Ott (1981).

60. And see Ott (1981: 185–186).

61. Coombe (1998: 169).

62. Coombe (1998: 169).

63. One farmstead cheesemaker told the following anecdote at the ACS meeting in 2007: "This spring during calving season we had a tough day, arguing about how much milk to feed the calves, who does what, fighting over which chores—and it's frustrating for [my wife] to try to manage all this. So she came in to the milk house, and she was red in the face and very agitated, and she said, "I'm so upset!" And I said, "I can see that." And she said, "But I don't want to take it out on the cheese today!"

64. Malinowski (1948: 29).

65. As modes of practical knowledge and activity, science and magic are not mutu-ally exclusive. Anthropologists have demonstrated the compatibility between scientific practice and magical thinking in such modern arenas as nuclear weapons science (e.g., Gusterson 1996).

66. National Research Council (2003: 234).

67. Escobar (1999: 6).

68. See Liz Thorpe's *The Cheese Chronicles* (2009) for a version of the Vermont Shep-herd story as well as a playful recounting of her day "helping" to make Vermont Shepherd.

69. Kurt Dammeier, speaking on the panel, "Sustainability of Cheesemaking as a Business," annual meeting of the ACS, Burlington, Vt., August 2, 2007.

70. A brochure sent to me by Major Farm in late 2009 says of Vermont Shepherd, "It is created by several generations of the Major and Ielpi Families and friends who pasture and milk the sheep, make and age the cheese on their 250 acre farm in Westminster West, Vermont."

71. "Starting a Farmstead Cheese Business," July 12–13, Taylor Farm, Vt. The tale is elaborated in Major (2005).

72. Cheesemaker and business owner Allison Hooper (2005) makes the same point. A goat dairy farmer and cheesemaker who sells nearly all her cheese through farmers' markets told me in nearly identical words, "People aren't going to buy cheese just because you made it." It is essential to "have a kind of story" to sell, too. Cheesemakers and owners of cheesemaking farms who have published books to tell their story include Cahn (2003); Schwartz, Hausman, and Sabath (2009); and Miller (2010).

73. Angela Miller, co-owner of Consider Bardwell Farm in Vermont, writes of her customers in *Hay Fever*, "When they purchase a piece of Manchester or Rupert, they're buying a connection to us farmers and a vision of goats grazing on emerald Vermont fields and drinking from running brooks. We're their surrogates, living the life many of them aspire to. They don't realize what an exhausting and expensive life it is" (2010: 205).

74. Grasseni (2003: 260).

75. The previous year the Majors had hosted a summer intern whose French family had a home in the Pyrenees where the Majors could stay; she traveled with them to serve as translator.

76. The Majors also encountered newcomers to the craft who were part of a traditional-foods revival akin to what the Majors were then unwittingly kick-starting in the United States. See Cavanaugh (2007); Grasseni (2009).

77. Sandra Ott (1981: 184–185) describes this technique as practiced by Basque cheesemakers:

> When the milk reaches the correct temperature, the kettle is removed from the fire, and the shepherd plunges both forearms into the hot curdled milk. During this second heating, the "substance" or "material" *(materia)* of the milk settles as a thick sediment on the bottom of the kettle. The cheesemaker gradually amasses or gathers *(biltzen)* this substance into a round cake. If he does this too quickly, holes and cracks will form in the cheese and rotting will result. As it was often said to me, the shepherd must also have the patience of a woman towards her children when he amasses his cheese.
>
> Since this stage of the process occurs beneath the surface of the milk, I was unable to see exactly how the cheese is amassed. After about eight minutes, the shepherd suddenly pulls a steaming, wet, white cheese from the kettle.

78. These magazines are *Culture: The Word on Cheese, Cheese Connoisseur,* and *Say Cheese: For Cheese Lovers.*

79. "In gift transactions . . . the object given continues to be identified with the giver and indeed continues to be identified with the transaction itself" (Carrier 1995: 21).

80. Mauss ([1925] 2000).

81. Miller (2010: 205).

82. "Farmstead Appellation: Pros and Cons," ACS panel moderated by Jennifer Bice, Louisville, Ky., July 23, 2005.

83. Busch (2000) argues that agricultural grades and standards not only produce expectations for uniformity but also regulate a "moral economy" of good practice.

84. "In order for a cheese to be classified as 'farmstead,' as defined by the American Cheese Society, the cheese must be made with milk from the farmer's own herd, or flock, on the farm where the animals are raised. Milk used in the production of farmstead cheeses may not be obtained from any outside source. Farmstead cheeses may be made from all types of milk and may include various flavorings." From the ACS Web site, www.cheesesociety.org/displaycommon.cfm?an=1&subarticlenbr=51, accessed July 12, 2010.

85. In the United States, federal standards for labeling food products as "organically" produced are reductively based on approved inputs rather than on the principle of organic process; it is a cautionary tale for those who might want to establish a legally binding definition of "farmstead" or, for that matter, "artisanal" cheese. See Allen and Kovach (2000); Guthman (2004).

CHAPTER 3. ECONOMIES OF SENTIMENT

Epigraph: Schwartz, Hausman, and Sabath (2009: 223).

1. Survey conducted in February 2009.

2. I build here on Sylvia Yanagisako's insight that social and moral sentiments "operate simultaneously as material and cultural forces of production to incite, enable, constrain, and shape processes of production" (2002: 12). She continues, "As affective ideas and ideas with affect, sentiments are both emotional orientations and embodied dispositions" and include "concepts of selfhood and identity" (2002: 10).

3. Gudeman (2001: 1).

4. French sociologists Luc Boltanski and Laurent Thévenot (1991) suggest that other "conventions" or "orders of worth" include technological rationality, civic-mindedness, familial and other forms of loyalty, personal inspiration, and fame. See also Stark (2009).

5. Gudeman (2008). See also Gibson-Graham (1996).

6. On the crafting of artisan selves, see Kondo (1990), Terrio (2000), and Herzfeld (2004).

7. Margaret Radin speaks of this as "pervasive incomplete commodification" (1996: 113).

8. See Collier (1997).

9. As home-based entrepreneurs, farmers and artisans, write Smart and Smart, "regularly operate in the ambiguous boundaries between capital and labor, cooperation and exploitation, family and economy, tradition and modernity, friends and competitors" (2005: 1). They suggest that for such endeavors the category of "petty capitalist" offers more precision than "entrepreneur" (which could extend from a tamale vendor to a biotech start-up) or "family business" (which could cover a range in scale of operation and degree of owner-involvement in daily operations). According to Yanagisako, the under-

standing that "'modern family capitalism' is an oxymoron" has hampered social-science analysis of capitalist action and subjectivity (2002: 21).

10. Of the farmstead operations I surveyed, 70 percent are owned and operated by spouses or domestic partners, while 14 percent of farm-based operations involve the collaborative work of nonspouse family members—sibling teams, mother-son duos, grown children working with their parents. Only 20 percent of farm-based cheesemakers report working solo, compared to 36 percent of those running off-farm creameries.

11. Today's farmstead cheesemakers are not unlike their nineteenth-century counterparts, whose "idea of economy" "was conceptualized as a series of relationships with other people rather than as a process with the farm at the center where money came in and went out" (McMurry 1995: 53). Similarly, Yanagisako's analysis of Italian textile firms shows business operation to be guided as much by gendered, kin-based sentiment as by calculative reason; intrafamilial betrayal as well as trust and loyalty are both "products of the workings of Italian family capitalism" and "forces of production of Italian family capitalism" (2002: 11, italics omitted).

12. "Within any one business, a range of market and nonmarket transactions are enacted, various kinds of labor are deployed, and different class processes of production, appropriation, and distribution can coexist" (Gibson-Graham 2006: 74).

13. Robbins (2009: 284).

14. Gudeman (2001).

15. See Amin and Thrift (2004) for a similar argument that economic activity is also cultural activity, directed simultaneously at multiple goals (including prosperity) and, in the words of Clarke et al., "can be ordered by passions (desire and fear), moral sentiments (work hard, be honest, trust people), knowledge (understood as learnt culture—conventions, habits and so on) and disciplines (accountancy and similar technologies)" (2008: 225).

16. This quote from the owner-operator of a farmstead cheese business licensed in a western state in 2005 came in reply to my survey query, "What were your original goals in becoming a commercial cheesemaker?"

17. For a related survey of artisan food producers' goals in the United Kingdom, see Tregear (2005).

18. Compare Fred Turner's *From Counterculture to Cyberculture* (2006).

19. In his study of middle-class "lifestyle migrants" to the rural upper Midwest, Brian Hoey describes people who "find the relationship between economic life and a quest for deeper human values increasingly difficult to reconcile. Their economic commitments too often seem to impede the pursuit of other vital human needs," needs that include "developing and cherishing more intimate relationships with their families, a desire to feel belonging as part of a community while living in a physical environment that fosters an abiding sense of place, and a fundamental longing to better know themselves in order to see and experience personal growth" (2005: 605). While this characterization might seem to fit the rural in-migrant cheesemakers, my analysis differs from Hoey's on two counts. First, while Hoey draws on the philosophical writings of Charles Taylor and Alistair McIntyre to analyze the "moral narratives" that lifestyle migrants construct to bridge their outer (economic) and inner (moral) lives, I follow economic anthropologists

who reject an analytic division between "economic life" and "deeper human values"—economy *is* social, it is constituted by human values. What I see lifestyle migrants engaged in, then, is a reordering of values. Second, my analysis emphasizes that this moral project is not exclusive to lifestyle migrants but is also pursued by those who have lived and worked on farms for much of their lives.

20. A sampling of such goals reported in my survey include "Make great cheese"; "Best Farmstead Cheese in country"; "to produce a local, delicious cheese"; "to make an exceptional cheese at a regional level."

21. Many of the early "goat ladies," particularly in California, made cheese in their home kitchens for domestic consumption before launching commercial enterprises. Two early producers in Vermont, Allison Hooper and Laini Fondiller, became enamored of goat cheese and dairy farming after working in their early twenties on farms in France.

22. In Napa County, California, Barbara and Rex Backus began raising goats and making cheese in the 1970s. Recalling those early days, Barbara laughed at the naïveté of "these urban, overeducated types coming to the country"—meaning herself and her friends. Back then, "most of the people coming up here were really ignorant of what it meant to be a farmer. This, of course, isn't farmland," she said, indicating the arid, hilly landscape outside her kitchen window. Fortunately, they found it does sustain goats.

23. See Wilhelm (1985).

24. Warren Belasco calls this food economy the "countercuisine" (1989).

25. Belasco draws an analogy to how "the revival of midwifery" represented "a feminist defense against modern medical patriarchy" (1989: 54).

26. Quoted in Bilski (1986).

27. Julian and Riven (2001: 93).

28. Lawson, Jarosz, and Bonds (2008).

29. Nearly a third of my survey respondents obtained college degrees in the humanities, and one in eight reported work experience in the arts, design, or media. In Vermont, Woodcock Farm's Mark Fischer, a graduate of the Rhode Island School of Design, spent the 1970s shooting video footage of performances at the New York music venue CBGBs.

30. Sociologist Richard Sennett suggests that what unites craftspeople—the carpenter, the lab technician, the musical director—is dedication "to good work for its own sake. Theirs is a practical activity, but their labor is not simply a means to another end" (2008: 20).

31. "How Big Is Big Enough? Getting at Size for Farmstead Sustainability," panel at the meeting of the ACS, Burlington, Vt., August 2, 2007.

32. Csikszentmihalyi (1975).

33. David Major met his second wife after she moved nearby with her two children, wanting to start over after her first husband, a firefighter, died at the World Trade Center site. Seeking manual, mind-clearing labor, Yesenia started helping out in the cheese house, washing equipment and molding wheels of Vermont Shepherd alongside David. A flight attendant for American Airlines had also passed through Major Farm after 9/11, finding relief in a couple weeks of work.

34. "So You Want to Be a Cheesemaker? Stories from Dancing Cow Farm," presentation at the meeting of the ACS, Burlington, Vt., August 3, 2007.

35. Dancing Cow Farmstead has since folded.

36. See Ross (2003).

37. "European Forebears: Reinventing the Classics," panel at the meeting of the ACS, Chicago, Ill., July 25, 2008.

38. Barlett (1993: 79).

39. "Lifestyle is not a term which has much applicability to traditional cultures," asserts Giddens, "because it implies choice within a plurality of possible options, and is 'adopted' rather than 'handed down'" (1991: 81).

40. Collier (1997: 26).

41. At a 2007 workshop I attended for farmers considering cheese as a value-added enterprise, three New England dairy farmers, all milking about fifty cows, agreed that some sort of value-added project was the only path toward growth they would consider. "I can't expand to three hundred cows," one of them said. "Then you're no longer a dairy farmer, you're a manager" wishing you could "get out with the cows from time to time." Far from representing mutually exclusive sentiments, "necessity" and "lifestyle" shade into each other.

42. For example, see Miller (2010: 79); also Hewitt (2010).

43. About half the respondents to my survey spent at least part of their childhood in a rural area, often on a working farm; among them, 90 percent attended college or technical school. One-fourth of these studied business and nearly a third had work experience in business or management.

44. For a filmic depiction of the sort of sheep ranching operation Marcia's father may have grown up on, see *Sweetgrass* by Lucien Castaing-Taylor and Ilisa Barbash (2009).

45. For example, Schlosser (2001); Nabhan (2002); Pollan (2006); Kingsolver (2007); Patel (2007).

46. Schwartz, Hausman, and Sabath (2009: xi).

47. Cahn (2003: 8).

48. Similarly, Clarke et al. found in a study of organics consumption in England that "relatively ordinary concrete concerns—quality food, personal health—born out of practical experience (often within the family) dominate the narratives about being involved with organics" (2008: 224). On the feminist epistemology of situated knowledge, see Haraway (1988).

49. Gibson-Graham (2006: 54). See also Radin (1996).

50. Michel Callon and John Law (2005) have adopted the term "qualculation," introduced by market theorist Franck Cochoy (see, e.g., 2008), to speak to the qualitative character of calculative action.

51. While 39 percent of my survey respondents reported that their initial goals for starting a commercial cheese business have been met (only 7 percent saying their goals have not), 24 percent reported having to increase production over what they had originally anticipated in order to generate "necessary" income. Another 14 percent reported that they had become "more focused on money" or "more business-oriented" since starting the business.

52. The question for farmstead cheese, as the organizer posed it, is "what size operation," what scale of product line and how extensive a market network succeeds in creating

"a sustainable income and family stability," in striking an equilibrium between "quality of life and ability to make a living." The panelists were Greg Bernhardt, of Blue Ledge Farm, Karen Weinberg, from 3-Corner Field Farm, and Linda Dimmick, from Neighborly Farms.

53. "How Big Is Big Enough? Getting at Size for Farmstead Sustainability," panel at the ACS meeting, Burlington, Vt., August 2, 2007.

54. Kondo (1990: 57).

55. They built a milking parlor sized to goats, renovated existing space to serve as a cheese room ($1,750), renovated space as an apartment to house interns ($4,000), extended the cheese make room and added aging space ($25,000), and built a new barn ($17,000). In 2007 their farm was appraised for $415,000. To offset property taxes, they sold development rights to the Vermont Land Trust.

56. Dixon (n.d.) See also the appendix, table 6, for details on the start-up capital initially required to "build, equip and license" an artisan creamery, and table 7 for the sources from which this capital was acquired.

57. In regulatory terms, yogurt is classified with fluid milk rather than cheese.

58. "So You Want to Be a Cheesemaker? Stories from Dancing Cow Farm," presentation at the ACS meeting, Burlington, Vt., August 3, 2007.

59. Acknowledging much to same to me, Jon Wright said of his fifteen years running Taylor Farm: "I have to recognize where my strengths are, you know—and I'd love to be out there baling hay, but it's more important to me to be here right now, so one of my guys is doing that. Years ago I would have been all conflicted. I would have been out there trying to bale hay, and frustrated when I was here [in the office]. . . . You're constantly learning about your own personality and the business is very much a reflection of me and my personality, and the flaws [in the business] I see as flaws in me."

60. Of 124 farm-based cheesemaking operations surveyed in 2009, 43 percent reported only one or two employees, including owner-operators. An additional 36 percent reported three to six employees, including the owner-operators and part-time as well as full-time positions. The majority of on-farm cheesemaking operations are quite small.

61. College interns might suggest a more acceptable alternative to the exploitative employment of marginalized and legally vulnerable Mexican and Central American farmworkers, on which dairy farms are increasingly reliant, even in Vermont (Freidberg 2009; Radel, Schmook, and McCandless 2010). College interns may also approach farming and food-making as do the post-pastoral farmers who employ them, as something worth doing for reasons other than earning a paycheck (see Miller [2010] for a look at the sometimes strained labor relations on a cheesemaking farm). In 2012, Blue Ledge Farm's Web site indicated that seasonal interns were now also paid a small stipend: blueledge-farm.com/internships.html, accessed May 14, 2012.

62. Contrast the strict gendered division of labor among French chocolatiers studied by Terrio (2000): the men, working in backroom workshops, made the chocolates while their wives worked retail at the "front of the house."

63. Gender narratives were commonly employed to explain a preference for goats or sheep over cows, with cows deemed "too large" for women to handle easily—not that men ever lift cows up and carry them around! Then again, I heard men, too, describe cows as

"too intimidating." Historically, cow dairying was strictly gendered as feminine, as represented by the iconic rosy-cheeked dairymaid (McMurry 1995: 78). Dairying began to be gendered as masculine in the mid 1800s, when "the connections between female nurturance, lactation, and the milking of cows were replaced by suggestions on milking technique and procedure that increasingly showed a concern for discipline and system. This shift paralleled the rise of the notion of the cow as a machine: if cows were machines, then according to prevalent cultural canons they were properly men's province" (McMurry 1995: 80).

64. One woman responded to my survey invitation with the following e-mail message: "I am not producing cheese anymore. The reason I stopped is because I went through a divorce. Between the court system and my ex, they made it impossible for me to continue. I had been making cheese since 1997, so it was a difficult thing to do (to stop) but necessary. I am not producing anything. I sold/gave away most of my animals." When I e-mailed her back to ask if I might print her message in this book, she replied, "Absolutely. I think it's important for everyone to know that there is more to what happens in life than just money issues."

65. At the time of the presentation, 45 percent of Blue Ledge sales were wholesale to Vermont food stores; 20 percent were direct retail through three Vermont farmers' markets (open six months a year); and 10 percent were handled through a distributor.

66. Results from my survey, reporting on the year 2009 (note that 35 percent of survey respondents had become licensed within the previous five years), were as follows:

farmstead operations (n = 70): 54 percent reported profit; 46 percent did not turn a profit

dairy farms with cheese as value-added (n = 35): 57 percent reported profit; 43 percent did not turn a profit

independent creameries (n = 36): 78 percent reported profit; 22 percent did not turn a profit

67. As consultants from the University of Vermont summarize, a herd or flock "must cover its' [sic] own costs plus contribute to the family living expenses, plus pay back borrowed money plus replace depreciated equipment" (Delaney and Kauppila n.d.: 138).

68. Beyond initial investments in property, equipment, and infrastructure, annual or monthly working expenses may include

on farm: breeding costs (stud fees or semen); feed; hay and wood shavings; seed and fertilizer; testing fees (soil, milk); gas and fuel oil; electricity (can run very high for refrigeration); liability insurance; equipment repairs; veterinary and other animal expenses (e.g., shearing); property taxes

cheesemaking supplies: cultures, rennet, salt, molds, cheesecloth, sanitizer, hairnets, gloves, footwear—and milk if purchased from other farms

office: accounting; advertising and marketing; telephone and Internet; packaging; shipping and other transportation; farmers' market fees; office supplies

other potential expenses: consultant and workshop fees; wages, worker's compensation, and payroll taxes; private health insurance (for owners and/or employees); interest on loans; donations of cheese to community events;

entrance and other fees for awards competitions; reject product or wastage (i.e., cheese that ends up on the manure pile); product "loss" through sampling at farmers' markets and cheese festivals

69. Again we see qualities and quantities fold into each other: *good* cheese is made from *clean* and *flavorful* milk produced by *well*-tended animals that have *plenty* of space and *diverse* sources of food.

70. According to my survey data, farmstead producers who buy milk do so from an average of two other farms. As Kondo writes of family-owned artisan enterprises in Japan, "the distinction between small and large firms is a *culturally* meaningful one . . . laden with symbolic, cultural, and moral value" (1990: 53).

71. In 2008 Blue Ledge paid $40/cwt for goat's milk and $24/cwt for cow's milk, a bit higher than the going commodity price, which was relatively high that year.

72. "So You Want to Be a Cheesemaker? Stories from Dancing Cow Farm," presentation at the ACS meeting, Burlington, Vt., August 3, 2007.

73. Vickers (1990: 3).

74. Page 168; quoted in McMurry (1995: 52).

75. McMurry (1995: 52). See also Vickers (1990).

76. Although that is precisely what they did, in 2010.

77. Before they moved to the farm, they told me, "We had reached the point in our life where we didn't have to balance the checkbook. We could go to any restaurant we liked." That changed after they started the cheese business.

78. In my survey (n = 143), respondents reported a broad range of household incomes, but for only about a quarter of artisan business owners did income derived from cheese account for more than 75 percent of total household income. See the appendix, table 8.

79. Robbins (2009: 282–283).

80. Addressing this need, in October 2010 Wisconsin's Dairy Business Innovation Center (DBIC) held a pricing fundamentals seminar for cheesemakers in Madison, covering market-based and cost-plus pricing as well as how to calculate costs; see DBIC press release: www.dbicusa.org/press_releases.php, accessed October 10, 2010.

81. Stark (2009).

82. Among 153 survey respondents across all types of enterprise, 84 percent had expanded cheese production since opening or acquiring the business and (n = 155) 61 percent plan or hope for future expansion.

83. Then again, making cheese from pasteurized milk requires the addition of larger quantities of expensive freeze-dried bacterial cultures.

84. Asked whether they agreed with the statement "I feel secure about my savings and ability to retire when I want," survey respondents (n = 140) answered: disagree, 33 percent; disagree somewhat, 16.5 percent; feel neutral, 19 percent; agree somewhat, 13.5 percent; agree, 18 percent.

85. In September 2010, their 7.25 acres and home were up for sale for $795,000. The dairy operation, including cheesemaking equipment and "secret cheese recipes," was available for an additional $65,000. http://activerain.com/blogsview/1604642/pugs-leap -goat-cheese-dairy-and-a-7-acre-healdsburg-view-site, accessed September 26, 2010. In 2011, the new owners were moving the dairy business to Petaluma.

86. "How Big Is Big Enough? Getting at Size for Farmstead Sustainability," panel at the ACS meeting, Burlington, Vt., August 2, 2007.

87. "How Big Is Big Enough?" panel at the ACS meeting, Burlington, Vt., August 2, 2007.

88. Dudley (1996: 48); see also Barlett (1993: 120–128) on "cautious" versus "ambitious" or "entrepreneurial" farm management styles.

89. Villette and Vuillermot (2009).

90. Grasseni (2003).

91. Complicating matters, the state of California has its own milk pricing order. More often than not, California's prices are slightly lower than the national average—giving their cheese factories an edge over Wisconsin's.

92. Typical comments include, "to keep the dairy on the plus side" (entered the cheese business in 2000); "develop an additional source of income beyond selling milk" (2002); "stabilize our milk price and provide a decent on-farm income for myself" (2005); and "stabilize value of milk on the farm" (2006).

93. The 2002 Farm Bill authorized a Value-Added Agricultural Product Market Development Grants Program; see USDA press release at www.rurdev.usda.gov/ny/tool barpages/rbspages/valueadded.htm, accessed May 14, 2012.

94. Annual averages (per hundred pounds): 2006: $12.88; 2007: $19.13; 2008: $18.34. See "Understanding Dairy Markets" at http://future.aae.wisc.edu/data/monthly_values/by_area/10?grid=true&tab=prices&area=US, accessed May 14, 2012.

95. United States Department of Agriculture news release no. 0624.09, www.usda.gov/wps/portal/!ut/p/_s.7_0_A/7_0_1OB?contentidonly=true&contentid=2009/12/0624.xml, accessed May 14, 2012.

96. On December 18, 2009, Agriculture Secretary Tom Vilsack announced that the Commodity Credit Corporation would purchase sixty million dollars' worth of cheese and cheese products to distribute through domestic feeding programs, including food banks and the school lunch program.

97. Interest in value-added agriculture also "derives from changes in consumer preferences" owing, for example, to "increased incomes, out-migration from cities by affluent second-home owners, 'demassifying' of food markets into many small segments, general disaffection with foods associated with the 'agro-industrial complex,' the desire of consumers for more direct contact with producers of their food, increased desire for 'functional foods' that provide health and wellness benefits, consumer exposure to a broader variety of food flavors, and increased visibility of 'food-based media outlets and personalities'" (Nicholson and Stephenson 2006: 2).

98. "How Big Is Big Enough? Getting at Size for Farmstead Sustainability," panel at the ACS meeting, Burlington, Vt., August 2, 2007.

99. Nicholson and Stephenson (2006); Streeter and Bills (2003a and 2003b).

100. At the same time, as Dudley (2000: 114) writes of farmers in the 1980s, "The 'value' of secondhand consumption has less to do with the economic bargain that may be involved than with the moral 'thriftiness' it demonstrates." Thus, she explains, being "content to live in a hundred-year-old farmhouse" can signify the virtue of a farm couple's frugality.

101. Willetts (1997).

102. "Farm-Scale Cheese Making with Raw Milk from Grass-Fed Cows," Jersey Girls Dairy, Chester, Vt., July 22, 2007. Workshop cosponsored by the Vermont Pasture Network, Vermont Grass Farmers Association, and Rural Vermont.

103. See, for example, Guthman (2004).

104. LaFollette (2000: 401).

CHAPTER 4. TRADITIONS OF INVENTION

Epigraph: Norton and Dilley (2009: 3).

1. In 1995, volunteers video-recorded interviews with more than 250 former cheesemakers (who worked in the 1920s through the 1970s), dairy farmers, cheese graders, and wives of cheesemakers to generate an oral history library of the Green County, Wisconsin, cheese industry. I transcribed several of these interviews, available for viewing on VHS at the Historic Cheesemaking Center.

2. Apps (1998: 137); Marquis and Haskell (1964: 66).

3. Trewartha (1926).

4. Addressing the Wisconsin Dairymen's Association in 1885, T. H. Curtis (1885: 51), a consultant from Syracuse, New York, described this procedure of determining when curd has been "sufficiently 'cooked'": "Take a handful and squeeze the whey out. If it is firm enough, on opening your hand, it will at once rattle to pieces."

5. See Petrini (2007). A notable exception to this is Kindstedt (2005), with a historical chapter on cheesemaking in the United States.

6. Hobsbawm (1983).

7. See Parr (2009); Davies (2010).

8. Hirsch and Stewart (2005: 262).

9. Bushman (1998: 364).

10. Durand (1952: 265). Vermont farmers began exporting cheese to Montreal in the early nineteenth century (Kindstedt 2005: 25).

11. On July 20, 1801, the farmwives of Cheshire, Massachusetts, pooled their curd yielded from a single day's milking and, using a cider press, formed a mammoth cheese to be presented as a gift of appreciation to President Thomas Jefferson—and as an unforgettable advertisement for the town's principal agricultural commodity. The scheme was hatched by Elder John Leland, who made the presentation at the White House (and had excluded the cows of Federalists). One month after pressing, the cheese was weighed at 1,235 pounds (see Browne 1944).

12. Gilbert (1896: 12).

13. Gilbert (1896: 12), Durand (1952: 268). By 1850, on the eve of the factory system, New York was producing 47 percent of the nation's cheese (Gilbert 1896: 14).

14. Gilbert (1896: 9).

15. Gilbert (1896: 11). See also McMurry (1995: 46). On England, see Twamley (1784), Blundel and Tregear (2006), and Valenze (1991, 2011).

16. Per my survey data.

17. Arnold (1876: 16).

18. McMurry (1995: 123–124).

19. Durand (1939: 283).

20. Durand (1952). Cheese factories in England also began to emerge in the 1870s, although commercial cheesemaking farms had been working with consolidated milk since the seventeenth century, and the centralized cheese factory system never caught on in England as it did in the United States (Blundel and Tregear 2006).

21. Gilbert (1896: 16), Durand (1952: 272).

22. Proponents of the factory system tried, without much evidence, to forward this argument, similar to current advice to dairy farmers that they take up a value-added enterprise.

23. McMurry (1995: 137; also 135).

24. Quoted in McMurry (1995: 140–141) and also in Apps (1998: 26).

25. Bushman (1998: 374).

26. Arnold (1876: 17).

27. Crowley is a proprietary cheese factory, owned by an individual or partnership of individuals—often, though not necessarily, the cheesemaking family. Early cheese factories could be owned in two additional ways: as joint stock companies owned by stockholders, or as a cooperative of dairy-farmer patrons who hired a cheesemaker (and his family) on a percentage basis (Apps 1998: 111).

28. Crowley Cheese Company, Inc. was purchased in 2009 by Galen and Jill Jones (Galen Jones is a media management consultant) from an investor group of former Time, Inc. executives who had owned it for fifteen years. In 2008, production was suspended for the first time in the factory's 126-year history before the Jones purchase. Cheesemakers Ken Hart and Kimberly Farrar were returned to their jobs after the purchase was concluded (Edwards 2009; Widness 2010).

29. According to the *Merriam-Webster Dictionary,* a second meaning of *slatternly* is "of, relating to, or characteristic of a slut or prostitute" (both definitions quoted in McMurry 1995: 168).

30. Fitzgerald (2003).

31. Valenze (1991: 143, 153).

32. Wood (2009a, 2009b).

33. Gilbert (1896: 11).

34. Curtis (1885: 64).

35. Curtis (1885: 64).

36. Dairy scientist John Decker's *Cheese Making* guide from 1909 notes, "Cheaper and stronger color is now being made from aniline, a coal-tar product. The public seems to be prejudiced against mineral coloring, but there is so little of it in the cheese that it is doubtful if it is injurious to health" (1909: 53–54).

37. Gilbert (1896: 22).

38. Gilbert (1896: 23). For an uncritical description of the process for "Oleomargarine Cheese," see Arnold (1876: 334).

39. Apps (1998: 39–40).

40. Gilbert (1896: 24).

41. Gilbert (1896: 12).

42. Wisconsin's percentage of the nation's cheese production picked up where New York left off: in 1899, Wisconsin accounted for 26.6 percent of U.S. cheese; in 1909, 46.6 percent; and in 1919, 61.3 percent (Apps 1998: 31).

43. Durand (1952: 279).

44. Trewartha (1926: 293).

45. Doane (1961).

46. Braverman (1974).

47. Marquis and Haskell (1964: 66).

48. McMurry (1995: 83). For a contemporary technical discussion, see Dixon (2005: 209–210).

49. Arnold (1876: 343).

50. Wood (2009b: 53–70). In Marin County, California, I visited the Giacomini dairy, home of Point Reyes Farmstead Cheese Company, and met with Jill Giacomini Basch, one of the farmer's four daughters (all work for the cheese business). As we stood on a staircase in the split-level cheese room built on the foundation of an old horse barn, Jill pointed out the gravity-flow system to move curd gently from the 1,500-gallon vat into circular cheese molds arrayed on a table set on the lower level, thereby saving the curd from the stress of mechanical pumping and saving the cheesemakers from the back strain of hooping curd by hand. Explaining that her family got the idea for this setup after touring an Amish cheese factory in Salemville, Wisconsin, Jill quipped, "We like to say we're doing things the high-tech, state-of-the-art, Amish way."

51. According to the Food and Drug Administration's Code of Federal Regulations, sec. 133.169, *pasteurized process cheese* is defined as "food prepared by comminuting and mixing, with the aid of heat, one or more cheeses of the same or two or more varieties . . . for manufacturing with an emulsifying agent . . . into a homogeneous plastic mass." Among process cheeses, "when cheddar cheese, washed curd cheese, colby cheese, granular cheese, or any mixture of two or more of these is combined with other varieties of cheese in the cheese ingredient, any of such cheeses or such mixture may be designated as 'American cheese.'"

52. Out of 10,435,941 pounds of cheese (excluding cottage cheese) produced in the United States in 2010, 3,488,484 pounds of it was mozzarella: National Agricultural Statistics Service (2011).

53. McMurry (1995: 129).

54. McMurry (1995: 96).

55. McMurry (1995).

56. Norton and Dilley (2009).

57. Crowley Cheese Web site, www.crowleycheese-vermont.com/, accessed May 15, 2012.

58. Ulin (1996, 2002).

59. Ulin (2002: 702).

60. Ulin (2002: 699).

61. Thorpe (2009: 141) writes, "When new kinds of cheese and new models of production began to sprout up in the early 1980s, they defined themselves in opposition to the old factory style."

62. Bourdieu (1984); Ulin (2002).

63. Werlin (2000); Tewksbury (2002); McCalman and Gibbons (2005); Ogden (2007); Wolf (2008); Hurt (2008); Parr (2009); Davies (2010).

64. Mintz (1985).

65. Mignon (1962).

66. Juliette Rogers reports running into similar numerical inconsistency during field-work among dairy farmers and cheesemakers in Normandy (2008: 77).

67. Boisard (2003: 10).

68. Hobsbawm (1983: 2).

69. In a letter to the townspeople of Camembert, Knirim explained: "Years ago, I suffered for several months from indigestion, and Camembert was practically the sole nourishment that my stomach and intestines were able to tolerate. Since then, I have sung the praises of Camembert, I have introduced it to thousands of gourmets, and I myself eat it two or three times a day" (Boisard 2003: 3).

70. See Rogers (2008).

71. On cheese, see Boisard (1991, 2003); Grasseni (2003, 2009); Rogers (2008). On wine, see Guy (2003); Ulin (2002).

72. Boisard (2003); Rogers (2008); Trubek and Bowen (2008); Grasseni (2009).

73. Boisard (1991).

74. As Hobsbawm writes, "It is the contrast between the constant change and innova-tion of the modern world and the attempt to structure at least some parts of social life within it as unchanging and invariant, that makes the 'invention of tradition' so interest-ing for historians of the past two centuries" (1983: 2). See also Sutton (1994); Collier (1997); Terrio (2000); Paxson (2004).

75. Previously an architect, Boyce spent ten years in the organic beef industry before taking on Marin French (he had studied at the University of California at Berkeley and long wanted to return to Marin County, where he spent many student days).

76. Kamp (2006: 171–172).

77. Roberts (2007: xiii).

78. "So You Want to Be a Cheesemaker? Stories from Dancing Cow Farm," presenta-tion at the meeting of the ACS, Burlington, Vt., August 3, 2007. Indeed, chapter 5, article 2 of France's decree no. 2007–628 relating to cheeses and specialty cheese houses (April 27, 2007) stipulates that "pyramid and truncated pyramid" forms are "reserved exclusively for goat's-milk cheeses."

79. "European Forebears: Reinventing the Classics," panel at the meeting of the ACS, Chicago, Ill., July 25, 2008.

80. On the power and politics of naming cheeses, see West et al. (2012).

81. Becker (1978: 865).

82. Nies (2008: 10).

83. Nies (2008: 10). Valenze (1991: 154) writes similarly of eighteenth-century English dairywomen, "Long accustomed to selling their products, if only on a local basis, they showed considerable sensitivity to the ever-elusive predilections of the market."

84. To be sure, "farmstead" cheeses have their own category in the ACS competition.

85. As Marquis and Haskell (1964: 18) write in *The Cheese Book*, "the story of cheese-making is a long history of imitation, ever since the first cheeses were made."

86. As Johannes Fabian has argued, such temporal distancing impedes communica-tion through a "denial of coevalness" (1983).

87. Boisard (2003: 166).

88. Grasseni (2003); Rogers (2008).

89. Grasseni (2003: 273).

90. According to oral history interviews from 1995 with Albert Deppeler and Myron Olson, Green County Historic Cheesemaking Center, Monroe, Wisconsin.

91. Boisard (1991: 174).

92. As Heath and Meneley (2007) put it, *techne* and technoscience are not mutually exclusive.

93. Wolf (2008: 159).

94. Apps (1998: 134).

95. Grasseni (2003: 260).

96. Strathern (1992b: 38).

97. See Taber (2006).

98. Strathern (1992b: 39).

99. Fabian (1983: 31) writes, "Communication is, ultimately, about creating shared Time." And time—or better, history—has not always been shared across these cheesemaking spaces.

100. Frederick Taylor's *The Principles of Scientific Management,* published in 1911, spurred a revolution in business management that saw artisanal "rule-of-thumb" methods in manufacturing labor replaced with streamlined, increasingly automated methods designed by managers based on scientific time-and-motion studies. "Taylorism" has become synonymous with his principle of "scientific management." For a critique, see Braverman (1974).

101. See "American Raw Milk Cheeses," www.slowfoodusa.org/index.php/programs/presidia_product_detail/american_raw_milk_cheeses/, accessed August 3, 2010.

102. Leitch (2003: 455).

103. Mintz (2006: 10).

104. With milk from the five grass-based dairy farms that have invested in his cooperative creamery, Bruce Workman also makes wheels of Gouda and Cheddar plus "some conventional cheeses to pay the bills"—shrink-wrapped deli loaves of Havarti, Pepper Jack, and Muenster that could be made "in your sleep."

105. "European Forebears: Reinventing the Classics," panel at the ACS meeting, Chicago, Ill., July 25, 2008.

106. Private labeling can be a boon. Swiss Colony, a midwestern specialty foods mail-order business, has helped several Wisconsin artisan factories, and Linda Dimmick has made a couple of fortuitous deals with national chains to buy large portions of a year's inventory. While this "paid a lot of bills," it is only a stopgap measure. It is no way to build a brand.

107. Wilk (2006b: 15).

CHAPTER 5. THE ART AND SCIENCE OF CRAFT

Epigraph: "From the Mountain," *nom de plume* of Harriet Martineau (Martineau 1863: 290).

1. ACS Web site, www.cheesesociety.org/displaycommon.cfm?an=1&subarticlenbr=51, accessed August 28, 2010. The definition was developed by ACS committee in the late 1990s.

2. Heath and Meneley (2007: 594).

3. Metcalf (2007: 5–6).

4. Becker (1978).

5. Metcalf (2007); Sally Markowitz (1994) adds that modern art is distinguished from craft by a "semantic criterion": objects of art—paintings, sculptures—demand interpretation, whereas objects of craft—pottery, furniture, textiles—do not.

6. "Washed-Rind Cheeses," March 22–23, 2007, Woodcock Farm, Weston, Vt.; "Starting a Farmstead Cheese Business," July 12–13, 2007, Taylor Farm, Vt.

7. I draw on a multidisciplinary body of work on the question of craft, notably Becker (1978); Dormer (1997); Ingold (2000); Markowitz (1994); Pye (1968); Alfondy (2007); Risatti (2007); Sennett (2008).

8. See Sutton (2001) on the synesthetic power of taste in preserving memory.

9. Becker (1978: 864).

10. "Because materials don't easily give themselves up to becoming the object the maker wishes," art historian Howard Risatti observes, craftspeople select and prepare the materials that will best lend themselves to the crafted object they have in mind to make (2007: 100). See also Markowitz (1994).

11. Pye (1968: 7).

12. On the technoscientific history of milk's materiality and standardization, see Atkins (2007).

13. In Liz Thorpe's words, "Artisanal cheesemakers change their recipe, and their cheesemaking technique, to accommodate the shifting fluid medium that is milk. Commodity cheesemakers take all possible steps to forcibly create a consistent fluid medium that can be made into a consistent final product, without modifying their approach" (2009: 135). Milk is said to express seasonal variation owing to the different compositions of early-lactation and late-lactation milk, and also from beta-carotene and other components traceable to the species of grasses, legumes, and wildflowers found seasonally in pastures, hay, and browse eaten by cows, sheep, and goats.

14. This is knowledge by personal acquaintance rather than abstract knowledge that something is so. Lesher (1969) draws a relevant distinction in Plato's *Theaetetus* between *gnosis* ("knowledge by acquaintance") and *episteme* ("knowledge that something is the case"). This sense of gnosis well captures the artisan's "knowledge" of materials—in the case of cheesemaking, "knowing" one's milk and curd, how it behaves under particular conditions.

15. Risatti (2007: 195).

16. Pye (1968: 66).

17. Kindstedt (2005: 37–38).

18. See West and Domingos (2012); Weiss (2012).

19. "As in any craft," writes Tim Ingold, "the skilled maker who has a feel for what she is doing is one whose movement is continually and subtly responsive to the modulations of her relation with the material" (2000: 357). Douglas Harper, writing of an artisan mechanic, calls this "knowledge in the body" a sort of "kinesthetic correctness" (1987: 117).

20. Willi Lehner made a similar multisensory shift in explaining that what sets apart a good cheesemaker is "*watching* how the milk is changing, and *feeling* how it affects the cheese."

21. Erin O'Connor writes, "Proficient glassblowers have often said that glassblowing is not about blowing the perfect piece of glass, but coming up with effective solutions to all the problems that consistently present themselves in the process of glassblowing. . . . They nudge towards the idea that *non-reflective anticipation* is the force of proficiency" (2007: 137).

22. Polanyi writes, "Although the expert . . . can indicate their clues and formulate their maxims, they know many more things than they can tell, knowing them only in practice, as instrumental particulars, and not explicitly, as objects. The knowledge of such particulars is therefore ineffable, and the pondering of a judgment in terms of such particulars is an ineffable process of thought" (1958: 88).

23. Grasseni (2004).

24. This recalls what James Scott describes as *metis:* "the ability and experience necessary to influence the outcome—to improve the odds—in a particular instance" (1998: 318).

25. Valenze (1991, 2011).

26. Loring (1866: 74–75).

27. What it means to be "handmade" is a historical and social question, not a technical one (Pye 1968: 11).

28. James Gibson writes, "The theory of affordances rescues us from the philosophical muddle of assuming fixed classes of objects, each defined by its common features and then given a name. . . . You do not have to classify and label things in order to perceive what they afford" (1986: 134).

29. Dormer (1997: 140).

30. Ingold (2000); Sutton (2006).

31. West and Domingos (2012: 131).

32. Bruce's artisanal use of automated machinery disrupts its "mechanical objectivity," to borrow a term from Lorraine Daston and Peter Galison, who define this as "the insistent drive to repress the willful intervention" of the knower in ascertaining the objective truth of objects of nature (2007: 121).

33. Juliette Rogers writes of the French context, "An artisanal cheesemaker is one who keeps close watch and control over the process of cheesemaking, and has the skills to 'read' the milk and developing cheese and respond to its changing needs. He molds, unmolds, salts and washes cheeses by hand in small batches, and output is relatively small. The particulars of this definition are in dialectic with the definition of industrial-scale cheesemaking, which is done by machines like conveyor belts, mechanical ladlers, and whey pumps, all orchestrated by computer. They produce large quantities of cheese that has barely come into contact with people, which lead critics to assert that quality suffers as a consequence. Cheesemakers whose productions hover in the middle are especially touchy about the terminology; one who installed a small but thoroughly automated system in the summer of 2005 dwelt upon the degree of personal control and physical oversight he had over every aspect of the process as he struggled to retain his claims to artisan status" (2008: 21).

34. This is the case in Europe as well. West and Domingos write of Portuguese makers of Serpa cheese who, while continuing to put sheep out to pasture, adapted—in advance of state enforcement of EU safety regulations—stainless steel work surfaces and refrigeration to ease cleaning and more easily achieve consistency "in their work environment and in their final product" (2012: 131–132).

35. Daston and Galison describe "epistemic virtue" as "norms that are internalized and enforced by appeal to ethical values, as well as to pragmatic efficacy in securing knowledge" (2007: 40–41).

36. Of those surveyed in 2009 (n = 146), 66 percent reported taking at least one workshop through a university program and/or with an independent instructor.

37. Dixon (2005: 199).

38. Ingold writes that skill "is a property not of the individual human body as a biophysical entity, a thing-in-itself, but of the total field of relations constituted by the presence of the organism-person, indissolubly body and mind, in a richly structured environment. That is why the study of skill, in my view, not only benefits from, but *demands* an ecological approach" (2000: 353).

39. For James Scott, "techne is characterized by impersonal, often quantitative precision and a concern with explanation and verification, whereas metis is concerned with personal skill, or 'touch,' and practical results" (1998: 320). This qualification parallels cheesemakers' distinction between the "science" and "art" that come together in crafting cheese. By insisting that artisanship encompasses a blend of science and art, or *techne* and *metis*—or, for that matter, what Ingold (2000: 315–316) distinguishes as technology and technique (Ingold's *technique* in particular closely resembles Scott's *metis*)—I am getting at the ability of the skilled artisan to make a particular style of cheese with a great deal of consistency when working with dynamic materials under fluctuating conditions.

40. This follows a Western epistemological convention going back to Aristotle's distinction in *Nichomachean Ethics* between *episteme* (a demonstrable, theoretical knowing about the natural world) and *techne* (a practical knowing-how that entails reasoning in making or doing something); *techne* is alternately translated as art, craft, or craftsmanship.

41. The lower the pH, the less rennet is needed per unit of milk.

42. Per 100 grams of cheese, Camembert contains 23.7 grams of fat and 75 mg of cholesterol while Cheddar contains 34.4 grams of fat and 100 mg of cholesterol (O'Brien and O'Connor 2004: 574).

43. Dixon (2005: 207).

44. "Objectivity and subjectivity are expressions of a particular historical predicament, not merely a rephrasing of some eternal complementarity between a mind and the world" (Daston and Galison 2007: 379).

45. Herzfeld (2004: 123).

46. Polanyi (1958: 31).

47. Maxims work to guide practice efficaciously only within a framework of what Polanyi calls "personal knowledge," a kind of passionately felt commitment to the task at hand.

48. Herzfeld (1997). To illustrate, Greeks share the knowledge that their coffee comes from the Ottomans but heaven help the foreign tourist who tries to order a "Turkish coffee" in a Greek café—it's *ena Ellenikó, Greek* coffee.

49. Heath and Meneley (2007). See also Polanyi (1958); Knorr (1979); Latour (1987); Schaffer (1989); Nutch (1996); Collins (2001a); Delamont and Atkinson (2001).

50. Latour (1987); Collins (2001a, 2001b, 2007). Not that actual cooking is a strict matter of following a recipe, either (see Short 2006; Sutton 2006).

51. James Scott writes: "It is doubtless reassuring to those who have both the intuition and access to formal measurement to know that their judgment can be checked. But the epistemic alternative to metis is far slower, more laborious, more capital intensive, and not always decisive. When rapid judgments of high (not perfect) accuracy are called for, when it is important to interpret early signs that things are going well or poorly, then there is no substitute for metis" (1998: 330).

52. Mauss (1973).

53. Mauss (1973); Bourdieu (1977).

54. Social theorists refer to this as an interface between social structure and individual agency.

55. Michael was stretching mozzarella for his father at Al Ducci's Italian Pantry in Manchester, Vt., when Joann Englert came into the store, visiting from Boston. So taken was Joann with Al Ducci's mozzarella that she persuaded Michael to go into business with her to produce it commercially for the Boston market.

56. Italian for "spun paste," *pasta filata* represents a technique of stretching curd used in the manufacture of many Italian cheeses.

57. See also Farrar and Trorey (2008: 45–46).

58. Glassblowing (O'Connor 2007), quilting (Staip 2006), and midwifery (M. MacDonald 2007) are all hands-on productive activities that engage synesthetic reason, but as an expensive hobby, blowing glass is shaped by different dynamics of class, gender, and power than the craft of the multitasking quilter pursuing a "serious leisure activity" in the midst of her gendered domestic responsibilities, or that of a lay midwife confronting the authority of biomedicine. Similarly, the varied sentiments, occupational backgrounds, and cultural as well as economic capital that cheesemakers bring to their craft shape a range of artisan sensibilities, including attitudes about mechanized tool use, technical intimacy with a pH meter, and calibrations of the sensory tool of taste.

59. Becker writes, "To speak of usefulness implies the existence of a person whose purposes define the ends for which the objects or activities will be useful. . . . Defining craft . . . [in this way] implies both an aesthetic, standards on which judgments of particular items of work can be based, and an organizational form in which the evaluative standards find their origin and logical justification" (1978: 864). For example, as Grasseni writes of cattle-breeders, "Good-looking cows become the objects of an intimate appreciation—of gut-feelings—even though these criteria eventually depend on the history of animal husbandry and on the economic imperatives of competitive productivity. . . . [And] standards change over time" (2004: 46).

60. See also Hennion (2007).

61. Terrio (1999); Creighton (2001); Grasseni (2003).

62. Dixon (2005: 198).

63. Barham (2003); Trubek (2008); Trubek and Bowen (2008); Bowen (2010).

64. This is similar to Pye's suggestion that quality of workmanship can be judged "by reference to the designer's intention" (1968: 13).

65. This root word is often interpreted in terms of the mold used to shape a wheel of cheese, also called a form.

66. Kindstedt (2005: 198).

CHAPTER 6. MICROBIOPOLITICS

Epigraphs: Tewksbury (2002: 27), Edgar (2010: 120).

1. Interview, January 24, 2011.

2. Dutton (2011: 77).

3. Kunzig (2001).

4. In fall 2010, raw-milk Gouda tainted with *E. coli* O157:H7 made by Bravo Farms in California and sold through Costco and Whole Foods stores sickened thirty-eight people in five states.

5. Sheehan is quoted in Bren (2004). See also "Raw Milk and You," at www.farm steadinc.com/raw-milk-and-you/, accessed December 12, 2011.

6. The Centers for Disease Control and Prevention dismisses claims that pasteurization reduces the nutrient value of milk and milk products, noting, for example, that while pasteurization diminishes levels of vitamin C, milk is not a significant source of vitamin C for humans. See "Raw Milk Questions and Answers" at www.cdc.gov/foodsafety/rawmilk/raw-milk-questions-and-answers.html, accessed December 13, 2011.

7. Foucault (1978).

8. Paxson (2008: 17).

9. At once revered as "nature's perfect food" for humans and reviled as the perfect nutrient broth for maleficent (as well as beneficent) bacteria, milk elicits strong feelings of love and fear. A number of books have recently been published on milk politics and materiality; see Atkins (2010); DuPuis (2002); Gumpert (2009); Mendelson (2008); Valenze (2011); Wiley (2011).

10. "ACS Statement on the Importance of Artisan, Farmstead, and Specialty Cheese," issued November 17, 2010. Available at www.cheesesociety.org/about-us/position-statements/, accessed May 17, 2012.

11. In November 2010, the ACS surveyed its cheesemaker members about audits and inspections. Results indicated that FDA testing concentrated on *Listeria*. Among those businesses that reported having been tested for pathogens, 59 percent were tested for *Listeria*, with 8 percent reporting a positive test result; no positive results were reported for any other pathogen. Survey results courtesy of the ACS.

12. In a radio interview, Mateo Kehler suggested that, with increased funding, the FDA has felt pressure to "show results" of heightened regulation, even setting "targets for criminal prosecution." In filling the ranks of FDA inspectors, criminal investigators rather than food scientists have been hired; these people know little about food, Kehler suggested, but they do know "how to put together a case." *Cutting the Curd,* episode 49, with Anne Saxelby on Heritage Radio Network, December 19, 2010. Available online at www.heritage radionetwork.com/episodes/1229-Cutting-the-Curd-Episode-49-Tia-Keenan-Daphne -Zepos-Matteo-Kehler, accessed January 11, 2011.

13. Sage (2007: 206).

14. Latour (1988).

15. Boisard (2003: 76–77).

16. Conn (1892: 260–261).

17. Conn (1892: 260).

18. Sage (2007: 211). While routine pasteurization of milk for drinking was a public-

health triumph, its effect on milk's "keeping quality" was what motivated the dairy industry to adopt it; in delaying souring, if not spoilage, pasteurization enabled regional milk sheds to consolidate and expand geographically, thus lowering the commercial cost of producing milk (DuPuis 2002: 81–82).

19. Writing of the 1950s push to pasteurize milk for Camembert, Boisard writes, "Raw milk is fragile, unstable, and difficult to work with industrially. By pasteurizing it, scientists believe, milk can be brought under control. Once rid of all of its microscopic hosts, it becomes controllable, obeying the instructions of scientific authorities rather than acting with a kind of unpredictable anarchy. Pasteurizing the milk intended for cheese therefore meant making it obedient to discipline" (2003: 162).

20. Sage (2007: 210).

21. Sage follows Latour's (1987) sociological formulation of a black box, a term that originated in cybernetics.

22. Sage (2007: 210, quoting Nestle 2003: 127).

23. U.S. Food and Drug Administration Web site, "Questions & Answers: Raw Milk." From March 1, 2007; the updated page as of March 26, 2010, toned down the language. www.fda.gov/Food/FoodSafety/Product-SpecificInformation/MilkSafety/ucm122062.htm, accessed June 16, 2010. The original wording comes from Sheehan (2007).

24. "Raw Milk Questions and Answers" on the CDC Web site, www.cdc.gov/foodsafety/rawmilk/raw-milk-questions-and-answers.html, accessed May 18, 2012. Raw milk can harbor *Salmonella, Staphylococcus aureus, Campylobacter,* and *Escherichia coli.*

25. Consumer-patients are often confronted with competing messages coming from the abstracted reason of authoritative knowledge and the concrete, anecdotal evidence of experiential knowledge; Abel and Browner (1998) have detailed similar conclusions with regard to women's reproductive decision-making.

26. O'Hagan (2010).

27. Wakin (2000: B1).

28. Baylis (2009: 295).

29. Nestle (2003: 16).

30. Neuman (2011: B1).

31. Mintz (2002: 27).

32. Also included in federal standards of definition for cheese are stipulations to prevent "filling" cheddar with lard or other dairy substitutes, as happened in the early years of the cheese factories.

33. National Research Council (2003: 226). For a review of food-borne illness outbreaks in North America and western Europe associated with cheese from 1971 to 1989, demonstrating that none were linked to aged raw-milk cheese, see D'Aoust (1989).

34. Sheehan, Childers, and Cianci (2004); Reitsma and Henning's paper concluded, "The current requirement for ripening of Cheddar cheese will not assure consumers of a safe product if the cheese is made from raw milk and a pathogen such as *E. coli* O157:H7 is present in the cheese at the beginning of ripening" (1996: 463).

35. Donnelly (2004: 548). In 2000, the ACS partnered with Oldways Preservation and Exchange and, later, Whole Foods to form the Cheese of Choice Coalition, dedicated to protecting Americans' right to make and eat raw-milk cheese.

36. In 2006, research scientists at the FDA's National Center for Food Safety and

Technology published a follow-up to the 1996 *E. coli* study that continued to question the efficacy of the 60-day aging period in eliminating unacceptable risk from O157:H7 (Schlesser et al. 2006). However, Baylis (2009: 300) notes that two of the strains inoculated by Schlesser et al. were particularly tolerant of acidic conditions (such as found in aged cheese), having been associated with infectious outbreaks in cider and fresh apple juice (which by U.S. law must also be pasteurized).

37. D'Amico, Druart, and Donnelly (2008).

38. From the FDA's "Bad Bug Book," www.fda.gov/food/foodsafety/foodborneillness/foodborneillnessfoodbornepathogensnaturaltoxins/badbugbook/ucm070064.htm, accessed January 3, 2010.

39. Donnelly (2005: 191); but see D'Amico, Druart, and Donnelly (2008) for evidence that raw-milk bloomy-rind cheese, such as Camembert, provides no better protection against *L. monocytogenes* than does pasteurized bloomy-rind cheese.

40. Nestle (2003: 36, 40); figures based on U.S. statistics for 1999.

41. The Washington State Department of Agriculture collected samples of cheese, brine, rennet, and environmental swabs on February 1 and 9 and March 1, 2010; each test returned positive results for *Listeria monocytogenes* (Elrand 2010). In response, Estrella Family Creamery initiated recalls on February 11 (Red Darla), February 17 (Brewleggio, Wynoochee River Blue, Domino), and on March 5 (Old Apple Tree Tomme): http://pnwcheese.typepad.com/cheese/2010/10/federal-court-filings-reveal-details-of-estrella-family-creamery-closure.html, accessed January 3, 2011.

42. Using pulsed field gel electrophoresis (PFGE), FDA laboratories ascertained that *L. mono* isolates collected on August 2 were "indistinguishable" from PFGE patterns associated with *L. mono* samples collected by the Washington state officials in February (Elrand 2010). On September 4, the FDA warned consumers that all lots of Estrella cheese "put consumers at risk for *Listeria monocytogenes*." Press release at www.fda.gov/News Events/Newsroom/PressAnnouncements/ucm224990.htm, accessed January 3, 2010.

43. See Department of Justice press release, "Feds Seize Product from Montesano Dairy Adulterated Due to the Presence of a Dangerous Pathogen," United States Attorney's Office, Western District of Washington, October 25, 2010, www.justice.gov/usao/waw/press/2010/oct/estrella.html, accessed January 10, 2011. While the FDA and the district attorney deemed all the Estrellas' cheese "adulterated" in that it "may have been contaminated . . . or rendered injurious" owing to the presence of minute and isolated—though persistent—traces of *Listeria monocytogenes,* jurisdiction over seizure (21 U.S.C. 334 (a)(1)) is granted when an article is "introduced into or while in interstate commerce or while held for sale (whether or not the first sale) after shipment in interstate commerce." In her seizure order, U.S. Attorney Jenny Durkan and Assistant Attorney David East cited the Estrellas' interstate purchase of rennet (from a Madison, Wisconsin, company) as a necessary condition in constituting the Estrellas' inventory as illegal and subject to seizure within the jurisdiction of the court. The 2011 Food Safety Modernization Act, giving the FDA new power to mandate recalls, was designed, in part, to obviate such legal acrobatics.

44. Acceptable amounts vary up to 100 or 1,000 cfu (colony-forming units) per gram of food at point of sale. See the report at http://ec.europa.eu/food/fs/sc/scv/out25_en.pdf, p. 19, accessed January 4, 2012.

45. Thorpe (2009: 50).

46. Ogden (2007: 11).

47. Question posted by "JGH" on October 13, 2005, www.babycenter.com, accessed February 1, 2007.

48. The Laughing Cow question continues to be posed; for example, posted on February 10, 2011: "Does anyone know if its safe to eat the laughing cow cheese while pregnant? I know its a soft cheese, which is a no no, but it says 'pasteurized' on it. Does that mean its safe to eat?" http://community.babycenter.com/post/a26351611/laughing_cow_cheese, accessed December 15, 2011.

49. Donnelly (2004).

50. www.cfsan.fda.gov/pregnant/whillist.html, accessed July 7, 2006. By 2012, the CDC had added to this wording the following clarification: "It is safe to eat hard cheeses, semi-soft cheeses such as mozzarella, pasteurized processed cheese slices and spreads, cream cheese, and cottage cheese." See "Listeriosis (Listeria) and Pregnancy," www.cdc.gov/ncbddd/pregnancy_gateway/infections-listeria.html, accessed May 30, 2012.

51. Meanwhile, dairy farmers have devised creative ways of selling raw milk in states where sales are prohibited or restricted. "Cow-shares" are legal contracts through which people who want to consume raw milk become owners of cows that a dairy farmer cares for and milks; the consumer pays the farmer for labor, not for the milk itself, since it (ostensibly) comes from a cow the consumer owns. "Milk clubs" can extend access to raw milk in states where it can be sold only direct from the farm; here, a club member takes responsibility for driving to the farm to pick up bottles of milk that are then delivered to urban club-members. I have also heard of raw goat's milk being sold at a farmers' market as "milk bath" (again, maintaining the fiction that the milk is not for human consumption).

52. D'Amico, Druart, and Donnelly (2008).

53. Latour (1988).

54. Shillinglaw (2003). The FDA sets limits for total bacteria count and somatic cell count for milk that will be pasteurized (whether for drinking or processing), but prepasteurized milk is not regulated for coliform (bacterial residue from fecal matter). While the FDA tests milk to check animal health (sick animals tend to shed somatic cells into their milk), it does not in this way regulate sanitary milking conditions. Pasteurized milk, such as we buy in supermarket cartons, may contain heat-treated or irradiated fecal bacteria. Owing to smaller-scale and differently configured ecologies of production, raw milk produced for farmstead cheesemaking routinely tests cleaner for coliform, somatic cells, and total bacteria than pasteurized milk purchased in a supermarket (D'Amico, Druart, and Donnelly 2008).

55. Dunn (2007).

56. Pritchard (2005: 148).

57. Sulik (2004: 50). Metal detection is used only in large industrial plants.

58. The fermentation step of developing lactic acid bacteria functions to eradicate pathogens; however, "the process of setting CLs [Control Limits] and monitoring is not as clear" as with pasteurization, which weakens fermentation's candidacy for CCP status (Schmidt and Newslow 2007: 2). See also Sulik (2004: 58).

59. Dunn (2007: 42–43).

60. Chapter 12 of Gianaclis Caldwell's *The Farmstead Creamery Advisor* (2010) is devoted to creating HACCP plans.

61. ACS, "Statement on Safe Cheesemaking," November 17, 2010, www.cheesesociety .org/wp-content/uploads/2011/02/ACS-Statement-on-Safe-Cheesemaking-for-Web.pdf, accessed May 17, 2012.

62. The survey had 130 ACS-member cheesemaker respondents.

63. On the implications for social relations of a modern preoccupation with managing risk, see Beck (1992).

64. "Certified Cheese Professional Exam," www.cheesesociety.org/events-education/ certification-2/, accessed January 4, 2012.

65. Cheesemakers' knowledge will translate into power only if regulators regard that practical knowledge as being efficacious.

66. See Paxson (2008) for a systematic if partial discussion of the microbiopolitics behind the making of Vermont Shepherd.

67. Senier (2008); Mnoonkin (2011).

68. In 1997, an outbreak of salmonellosis in Yakima County, Washington, began with a group of farmworkers making Mexican-style soft cheese with some of the raw milk from the dairy farm where they worked; they got sick from *Salmonella* but kept working, and the *Salmonella* circulated among the local dairy cattle. A huge outbreak of salmonellosis occurred in 1984 in Canada, reaching 2,700 cases. In that case, *Salmonella typhimurium* (a drug-resistant phage; "any drug you throw at it, they laugh," D'Amico said at the VIAC workshop) was eventually recovered from a shedding cow, cheese curd, and ill cheese factory workers. Employees had manually overridden pasteurization controls and transferred cheese curd to forming machines with their bare hands.

69. During a previous visit to his lab, D'Amico told me about a farm whose cheese suddenly tested positive for high levels of coliform. The source turned out to be contaminated well water. No one was sickened, but the organoleptic qualities of the cheese had suffered.

70. During the decade of the 1930s, bovine tuberculosis *(Mycobacterium bovis)* was accountable for 50,000 new tuberculosis infections and 2,500 deaths per year among humans in the United Kingdom (Sage 2007: 212). Dairy herds are tested regularly for *Mycobacterium bovis*.

71. The FDA's tolerance level for other species of *E. coli* varies from greater than 1×10^4 to 1×10^3 per gram (D'Amico, Druart, and Donnelly 2008). The European Union has some tolerance for *E. coli* O157:H7.

72. De Buyser et al. (2001).

73. In testing of Vermont farmstead cheese producers that D. J. D'Amico conducted in 2006 for VIAC, he found *Staphylococcus aureus* present in 17 of 62 (26.4 percent) of raw cow's-milk samples; 9 of 49 (18.4 percent) of raw goat's-milk samples, and 18 of 21 (85.7 percent) of raw sheep's-milk samples (including multiple samples from the same farms). Typically, the *S. aureus* in a contaminated sample amounted to less than 50 cells per milliliter, well under the legal limit of 10^4.

74. Sulik (2004: 11).

75. Sulik (2004: 51–52).

76. Rapp (1999: 70).

77. Cheesemakers with a background in the medical professions carry over a habituated hygiene into cheesemaking. When I asked Gail Holmes, former maker of Ascutney Mountain, whether she found anything from her nursing career useful in making cheese, she replied: "I did. I was aware of sterile fields and techniques from working in the operating room. So I was a bit obnoxious as far as the other partners [at Cobb Hill cooperative] were concerned, because I kept saying, 'Nope, you can't do that, you'll contaminate it.' And they would roll their eyes, saying, 'I'm clean as I have to be.' I thought, *Oh, my God! We're all making cheese in this room and it's right next to the road, and cars drive by, and dust gets kicked up into the air*. It *is* a farm, you know. You've got cows, sheep, chickens, all right there. I was thinking, *Well, this is a recipe for disaster*. But we survived."

78. Tomes (1998), especially chapter 6, "The Domestication of the Germ."

79. Kohler (2002: 6).

80. Kohler (2002: 7).

81. Elrand (2010). The original inspection report, filed by FDA inspector Scott W. Fox on September 10, 2010, elaborates, "the owner was observed on 9/1/10 removing a core of cheese from a wheel with a trier, placed a portion of cheese into her mouth, and replaced the cheese plug in the wheel, before loading it for transport to market. The trier was wiped with a rag after each use without apparent washing or sanitizing and no hand washing was observed before a repeat of this process."

82. Sanitizing is not synonymous with cleaning. Only clean surfaces may be properly sanitized. Dirt and visible soil (e.g., milk fat and protein residue) are removed by cleaning agents; microorganisms are eradicated through sanitizing. A sanitizer's "directions for use" is a legal document; it is unlawful to use sanitizer in any method other than what is specified on the label. Routine use of diluted sanitizing agents can encourage the flourishing of resistant strains; use of overly strong sanitizer can result in the chemical contamination of food.

83. Undergirding much of what I have described in terms of post-pastoral and post-Pasteurian thinking, Beck writes, "At the end of the twentieth century, nature is *neither* given *nor* ascribed, but has instead become a historical product, the *interior* furnishings of the civilizational world, destroyed or endangered in the natural conditions of its reproduction. But that means that the destruction of nature, integrated into the universal circulation of industrial production, ceases to be 'mere' destruction of nature and becomes an integral component of the social, political and economic dynamic. The unseen side effect of the societalization *[Vergesellschaftung]* of nature is the *societalization of the destruction and threats to nature*, their transformation into economic, social and political contradictions and conflicts. Violations of the natural conditions of life turn into global social, economic and medical threats to people—with completely new sorts of challenges to the social and political institutions of highly industrialized global society" (1992: 80).

84. See Paxson (2008) for a discussion of Marcellino's cheese microbiology research.

85. Harry West writes, "For many, protection of diverse micro-cultures in raw-milk cheeses is bound up with the protection of diverse macro-cultures in the form of human communities and component livelihoods" (2008: 28).

86. In *Alien Ocean* (2009), Stefan Helmreich explores how new relations among

256 NOTES TO CHAPTER 7

humans and other living things are entangled "symbiopolitically"; microbes, including halophiles (such as *Halomonas*) found in hydrothermal deep-sea vent sites, become entities through which governance—environmental as well as economic—is threaded.

87. Enserink (2002: 90).

CHAPTER 7. PLACE, TASTE, AND THE PROMISE OF *TERROIR*

Epigraph: Kessler (2009: 157).

1. Held March 19–22, 2009, in Petaluma, California.

2. Guy (2003: 42).

3. Bérard and Marchenay (2000, 2006); Guy (2003: 42); Trubek (2008); Demossier (2011).

4. Johnson (1998: 4).

5. Trubek (2008: 18).

6. Trubek (2008: 18). See "A Traditional Craft over a Thousand Years Old" on the Web site of the Comté Cheese Association, www.lesroutesducomte.com/routes-du-comte -1st-aop-cheese-tour-on-gastronomy-in-jura-s-mountains-a-heritage-shared-by-every body,6,0,0,2,2.html, accessed January 5, 2012.

7. The selection of Peoria, Illinois, as a stand-in for placeless or mainstream America may have been inspired by the catchphrase, "Will it play in Peoria?" In the 1960s and 1970s Peoria was a favorite test market for the audience reception of new films and concert performances.

8. Four facets of production are considered in evaluating cheese *terroir*: physical environment (climate, soils, water, bedrock), animal fodder (grazing conditions, grain rations), breed of animal milked, and customary cultural "know-how" in dairy farming and cheesemaking. See Bérard et al. (2008); Boisard (2003); Rogers (2008); on Italian DOC cheese, Grasseni (2003, 2012); on Portuguese DOC cheese, West and Domingos (2012); on Greek PDO cheese, Petridou (2012).

9. See Ott (1981) for a full description and analysis.

10. See Major (2005).

11. Not only were guild members as entrepreneurially minded as the Majors, the price they received without the boost of government subsidy was insufficient compensation for the artisan labor they added to milk.

12. Point Reyes Farmstead Cheese Company homepage, www.pointreyescheese.com/, accessed June 8, 2011.

13. In posing this question of pasture-raised pork in North Carolina, Brad Weiss (2011) calls attention to African American farmers who have sustained households for generations by raising pigs, but whose economic marginalization may be exacerbated by fresh excitement over so-called "local" and "sustainable" farming, practiced often though not exclusively by rural newcomers sharing similar sentiments and economic security with many farmstead cheesemakers.

14. Barham (2003); Trubek (2008); Trubek and Bowen (2008).

15. Bérard and Marchenay (2000); Rogers (2008); Teil (2010); Demossier (2011).

16. The "*terroir* question" was first brought to my attention at the 2005 meeting of the

ACS in Louisville, Ky., at a session titled "Nurturing Terroir: Encouraging Local Influences to Create Unique Cheeses" (see Paxson 2010).

17. See also Trubek (2008).

18. Methane, a greenhouse gas, is released as cow manure decomposes. The methane digester converts the liquid components of cow manure to methane gas, which fuels the combustion engine of a generator that produces electricity and hot water for the dairy; solid wastes are turned into organic fertilizer for the pastures. The manure lagoons of livestock farms contribute 7 percent of the nation's anthropogenic methane emissions (2001 U.S. Greenhouse Gas Inventory Report of the Environmental Protection Agency, http://epa.gov/climatechange/emissions/downloads11/US-GHG-Inventory-2011-Chapter-6-Agriculture.pdf, accessed January 5, 2011).

19. Terrio (1996: 71).

20. Terrio (1996: 74).

21. Consumer survey research by Ann Colonna (2011) is suggestive. In a blind tasting (n = 901), 56 percent of tasters expressed a preference for the pasteurized versions of particular cheeses when compared to raw-milk counterparts (with 44 percent preferring the raw-milk versions), whereas when the cheeses were labeled as either "raw" or "pasteurized," only 41 percent expressed preference for the pasteurized cheeses, with 59 percent now "preferring" the raw-milk versions. This suggests that consumers tend to prefer the *idea* of raw-milk cheese over the actual taste, odor, and texture of it.

22. Jeffrey Roberts, "Blind Cheese Tasting: Raw vs. Pasteurized," workshop held at Rendezvous restaurant in Cambridge, Massachusetts, August 16, 2007.

23. For a related discussion of the California wine industry, see Trubek (2008), chapter 3.

24. Trubek (2008: 113).

25. Quoted in Cox (2000).

26. Delmas and Grant (forthcoming).

27. Delmas and Grant (forthcoming).

28. Delmas and Grant (forthcoming).

29. See also Warner (2007).

30. Lynn Margulis, quoted in White (1994: 76).

31. Allen and Kovach (2000); Guthman (2004).

32. Ulin (1996: 39).

33. For example, at the 2005 ACS panel on "Nurturing Terroir: Encouraging Local Influences to Create Unique Cheeses," Louisville, Ky.; see Paxson (2010).

34. See Mol (2009) on the possibility of cultivating the "good" taste of a consumer-citizen.

35. See also Cazaux (2011).

36. Hintz and Percy (2008: ix).

37. Trubek (2008: 212–222).

38. Davey (2006).

39. Nohl (2005).

40. Nohl (2005: 65).

41. The resulting topography is said to be "marked by abrupt hills and meandering

waterways, steep-sided ridges, caves, subsurface caverns and towering bluffs," elements that "combine to provide an area of many diverse microclimates" (Cazaux 2011: 36).

42. Tenenbaum (2011).

43. Tenenbaum (2011).

44. Cazaux (2011).

45. Feurer et al. (2004: 555).

46. Noella Marcellino (2003) has studied the diversity of strains of *Geotrichum candidum,* a fungus that colonizes cheese rinds and contributes to a cheese's flavor development. Marcellino sampled cheesemaking facilities in seven regions in France and tested the following hypothesis: that the diversity of strains of *G. candidum* found on a particular cheese is predominantly either a function of geographic region or of the class of cheese sampled. DNA sequencing revealed no geographic clustering patterns, leading Marcellino to conclude, "similar or identical strains are ubiquitous throughout France and probably the world" (Marcellino et al. 2001: 4756; see Paxson 2008 for discussion).

47. McKnight (2006: 5).

48. Warner (2007).

49. Weiss (2011).

50. *Hands on the Land* is the title of Albers's (2000) history of the Vermont landscape. Numerous geographers and historians cover this terrain, e.g., Anderson (2004); Cronon (1983); Mitchell (1996); and Williams (1973).

51. On California's Central Valley, see Nash (2006).

52. Marks (2002).

53. Feurer et al. (2004). It is more likely that the environmental conditions of smear-ripening cheese are conducive to the growth of these bacteria than that "Irish" microbes were somehow transported to France, where they landed on cheese.

54. Feurer et al. (2004).

55. On the promissory projects of microbial bioprospecting, which draws on similar cultural reasoning, see Hayden (2003) and Helmreich (2009).

56. Galison (1997: 783).

57. Barham (2003: 131).

58. Ingold (2000: 195).

59. Demossier (2000: 146); but see Laudan (2004) for a critique.

60. Kehler (2005).

61. Interview with Sasha Davies, http://cheesebyhand.com/?attachment_id=25, accessed July 23, 2011.

62. Marcel (2008).

63. See also Trubek (2008).

64. Farm Summit Meeting, held at the Brattleboro Museum and Art Center, June 3, 2004, in conjunction with the annual "Strolling of the Heifers" parade. That year's theme, "The True Value of Vermont Dairy Farms: 'It's More Than the Milk!'" addressed the economic impact of dairy farms on the community and state at large.

65. *Imagining Vermont: Values and Vision for the Future,* final report of the Council on the Future of Vermont, Vermont Council on Rural Development, 2009. Available online: http://vtrural.org/sites/default/files/library/files/futureofvermont/documents/Imagining _Vermont_FULL_Report1.pdf, accessed August 3, 2011.

66. Vermont Agency of Agriculture, www.vermontdairy.com/learn/number-of-farms/, accessed May 31, 2011.

67. Before Vermont was a dairy state, it was a woolly state. Sheep flourished where wheat did not on the region's thin-soiled, rocky hilltops. After the wool market crashed in the mid-nineteenth century, when new railroads flooded markets with cheap wool from the West, Vermont's hilltop farms were abandoned to tree regrowth and property values plummeted (Albers 2000: 203).

68. Susanna McCandless estimates as many as two-thirds of Vermont's dairy farms employ Mexican immigrants (Radel, Schmook, and McCandless 2010: 189–191); see also Freidberg (2009: 234).

69. Cellars at Jasper Hill homepage, www.cellarsatjasperhill.com/, accessed February 10, 2010.

70. Rathke (2008).

71. Trubek (2008: 61).

72. See Miller (2010: chapter 12) for an account from the perspective of Consider Bardwell Farm.

73. Barham (2007: 279).

74. Interview with Frank Bryan: Real Vermonters and Real Democracy. *Window of Vermont* (Winter–Spring 1984–1985): 2.

75. Between the farm, the Cellars, and the house that Andy built on an adjacent hill, the Kehlers paid $60,000 in property taxes in 2010.

76. At the Farm Summit, "tax structures" came fourth on Robert Wellington's list of the "true values" of Vermont dairy farms. Working farms keep everyone's taxes low, he declared: "I've never seen a cow call 911. And stalks of corn don't go to school."

77. A few of Jasper Hill's sales and marketing people have moved to the Greensboro area from Boston and New York City in order to take up jobs there; the head cheesemaker and farm employees are local to the area.

78. Hewitt (2010).

79. At the time, Cabot paid the Cellars an eight-dollar aging fee per month per wheel; when the Cellars sold a cheese, they returned the accumulated aging fee to Cabot and also paid for the green wheel. Jasper Hill kept the economic return on the value added through *affinage* and marketing. The arrangement was designed to give Cabot added cachet and Jasper Hill a line of credit from Cabot tied to volume; the deal enabled the Kehlers to secure a bank loan to build the Cellars in the first place. In spring 2011 the Kehlers were anticipating that Cabot might (reasonably) seek a higher return for the green wheels; indeed, that year Cabot stopped giving advances on inventory.

80. Escobar (1999: 4).

81. Gray (2008: 112).

82. Topham (2000).

83. Graeber (2001: 45).

84. Gray (1999); Hirsch (1995).

85. As with communication in Daniel Miller's (2008: 1131) analysis of "the uses of value," *terroir* "adds value when it is used as a bridge between forms of value that are otherwise difficult to reconcile."

CHAPTER 8. BELLWETHER

1. Kessler (2009: 127).

2. Kessler (2009: 238).

3. Roberts (2007: xix).

4. Heldke (1992).

5. According to my 2009 survey, 45 percent of self-described farmstead cheesemakers produce fewer than 6,000 pounds of cheese a year, and another 27 percent make 6,000 to 12,000 pounds of cheese a year.

6. On August 20, 2010, it was announced that Keehn had sold Cypress Grove to Emmi, a Swiss dairy company. See http://arcataeye.com/2010/08/cypress-grove-chevre -aquired-by-swiss-company—august-20–2010/, accessed August 26, 2010.

7. Lyson (2004: 85).

8. DeLind (2006). In Doreen Massey's words, "This is a notion of place where specificity (local uniqueness, a sense of place) derives not from some mythical roots nor from a history of relative isolation—now to be disrupted by globalization—but precisely from the absolute particularity of the mixture of influences found together there" (1999: 22).

9. See DeLind (2002).

10. In a study of an organic produce delivery scheme in England, Clarke et al. found, "When people talk about the ethics of consumption they predominantly refer to . . . 'ordinary' ethics—caring for the family, caring about value and taste, linking health to everyday choices, cross-cutting concerns between the values of the workplace and the values of the home, and so on—rather than about strongly held ideological or spiritual blueprints for action" (2008: 223–224).

BIBLIOGRAPHY

Abel, Emily K., and Carole H. Browner. 1998. Selective Compliance with Biomedical Authority and the Uses of Experiential Knowledge. Pp. 310–326 in *Pragmatic Women and Body Politics,* edited by Margaret Lock and Patricia A. Kaufert. Cambridge: Cambridge University Press.

Albers, Jan. 2000. *Hands on the Land: A History of the Vermont Landscape.* Cambridge, Mass.: MIT Press.

Alexandre, Sandy. 2012. *The Properties of Violence: Claims to Ownership in Representations of Lynching.* Jackson: University Press of Mississippi.

Alfondy, Sandra, ed. 2007. *NeoCraft: Modernity and the Crafts.* Halifax: Nova Scotia College of Art and Design Press.

Allen, Patricia, Margaret FitzSimmons, Michael Goodman, and Keith Warner. 2003. Shifting Plates in the Agrifood Landscape: The Tectonics of Alternative Agrifood Initiatives in California. *Journal of Rural Studies* 19 (1): 61–75.

Allen, Patricia, and Martin Kovach. 2000. The Capitalist Composition of Organic: The Potential of Markets in Fulfilling the Promise of Organic Agriculture. *Agriculture and Human Values* 17: 221–232.

Allison, Anne. 1991. Japanese Mothers and *Obentos:* The Lunch Box as Ideological State Apparatus. *Anthropological Quarterly* 64 (4): 195–208.

Amin, Ash, and Nigel Thrift. 2004. *Blackwell Cultural Economy Reader.* Oxford: Blackwell Publishing.

Anderson, Virginia DeJohn. 2004. *Creatures of Empire: How Domestic Animals Transformed Early America.* Oxford: Oxford University Press.

Appadurai, Arjun. 1981. Gastro-Politics in Hindu South Asia. *American Ethnologist* 8 (3): 494–511.

———. 1986. Introduction: Commodities and the Politics of Value. Pp. 3–63 in *The Social*

Life of Things: Commodities in Cultural Perspective, edited by Arjun Appadurai. Cambridge: Cambridge University Press.

Apps, Jerry. 1998. *Cheese: The Making of a Wisconsin Tradition.* Amherst, Wisc.: Amherst Press.

Arnold, Lauren Briggs. 1876. *American Dairying: A Manual for Butter and Cheese Makers.* Rochester, N.Y.: Rural Home Publishing.

Atkins, Peter J. 2007. Laboratories, Laws, and the Career of a Commodity. *Environment and Planning D: Society and Space* 25: 967–989.

———. 2010. *Liquid Materialities: A History of Milk, Science and the Law.* Farnham, U.K.: Ashgate.

Barham, Elizabeth. 2003. Translating Terroir: The Global Challenge of French AOC Labeling. *Journal of Rural Studies* 19 (1): 127–138.

———. 2007. The Lamb That Roared: Origin-Labeled Products and Place-Making Strategy in Charlevoix, Quebec. Pp. 277–297 in *Remaking the North American Food System: Strategies for Sustainability,* edited by C. Clare Hinrichs and Thomas Lyson. Lincoln: Nebraska University Press.

Barlett, Peggy F. 1993. *American Dreams, Rural Realities: Family Farms in Crisis.* Chapel Hill: University of North Carolina Press.

Barndt, Deborah. 2002. *Tangled Routes: Women, Work, and Globalization on the Tomato Trail.* New York: Rowman and Littlefield.

Barron, Hal S. 1984. *Those Who Stayed Behind: Rural Society in Nineteenth-Century New England.* Cambridge: Cambridge University Press.

Baylis, Christopher L. 2009. Raw Milk and Raw Milk Cheeses as Vehicles for Infection by Verocytotoxin-Producing *Escherichia coli. International Journal of Dairy Technology* 62 (3): 293–307.

Beck, Ulrich. 1992. *Risk Society: Towards a New Modernity.* Translated by Mark Ritter. London: Sage Publications.

Becker, Howard S. 1978. Arts and Crafts. *American Journal of Sociology* 83 (4): 862–889.

———. 1982. *Art Worlds.* Berkeley: University of California Press.

Begon, Michael, Colin R. Townsend, and John L. Harper. 2006. *Ecology: From Individuals to Ecosystems.* 4th edition. Oxford: Blackwell Publishing.

Belasco, Warren J. 1989. *Appetite for Change: How the Counterculture Took on the Food Industry 1966–1988.* New York: Pantheon.

Bell, David, and Gill Valentine. 1997. *Consuming Geographies: We Are Where We Eat.* London: Routledge.

Benson, Michaela, and Karen O'Reilly. 2009. *Lifestyle Migration: Expectations, Aspirations and Experiences.* Farnham, U.K.: Ashgate.

Bérard, Laurence, François Casabianca, Rémi Bouche, Marie-Christine Montel, Philippe Marchenay, and Claire Agabriel. 2008. Salers PDO Cheese: The Diversity and Paradox of Local Knowledge. Pp. 289–297 in 8th European IFSA Symposium, *Empowerment of the Rural Actors: A Renewal of Farming System Perspectives,* 6–10 July, Clermont-Ferrand, France. Available online: www.ethno-terroirs.cnrs.fr/IMG/pdf/Salers_IFSA_2008.pdf. Accessed May 10, 2012.

Bérard, Laurence, and Philippe Marchenay. 2000. A Market Culture: *Produits de terroir* or the Selling of Heritage. Pp. 154–167 in *Recollections of France: Memories, Identities and Heritage in Contemporary France,* edited by Sarah Blowen, Marion Demossier, and Jeanine Picard. Oxford: Berghahn Books.

———. 2006. Local Products and Geographical Indications: Taking Account of Local Knowledge and Biodiversity. *International Social Science Journal* 187: 109–116.

Bestor, Theodore. 2004. *Tsukiji: The Fish Market at the Center of the World.* Berkeley: University of California Press.

Biersack, Aletta. 2006. Reimagining Political Ecology: Culture/Power/History/Nature. Pp. 3–40 in *Reimagining Political Ecology,* edited by Aletta Biersack and James B. Greenberg. Durham, N.C.: Duke University Press.

Bilski, Tory. 1986. Profile of Marian Pollack and Marjorie Susman in *Vermont Woman,* April.

Blundel, Richard, and Angela Tregear. 2006. From Artisans to "Factories": The Interpenetration of Craft and Industry in English Cheese-Making, 1650–1950. *Enterprise and Society* 7 (4): 705–739.

Boisard, Pierre. 1991. The Future of a Tradition: Two Ways of Making Camembert, the Foremost Cheese of France. *Food and Foodways* 4 (3 and 4): 173–207.

———. 2003. *Camembert: A National Myth.* Translated by Richard Miller. Berkeley: University of California Press.

Boltanski, Luc, and Laurent Thévenot. 1991. *On Justification: Economies of Worth.* Translated by Catherine Porter. Princeton, N.J.: Princeton University Press, 2006.

Boulding, Kenneth. 1966. The Economics of the Coming Spaceship Earth. Pp. 3–14 in *Environmental Quality in a Growing Economy, Essays from the Sixth RFF Forum,* edited by Henry Jarrett. Baltimore, Md.: Johns Hopkins Press, for Resources for the Future.

Bourdieu, Pierre. 1977. *Outline of a Theory of Practice.* Translated by Richard Nice. Cambridge: Cambridge University Press.

———. 1984. *Distinction: A Social Critique of the Judgment of Taste.* Translated by Richard Nice. New York: Routledge.

Bowen, Sarah. 2010. Embedding Local Places in Global Spaces: Geographical Indications as a Territorial Development Strategy. *Rural Sociology* 75 (2): 209–243.

Braverman, Harry. 1974. *Labor and Monopoly Capital: The Degradation of Work in the Twentieth Century.* New York: Monthly Review Press.

Bren, Linda. 2004. Got Milk? Make Sure It's Pasteurized. *FDA Consumer* 38 (5, September–October). Electronic document, www.fda.gov/fdac/features/2004/504_milk.html. Accessed January 4, 2012.

Brooks, David. 2001. *Bobos in Paradise: The New Upper Class and How They Got There.* New York: Simon and Schuster.

Browne, C. A. 1944. Elder John Leland and the Mammoth Cheshire Cheese. *Agricultural History* 18 (4): 145–153.

Burros, Marian. 2004. Say Cheese, and New England Smiles. *New York Times,* June 23, Dining section, F1.

Busch, Lawrence. 2000. The Moral Economy of Grades and Standards. *Journal of Rural Studies* 16 (3): 273–283.

Bushman, Richard L. 1998. Markets and Composite Farms in Early America. *The William and Mary Quarterly* 55 (3): 351–374.

Bushnell, Mark. 2002. The Cheese Has an Ally: UVM Researcher Fights Possible Ban on Unpasteurized Cheese by FDA. *Rutland [Vt.] Herald* Sunday Magazine, February 23.

Cahn, Miles. 2003. *The Perils and Pleasures of Domesticating Goat Cheese: Portrait of a Hudson Valley Dairy Goat Farm.* New York: Catskill Press.

Caldwell, Gianaclis. 2010. *The Farmstead Creamery Advisor: The Complete Guide to Building and Running a Small, Farm-Based Cheese Business.* White River Junction, Vt.: Chelsea Green.

Callon, Michel. 1986. Some Elements of a Sociology of Translation: Domestication of the Scallops and the Fishermen of St. Brieuc Bay. Pp. 196–223 in *Power, Action, and Belief: A New Sociology of Knowledge?* edited by John Law. London: Routledge.

Callon, Michel, Cécile Méadel, and Vololona Rabeharisoa. 2002. The Economy of Qualities. *Economy and Society* 31 (2): 194–217.

Callon, Michel, and John Law. 2005. On Qualculation, Agency, and Otherness. *Environment and Planning D: Society and Space* 23: 717–733.

Campbell, John. 1964. *Honour, Family, and Patronage: A Study of Institutions and Moral Values in a Greek Mountain Community.* Oxford: Oxford University Press.

Candea, Matei. 2010. "I Fell in Love with Carlos the Meerkat": Engagement and Detachment in Human-Animal Relations. *American Ethnologist* 37 (2): 241–258.

Carman, Ezra A., H. A. Heath, and John Minto. 1892. *Special Report on the History and Present Condition of the Sheep Industry of the United States, for the U.S. Department of Agriculture, Bureau of Animal Husbandry.* Washington, D.C.: Government Printing Office.

Carney, Judith A. 2001. *Black Rice: The African Origins of Rice Cultivation in the Americas.* Cambridge, Mass.: Harvard University Press.

Carrier, James G. 1995. *Gifts and Commodities: Exchange and Western Capitalism since 1700.* London: Routledge.

Carroll, Ricki. 1999. The American Cheese Society: A History. *Newsletter of the American Cheese Society* 1 (October): 12–13.

Cavanaugh, Jillian. 2007. Making Salami, Producing Bergamo: The Production and Transformation of Value in a Northern Italian Town. *Ethnos* 72 (2): 114–139.

Cazaux, Gersende. 2011. *Application of the Concept of Terroir in the American Context: Taste of Place and Wisconsin Unpasteurized Milk Cheeses.* Dairy Business Innovation Center, Madison, Wisconsin. Available online: www.dbicusa.org/documents/Gigis-thesis-non-confidential.pdf. Accessed November 10, 2011.

Chiappe, Marta B., and Cornelia Butler Flora. 1998. Gendered Elements of the Alternative Agriculture Paradigm. *Rural Sociology* 63 (3): 372–393.

Clark, Nigel. 2007. Animal Interface: The Generosity of Domestication. Pp. 49–70 in *Where the Wild Things Are Now: Domestication Reconsidered,* edited by Rebecca Cassidy and Molly Mullin. Oxford: Berg.

Clarke, Nick, Paul Cloke, Clive Barnett, and Alice Malpass. 2008. The Spaces and Ethics of Organic Food. *Journal of Rural Studies* 24 (3): 219–230.

Cochoy, Franck. 2008. Calculation, Qualculation, Calqulation: Shopping Cart Arithmetic, Equipped Cognition and the Clustered Consumer. *Marketing Theory* 8 (1): 15–44.

Collier, Jane. 1997. *From Duty to Desire: Remaking Families in a Spanish Village*. Princeton, N.J.: Princeton University Press.

Collins, Harry M. 2001a. Tacit Knowledge, Trust and the Q of Sapphire. *Social Studies of Science* 31 (1): 71–85.

———. 2001b. What Is Tacit Knowledge? Pp. 107–119 in *The Practice Turn in Contemporary Theory*, edited by Theodore R. Schatzki. New York: Routledge.

———. 2007. Bicycling on the Moon: Collective Tacit Knowledge and Somatic-Limit Tacit Knowledge. *Organizational Studies* 28 (2): 257–262.

Colonna, Ann. 2011. Consumer Preference for and Attitudes about Pasteurized vs. Raw Milk Cheese. Presented at the session "Raw Milk Cheese Trends around the World" at the annual meeting of the American Cheese Society, Montreal, Canada, August 5.

Conn, Herbert W. 1892. Some Uses of Bacteria. *Science* 16 (483): 258–263.

Coombe, Rosemary. 1998. *The Cultural Life of Intellectual Properties: Authorship, Appropriation, and the Law*. Durham, N.C.: Duke University Press.

Counihan, Carole. 1999. *The Anthropology of Food and Body: Gender, Meaning, and Power*. New York: Routledge.

Cox, Jeff. 2000. Organic Winegrowing Goes Mainstream. Wine News, August–September. www.thewinenews.com/augsepoo/cover.html. Accessed May 10, 2012.

Crawford, Matthew B. 2009. *Shop Class as Soulcraft: An Inquiry into the Value of Work*. New York: Penguin.

Creighton, Millie. 2001. Spinning Silk, Weaving Selves: Nostalgia, Gender, and Identity in Japanese Craft Vacations. *Japanese Studies* 21 (1): 5–29.

Cronon, William. 1983. *Changes in the Land: Indians, Colonists, and the Ecology of New England*. New York: Hill and Wang.

———. 1991. *Nature's Metropolis: Chicago and the Great West*. New York: W. W. Norton.

Cross, John A. 2004. The Expansion of Amish Dairy Farming in Wisconsin. *Journal of Cultural Geography* 21: 77–104.

Csikszentmihalyi, Mihaly. 1975. *Beyond Boredom and Anxiety: Experiencing Flow in Work and Play*. San Francisco: Jossey-Bass.

Curtis, T. H. 1885. Cheese Factories and Cheese-Makers as I Found Them in Wisconsin. Address at the Thirteenth Annual Convention of the Wisconsin Dairymen's Association. Pp. 41–65 in the *Thirteenth Annual Report of the Wisconsin Dairymen's Association*. Madison, Wisc.: Democrat Printing Co.

Cutts, Mary Pepperrell Sparhawk. 1869. *The Life and Times of Hon. William Jarvis, of Weathersfield, Vermont, by His daughter, Mary Pepperrell Sparhawk Cutts*. New York: Hurd and Houghton.

D'Amico, Dennis J., Marc J. Druart, and Catherine W. Donnelly. 2008. 60-Day Aging Requirement Does Not Ensure Safety of Surface-Mold-Ripened Soft Cheeses Manufactured from Raw or Pasteurized Milk when *Listeria monocytogenes* Is Introduced as a Postprocessing Contaminant. *Journal of Food Protection* 71 (8): 1563–1571.

D'Aoust, J. Y. 1989. Manufacture of Dairy Products from Unpasteurised Milk: A Safety Assessment. *Journal of Food Protection* 52: 906–914.

Daston, Lorraine, and Peter Galison. 2007. *Objectivity*. New York: Zone Books.

Davey, Monica. 2006. Wisconsin's Crown of Cheese Is within California's Reach. *New York Times*, September 30, A1.

Davies, Sasha. 2010. *The Guide to West Coast Cheese: More Than 300 Cheeses Handcrafted in California, Oregon, and Washington.* Portland, Ore.: Timber Press.

De Buyser, M.-L., B. Dufour, M. Maire, and V. Lafarge. 2001. Implication of Milk and Milk Products in Food-Borne Diseases in France and in Different Industrialized Countries. *International Journal of Food Microbiology* 67: 1–17.

Decker, John Wright. 1909. *Cheese Making: Cheddar, Swiss, Brick, Limburger, Edam, Cottage.* Columbus, Ohio: by the author.

Delamont, Sara, and Paul Atkinson. 2001. Doctoring Uncertainty: Mastering Craft Knowledge. *Social Studies of Science* 31 (1): 87–107.

Delaney, Carol, and Dennis Kauppila. n.d. Start-up and Operating Costs of Small Farmstead Cheese Operations for Dairy Sheep. Pp. 127–140 of report funded by the Vermont Sustainable Jobs Fund and the UVM Center for Sustainable Agriculture, Small Ruminant Dairy Project. Available online: www.ansci.wisc.edu/Extension-New%20 copy/sheep/Publications_and_Proceedings/Pdf/Dairy/Management/Startup%20and %20operating%20costs%20of%20small%20farmstead%20cheese%20operations%20for %20dairy%20sheep.pdf. Accessed February 18, 2010.

DeLind, Laura B. 2002. Place, Work, and Civic Agriculture: Common Fields for Cultivation. *Agriculture and Human Values* 19: 217–224.

———. 2006. Of Bodies, Place, and Culture: Re-Situating Local Food. *Journal of Agricultural and Environmental Ethics* 19 (2): 121–146.

DeLind, Laura B., and Jim Bingen. 2008. Place and Civic Agriculture: Re-thinking the Context for Local Agriculture. *Journal of Agricultural and Environmental Ethics* 21 (2): 127–151.

Delmas, Magali A., and Laura E. Grant. Forthcoming. Eco-Labeling Strategies and Price-Premium: The Wine Industry Puzzle. *Business and Society.* Available online: http:// bas.sagepub.com/content/early/2010/03/04/0007650310362254.abstract. Accessed July 7, 2011.

Demossier, Marion. 2000. Culinary Heritage and *Produits de Terroir* in France: Food for Thought. Pp. 141–153 in *Recollections of France: Memories, Identities and Heritage in Contemporary France,* edited by Sarah Blowen, Marion Demossier, and Jeanine Picard. Oxford: Berghahn Books.

———. 2011. Beyond *Terroir*: Territorial Construction, Hegemonic Discourses, and French Wine Culture. *Journal of the Royal Anthropological Institute* 17: 685–705.

Despret, Vinciane. 2005. Sheep Do Have Opinions. Pp. 360–368 in *Making Things Public,* edited by Bruno Latour and Peter Weibel. Cambridge, Mass.: ZKM Center for the Arts/MIT Press.

DeVault, Marjorie. 1991. *Feeding the Family: The Social Organization of Caring as Gendered Work.* Chicago: University of Chicago Press.

Dixon, Peter. 2005. The Art of Cheesemaking. Pp. 197–225 in *American Farmstead Cheese: The Complete Guide to Making and Selling Artisan Cheeses,* edited by Paul Kindstedt. White River Junction, Vt.: Chelsea Green.

———. n.d. The Business of Farmstead Cheese, Yogurt and Bottled Milk Products: Considerations for Starting a Milk Processing Business. Unpublished MS.

Doane, Phyllis. 1961. The Beginning and Growth of Kraft Foods. *Journal of the American Oil Chemists' Society* 38 (8): 4–5.

Donnelly, Catherine W. 2004. Growth and Survival of Microbial Pathogens in Cheese. Pp. 541–559 in *Cheese: Chemistry, Physics and Microbiology,* 3rd ed., vol. 1: *General Aspects,* edited by Patrick F. Fox, Paul McSweeney, Timothy Cogan, and Timothy Guinee. London: Elsevier.

———. 2005. The Pasteurization Dilemma. Pp. 173–195 in *American Farmstead Cheese: The Complete Guide to Making and Selling Artisan Cheeses,* edited by Paul Kindstedt. White River Junction, Vt.: Chelsea Green.

Dormer, Peter, ed. 1997. *The Culture of Craft.* Manchester, U.K.: Manchester University Press.

Dudley, Kathryn Marie. 1996. The Problem of Community in Rural America. *Culture & Agriculture* 18 (2): 47–57.

———. 2000. *Debt and Dispossession: Farm Loss in America's Heartland.* Chicago: University of Chicago Press.

Dunn, Elizabeth. 2007. *Escherichia coli,* Corporate Discipline and the Failure of the Sewer State. *Space and Polity* 11 (1): 35–53.

DuPuis, E. Melanie. 2002. *Nature's Perfect Food: How Milk Became America's Drink.* New York: New York University Press.

DuPuis, E. Melanie, and David Goodman. 2005. Should We Go "Home" to Eat? Toward a Reflexive Politics of Localism. *Journal of Rural Studies* 21 (3): 359–371.

Durand, Loyal, Jr. 1939. Cheese Region of Southeastern Wisconsin. *Economic Geography* 15 (3): 283–292.

———. 1952. The Migration of Cheese Manufacture in the United States. *Annals of the Association of American Geographers* 42 (4): 263–282.

Dutton, Rachel. 2011. Small World: A Rind Researcher Captures the Microscopic Residents of Cheese. *Culture: The Word on Cheese* 3 (2): 74–81.

Edgar, Gordon. 2010. *Cheesemonger: Life on the Wedge.* White River Junction, Vt.: Chelsea Green.

Edwards, Bruce. 2009. Crowley Cheese Factory Resumes Production. *Rutland [Vt.] Herald,* November 2. Available online: www.rutlandherald.com/article/20091102/BUSINESS/911020309. Accessed July 17, 2011.

Elrand, Lisa. 2010. Affidavit in Support of Verified Complaint for Forfeiture *In Rem,* filed with the U.S. Attorney's office in Seattle, Washington, October 21. Available online: http://pnwcheese.typepad.com/cheese/2010/10/federal-court-filings-reveal-details-of-estrella-family-creamery-closure.html. Accessed January 3, 2010.

Enserink, Martin. 2002. What Mosquitoes Want: Secrets of Host Attraction. *Science* 298 (5591): 90–92.

Escobar, Arturo. 1999. After Nature: Steps to an Antiessentialist Political Ecology. *Current Anthropology* 40 (1): 1–30.

Fabian, Johannes. 1983. *Time and the Other: How Anthropology Makes Its Object.* New York: Columbia University Press.

Fajans, Jane. 1988. The Transformative Value of Food: A Review Essay. *Food and Foodways* 3 (1–2): 143–166.

Farrar, Nicholas, and Gill Trorey. 2008. Maxims, Tacit Knowledge and Learning: Developing Expertise in Dry Stone Walling. *Journal of Vocational Education and Training* 60 (1): 35–48.

Farquhar, Judith. 2002. *Appetites: Food and Sex in Post-Socialist China.* Durham, N.C.: Duke University Press.

———. 2006. Food, Eating, and the Good Life. Pp. 145–160 in *Handbook of Material Culture,* edited by Chris Tilley, Webb Keane, Susanne Kücher, Mike Rowlands, and Patricia Spyer. London: Sage.

Ferry, Elizabeth Emma. 2002. Inalienable Commodities: The Production and Circulation of Silver and Patrimony in a Mexican Mining Cooperative. *Cultural Anthropology* 17 (3): 331–358.

Feurer, C., F. Irlinger, H. E. Spinnler, P. Glaser, and T. Vallaeys. 2004. Assessment of the Rind Microbial Diversity in a Farmhouse-Produced vs. a Pasteurized Industrially Produced Soft Red-Smear Cheese Using Both Cultivation and rDNA-Based Methods. *Journal of Applied Microbiology* 97: 546–556.

Finn, Daniel K. 2006. *The Moral Ecology of Markets: Assessing Claims about Markets and Justice.* Cambridge: Cambridge University Press.

Fischer, Michael M. J. 2003. *Emergent Forms of Life and the Anthropological Voice.* Durham, N.C.: Duke University Press.

Fisher, Carolyn. 2007. Selling Coffee, or Selling Out? Evaluating Different Ways to Analyze the Fair-Trade System. *Culture & Agriculture* 29 (2): 78–88.

Fishman, Charles. 2006. *The Wal-Mart Effect: How the World's Most Powerful Company Really Works—and How It's Transforming the American Economy.* New York: Penguin.

Fitzgerald, Deborah. 2003. *Every Farm a Factory: The Industrial Ideal in American Agriculture.* New Haven, Conn.: Yale University Press.

Florida, Richard. 2002. *The Rise of the Creative Class and How It's Transforming Work, Leisure, Community, and Everyday Life.* New York: Basic Books.

Foucault, Michel. 1978. *The History of Sexuality,* vol. 1, translated by Robert Hurley. New York: Vintage.

Franklin, Sarah. 2007. *Dolly Mixtures: The Remaking of Genealogy.* Durham, N.C.: Duke University Press.

Freidberg, Susanne. 2004. *French Beans and Food Scares: Culture and Commerce in an Anxious Age.* Oxford: Oxford University Press.

———. 2009. *Fresh: A Perishable History.* Cambridge, Mass.: Belknap Press.

Galison, Peter. 1997. *Image and Logic: A Material Culture of Microphysics.* Chicago, Ill.: University of Chicago Press.

Gewertz, Deborah, and Frederick Errington. 2010. *Cheap Meat: Flap Food Nations in the Pacific Islands.* Berkeley: University of California Press.

Gibson, James J. 1986. *The Ecological Approach to Visual Perception.* Hillsdale, N.J.: Lawrence Erlbaum Associates.

Gibson-Graham, J. K. 1996. *The End of Capitalism (as We Knew It): A Feminist Critique of Political Economy.* Minneapolis: University of Minnesota Press.

———. 2006. *A Postcapitalist Politics.* Minneapolis: University of Minnesota Press.

Giddens, Anthony. 1991. *Modernity and Self-Identity: Self and Society in the Late Modern Age.* Stanford, Calif.: Stanford University Press.

Gifford, Terry. 1999. *Pastoral: The New Critical Idiom.* New York: Routledge.

———. 2006. *Reconnecting with John Muir: Essays in Post-Pastoral Practice.* Athens: University of Georgia Press.

Gilbert, B. D. 1896. *The Cheese Industry of the State of New York*. Washington, D.C.: Government Printing Office.

Gillette, Maris. 2000. *Between Mecca and Beijing: Modernization and Consumption among Urban Chinese Muslims*. Stanford, Calif.: Stanford University Press.

Goode, J. J. 2010. The Stellar American-Made Cheese Plate: The United States Can Finally Boast about Some World-Class Wheels. May issue of *Details*. Available online: www.details.com/style-advice/food-and-drinks/201005/the-ultimate-guide-to-buying-cheese-the-stellar-american-made-cheese-plate. Accessed May 28, 2011.

Goodman, David. 1999. Agro-Food Studies in the "Age of Ecology": Nature, Corporeality, Bio-Politics. *Sociologia Ruralis* 39 (1): 17–38.

Gould, Rebecca Kneale. 2005. *At Home in Nature: Modern Homesteading and Spiritual Practice in America*. Berkeley: University of California Press.

Graeber, David. 2001. *Toward an Anthropological Theory of Value: The False Coin of Our Own Dream*. New York: Palgrave Macmillan.

Grasseni, Cristina. 2003. Packaging Skills: Calibrating Cheese to the Global Market. Pp. 259–288 in *Commodifying Everything: Relationships of the Market*, edited by Susan Strasser. New York: Routledge.

———. 2004. Skilled Vision: An Apprenticeship in Breeding Aesthetics. *Social Anthropology* 12 (1): 41–55.

———. 2005. Designer Cows: The Practice of Cattle Breeding between Skill and Standardization. *Society & Animals* 13 (1): 33–49.

———. 2009. *Developing Skill, Developing Vision: Practices of Locality at the Foot of the Alps*. Oxford: Berghahn Books.

———. 2012. Resisting Cheese: Boundaries, Conflict and Distinction at the Foot of the Alps. *Food, Culture & Society* 15 (1): 23–29.

Gray, John. 1999. Open Spaces and Dwelling Places: Being at Home on Hill Farms in the Scottish Borders. *American Ethnologist* 26 (2): 440–460.

Gray, Rebecca. 2008. *American Artisanal: Finding the Country's Best Real Food, from Cheese to Chocolate*. New York: Rizzoli International.

Gudeman, Stephen. 2001. *The Anthropology of Economy*. Malden, Mass.: Blackwell Publishing.

———. 2008. *Economy's Tension: The Dialectics of Community and Market*. New York: Berghahn Books.

Gumpert, David E. 2009. *The Raw Milk Revolution: Behind America's Emerging Battle over Food Rights*. White River Junction, Vt.: Chelsea Green.

Gusterson, Hugh. 1996. Nuclear Weapons Testing—Scientific Experiment as Political Ritual. Pp. 131–146 in *Naked Science: Anthropological Inquiries into Boundaries, Power, and Knowledge*, edited by Laura Nader. New York: Routledge.

Guthman, Julie. 2004. *Agrarian Dreams: The Paradox of Organic Farming in California*. Berkeley: University of California Press.

———. 2008. Bringing Good Food to Others: Investigating the Subjects of Alternative Food Practice. *Cultural Geographies* 15 (4): 431–447.

Guy, Kolleen M. 2003. *When Champagne Became French: Wine and the Making of a National Identity*. Baltimore, Md.: Johns Hopkins University Press.

Hamilton, Shane. 2008. *Trucking Country: The Road to America's Wal-Mart Economy.* Princeton, N.J.: Princeton University Press.

Haraway, Donna. 1988. Situated Knowledges: The Science Question in Feminism and the Privilege of Partial Perspective. *Feminist Studies* 14 (3): 575–599.

———. 1998. *How Like a Leaf: An Interview with Thyrza Nichols Goodeve.* Milan, Italy: La Tartaruga/Baldini and Castoldi International.

———. 2003. *The Companion Species Manifesto: Dogs, People, and Significant Otherness.* Chicago: Prickly Paradigm Press.

———. 2008. *When Species Meet.* Minneapolis: University of Minnesota Press.

Harper, Douglas. 1987. *Working Knowledge: Skill and Community in a Small Shop.* Berkeley: University of California Press.

———. 2001. *Changing Works: Visions of a Lost Agriculture.* Chicago: University of Chicago Press.

Hayden, Cori. 2003. *When Nature Goes Public: The Making and Unmaking of Bioprospecting in Mexico.* Princeton, N.J.: Princeton University Press.

Heath, Deborah, and Anne Meneley. 2007. Techne, Technoscience, and the Circulation of Comestible Commodities: An Introduction. *American Anthropologist* 109 (4): 593–602.

———. 2010. The Naturecultures of Foie Gras: Techniques of the Body and a Contested Ethics of Care. *Food, Culture and Society* 13 (3): 421–452.

Heldke, Lisa. 1992. Foodmaking as a Thoughtful Practice. Pp. 203–229 in *Cooking, Eating, Thinking: Transformative Philosophies of Food,* edited by Deane W. Curtin and Lisa M. Heldke. Bloomington: Indiana University Press.

Helmreich, Stefan. 2007. Blue-Green Capital, Biotechnology Circulation and an Oceanic Imaginary: A Critique of Biopolitical Economy. *BioSocieties* 2 (3): 287–302.

———. 2008. Species of Biocapital. *Science as Culture* 17 (4): 463–478.

———. 2009. *Alien Ocean: Anthropological Voyages in Microbial Seas.* Berkeley: University of California Press.

Hennion, Antoine. 2007. Those Things That Hold Us Together: Taste and Sociology. *Cultural Sociology* 1 (1): 97–114.

Herzfeld, Michael. 1997. *Cultural Intimacy: Social Poetics in the Nation-State.* New York: Routledge.

———. 2004. *The Body Impolitic: Artisans and Artifice in the Global Hierarchy of Value.* Chicago: University of Chicago Press.

Herzog, Karen. 2009. Immigrants Add New Flavors to Wisconsin's Cheesemaking Legacy. *Milwaukee Journal Sentinel,* March 17. Available online: www.jsonline.com/news/wisconsin/41352337.html. Accessed October 3, 2010.

Hewitt, Ben. 2008. A Giant Cheese Cave. *Gourmet,* October 20. Available online: www.gourmet.com/travel/2008/10/Vermont-cheese-cave. Accessed May 21, 2011.

———. 2010. *The Town That Food Saved: How One Community Found Vitality in Local Food.* New York: Rodale.

Hinrichs, C. Clare. 2007. Practice and Place in Remaking the Food System. Pp. 1–15 in *Remaking the North American Food System: Strategies for Sustainability,* edited by C. Clare Hinrichs and Thomas Lyson. Lincoln: Nebraska University Press.

Hinrichs, C. Clare, and Thomas Lyson, eds. 2007. *Remaking the North American Food System: Strategies for Sustainability.* Lincoln: Nebraska University Press.

Hintz, Martin, and Pam Percy. 2008. *Wisconsin Cheese: A Cookbook and Guide to the Cheeses of Wisconsin.* Guilford, Conn.: Morris Books.

Hirsch, Eric. 1995. Landscape: Between Place and Space. Pp. 1–30 in *The Anthropology of Landscape: Perspectives on Place and Space,* edited by Eric Hirsch and Michael O'Hanlon. Oxford: Clarendon Press.

Hirsch, Eric, and Charles Stewart. 2005. Introduction: Ethnographies of Historicity. *History and Anthropology* 16 (3): 261–274.

Hobsbawm, Eric. 1983. Introduction: Inventing Traditions. Pp. 1–14 in *The Invention of Tradition,* edited by Eric Hobsbawm and Terence Ranger. Cambridge: Cambridge University Press.

Hoey, Brian A. 2005. From Pi to Pie: Moral Narratives of Noneconomic Migration and Starting over in the Postindustrial Midwest. *Journal of Contemporary Ethnography* 34: 586–624.

———. 2008. American Dreaming: Refugees from Corporate Work Seek the Good Life. Pp. 117–139 in *The Changing Landscape of Work and Family in the American Middle Class: Reports from the Field,* edited by Elizabeth Rudd and Lara Descartes. Lanham, Md.: Lexington Books.

Holloway, Lewis, Moya Kneafsey, Laura Venn, Rosie Cox, Elizabeth Dowler, and Helena Tuomainen. 2007. Possible Food Economies: A Methodological Framework for Exploring Food Production-Consumption Relationships. *Sociologia Ruralis* 47 (1): 1–19.

Holtzman, Jon. 2009. *Uncertain Tastes: Memory, Ambivalence, and the Politics of Eating in Samburu, Northern Kenya.* Berkeley: University of California Press.

Hooper, Allison. 2005. The Business of Farmstead Cheesemaking. Pp. 227–246 in *American Farmstead Cheese: The Complete Guide to Making and Selling Artisan Cheeses,* edited by Paul Kindstedt. White River Junction, Vt.: Chelsea Green.

Hurt, Jeanette. 2008. *The Cheeses of Wisconsin: A Culinary Travel Guide.* Woodstock, Vt.: Countryman Press.

Ingold, Tim. 2000. *The Perception of the Environment: Essays in Livelihood, Dwelling and Skill.* London: Routledge.

Jarosz, Lucy. 2008. The City in the Country: Growing Alternative Food Networks in Metropolitan Areas. *Journal of Rural Studies* 24 (3): 231–244.

Jarosz, Lucy, and Victoria Lawson. 2002. Sophisticated People versus Rednecks: Economic Restructuring and Class Difference in America's West. *Antipode* 34 (1): 8–27.

Johnson, Hugh. 1998. Foreword. P. 4 in *Terroir: The Role of Geology, Climate, and Culture in the Making of French Wines,* by James Wilson. Berkeley: University of California Press.

Julian, Sheryl, and Julie Riven. 2001. Blessed Are the Cheese Makers: Two Dairy Farmers Struggled for Years Selling Milk but Their Tangy Raw-Milk Cheese Turned Their Fortunes. *Boston Globe Magazine,* May 20, 93.

Kahn, Miriam. 1986. *Always Hungry, Never Greedy: Food and the Expression of Gender in a Melanesian Society.* Cambridge: Cambridge University Press.

Kamp, David. 2006. *The United States of Arugula: The Sun-Dried, Cold-Pressed, Dark-Roasted, Extra Virgin Story of the American Food Revolution.* New York: Broadway Books.

Keen, W. E. 1999. Lessons from Investigations of Foodborne Disease Outbreaks. *Journal of the American Medical Association* 281: 1845–1847.

Kehler, Mateo. 2010. Banking on Sunshine. *Diner Journal* 15: 8–10.

Kessler, Brad. 2009. *Goat Song: A Seasonal Life, a Short History of Herding, and the Art of Making Cheese.* New York: Scribner.

Kindstedt, Paul. 2005. *American Farmstead Cheese: The Complete Guide to Making and Selling Artisan Cheeses.* White River Junction, Vt.: Chelsea Green.

Kingsolver, Barbara. 2007. *Animal, Vegetable, Miracle: A Year of Food Life.* New York: HarperCollins.

Kirksey, S. Eben, and Stefan Helmreich. 2010. The Emergence of Multispecies Ethnography. *Cultural Anthropology* 25 (4): 545–575.

Kloppenburg, Jack. 1988. *First the Seed: The Political Economy of Plant Biotechnology.* Madison: University of Wisconsin Press.

Kloppenburg, Jack, Sharon Lezberg, Kathryn De Master, George Stevenson, and John Hendrickson. 2000. Tasting Food, Tasting Sustainability: Defining the Attributes of an Alternative Food System with Competent, Ordinary People. *Human Organization* 59 (2): 177–186.

Knight, John, ed. 2005. *Animals in Person: Cultural Perspectives on Human-Animal Intimacy.* Oxford: Berg.

Knorr, Karin. 1979. Tinkering toward Success: Prelude to a Theory of Scientific Practice. *Theory and Society* 8: 347–376.

Kohler, Robert E. 2002. *Landscapes and Labscapes: Exploring the Lab-Field Border in Biology.* Chicago: University of Chicago Press.

———. 2006. *All Creatures: Naturalists, Collectors, and Biodiversity 1850–1950.* Princeton, N.J.: Princeton University Press.

Kondo, Dorinne. 1990. *Crafting Selves: Power, Gender, and Discourses of Identity in a Japanese Workplace.* Chicago: University of Chicago Press.

Kopytoff, Igor. 1986. The Cultural Biography of Things: Commoditization as a Process. Pp. 64–91 in *The Social Life of Things: Commodities in Cultural Perspective,* edited by Arjun Appadurai. Cambridge: Cambridge University Press.

Kunzig, Robert. 2001. The Biology of . . . Cheese: Safety vs. Flavor in the Land of Pasteur. *Discover* 22 (11 November). Available online: http://discovermagazine.com/2001/nov/featbiology. Accessed May 29, 2012.

LaFollette, Hugh. 2000. Pragmatic Ethics. Pp. 400–419 in *The Blackwell Guide to Ethical Theory,* edited by Hugh LaFollette. Malden, Mass.: Blackwell Publishing.

Latour, Bruno. 1987. *Science in Action: How to Follow Scientists and Engineers through Society.* Cambridge, Mass.: Harvard University Press.

———. 1988. *The Pasteurization of France.* Translated by Alan Sheridan and John Law. Cambridge, Mass.: Harvard University Press.

———. 1993. *We Have Never Been Modern.* Translated by Catherine Porter. Cambridge, Mass.: Harvard University Press.

———. 2005. *Reassembling the Social: An Introduction to Actor-Network Theory.* Oxford: Oxford University Press.

Laudan, Rachel. 2004. Slow Food: The French Terroir Strategy, and Culinary Modernism. *Food, Culture & Society* 7 (2): 133–144.

Lave, Jean, and Étienne Wenger. 1991. *Situated Learning: Legitimate Peripheral Participation*. Cambridge: Cambridge University Press.

Law, John. 1992. Notes on the Theory of the Actor Network: Ordering, Strategy, and Heterogeneity. *Systems Practice* 5 (4): 379–393.

Lawson, Victoria, Lucy Jarosz, and Anne Bonds. 2008. Building Economies from the Bottom Up: (Mis)representations of Poverty in the Rural American Northwest. *Social & Cultural Geography* 9 (7): 737–753.

Leitch, Alison. 2003. Slow Food and the Politics of Pork Fat: Italian Food and European Identity. *Ethnos* 68 (4): 437–462.

Lesher, J. H. 1969. ΓΝΩΣΙΣ and ΕΠΙΣΤΗΜΗ in Socrates' Dream in the Theaetetus. *The Journal of Hellenic Studies* 89: 72–78.

Lévi-Strauss, Claude. 1969. *The Raw and the Cooked: Mythologiques,* vol. 1, translated by John Weightman and Doreen Weightman. New York: Harper and Row.

Little, Jane Braxton. 2011. Message in a Bottle. *Audubon* (March–April): 76–81.

Locke, John. (1689) 1982. *Second Treatise of Government,* edited by Richard Cox. Arlington Heights, Ill.: Harlan Davidson.

Loring, Geo. B. 1866. Address at the Cattle Show opening, September 13, 1865. Recorded in *Transactions of the Rhode Island Society for the Encouragement of Domestic Industry in the Year 1865.* Providence, R.I.: Anthony Knowles.

Lyson, Thomas. 2004. *Civic Agriculture: Reconnecting Farm, Food, and Community.* Medford, Mass.: Tufts University Press.

Lyson, Thomas A., and Gilbert W. Gillespie. 1995. Producing More Milk on Fewer Farms: Neoclassical and Neostructural Explanations of Changes in Dairy Farming. *Rural Sociology* 60 (3): 493–504.

MacDonald, James M., Erik J. O'Donoghue, William D. McBride, Richard F. Nehring, Carmen L. Sandretto, and Roberto Mosheim. 2007. *Profits, Costs, and the Changing Structure of Dairy Farming.* Economic Research Report no. ERR-47, United States Department of Agriculture. Available online: www.ers.usda.gov/publications/err47/err47b.pdf. Accessed May 17, 2010.

MacDonald, Kenneth Iain. 2007. Mondo Formaggio: Windows on the Circulation of Cheese in the World. Presented at "Critical Fetishism and Value: Embodied Commodities in Motion," Amherst College, Amherst, Mass., October 19–20.

MacDonald, Margaret. 2007. *At Work in the Field of Birth: Midwifery Narratives of Nature, Tradition, and Home.* Nashville, Tenn.: Vanderbilt University Press.

Madigan, Carleen. 2009. *The Backyard Homestead: Produce All the Food You Need on Just a Quarter Acre!* North Adams, Mass.: Storey Publishing.

Major, Cindy. 2005. Putting It All Together: The Vermont Shepherd Story. Pp. 247–261 in *American Farmstead Cheese: The Complete Guide to Making and Selling Artisan Cheeses,* edited by Paul Kindstedt. White River Junction, Vt.: Chelsea Green.

Malinowski, Bronislaw. 1948. *Magic, Science, and Religion, and Other Essays.* Glencoe, Ill.: The Free Press.

Manning, Paul. 2010. The Semiotics of Brand. *Annual Review of Anthropology* 39: 33–49.

Mansfield, Becky. 2011. Is Fish Health Food or Poison? Farmed Fish and the Material Production of Un/Healthy Nature. *Antipode* 43 (2): 413–434.

Marcel, Joyce. 2008. Milk Money: The Kehler Brothers' Cheese Cave. *Vermont Busi-*

ness Magazine, May. Available online: http://findarticles.com/p/articles/mi_qa3675/is
_200805/ai_n25501760/. Accessed February 10, 2010.

Marcellino, Noella. 2003. Biodiversity of *Geotrichum candidum* Strains Isolated from
Traditional French Cheese. PhD diss., University of Connecticut.

Marcellino, Noella, E. Beauvier, R. Grappin, M. Guéguen, and D. R. Benson. 2001. Diversity of *Geotrichum candidum* Strains Isolated from Traditional Cheesemaking Fabri-
cations in France. *Applied and Environmental Microbiology* 67 (10): 4752–4759.

Markowitz, Lisa. 2008. Produce(ing) Equity: Creating Fresh Markets in a Food Desert.
Research in Economic Anthropology 28: 195–211.

Markowitz, Sally J. 1994. The Distinction between Art and Craft. *Journal of Aesthetic
Education* 28 (1): 55–70.

Marks, Jonathan. 2002. *What It Means to Be 98 Percent Chimpanzee.* Berkeley: University
of California Press.

Marquis, Vivienne, and Patricia Haskell. 1964. *The Cheese Book: A Definitive Guide to the
Cheeses of the World.* New York: Simon and Schuster.

Martineau, Harriet. 1863. An Industrial Chance for Gentlewomen. In *Once a Week: An
Illustrated Miscellany of Literature, Art, Science, & Popular Information,* 9 (June–
December): September 5. London: Bradbury & Evans.

Marx, Karl. (1857–1858) 1978. *The Grundrisse.* Excerpted (pp. 221–293) in *The Marx-Engels
Reader,* 2nd ed., edited by Robert C. Tucker. New York: W. W. Norton.

———. (1867) 1976. *Capital,* vol. 1, translated by Ben Fowkes. London: Penguin.

Marx, Leo. 1964. *The Machine in the Garden: Technology and the Pastoral Ideal in America.* Oxford: Oxford University Press.

Massey, Doreen. 1999. *Power-Geometries and the Politics of Space-Time.* Hettner-Lectures,
2. Heidelberg: Department of Geography, University of Heidelberg.

Maurer, Bill. 2005. *Mutual Life, Limited: Islamic Banking, Alternative Currencies, Lateral
Reason.* Princeton, N.J.: Princeton University Press.

Mauss, Marcel. (1925) 2000. *The Gift: Forms and Functions of Exchange in Archaic Societies,* translated by W. D. Halls. New York: W. W. Norton.

———. 1973. Techniques of the Body. *Economy and Society* 2 (1): 70–88.

McCalman, Max, and David Gibbons. 2005. *Cheese: A Connoisseur's Guide to the World's
Best.* New York: Clarkson Potter.

———. 2009. *Mastering Cheese: Lessons for Connoisseurship from a Maître Fromager.* New
York: Clarkson Potter.

McKnight, Qui'tas. 2006. *The Art of Farmstead Cheese Making in the British Isles.* Madison, Wisc.: Babcock Institute for International Dairy Research and Development.

McMurry, Sally. 1995. *Transforming Rural Life: Dairying Families and Agricultural
Change, 1820–1885.* Baltimore, Md.: Johns Hopkins University Press.

Mead, Margaret. 1970. The Changing Significance of Food. *American Scientist* 58 (2):
176–181.

Meigs, Anna. 1987. Food as a Cultural Construction. *Food and Foodways* 2 (1): 341–357.

Mendelson, Anne. 2008. *Milk: The Surprising Story of Milk through the Ages.* New York:
Knopf.

Meneley, Anne. 2004. Extra Virgin Olive Oil and Slow Food. *Anthropologica* 46 (2):
165–176.

Metcalf, Bruce. 2007. Replacing the Myth of Modernism. Pp. 4–32 in *NeoCraft: Modernity and the Crafts*, edited by Sandra Alfoldy. Halifax: Nova Scotia College of Art and Design Press.

Mignon, Ernest. 1962. *Les mots du général*. Paris: A. Fayard.

Miller, Angela, with Ralph Gardner Jr. 2010. *Hay Fever: How Chasing a Dream on a Vermont Farm Changed My Life*. Hoboken, N.J.: Wiley & Sons.

Miller, Daniel. 1987. *Material Culture and Mass Consumption*. Oxford: Basil Blackwell.

———. 2008. The Uses of Value. *Geoforum* 39: 1122–1132.

Mintz, Sidney. 1985. *Sweetness and Power: The Place of Sugar in Modern History*. New York: Penguin Books.

———. 2002. Food and Eating: Some Persisting Questions. Pp. 24–32 in *Food Nations: Selling Taste in Consumer Society*, edited by Warren Belasco and Philip Scranton. New York: Routledge.

———. 2006. Food at Moderate Speeds. Pp. 3–11 in *Fast Food/Slow Food: The Cultural Economy of the Global Food System*, edited by Richard Wilk. Lanham, Md.: AltaMira Press.

Mitchell, Don. 1996. *The Lie of the Land: Migrant Workers and the California Landscape*. Minneapolis: University of Minnesota Press.

Mnoonkin, Seth. 2011. *The Panic Virus: A True Story of Medicine, Science, and Fear*. New York: Simon and Schuster.

Mol, Annemarie. 2008. *The Logic of Care: Health and the Problem of Patient Choice*. New York: Routledge.

———. 2009. Good Taste: The Embodied Normativity of the Consumer-Citizen. *Journal of Cultural Economy* 2 (3): 269–283.

Mullin, Molly. 1999. Mirrors and Windows: Sociocultural Studies of Human-Animal Relationships. *Annual Review of Anthropology* 28: 201–224.

Munn, Nancy D. 1986. *The Fame of Gawa: A Symbolic Study of Value Transformation in a Massim (Papua New Guinea) Society*. Durham, N.C.: Duke University Press.

Murdoch, Jonathan. 1997. Inhuman-Nonhuman-Human: Actor-Network Theory and the Prospects for a Nondualistic and Symmetrical Perspective on Nature and Society. *Environment and Planning D: Society and Space* 15 (6): 731–756.

Murdoch, Jonathan, and Mara Miele. 2004. A New Aesthetic of Food? Relational Reflexivity in the "Alternative" Food Movement. Pp. 156–175 in *Qualities of Food*, edited by Mark Harvey, Andrew McMeekin, and Alan Warde. Manchester, U.K.: Manchester University Press.

Myers, Fred R., ed. 2001. *The Empire of Things: Regimes of Value and Material Culture*. Santa Fe, N.M.: School of American Research Press.

Nabhan, Gary Paul. 2002. *Coming Home to Eat: The Pleasures and Politics of Local Foods*. New York: W. W. Norton.

Nash, Linda. 2006. *Inescapable Ecologies: A History of Environment, Disease, and Knowledge*. Berkeley: University of California Press.

National Agricultural Statistics Service. 2011. *Dairy Products 2010 Summary*. United States Department of Agriculture. Available online: http://usda.mannlib.cornell.edu/usda/current/DairProdSu/DairProdSu-04-27-2011.pdf. Accessed June 15, 2011.

National Research Council. 2003. Scientific Criteria to Ensure Safe Food. Committee on the Review of the Use of Scientific Criteria and Performance Standards for Safe Food, Institute of Medicine, National Research Council. Washington, D.C.: National Academies Press.

Nestle, Marion. 2002. *Food Politics: How the Food Industry Influences Nutrition and Health*. Berkeley: University of California Press.

———. 2003. *Safe Food: Bacteria, Biotechnology, and Bioterrorism*. Berkeley: University of California Press.

Neuman, William. 2011. Raw Milk Cheesemakers Fret over Possible New Rules. *New York Times*, February 4, B1.

Nicholson, Charles, and Mark Stephenson. 2006. *Financial Performance and Other Characteristics of On-Farm Dairy Processing Enterprises in New York, Vermont and Wisconsin. Department of Applied Economics and Management*. Ithaca, N.Y.: College of Agriculture and Life Sciences, Cornell University. Available online: http://purl.umn.edu/121583. Accessed May 21, 2012.

Nies, Kristina. 2008. Chore, Craft & Business: Cheesemaking in 18th Century Massachusetts. Master's thesis, Boston University.

Nohl, Mary Van de Kamp. 2005. The Big Cheese: California Wants to Steal Our Identity as the Top Cheesemaker: Why Our State Won't Be Beat. *Milwaukee Magazine* 30 (9): 56–65.

Norton, James, and Becca Dilley. 2009. *The Master Cheesemakers of Wisconsin*. Madison: University of Wisconsin Press.

Noske, Barbara. 1993. The Animal Question in Anthropology. *Society & Animals* 1 (2): 185–190.

Nutch, Frank. 1996. Gadgets, Gizmos, and Instruments: Science for the Tinkering. *Science, Technology, & Human Values* 21 (2): 214–228.

O'Brien, Nora N. and Thomas P. O'Connor. 2004. Nutritional Aspects of Cheese. Pp. 573–581 in *Cheese: Chemistry, Physics and Microbiology*, 3rd ed., vol. 1: *General Aspects*, edited by Patrick Fox, Paul McSweeney, Timothy Cogan, and Timothy Guinee. London: Elsevier.

O'Connor, Erin. 2007. Embodied Knowledge in Glassblowing: The Experience of Meaning and the Struggle towards Proficiency. *The Sociological Review* 55: 126–141.

Ogden, Ellen Ecker. 2007. *The Vermont Cheese Book*. Woodstock, Vt.: Countryman Press.

O'Hagan, Maureen. 2010. Is Raw, Unpasteurized Milk Safe? *Seattle Times*, March 20. Available online: http://seattletimes.nwsource.com/html/localnews/2011399591_rawmilk21m.html. Accessed June 16, 2010.

Ohnuki-Tierny, Emiko. 1993. *Rice as Self: Japanese Identities through Time*. Princeton, N.J.: Princeton University Press.

Orlean, Susan. 2009. The It Bird: The Return of the Back-yard Chicken. *The New Yorker* (September 28): 26–31.

Orzech, Kathryn M., and Mark Nichter. 2008. From Resilience to Resistance: Political Ecological Lessons from Antibiotic and Pesticide Resistance. *Annual Review of Anthropology* 37: 267–282.

Ott, Sandra. 1979. Aristotle among the Basques: The "Cheese Analogy" of Conception. *Man* 14 (4): 699–711.

———. 1981. *The Circle of Mountains: A Basque Shepherding Community.* Reno: University of Nevada Press.

Parr, Tami. 2009. *Artisan Cheese of the Pacific Northwest: A Discovery Guide.* Woodstock, Vt.: Countryman Press.

Patel, Raj. 2007. *Stuffed and Starved: The Hidden Battle for the World Food System.* London: Portobello Books.

Paxson, Heather. 2004. *Making Modern Mothers: Ethics and Family Planning in Urban Greece.* Berkeley: University of California Press.

———. 2008. Post-Pasteurian Cultures: The Microbiopolitics of Raw-Milk Cheese in the United States. *Cultural Anthropology* 23 (1): 15–47.

———. 2010. Locating Value in Artisan Cheese: Reverse-Engineering *Terroir* for New-World Landscapes. *American Anthropologist* 112 (3): 444–457.

———. 2012. Nicknames and Trademarks: Establishing American Originals. *Food, Culture & Society* 15 (1): 12–18.

Petridou, Eleni. 2012. What's in a Place Name? Branding and Labeling in Greece. *Food, Culture & Society* 15 (1): 29–34.

Petrini, Carlo. 2007. Foreword. Pp. ix–x in *The Atlas of American Artisan Cheese,* by Jeffrey P. Roberts. White River Junction, Vt.: Chelsea Green.

Polanyi, Michael. 1958. *Personal Knowledge: Towards a Post-Critical Philosophy.* Chicago: University of Chicago Press.

Pollan, Michael. 2006. *The Omnivore's Dilemma: A Natural History of Four Meals.* New York: Penguin.

Poppendieck, Janet. 1998. *Sweet Charity? Emergency Food and the End of Entitlement.* New York: Penguin.

Pritchard, Todd Jay. 2005. Ensuring Safety and Quality 1: Hazard Analysis Critical Control Point and the Cheesemaking Process. Pp. 139–151 in *American Farmstead Cheese: The Complete Guide to Making and Selling Artisan Cheeses,* edited by Paul Kindstedt. White River Junction, Vt.: Chelsea Green.

Pye, David. 1968. *The Nature and Art of Workmanship.* London: Studio Vista.

Rabinow, Paul. 1992. Artificiality and Enlightenment: From Sociobiology to Biosociality. Pp. 234–252 in *Incorporations,* edited by Jonathan Crary and Sanford Kwinter. New York: Zone.

Radel, Claudia, Birgit Schmook, and Susannah McCandless. 2010. Environment, Transnational Labor Migration, and Gender: Case Studies from Southern Yucatán, Mexico and Vermont, USA. *Population and Environment* 32 (2–3): 177–197.

Radin, Margaret Jane. 1996. *Contested Commodities: The Trouble with Trade in Sex, Children, Body Parts, and Other Things.* Cambridge, Mass.: Harvard University Press.

Rapp, Rayna. 1999. *Testing Women, Testing the Fetus: The Social Impact of Amniocentesis in America.* New York: Routledge.

Rathke, Lisa. 2008. Giant Cheese Cave Gives Small Makers New Opportunities. *Boston Globe,* February 29. Available online: www.boston.com/news/local/vermnt/articles/2008/02/29/giant_cheese_cave_gives_small_makers_new_opportunities/. Accessed February 10, 2010.

Reitsma, Christine J. and David R. Henning. 1996. Survival of Enterohemorrhagic *Esch-*

erichia coli O157:H7 during the Manufacture and Curing of Cheddar Cheese. *Journal of Food Protection* 59 (5): 460–464.

Ring, Wilson. 2009. Vermont Dairy Farms Count on Illegal Immigrants. *The Bay State Banner,* October 22, vol. 45, no. 11.

Risatti, Howard. 2007. *A Theory of Craft: Function and Aesthetic Expression.* Chapel Hill: University of North Carolina Press.

Ritvo, Harriet. 1987. *The Animal Estate: The English and Other Creatures in the Victorian Age.* Cambridge, Mass.: Harvard University Press.

———. 1995. Possessing Mother Nature: Genetic Capital in Eighteenth-Century Britain. Pp. 413–426 in *Early Modern Conceptions of Property,* edited by J. Brewer and S. Staves. London: Routledge.

Robbins, Joel. 2007. Between Reproduction and Freedom: Morality, Value, and Radical Cultural Change. *Ethnos* 72 (3): 293–314.

———. 2009. Value, Structure, and the Range of Possibilities: A Response to Zigon. *Ethnos* 74 (2): 277–285.

Roberts, Jeffrey P. 2007. *The Atlas of American Artisan Cheese.* White River Junction, Vt.: Chelsea Green.

Rogers, Juliette. 2008. The Political Lives of Dairy Cows: Modernity, Tradition, and Professional Identity in the Norman Cheese Industry. PhD diss., Brown University.

Ross, Andrew. 2003. *No-Collar: The Humane Workplace and Its Hidden Costs.* New York: Basic Books.

Rouse, Carolyn, and Janet Hoskins. 2004. Purity, Soul Food, and Sunni Islam: Explorations at the Intersection of Consumption and Resistance. *Cultural Anthropology* 19 (2): 226–249.

Russell, Jenna. 2007. On New England's Dairy Farms, Foreign Workers Find a Home. *Boston Globe,* September 22. Available online: www.boston.com/news/local/articles/2007/09/22/on_new_englands_dairy_farms_foreign_workers_find_a_home?mode=PF. Accessed October 3, 2010.

Russell, Nerissa. 2007. The Domestication of Anthropology. Pp. 27–48 in *Where the Wild Things Are Now: Domestication Reconsidered,* edited by Rebecca Cassidy and Molly Mullin. Oxford: Berg.

Sage, Colin. 2007. "Bending Science to Match Their Convictions": Hygienist Conceptions of Food Safety as a Challenge to Alternative Food Enterprises in Ireland. Pp. 205–223 in *Alternative Food Geographies: Representation and Practice,* edited by D. Maye, L. Holloway, and M. Kneafsey. London: Elsevier.

Schaffer, Simon. 1989. Glass Works: Newton's Prisms and the Uses of Experiment. Pp. 67–103 in *The Uses of Experiment,* edited by David Gooding, Trevor Pinch, and Simon Schaffer. Cambridge: Cambridge University Press.

Schlesser, Joseph E., R. Gerdes, S. Ravishankar, K. Madsen, J. Mowbray, and A. Y. Teo. 2006. Survival of a Five-Strain Cocktail of Escherichia coli O157:H7 during the 60-Day Aging Period of Cheddar Cheese Made from Unpasteurized Milk. *Journal of Food Protection* 69 (5): 990–998.

Schlosser, Eric. 2001. *Fast Food Nation: The Dark Side of the All-American Meal.* New York: Houghton Mifflin.

Schmidt, Ronald H. and Debby L. Newslow. 2007. Hazard Analysis Critical Control Points (HACCP) Principle 2: Determine Critical Control Points (CCPs). Department of Food Science and Human Nutrition, Florida Cooperative Extension Service, IFAS, University of Florida. Available online: edis.ifas.ufl.edu/pdffiles/FS/FS14000.pdf. Accessed May 17, 2012.

Schor, Juliet. 2010. *Plentitude: The New Economics of True Wealth*. New York: Penguin.

Schwartz, Lisa, Judith Hausman, and Karen Sabath. 2009. *Over the Rainbeau: Living the Dream of Sustainable Farming*. Bedford Hills, N.Y.: Rainbeau Ridge Publishing.

Scott, James C. 1998. *Seeing Like a State: How Certain Schemes to Improve the Human Condition Have Failed*. New Haven, Conn.: Yale University Press.

Senier, Laura. 2008. "It's Your Most Precious Thing": Worst-Case Thinking, Trust, and Parental Decision-Making about Vaccinations. *Sociological Inquiry* 78 (2): 207–229.

Sennett, Richard. 2008. *The Craftsman*. New Haven, Conn.: Yale University Press.

Sheehan, John F. 2007. Testimony of John F. Sheehan, B.Sc. (Dy.), J.D., Director, Division of Plant and Dairy Food Safety, Office of Food Safety, Center for Food Safety and Applied Nutrition, U.S. Food and Drug Administration, before the Health and Government Operations Committee, Maryland House of Delegates, March 15. P. 2. Available online: www.fda.gov/downloads/Food/FoodSafety/Product-SpecificInformation/MilkSafety/ConsumerInformationAboutMilkSafety/UCM185696.pdf. Accessed January 4, 2012.

Sheehan, John, Robert Childers, and Sebastian Cianci. 2004. Ask the Regulators: Enhancing the Safety of Dairy and Other Animal Based Foods. *Food Safety Magazine* (August–September). Available online: www.foodsafetymagazine.com/article.asp?id=1354&sub=sub1. Accessed June 16, 2010.

Shillinglaw, Brian. 2003. Raw Milk and the Survival of Dairy Farming in New England. *The Natural Farmer* (Spring). Electronic document: www.nofamass.org/programs/rawmilk/tnf.php. Accessed August 20, 2007.

Short, Frances. 2006. *Kitchen Secrets: The Meaning of Cooking in Everyday Life*. Oxford: Berg.

Smart, Alan, and Josephine Smart. 2005. Introduction. Pp. 1–22 in *Petty Capitalists and Globalization: Flexibility, Entrepreneurship, and Economic Development*, edited by Alan Smart and Josephine Smart. Albany: State University of New York Press.

Sonnino, Roberta, and Terry Marsden. 2006. Beyond the Divide: Rethinking Relationships between Alternative and Conventional Food Networks in Europe. *Journal of Economic Geography* 6: 181–199.

Staip, Marybeth. 2006. Negotiating Time and Space for Serious Leisure: Quilting in the Modern U.S. Home. *Journal of Leisure Research* 38 (1): 104–132.

Stanford, Lois. 2006. The Role of Ideology in New Mexico's CSA (Community Supported Agriculture) Organizations: Conflicting Visions between Growers and Members. Pp. 181–200 in *Fast Food/Slow Food: The Cultural Economy of the Global Food System*, edited by Richard Wilk. Lanham, Md.: AltaMira Press.

Stark, David. 2009. *The Sense of Dissonance: Accounts of Worth in Economic Life*. Princeton, N.J.: Princeton University Press.

280 BIBLIOGRAPHY

Strathern, Marilyn. 1988. *The Gender of the Gift: Problems with Women and Problems with Society in Melanesia.* Berkeley: University of California Press.

———. 1992a. *After Nature: English Kinship in the Late Twentieth Century.* Cambridge: Cambridge University Press.

———. 1992b. *Reproducing the Future: Anthropology, Kinship, and the New Reproductive Technologies.* New York: Routledge.

Streeter, Deborah, and Nelson Bills. 2003a. Value-Added Ag-Based Economic Development: A Panacea or False Promise? Part One of a Two-Part Companion Series: What Is Value-Added and How Should We Study It? Working Paper, Department of Applied Economics and Management, Cornell University, Ithaca, N.Y.

———. 2003b. Value-Added Ag-Based Economic Development: A Panacea or False Promise? Part Two of a Two-Part Companion Series: What Is Value-Added and How Should We Study It? Working Paper, Department of Applied Economics and Management, Cornell University, Ithaca, N.Y.

Striffler, Steve. 2005. *Chicken: The Dangerous Transformation of America's Favorite Food.* New Haven, Conn.: Yale University Press.

Sulik, Patricia. 2004. Hazard Analysis Critical Control Point for New England Artisanal Farmstead Cheese Makers. *University of Connecticut Health Center Graduate School Masters Theses,* paper 110. Available online: http://digitalcommons.uconn.edu/uchcgs_masters/110/. Accessed May 17, 2012.

Sutton, David. 1994. "Tradition" and "Modernity": Kalymnian Constructions of Identity and Otherness. *Journal of Modern Greek Studies* 12 (2): 239–260.

———. 2001. *Remembrance of Repasts: An Anthropology of Food and Memory.* Oxford: Berg.

———. 2006. Cooking Skill, the Senses and Memory: The Fate of Practical Knowledge. Pp. 87–118 in *Sensible Objects: Colonialism, Museums and Material Culture,* edited by Elizabeth Edwards, Chris Gosden, and Ruth Phillips. Oxford: Berg.

Taber, George M. 2006. *The Judgment of Paris: California v. France and the Historic 1976 Paris Tasting That Revolutionized Wine.* New York: Scribner.

Teil, Geneviève. 2010. The French Wine "Appellations d'Origine Contrôlée" and the Virtues of Suspicion. *The Journal of World Intellectual Property* 13 (2): 253–274.

Tenenbaum, David. 2011. Wisconsin Cheese Could Get Boost from "Driftless" Label. University of Wisconsin-Madison News, February 4. Available online: www.news .wisc.edu/18935. Accessed June 9, 2011.

Terrio, Susan J. 1996. Crafting Grand Cru Chocolates in Contemporary France. *American Anthropologist* 98 (1): 67–79.

———. 1999. Performing Craft for Heritage Tourists in Southwest France. *City and Society* 11 (1–2): 125–144.

———. 2000. *Crafting the Culture and History of French Chocolate.* Berkeley: University of California Press.

Tewksbury, Henry. 2002. *The Cheeses of Vermont: A Gourmet Guide to Vermont's Artisanal Cheesemakers.* Woodstock, Vt.: Countryman Press.

Theodossopoulos, Dimitrios. 2005. Care, Order and Usefulness: The Context of the Human-Animal Relationship in a Greek Island Community. Pp. 15–35 in *Animals in*

Person: Cultural Perspectives on Human-Animal Intimacies, edited by John Knight. Oxford: Berg.

Thorpe, Liz. 2009. *The Cheese Chronicles: A Journey through the Making and Selling of Cheese in America, Field to Farm to Table.* New York: HarperCollins.

Tomes, Nancy. 1998. *The Gospel of Germs: Men, Women, and the Microbe in American Life.* Cambridge, Mass.: Harvard University Press.

Topham, Anne. 2000. Taste, Technology and Terroir: A Transatlantic Dialogue on Food and Culture. Paper presented at the European Union Center at the University of Wisconsin-Madison, September 8. Available online: www.fantomefarm.com/text .htm. Accessed June 5, 2008.

Tregear, Angela. 2005. Lifestyle, Growth, or Community Involvement? The Balance of Goals of UK Artisan Food Producers. *Entrepreneurship & Regional Development* 17: 1–15.

Trewartha, Glenn T. 1926. The Green County, Wisconsin, Foreign Cheese Industry. *Economic Geography* 2 (2): 292–308.

Trubek, Amy. 2008. *The Taste of Place: A Cultural Journey into Terroir.* Berkeley: University of California Press.

Trubek, Amy B., and Sarah Bowen. 2008. Creating the Taste of Place in the United States: Can We Learn from the French? *GeoJournal* 73: 23–30.

Turner, Fred. 2006. *From Counterculture to Cyberculture: Stewart Brand, the Whole Earth Network, and the Rise of Digital Utopianism.* Chicago: University of Chicago Press.

Twamley, Josiah. 1784. *Dairying Exemplified, or The Business of Cheesemaking: Laid down from Approved Rules, Collected from the Most Experienced Dairy-Women, of Several Counties.* Warwick, Eng.: J. Sharp.

Ulin, Robert. 1996. *Vintages and Traditions: An Ethnohistory of Southwest French Wine Cooperatives.* Washington, D.C.: Smithsonian Institution.

———. 2002. Work as Cultural Production: Labour and Self-Identity among Southwest French Wine Growers. *The Journal of the Royal Anthropological Institute* 8 (4): 691–712.

Valenze, Deborah. 1991. The Art of Women and the Business of Men: Women's Work and the Dairy Industry. *Past and Present* 130 (1): 142–169.

———. 2011. *Milk: A Local and Global History.* New Haven, Conn.: Yale University Press.

Van Esterik, Penny. 1999. Right to Food; Right to Feed; Right to be Fed: The Intersection of Women's Rights and the Right to Food. *Agriculture and Human Values* 16: 225–232.

Vickers, Daniel. 1990. Competency and Competition: Economic Culture in Early America. *The William and Mary Quarterly* 47 (1): 3–29.

Villette, Michel, and Catherine Vuillermot. 2009. *From Predators to Icons: Exposing the Myth of the Business Hero,* translated by George Holoch. Ithaca, N.Y.: Cornell University Press.

Wakin, Daniel J. 2000. New Scrutiny of Cheese Offends Refined Palates: Epicures Defend Unpasteurized Varieties as Regulators Look for Health Risks. *New York Times,* July 14, B1.

Walley, Christine. 2012. *Exit Zero: Family and Class in Postindustrial Chicago.* Chicago: University of Chicago Press.

Warner, Keith Douglass. 2007. The Quality of Sustainability: Agroecological Partnerships and the Geographic Branding of California Winegrapes. *Journal of Rural Studies* 23 (2): 142–155.

Watts, Michael. 2000. Political Ecology. Pp. 257–274 in *A Companion to Economic Geography*, edited by Eric Sheppard and Trevor Barnes. Oxford: Blackwell.

Weiss, Brad. 1996. *The Making and Unmaking of the Haya Lived World: Consumption, Commoditization, and Everyday Practice*. Durham, N.C.: Duke University Press.

———. 2011. Making Pigs Local: Discerning the Sensory Character of Place. *Cultural Anthropology* 26 (3): 438–461.

———. 2012. Configuring the Authentic Value of Real Food: Farm-to-Fork, Snout-to-Tail, and Local Food Movements. *American Ethnologist* 39 (3): 614–626.

Werlin, Laura. 2000. *The New American Cheese: Profiles of America's Great Cheesemakers and Recipes for Cooking with Cheese*. New York: Stewart, Tabori, and Chang.

West, Harry. 2008. Food Fears and Raw-Milk Cheese. *Appetite* 51 (1): 25–29.

West, Harry, and Nuno Domingos. 2012. Gourmandizing Poverty Food: The Serpa Cheese Slow Food Presidium. *Journal of Agrarian Change* 12 (1): 120–143.

West, Harry G., Heather Paxson, Joby Williams, Cristina Grasseni, Elia Petridou, and Susan Cleary. 2012. Naming Cheese. *Food, Culture and Society* 15 (1): 7–41.

White, Jonathan. 1994. *Talking on the Water: Conversations about Nature and Creativity*. San Francisco, Calif.: Sierra Club Books.

Widness, Sara. 2010. Veteran Cheese Maker Back in Business. *Rutland [Vt.] Business Journal*, January 14. Available online: www.vermonttoday.com/apps/pbcs.dll/article ?AID=/20100114/RBJ/100119971. Accessed May 31, 2012.

Wiley, Andrea S. 2011. *Re-Imagining Milk: Cultural and Biological Perspectives*. New York: Routledge.

Wilhelm, Douglas. 1985. Women Assume a Bigger Role in Vermont Farming. *Boston Globe*, March 31, 63–64.

Wilk, Richard. 2006a. *Home Cooking in the Global Village: Caribbean Food from Buccaneers to Ecotourists*. Oxford: Berg.

———. 2006b. From Wild Weeds to Artisanal Cheese. Pp. 13–27 in *Fast Food/Slow Food: The Cultural Economy of the Global Food System*, edited by Richard Wilk. Oxford: AltaMira Press.

Willetts, Anna. 1997. "Bacon Sandwiches Got the Better of Me": Meat-Eating and Vegetarianism in South-East London. Pp. 111–130 in *Food, Health & Identity*, edited by Pat Caplan. London: Routledge.

Williams, Raymond. 1973. *The Country and the City*. Oxford: Oxford University Press.

Woginrich, Jenna. 2008. *Made from Scratch: Discovering the Pleasures of a Handmade Life*. North Adams, Mass.: Storey Publishing.

Wolf, Clark. 2008. *American Cheeses: The Best Regional, Artisan, and Farmhouse Cheeses: Who Makes Them and Where to Find Them*. New York: Simon and Schuster.

Wood, Paul. 2009a. Cheese-Making Tools and Machinery, Part 1. *The Chronicle of the Early American Industries Association* 62 (1): 17–28.

———. 2009b. Cheese-Making Tools and Machinery, Part 2. *The Chronicle of the Early American Industries Association* 62 (2): 53–70.

Wooster, Chuck. 2005. *Living with Sheep: Everything You Need to Know to Raise Your Own Flock*. Guilford, Conn.: Lyons Press.

Yanagisako, Sylvia. 2002. *Producing Culture and Capital: Family Firms in Italy*. Princeton, N.J.: Princeton University Press.

Yanagisako, Sylvia, and Carol Delaney. 1995. Naturalizing Power. Pp. 1–22 in *Naturalizing Power: Essays in Feminist Cultural Analysis*, edited by Sylvia Yanagisako and Carol Delaney. New York: Routledge.

INDEX

acidification, 47, 144, 162. *See also* fermentation process

acidity, 144; acidity testing, 50, 146, 148, 149, 206; pathogens and, 169, 171, 172, 173*table*, 251–52n36

ACS. *See* American Cheese Society

actor-network theory, 228n5

affinage, 50, 53. *See also* aging and ripening

African American farmers, 256n13

African American slavery, 225n71

agency, 5, 44, 152, 249n54

aging and ripening, 49–54, 51*fig.*, 85, 102–3, 151; aging facilities/environments, 50, 166–67; Cellars at Jasper Hill, 203–9, 205*figs.*, 211; factory cheeses, 102–3; mandatory aging periods, 54, 161–62, 165, 167–70, 173–74, 175–76, 177; microorganisms in, 103, 158, 166–67, 168–69; safety of mold-ripened cheeses, 171, 172, 173, 174, 176, 177, 252n39; seasonal variation and, 174; tasting during, 184, 255n81

agricultural preservation, 11, 17, 25, 192–93, 223n42; land trusts, 25, 33, 225–26n78

agricultural subsidies, 12

agriculture: aestheticization of, 16; as stewardship, 193–94. *See also* animal husbandry; farming practices; industrial agriculture; *specific dairy animals*

Agri-Mark, 202, 206, 208

Albers, Jan, 258n50

allergies, 46, 165, 167, 171

Allerton, Mrs. E. P., 101

"American cheese," 107, 243n51

American cheesemaking traditions, 95–127, 153; diversification and American indigenous cheeses, 103–5; emergence of factories, 100–103; historical overviews, 9, 99–107; invented traditions, 98, 113–14; lack of continuity within, 96, 98–99, 107–11, 113, 114, 117, 124; oral history interviews, 241n1; valorization of cheesemaking skill, 101–2; west coast, 98, 103, 104–5, 113; Wisconsin, 95–96, 98, 102, 103, 104, 105, 197, 242n42. *See also* artisan factories

American Cheese Society (ACS), 24, 79; competitions, 23, 24, 58–59, 114, 116, 123, 227n104; definition of artisan(al), 128; farmstead designation and, 60, 233n84; membership statistics, 221n5; safety standards development efforts, 175–79; statement "On the Importance of Artisan, Farmstead, and Specialty Cheese," 160

American Originals competitions, 114, 116

Amish cheesemaking, 22, 221n4, 243n50

aniline colorings, 242n36

animal husbandry, 230n42; animal welfare, 60–61, 64; anthropology of, 40–46; consumer attitudes about, 38–39; farmstead appellation and, 60; Humane Certification, 61;

vs. how, 144, 145, 146. *See also* know-how;
    scientific knowledge; sensory evaluation;
    synesthetic reason
Koch, Robert, 163
Kohler, Robert, 19, 183, 225–26n78
Kohl, Herb, 196
Kondo, Dorinne, 79–80, 239n70
Kraft, 105, 106*fig.*, 107, 118–19, 121
Kraft, James L., 105
Kraft, Norman, 118–19, 183
Krahenbuhl, Randy, 105, 107

labeling: organic labeling, 194, 233n85; *terroir*
    as label term, 194–95. *See also* farmstead
    designation; regional designations
labor, 108, 109–10; divisions of labor, 53, 81,
    237n62; in domestic settings, 65–66, 233–
    34n9; engaged labor, 72–75, 81; highlighting
    in marketing, 14, 49; labor alienation, 14,
    72; labor self-sufficiency, 81, 237n60; mak-
    ers' valuation of their own labor, 64–65;
    microorganisms as co-laborers, 28, 50, 51,
    64; as value creator, 33, 39–40, 49, 87–88, 90;
    women's labor asserted, 69, 235n25. *See also*
    farm labor
Lactobacillus, lactic acid bacteria, 47, 162, 163,
    253n58
lamb, 38–39
lambing, 37–38, 228n18
land and landscape: pastoral views of, 16; post-
    pastoral views of, 17–20; reterritorialization
    notion, 201–2, 208–9, 211; sheep farmers'
    attachment to, 40, 43; stewardship, 64,
    190, 191, 192–95, 211; working landscapes,
    13, 15, 17–20, 32–33, 36, 201–2, 206. *See also*
    pastoral imagery/mythology; post-pastoral
    ethos; *terroir*
land trusts, 25, 33, 191, 225–26n78, 237n55
Lange, Randy, 193, 194
Lange Twins Winery, 193, 194
Larcher, Ivan, 197
lard: filled cheeses, 103, 251n32
Latour, Bruno, 162, 251n21
Laughing Cow (La Vache Qui Rit), 112, 171,
    253n48
Law, John, 236n50
Lee, Michael, 45
Lehner, Willi, 198, 199, 200, 211, 246n20
Leitch, Alison, 125
Leland, John, 17
Lévi-Strauss, Claude, 50
licensing: individual, 22, 25; statistics, 3, 3*fig.*,

221n5; unlicensed producers and facilities,
    171–72, 175
lifestyle objectives, 65, 66–67, 75, 108, 236n41;
    getting back to the land, 68–72; lifestyle
    migrants, 11, 67–68, 234–35n19
Limburger-style cheeses, 95, 98, 104; Chalet
    Cheese Co-op, 117–20, 125, 183–84
Listeria, 170, 181, 184; cheese categories and,
    170–73, 253n50; Estrella Family Creamery
    shutdown, 159, 167, 169–70, 184, 252n41,
    252n42, 252n43, 255n81; *L. monocytogenes,*
    159, 161, 169–70, 181, 199, 250n11; mold-
    ripened cheeses and, 172
listeriosis, 169, 170, 171, 172, 253n50
Litchfield cheese, 100
Little Darling, 127
livestock, 35, 39, 40–46; anthropocentric views
    of, 42, 230n39; anthropomorphizing views
    of, 41–42, 230n34, 230n40; breeds and *ter-
    roir,* 188, 256n8; as co-laborers, 28, 39–40,
    41, 45, 64; farmers' livestock affinities,
    40–46, 230n34, 237–38n63; in quantitative
    calculations, 82, 238n67. *See also* animal
    husbandry; *specific animals*
Living with Sheep (Wooster), 38, 42
localism, 77, 186. *See also* place; *terroir*
Locke, John, 33
Loring, George B., 137
Luis, Cesar, 22–23

machine in the garden, 15, 17, 35, 206
The Machine in the Garden (Marx), 213
mad cow disease, 47–48
magic and magical thinking, 53–54, 150–51, 231
mail order sales, 85
Major, Cynthia (Cindy), 30, 33, 53, 55, 56–59, 138.
    See also Major Farm; Vermont Shepherd
Major, David, 30–31, 33, 52, 54, 138, 235n33;
    background, 30, 56, 64; on livestock
    choices, 40–41. *See also* Major Farm; Ver-
    mont Shepherd
Major Farm, 28, 30–59, 166, 235n33; author's
    residency at, 23–24, 32, 46–49; business
    expansion, 33; cheese aging process, 49–54,
    51*fig.*, 166–67; cheesemaking process, 46–49,
    47*fig.*; cheese recalls, 54, 181; facilities and
    equipment, 34–35, 56; founding and product
    development, 44, 56–59, 138; products, 31,
    228n1; sheep management at, 30–31, 33–38,
    42, 46–47. *See also* Vermont Shepherd
Major, Yesenia Ielpi, 30, 235n33. *See also* Major
    Farm; Vermont Shepherd

Ott, Sandra, 52, 230n40, 232n77
Over the Rainbeau (Schwartz), 63, 77

packaging, 105
packaging skills, 88, 91, 123, 200–201
Parant, Charlie, 157
Parmesan, grated (Kraft), 105
Pasteur Institute, 162
Pasteurian: attitude, 161; approach to hygiene,
    161–62, 164, 166, 180; views of raw milk,
    164–65
pasteurization, 17, 132, 162; AOC rules, 188;
    environmental contamination and, 169–70;
    in factory cheesemaking, 163–64; of milk
    for drinking, 163, 250–51n18; perceived
    infallibility of, 164, 166, 170; potential
    pro-pathogenic effects, 169; as symbol of
    modernity, 166; toxins that survive, 181
The Pasteurization of France (Latour), 162
pasteurized-milk cheeses, 84–85, 93, 163–64,
    239n83; consumer preference for, 257n21; in
    Europe, 118; *terroir* and, 192. *See also* factory
    cheeses; pasteurization; *specific types and
    producers*
pasteurizers, 84, 168, 174
Pasteur, Louis, 103, 162
pastoral imagery/mythology, 15–16, 19, 20, 111,
    203, 213–14, 225n71; marketing of, 8, 20, 32,
    55–56, 57*fig.*, 62. *See also* post-pastoral ethos
pathogens, 163, 180, 199, 251n24; aging and, 54,
    168–69, 170, 174, 251–52n36; antibiotics and,
    231n48; environmental contamination and
    management, 169–70, 172, 177–78, 181, 182;
    heat-resistant, 181; introduction points/
    paths, 163, 166, 169, 254n69; newly virulent
    pathogens, 168–69; testing for, 129, 161,
    164, 167, 184, 250n11. *See also* food-borne
    illness; food safety; risk reduction; *specific
    pathogens*
Pawlet, 152
Pecorino, 34
Penicillium, 162
*Perils and Pleasures of Domesticating Goat
    Cheese* (Cahn), 16, 77
Petrini, Carlo, 9
pH, 144. *See also* acidity
Phelps, Elizabeth Porter, 116
physical (bodily) knowledge, 135–36, 141,
    246n20
pioneering cheesemakers, 11, 66–67
pizza cheese, 108, 172, 243n52
place: creation/remaking of, 201, 216, 260n8;

localism, 77. *See also* land and landscape;
    regional designations; rural communities;
    taste of place; *terroir*
Pleasant Ridge Reserve, 120
Point Reyes Farmstead Cheese Company, 132–
    33, 189, 243n50
Polanyi, Michael, 247n22, 248n47
Pollack, Marian, 69–72, 70*fig.*, 109, 125
Pollan, Michael, 77
Pondhopper, 115, 117
pork, 256n13
Portuguese cheesemakers, 50, 141, 247n34
post-Pasteurian: attitude, 161–62, 165, 166–67,
    175; views of raw milk and raw-milk cheese,
    166, 199
post-pastoral ethos, 8, 17–20, 62, 113, 222n28;
    animal husbandry, 44–45; Jasper Hill's
    vision, 201–2, 206–9; working landscapes,
    13, 15, 17–20, 32–33, 36, 201–2, 206
pregnancy, cheese safety warnings and, 171–72,
    173*table*, 253n48
prices: qualitative value and, 92; wool and wool
    processing, 37, 228n11, 228n17, 259n67. *See
    also* cheese prices; food prices; milk prices
pricing practices, 84–87
private-label sales, 85, 245n106
process cheese, 105, 107, 243n51
product development, 46–49, 115, 123. *See also*
    innovation
product diversity, 85, 123
production costs. *See* costs
production volume: statistics, 26, 100, 227n106.
    See also scale
profit and profitability, 82, 83, 86–87, 90, 238n66
progress, valorization of, 113
property taxes, 207, 237n55, 259n75
property values, 85
public health issues. *See* food-borne illness;
    food safety; health
Pugs Leap Farm, 86, 239n85
Putnam, Janine, 73
Putnam, John, 72–73, 96, 97*fig.*, 120, 142, 155. *See
    also* Thistle Hill Farm
Pye, David, 132, 133, 249n64

Quaker industry, 222n22
qualculation, 236n50
qualitative calculations, 81, 84, 146; pricing
    practices, 84–87; sustainability decisions,
    78–79, 236n50; value-added dairying, 87–92.
    See also business needs and decisions
quality, 123; adulteration, 103, 251n32; human-

animal relations and, 46; intangible influences on, 46, 231n63; microbial activity and, 159, 163; organic methods and, 193–94; quality maintenance difficulties, 204, 206; taste quality linked to production values, 191, 192–95, 198–99
Queso del Invierno, 228n1
queso fresco, 22, 171, 172
Queso Oaxaca, 23
quilting, 249n58

Rabeharisoa, Vololona, 225n58, 225n59
racial diversity, 22, 226n94
Radin, Margaret, 222n27, 224n53, 233n7
Rainbeau Ridge, 77. *See also* Schwartz, Lisa
Rance, Patrick, 57–58, 167
Rapp, Rayna, 182
raw milk, 45; circumvention of sales restrictions, 253n51; nutrient value, 160, 250n6; Pasteurian view of, 159–60, 164–65; post-Pasteurian views of, 165, 166–67; potential pathogens in, 181, 251n24, 254n73; related illness outbreaks, 164, 165, 168, 251n33; routine pasteurization of, 163, 250–51n18; typical test results, 253n54
raw-milk cheeses, 28–29, 217; blind tasting results, 257n21; European, 118, 167, 168; FDA view of, 159–60; hard, safety of, 172, 173*table*; mandatory aging requirements, 54, 161–62, 165, 167–70, 173–74, 175–76, 177; microbiology of, 159; related illness outbreaks, 159, 250n4; safety debate, 159–61; Slow Food USA preservation/marketing efforts, 125; *terroir* and, 192. *See also* food-borne illness; food safety; regulation; *specific types and producers*
raw-milk debate: ACS position paper, 160; nature-culture opposition in, 161–62, 165, 166, 167; polarized nature of, 159–60, 161, 164–65
Razionale, Vince, 204
Reagan-era surplus cheese giveaway, 10
real estate taxes, 207, 237n55, 259n75
real estate values, 85
recalls, 59, 175; FDA authority, 252n43; voluntary, 54, 181. *See also* Estrella Family Creamery shutdown
recipes, 5, 117, 128, 135, 143, 147–48, 248n50; adapting, 145, 147, 151, 156
record keeping, 50, 134, 177
recreation, in rural landscapes, 19, 22, 225–26n78

regional designations and branding, 194; French AOC system, 112, 188, 194; Jasper Hill Farm's Cellars initiative, 203–9, 205*figs.*, 211; Wisconsin DBIC effort, 196–97, 200–201, 211, 215. *See also* terroir
regulation, 28–29, 160–61, 167, 175–76, 217; antibiotics testing, 46, 231n48; AOC system, 112, 188, 194; cheese classification and, 165, 170–73, 174, 176; circumvention of, 174–75, 253n51; in Europe, 112, 114–15, 116–17, 118, 167, 170, 184; facilities requirements, 80; FDA enforcement activities, 159, 160–61, 250n11, 250n12; HACCP as tool for, 176, 177; industry safety standards development, 175–79; mandatory aging periods, 54, 161–62, 165, 167–70, 173–74, 175–76, 177; nineteenth century, 103; organic certification and labeling, 194, 214, 233n85; raw-milk/pasteurized-milk distinction and, 165, 170; waste regulations, 48. *See also* Estrella Family Creamery shutdown; food safety; U.S. Food and Drug Administration
renaissance rhetoric, 98, 117. *See also* innovation; tradition
rennet, 47–48, 119, 129, 144, 145, 146
restaurants, 27, 59, 69, 85
retailers and retail sales, 25–26, 59, 85, 123, 178–79
ripening. *See* aging and ripening
Risatti, Howard, 133, 246n10
risk, 180, 182; in craft practice, 132, 133, 155, 163, 177–78; risk taking as innovation, 114; risk tolerance and risk-taking behavior, 87, 133, 182–83. *See also* food safety; risk reduction
risk reduction, 162, 182, 184; environmental management, 177–78, 181; industry initiatives, 176–79; VIAC workshop, 179–81, 184
Roberts, Jeffrey, 3, 114, 175, 192, 214, 216–17
Rodale Press, 68, 77
Rogers, Juliette, 244n66, 247n33
Rome, New York: Williams cheese factory, 100–101
Roquefort, 34, 58
rotational grazing, 35–36
Rouge et Noir Camembert, 116
rural communities: depopulation, 9; economic development initiatives, 11; parents who left, 76; *terroir* and reterritorialization, 189, 190, 201–2, 208–9, 211, 216–17; vacationing and second homes, 19, 22, 207, 225–26n78
rural in-migrants, 11, 18–19; back-to-the-land movement, 3, 11, 66–67; community engagement, 75, 91–92, 94, 206–7, 234–35n19;

CALIFORNIA STUDIES IN FOOD AND CULTURE

Darra Goldstein, Editor

CPSIA information can be obtained
at www.ICGtesting.com
Printed in the USA
LVHW02s1906190118
563184LV00001B/4/P

9 780520 270183